RECLAIMING THE GREAT WORLD HOUSE

RECLAIMING THE GREAT WORLD HOUSE

THE GLOBAL VISION OF MARTIN LUTHER KING JR.

VICKI L. CRAWFORD AND
LEWIS V. BALDWIN, EDITORS

FOREWORD BY
ROBERT M. FRANKLIN

THE UNIVERSITY OF GEORGIA PRESS ATHENS

A Sarah Mills Hodge Fund Publication

This publication is made possible in part through a grant from the
Hodge Foundation in memory of its founder, Sarah Mills Hodge,
who devoted her life to the relief and education of
African Americas in Savannah, Georgia.

Publication of this book was also made possible in part
through the support of Morehouse College.

Set in 9.5/13.5 Utopia Std by Kaelin Chappell Broaddus
Printed and bound by Sheridan Books, Inc.
The paper in this book meets the guidelines for permanence
and durability of the Committee on Production Guidelines for
Book Longevity of the Council on Library Resources.

Most University of Georgia Press titles are
available from popular e-book vendors.

Printed in the United States of America
23 22 21 20 19 P 5 4 3 2 1

Library of Congress Cataloging-in-Publication Data

Names: Baldwin, Lewis V., 1949–, editor. | Crawford, Vicki, editor.
Title: Reclaiming the great world house : the global vision of
    Martin Luther King Jr. / Vicki L. Crawford and Lewis V. Baldwin,
    editors ; foreword by Robert M. Franklin.
Description: Athens : The University of Georgia Press, [2019] |
    Series: The Morehouse College King collection series on civil &
    human rights | Includes bibliographical references and index.
Identifiers: LCCN 2019010663 | ISBN 9780820356020 (hardcover) |
    ISBN 9780820356044 (paperback) | ISBN 9780820356037 (ebook)
Subjects: LCSH: King, Martin Luther, Jr., 1929–1968—Philosophy. |
    Human rights and globalization. | Human rights—Social aspects.
Classification: LCC E185.97.K5 R397 2019 | DDC 323.092—dc23
LC record available at https://lccn.loc.gov/2019010663

For the Office of the Martin Luther King Jr. Collection at Morehouse College,
a monument to the legacy of a drum major

CONTENTS

FOREWORD

Whenever I sit down with a new book in hand, I recall Franz Kafka's sobering admonition: "I think we ought to read only books that bite and sting us. If the book we are reading doesn't shake us awake like a blow on the skull, why bother reading it in the first place? A book must be the axe for the frozen sea within us."[1] This new and important volume on Martin Luther King Jr. as a globalist meets the Kafka test. In contrast to most King studies, which focus primarily on King's heroic and epic freedom struggle in the U.S. South, and others that suggest that King's globalism developed only in his later years, this book takes as its central premise that King's global perspective was evident long before he achieved national and international prominence. As the chapters unfold, each contributor expands and deepens our appreciation for the ways in which King's global vision and human-ethical ideal hold relevance for the world today. This book arrives at a time of enormous moral challenge and urgency, as our world appears to fracture into a multitude of premodern shards. That is where the "bite and sting" of the pages of *Reclaiming the Great World House* make unrelenting demands on our moral discernment and agency.

Lewis V. Baldwin and Vicki L. Crawford are wise and probing scholars. Baldwin has spent decades significantly interpreting King's life, while Crawford has helped to expand King's legacy in the classroom, in her capacity as director of the Morehouse College Martin Luther King Collection, and for public audiences. Here, like a team of master jewelers, they have curated and arranged gems that will illumine and provide hope as we contemplate the future. Faithful to the purpose and spirit of the book, the editors have assembled both established and younger, emerging King scholars from an ensemble of disciplines, including ethics, theology, economics, history, cultural studies, communications, and homiletics. Also congruent with the substance and spirit of both the volume and King's vision of a great "world house," the contributors are not only African Americans and Caucasians but also scholars from Africa, the Bahamas, Puerto Rico, Great Britain, and Korea. Clearly, the global perspective is central to this collection.

This diversity reminds us of the sophisticated, multidisciplinary cast of Dr. King's mind. Students of King will recall that he majored in sociology at Morehouse, where his world vision began to take shape. Given his options, that choice of sociology is striking. One could reasonably infer that King would have found more familiar and inviting intellectual tools and symbols in the fields of philosophy and religion. There he would have been enriched by exposure to Aristotle, Saint Augustine, and Saint Thomas Aquinas. Of course, King *did* study these subjects with Morehouse's distinguished faculty in religion, but he ultimately chose not to major in philosophy. Surely the field of political science too would have been appealing since there King would have encountered Niccolo Machiavelli, John Locke, Thomas Hobbes, and Harold Laswell, all of whom would have provided the precocious undergraduate with powerful tools for understanding the art of "who gets what, when, and how" (Laswell's classic definition of politics in 1956). But King chose to major neither in politics nor economics. Instead he decided to focus on sociology while drawing from and synthesizing the insights of the other disciplines.

Why is sociology important for understanding global realities? My own sociology professor used to define the discipline, self-deprecatingly, as the "systematic elaboration of the obvious." Under the guidance of Walter R. Chivers, Morehouse's brilliant sociology professor, King found hidden power and shadowy forces lurking behind the obvious. One could argue that King learned a unique approach to classical sociology in a historically black college situated in a racist southern environment. King's experience at Morehouse would figure prominently in the development of his global outlook. Ultimately King's major in sociology led him to his classic formulation of the "triple evils" that plague the human condition worldwide: namely racism, poverty, and war. *Reclaiming the Great World House* examines this view in light of the complexity and injustices of our contemporary world.

Later, after feasting at the tables of liberal theological education at Crozer Theological Seminary and Boston University, King was equipped to reflect profoundly on how "the evil triumvirate," as he also called it, represented distortions of human personality and thus required multidisciplinary analysis and action. In addressing this he fused the richest insights from his sociological and theological education. King's probing study of the Bible, theology, the history of religions, and ethics provided insights on the predicaments and possibilities of human beings as finite creatures. As this book shows, these insights had major implications for the struggle against racism, poverty, and war, which King saw as the major external barriers to community and peace in the great world house of human diversity. Theology unlocked and decoded a dimension of the human spirit that sociology did not aspire to address. King came to embrace a vision of radical personal and social transformation grounded in the conviction that humans are made for God and each other, thus leading to the rejection of racialized state power and inequality alike. For King, the cruel, violent, and self-righteous, even murderers, are potential servants of God and can become instruments of love, justice, and reconciliation. King was fascinated by the profound human possibility of metanoia, or deep change and renewal. It strikes me that in an era marked by multiple forms of terrorism, not the least of which is state terrorism, the radical possibilities of personal change and social transformation deserve consideration. These possibilities drive the essays in *Reclaiming the Great World House*.

But before finding definitive answers in theology, King sought to crystallize the big questions, and that task fell back to sociology. He respected the careful attention to human behavior evident in the works of pioneering sociologists such as Max Weber, W. E. B. Du Bois, Emile Durkheim, and E. Franklin Frazier. In various ways these helped King, the young theologian, to avoid naïveté concerning the nature of societies, violence, and the deep flaws of racism and classism. The making of King's global mind, imprinted by the Morehouse faculty and further refined at Crozer, Boston, and in the crucible of struggle, is wonderfully summarized in Vicki L. Crawford's introductory essay before she provides a useful synopsis of each chapter in this book. Readers who prefer to consult a roadmap before traveling will appreciate this.

The essays comprising this book rely on some of the lesser-known writings and thoughts of Martin Luther King Jr. Since his death a half century ago, institutions like Morehouse, Boston University, Stanford University, and the Martin Luther King Jr. Center for Nonviolent Social Change have documented and disseminated his most notable works. For their labors and investments, we can all be grateful. The massive Martin Luther King Jr. Papers Project, now being published by Clayborne Carson at Stanford, represents a treasure trove of resources for those seeking to know the mind and imagination of an extraordinary global public moralist. So does the Martin Luther King Jr. Collection at Morehouse College. When I was the president of Morehouse from 2007 to 2012, we received most of those materials comprising this collection, and I had the wonderful opportunity to provide a few guided tours of the King papers in the Atlanta University Center Robert W. Woodruff Library and during an inaugural display of the original documents at the Atlanta History Center. Two of those occasions are especially memorable to me and also relevant to the focus of this book: during Atlanta visits by the Nobel Prize for Literature winner Salmon Rushdie and UN General Secretary Ban Ki-moon.

In 2008 it was fascinating to observe how these two global thought leaders from very different cultural backgrounds, one Iranian and the other Korean, gravitated toward Dr. King as a guide and mentor from whom they could recalibrate their own moral compass. Rushdie observed the voluminous note cards King kept and chuckled about how well organized King had been as a young student. Rushdie remarked that, by comparison, he had been quite the opposite in his youth, and he was surprised he had ever managed to write anything. He was also deeply impressed by King's courage in the face of racist and violent opposition backed by the political and religious establishments. One can imagine that Rushdie understood King's sense of living under the weight of a virtual death sentence by his opponents.[2]

Similarly, Ban Ki-moon was fascinated, almost mesmerized, as he read King's correspondence with Ralph Bunche, who was director of the UN Department of Trusteeship and the first African American to receive the Nobel Peace Prize, in 1950.[3] Ban was so focused on the Bunche letters that he could not be torn away so that our planned itinerary could remain on track. It appeared that some voice or strange currents from the past had surged upward and seized him. I was moved by the depth of his emotional response as he walked away afterward, eyes glistening. From these observations, it was quite apparent that forty years after his assassination in Memphis, King continued to speak to global leaders.

Reclaiming the Great World House arrives at a time when America's world leadership is being diminished and redefined, and there is perhaps an even more pressing need than ever for global leaders to hear King's voice. Undoubtedly, King would regard America's growing isolationism as a retreat from moral responsibility on the world stage. People around the globe shudder in fear when they realize that the most powerful nation on earth is led by a man who is ignorant of history and mistrustful of the larger world. Commenting on America's distinctive moral culture, nineteenth-century French historian Alexis de

Tocqueville concluded that the greatness of America consisted not in its being more enlightened than any other country but, rather, in its ability to repair its imperfections and "weaknesses of the human heart," while also correcting the defects in its democracy.[4] It could be argued that King's justly famous "Letter from Birmingham Jail" (1963) and one of his last two books, *Where Do We Go from Here: Chaos or Community?* (1967), were prescriptions for such healing, for in both he highlighted the necessity for a more compassionate, democratic, and inclusive America, as well as more creative and harmonious living in the world house.

This book deepens our understanding of the continuing social evils of racism, poverty, and war, which seem strangely resistant to American self-reparation. It reminds us that these evils still haunt the global community. But the authors also train an analytical eye on the problems of religious bigotry and intolerance, sexism, homophobia, xenophobia, Islamophobia, environmental destruction, and other social ills that threaten human dignity, welfare, and survival in the world house. In his own time, King himself addressed many of the root issues that still give rise to these social problems. Clearly his words contain an "access and permanence of meaning," as philosopher Martin Heidegger put it, that resonates with our times and at all times and situations.[5] This is the essential point of *Reclaiming the Great World House.* Coeditor Lewis V. Baldwin may be the nation's most prolific King scholar, and his persistent message has been, as it is in this volume, that King must continue to speak beyond his own time and context. A voice that cries in the wilderness can be more easily heard when the entire civilization devolves into wilderness.

Universities and congregations around the globe should make this book required reading because students and all citizens need texts that will help them recalibrate their own moral compass. We all desperately need books that offer visions of multinational hope, peace, justice, equal opportunity for all, and community, especially for those at the bottom of the socioeconomic pyramid. In this respect, reclaiming King's vision of the world house is not only serious ethical work for the reader but also a critical therapeutic project, one capable of healing rifts within and between nations.

In December 1964 Martin Luther King Jr. became the youngest person to receive the Nobel Peace Prize. He used the power of moral suasion and high rhetoric to challenge world leaders to seriously consider human interconnectedness and shared destiny, and to thus act appropriately. Forty-five years later, Barack Hussein Obama, a self-described student of King and president of the United States, also received a Nobel Peace Prize. Many were surprised that after only nine months in the White House, Obama stood at the podium in Oslo, Norway where King once stood. But shrewd observers saw something in the decision by the Nobel Committee. This was in essence an affirmation of King's vision of global cooperation and of the racial progress America had made over four decades, at least to the degree that Obama could be elected president. It was also a vote of confidence in the promise and hope that the new president symbolized. The reins of a global superpower were now in the hands of one who could use hard power to effect change, thus moving what King called "the arc of the moral universe" closer toward justice.[6]

President Obama accomplished much on the national and international stages, but much remains to be done for the health and salvation of the great world house. Now demagogues are emerging worldwide who knew not Martin. They speak of building walls of isolation and ethnic separatism, not bridges of reconciliation, cooperation, and solidarity. Winter is coming. That is why I have looked forward to a volume like *Reclaiming the Great World House* for some time. We need the wisdom of these pages. We need them to be, as Kafka said, "the axe for the frozen sea within us."[7] May it be so.

Robert M. Franklin

President Emeritus, Morehouse College

James T. and Berta R. Laney Professor of

Moral Leadership, Emory University

NOTES

1. Franz Kafka, *Letters to Friends, Family, and Editors* (New York: Schocken Books, 1977), 16.

2. Following the 1988 publication of his fourth novel, *The Satanic Verses*, Rushdie was the subject of a fatwa, issued by Ayatollah Khomeini of Iran, calling for his assassination.

3. It is also worth noting that the second person of color to receive a Nobel Peace Prize was South Africa's ANC president Albert J. Lithuli, for his leadership of the nonviolent struggle against apartheid in his country. King exchanged letters with Lithuli as early as the late 1950s and was a cosponsor with him of the American Committee on Africa's "Appeal for Action against Apartheid" (1962), a document designating December 10, 1962, Human Rights Day, a "day of protest" against the South African government and its apartheid policies. See Irwin Abrams, ed., *The Words of Peace: Selections from the Speeches of the Winners of the Nobel Peace Prize* (New York: Newmarket Press, 1990), 36–38, 104; and Lewis V. Baldwin, *Toward the Beloved Community: Martin Luther King Jr. and South Africa* (Cleveland: Pilgrim Press, 1995), 17–19, 25–29, 34–38.

4. Alexis De Tocqueville, *Democracy in America*, translated and edited by Harvey C. Mansfield and Delba Wintrop (Chicago: The University of Chicago Press, 2000), 297. Also quoted in Clay Stauffer, "As President, Trump's Challenge Will Be Spiritual: Message of the Week," *Tennessean*, January 21, 2017.

5. Heiddeger felt that some cultural classics possess a permanence of meaning that renders them accessible to all rational human beings. See Martin Heidegger, *Being and Time,* translated by John MacQuarrie and Edward Robinson (New York: Harper, 1962).

6. Martin Luther King Jr., *Stride toward Freedom: The Montgomery Story* (New York: Harper & Row, 1958), 106–7.

7. Kafka, *Letters to Friends, Family, and Editors,* 16.

ACKNOWLEDGMENTS

Every book is the product of a collective endeavor, and the effort, expertise, and goodwill of a number of persons contributed to *Reclaiming the Great World House*. We exceeded the all too common scholarly provincialism in King studies by organizing a group of established and emerging King scholars for an interdisciplinary treatment of Martin Luther King Jr.'s vision of the great world house and its potential meaningfulness and/or relevance for contemporary and future generations. The contributors to this volume represent various fields of study, and their diversity of race, gender, nationality, and generation is ideally suited for engaging the more specific and different elements of King's global vision. We thank all for their planning, research, and writing and are grateful for how congenial and generous they have been in this effort. The contributors also approved of this book's dedication to the Office of the Morehouse Martin Luther King Jr. Collection, and we are thankful for this kind gesture as well. We hope this will be an asset to the Office of MLK Collection as it continues to develop and implement programming that advances the teachings and philosophy of Dr. King in the twenty-first century.

A hearty word of gratitude is extended to the estate of Dr. Martin Luther King Jr. and to staff persons in the library and archives of the Martin Luther King Jr. Center for Nonviolent Social Change in Atlanta. Eric D. Tidwell, the licensing manager of the King estate, was gracious in responding to our request for the use of Dr. King's image on the book's cover. Cynthia Lewis and Elaine Hall, who work in the King Center's library and archives, were equally helpful in this regard, and they also provided much-needed assistance in locating and copying important source materials.

Also, we wish to acknowledge the expertise and assistance of the archival staff at the Atlanta University Center's Robert W. Woodruff Library, which houses and preserves the Morehouse College Martin Luther King Jr. Collection. Sara Tanner, Tiffany Atwater, and Stacy Jones have generously supported the collection's director and the curricular and programmatic initiatives associated with the collection. Special thanks to library director and CEO Loretta Parham as well.

Warmest thanks to Robert M. Franklin and Rosetta E. Ross for generously writing the foreword and afterword to our book. Both are first-rate scholars in the fields of religion, African American studies, and civil rights, and their involvement with this volume demonstrates their faithfulness to the seriousness and high quality of King scholarship.

A special word of appreciation goes to Lisa Bayer, director of the University of Georgia Press, for her early support in the creation and development of the Morehouse College King Collection Series on Civil and Human Rights. Also, we are grateful to Walter Biggins, senior acquisitions editor at the University of Georgia Press, who saw the need for this volume, agreed that it should serve as the foundational text for the series, and urged us to meet our deadlines.

Jacqueline Laws Baldwin, the spouse of Lewis V. Baldwin, one of the coeditors of this book, deserves our deep appreciation for reading parts of our manuscript, correcting misspellings, imposing some consistency on the endnote citations, and making sure that we were taking seriously other guidelines set by the press for manuscript preparation. In addition, we wish to acknowledge the support of Vicki L. Crawford's mother, Ruth Crawford, who has been an unwavering source of strength and encouragement throughout her personal and professional life. Throughout life's journey, Ruth has offered a listening ear, helpful advice, and loving-kindness in this and other endeavors. Vicki is the other coeditor of this volume.

Reclaiming the Great World House has been for us a labor of love, and we can only hope that it will be as significant for readers as it is for those of us who worked so hard to bring it to fruition. If this turns out to be the case, this book will become yet another resource through which King's legacy of ideas and struggle continues to bless us, and our collective effort will have been more than richly rewarded.

RECLAIMING THE GREAT WORLD HOUSE

INTRODUCTION

VICKI L. CRAWFORD

But we do not have much time. The revolutionary spirit is already world-wide.
If the anger of the peoples of the world at the injustice of things is to be
channeled into a revolution of love and creativity, we must begin now
to work, urgently, with all the peoples, to shape a new world.
MARTIN LUTHER KING JR., *The Trumpet of Conscience*

The life and legacy of Martin Luther King Jr. remains a source of great insight and inspiration as we confront the continuing challenges of the twenty-first century. There is a growing interest in King beyond his prominence as a national civil rights leader, and specifically his stature in the global movement for justice and human rights. This book expands King scholarship in its elaboration on King as a global citizen.[1] *Reclaiming the Great World House: The Global Vision of Martin Luther King Jr.* contextualizes King historically and contemporarily through an examination of his ideas and social praxis. It seeks to discern new appropriations of King in today's world, with some attention to the future as well. Centered around King's concept of "the great world house," with its focus on eliminating the triple evils of racism, poverty, and war through nonviolent resistance, this volume extends the purview of King's "evil triumvirate" to address social, political, economic, and cultural injustice. The overall framework is King's all-inclusive vision of human rights, which he articulated alternately as "the world house," "a single neighborhood," "the human family," a "new world order," "the Kingdom of God on earth," and the "beloved community," among other similar expressions. These articulations reflected King's conception of a diverse, multiracial, multiethnic, multireligious global community extending beyond geopolitical boundaries and national and sectarian interests. *Reclaiming the Great World House* examines King's concept of one human family, globally connected, integrated, and united around a core of universally shared values.

One of King's most succinct statements concerning the "great world house" may be found in the final chapter of his book *Where Do We Go from Here: Chaos or Community?*[2] In the chapter, titled "The World House," King reflects on the global challenges of his day and warns that persistent injustice will ultimately threaten the survival of all humanity. He opens the chapter by comparing a real-world crisis to that of a large family that cannot get along but are forced to live together. King states: "All inhabitants of the world are now neighbors . . . . This is the great new problem of mankind. We have inherited a large house, a great 'world house' in which we have to live together—black and white, Easterner and Westerner, Gentile and Jew, Catholic and Protestant, Muslim and Hindu—a family unduly separated in ideas, culture and interest, who, because we can never again live apart, must learn somehow to live with each other in peace."[3] King later notes the ethical demands this places on peoples of all nationalities: "Every nation must now develop an overriding loyalty to mankind as a whole in order to preserve the best in their individual societies . . . . This call for a worldwide fellowship that lifts neighborly concern beyond one's tribe, race, class and nation is in reality a call for an all-embracing and unconditional love for all men."[4] With this understanding, King grounded his thought and action in a vision of human potentiality that remains timeless and all-encompassing. His nonviolent approach to peacebuilding, strong emphasis on individual and collective freedom, and uncompromising embrace of human dignity provide relevant standpoints for contemporary and possibly future analyses of global injustice.

Representing a diverse group of contributors and advantaged by multidisciplinary perspectives, this volume offers breadth and depth as it seeks new understandings of King's world house ideal and possible lessons for today and tomorrow. The convergence of King's ideas and action is not only pertinent but also indispensable among those seeking nonviolent means for addressing inequalities in the twenty-first century. The contributors to this volume affirm that King advances a unique perspective as we continue to work to eradicate racism, sexism, classism, homophobia, xenophobia, religious bigotry and intolerance, and other forms of human inequality and injustice.

The Great World House in Historical Context

The foundation for King's concept of the world house may be found in his family, church, and community experiences, wherein the problems confronting blacks in America were always understood in relation to those of oppressed peoples everywhere.[5] While he did not employ the term "world house" until the mid-1960s, the genesis of this idea can be traced back to King's socially and politically conscious upbringing and close-knit familial influences. King's deep faith and black Southern Baptist roots helped shape a moral and ethical outlook that would later express itself in his enlarged humanitarian vision. While he came of age in a racially hostile, segregated world, King grew up in a nurturing family environment where he received lifelong lessons about love, courage, justice, and other human virtues. This was perhaps King's introduction to the intrinsically valuable human traits that inspired his thinking and the development of his world house vision.

Later, Morehouse College, the all-male and historically black institution, would play an important role in King's intellectual and spiritual development while also contributing to his global consciousness. When King was a student there from 1944 to 1948, his world perspective continued to mature, thanks to the institution's faculty and strong liberal arts curriculum. It was at Morehouse that King was first introduced to the teachings of Mohandas K. Gandhi and Henry David Thoreau, whose essay on civil disobedience influenced his early ideas on nonviolence. Walter Chivers, professor and chair of the Morehouse Department of Sociology, would shape King's understanding of economic injustice and the intersection of race and class, while philosophy professor Samuel Williams introduced him to ideas in ethics and social philosophy. Theologian and professor of religion George D. Kelsey profoundly influenced King's theological views. Kelsey's approach to religious studies and the Bible included literary and historical insights, and it provided a critical method that King later adopted and used in his interviews, sermons, speeches, and writings throughout his life.[6]

Along with religion and philosophy, King studied literature and held a deep appreciation for the arts (including music) and the humanities, which figured into his openness to peoples of different nationalities and cultures. He frequently referenced and quoted Plato, Aristotle, Immanuel Kant, Georg Hegel, and other great philosophers, literary texts by the likes of James Russell Lowell, Langston Hughes, and John Donne, and activists such as Nannie Helen Burroughs. Perhaps through a liberal arts education and study of literature at Morehouse, King developed his brilliant mastery of language that became the hallmark of his exceptional oratory and writing.[7] The evolution of his conception of the world house may in some measure be attributed to this liberal education.

King was also deeply influenced by Morehouse president Dr. Benjamin Elijah Mays, whom he would later describe as his "spiritual and intellectual father." As president of the college from 1940 to 1967, Mays was an internationally recognized Baptist minister and academic leader who taught and motivated generations of young men who later themselves excelled as leaders. Born in the Jim

Crow South to sharecropper parents, Mays rose to become one of the preeminent ethical leaders of the twentieth century. During King's time at Morehouse, Mays's influence was greatest when he presided over the Tuesday morning chapel services, at which student attendance was mandatory. There Mays delivered reflective, powerful sermons and speeches that became memorable, for King and others, for their emphasis on social justice and human rights worldwide. He consistently urged students to resist segregation and cautioned them against complicity with a system designed to subjugate human beings. In 1939 Mays traveled to Mysore, India, where he met Mohandas Gandhi and spoke with him about his philosophy and practice of satyagraha ("holding on to truth" or "truth-force") and nonviolence. Upon his return, Mays shared his insights with the students. This was one of King's earliest introductions to Gandhi's ideology and practice.[8] Later, upon graduation from Morehouse, King deepened his understanding of Gandhi and the principles and practice of both satyagraha and nonviolent resistance through reading, travel, and firsthand experience.

While at Crozer Theological Seminary in Chester, Pennsylvania, from 1948 to 1951, King studied the theory and philosophy of personalism, which would become the fundamental theological underpinning for both his global vision and his lifelong social justice activism.[9] Personalism, as King understood it, involved ideas that included a belief in "God as personal, the sacredness of persons, the fundamental morality of the universe, and the significance of moral laws and freedom."[10] Early ruminations on the world house as a human-ethical ideal may be found among King's theological class notes, sermon drafts, and various other writings during his Crozer years. In a draft paper or sermon titled "Civilization's Great Need," King wrote: "The greatest need of civilization today is not political security; the greatest need of civilization today is not a well-rounded United Nations organization; the greatest need of civilization today is not a multiplicity of material goods; the greatest need of civilization today is not the superb genius of science as important as it is; the greatest need of civilization today is moral progress."[11]

Among King's notes are references for suggested sermon introductions, including one for a possible sermon titled "The House We are Building."[12] Several other papers submitted at Crozer bear evidence of King's pondering the role of the church in society, the nature of war and peace, and the face-off of communism and capitalism, precursors to his formulation of the "triple evils" idea. During his years at Crozer, King heard a sermon preached by fellow Morehouse alumnus Mordecai Johnson, who by that time had become president of Howard University. Like Benjamin Mays and theologian Howard Thurman two decades earlier, Mordecai Johnson was among the few African Americans who had traveled to India in the 1950s and was conversant with the philosophy and praxis of Gandhi. King was mesmerized by what he learned of Gandhi through Johnson and soon was reading widely on Gandhi's theory and philosophy of nonviolence. He would later remark:

> Prior to reading Gandhi, I had about concluded that the ethics of Jesus were only effective in individual relationships. The "turn the other cheek" philosophy and the "love your enemies" philosophy were only valid, I felt, when individuals were in conflict with other individuals; when racial groups and nations were in conflict, a more realistic approach seemed necessary. Gandhi was probably the first person in history to lift the love ethic of Jesus above mere interaction between individuals to a powerful and effective social force on a large scale. Love for Gandhi was a potent instrument for social and collective transformation. It was in this Gandhian emphasis on love and nonviolence that I discovered the method for social reform that I had been seeking.[13]

Following Crozer, King's formal study of systematic theology at Boston University provided further opportunities for him to refine his thinking on ethics and social justice and expand his personalist theology with global implications. While studying in Boston, King met and married Coretta Scott, who was in the city studying voice at the New England Conservatory of Music. In tracing the trajectory of King's conception of the world house, it is important to acknowledge the influence of Coretta, who shared his worldview and had similar moral and ethical values. While an undergraduate student at Antioch College, Coretta Scott had been involved in peace activism through Women Strike for Peace and the NAACP, among other organizations. Having grown up in the rural South, she was attuned to many of the same issues that King embraced, becoming an important conversation partner and sounding board for his ideas. For example, regarding Coretta's gift of Edward Bellamy's utopian novel *Looking Backward*, King wrote: "I welcomed the book because much of its content is in line with my basic ideas. I imagine you already know that I am much more socialistic in my economic theory than capitalistic. And yet I am not so opposed to capitalism that I have failed to see its relative merits."[14]

After King and Coretta exchanged wedding vows in June 1953, the couple continued to make evident their shared interests in addressing not only regional and national issues but global concerns as well. This became increasingly evident throughout the mid- to late 1950s, when King served as pastor of the Dexter Avenue Baptist Church in Montgomery, Alabama. "Martin always saw a close relationship between the black struggle in America and the struggle for independence in Africa," Coretta would later write as she reflected on their years at

Dexter. "In his early speeches and sermons he had often compared European colonialism [in Africa and Asia] with black oppression in America."[15] During the Montgomery bus boycott in 1955–56, King's ministerial and leadership roles expanded significantly as he also assumed the presidency of the Montgomery Improvement Association, the organization created to spearhead the boycott, and his growing national and international fame reinforced his world outlook and heightened his sense of being increasingly involved in a global human struggle. "The people of the Third World are now rising up," King declared in May 1956, "and at many points I feel that this movement in Montgomery is a part of this overall movement in the world in which oppressed people are revolting against the imperialism and colonialism that have too long existed."[16] By the time King and other ministers organized the Southern Christian Leadership Conference (SCLC) in 1957, an organization designed to coordinate local protests and to bring Christian discipline to the freedom struggle across the South, King had become known internationally as the southern black preacher whose ideas and activities were especially fruitful for rethinking and reshaping the global human condition.[17]

King's travels and experiences abroad were indisputably important to the formulation of his world house vision and inspired his deep interest in and affinity for national liberation movements in Africa, Asia, and Latin America. While King did not attend the influential Bandung Conference in Indonesia in April 1955, he was very much aware and supportive of the conference's goals to promote Afro-Asian economic partnerships. Prior to King's travels, he was asked by Nannie Helen Burroughs, president of the Women's Auxiliary of the National Baptist Convention, to deliver a speech on the convention's theme, "Vision of the World Made New." King spoke about his optimism that segregation, colonialism, and other forms of domination and oppression would ultimately fall. He envisioned the decline of segregation, along with an end to colonialism and imperialism. He stated: "Today we stand between two worlds, a world that is gradually passing away and a world that is being born. We stand between the dying old and the emerging new."[18]

In 1957, at the invitation of Ghana's new head of state, Kwame Nkrumah, the Kings traveled to West Africa where they attended the independence ceremonies marking Ghana's liberation from British colonial rule. Two years later, they traveled to India where they witnessed dire poverty and the daily mistreatment and abuse of the Untouchables (Dalits), which deepened Dr. King's understanding of the philosophy of Gandhi and how it might be applied to injustice and inequality worldwide. These experiences also helped King to develop an expansive transnational lens for linking racism in the United States with colonialism and imperialism in Asia, Africa, and other parts of the world. Moreover, they further convinced King of the power and potential of nonviolent resistance as a force for international peace, for he, by his own admission, had already denounced war as the "most colossal of all evils" and had "signed numerous statements with other Americans condemning nuclear testing."[19]

King's deep and far-reaching support of the South African anti-apartheid movement in the 1950s and 1960s offers yet another important lens for understanding his global perspective on injustice. Upon his return to Montgomery from Ghana in 1957, King, who had become the president of the SCLC, devoted extensive time and attention to the struggle of poor and oppressed people in South Africa. He spoke out against apartheid in numerous public speeches and interviews and developed a friendship with Chief Albert Lutuli of the African National Congress, though the two never met face-to-face. King greatly admired and respected the work of anti-apartheid activists Nelson Mandela and Robert Sobukwe and joined organizations such as the American Committee on Africa in 1957 and the American Negro Leadership Conference on Africa in 1962. Both organizations provided moral and financial support for anti-apartheid and anticolonial struggles in Africa. King, who joined his father and brother, Martin Sr. and Alfred D. King, as copastors of Atlanta's Ebenezer Baptist Church in January 1960, perceptively recognized and addressed the commonalities between the African American freedom struggle and the South African struggle to end apartheid throughout the late fifties and early sixties. His growing concern for the plight of oppressed South Africans and Africans as a whole reflected his expanding interest in the interconnectedness of oppressed people around the world.[20]

King's acceptance of the Nobel Peace Prize in December 1964 provided a solid platform for advancing his idea of the world house. In his Nobel lecture delivered at the University of Oslo, "The Quest for Peace and Justice," King stated that in spite of scientific and technological strides achieved over the preceding century, moral and spiritual progress had been absent, as had any increase in human mastery of the "simple art of living together." He outlined the problems of racism, poverty, and war, which he would mention even more emphatically in the subsequent years of his life. He argued:

> The struggle to eliminate the evil of racial injustice constitutes one of the major struggles of our time. The present upsurge of the Negro people of the United States grows out of a deep and passionate determination to make freedom and equality a reality "here" and "now." In one sense the civil rights movement in the United States is a special American phenomenon which must be understood in

the light of American history and dealt with in terms of the American situation. But on another and more important level, what is happening in the United States today is a relatively small part of a world development.[21]

In addressing the challenge of economic inequality that confronted the world house, King, drawing on the *imago Dei* concept (humans made in the image of God), stated:

> The time has come for an all-out world war against poverty. The rich nations must use their vast resources of wealth to develop the underdeveloped, school the unschooled, and feed the unfed. Ultimately a great nation is a compassionate nation. No individual or nation can be great if it does not have a concern for "the least of these." Deeply etched in the fiber of our religious tradition is the conviction that men are made in the image of God and that they are souls of infinite metaphysical value, the heirs of a legacy of dignity and worth. If we feel this as a profound moral fact, we cannot be content to see men hungry, to see men victimized with starvation and ill health when we have the means to help them. The wealthy nations must go all out to bridge the gulf between the rich minority and the poor majority.[22]

Finally, King's stance on war and rising militarism were the last of the three evils he addressed in the context of the world house. With a rising sense of urgency, he asserted: "Man's proneness to engage in war is still a fact. But wisdom born of experience should tell us that war is obsolete. There may have been a time when war served as a negative good by preventing the spread and growth of an evil force, but the destructive power of modern weapons has eliminated even the possibility that war may serve as a negative good. If we assume that life is worth living and that man has a right to survive, then we must find an alternative to war."[23]

Following King's acceptance of the Nobel Peace Prize, he became more direct and intentional in his use of the term "great world house." During this period, 1964 until his death some four years later, King spoke out on both domestic and international violence, particularly addressing rising militarism as he denounced the war in Vietnam. In a pivotal speech titled "Beyond Vietnam: A Time to Break Silence," delivered at New York's Riverside Church on April 4, 1967, exactly a year before he would be assassinated, King expressed his discontent with America's position on the war:

> A true revolution of values will lay hands on the world order and say of war: "This way of settling differences is not just." This business of burning human beings with napalm, of filling our nation's homes with orphans and widows, of injecting

poisonous drugs of hate into the veins of peoples normally humane, of sending men home from dark and bloody battlefields physically handicapped and psychologically deranged, cannot be reconciled with wisdom, justice, and love. A nation that continues year after year to spend more money on military defense than on programs of social uplift is approaching spiritual death.[24]

In the final years of King's life, he developed a greater sense of his role as a citizen of the world and what that entailed for all humanity. At the time of his death in April 1968, he was not only involved in mounting protests against the U.S. involvement in Vietnam but had also agreed to participate in a mission to achieve "a negotiated settlement" between warring factions in Nigeria.[25] Moreover, his indictment of the evils of global capitalism grew louder and louder, as he also highlighted the strengths of the democratic socialism he had witnessed in the Scandinavian countries (e.g., insuring a guaranteed income for every family and universal education and health care), claiming that this was more consistent with the Christian ethic. King melded his expanded global identity with his moral commitment to eradicating every form of injustice and framed this in language reflecting a broad vision of the entire human family. As such, he consistently challenged Americans and peoples throughout the world to embrace their cosmopolitanism. This would necessitate a genuine adherence to the highest ethical ideals and a moral obligation to speak and act against injustice everywhere.

Obviously, King's world vision and outreach were not antithetical to his work as a Baptist preacher and pastor. In an interview in London in the winter of 1968 he commented extensively on the global threat of white supremacy, poverty, and war and spoke of his mission to uplift and empower humanity. That, he said, was part of his "commitment to the Christian ministry."[26] Some five years earlier, in his celebrated "Letter from Birmingham Jail," he had suggested as much and more, insisting that God's calling on his life demanded a loyalty and dedication not confined by vocational preferences or local, regional, and national considerations: "Just as the prophets of the eighth century B.C. left their villages and carried their 'thus saith the Lord' far beyond the boundaries of their home towns, and just as the Apostle Paul left his village of Tarsus and carried the gospel of Jesus Christ to the far corners of the Greco-Roman world, so am I compelled to carry the gospel of freedom beyond my own home town. Like Paul, I must constantly respond to the Macedonian call for aid."[27] Undoubtedly, responding to "the Macedonian call," in King's mind, involved speaking to and combating those evils that undermined the well-being and survival of the great world house.[28] It was, in other words, a challenge to fully realize a new and more vital human and global ideal.

Contents of This Book

Reclaiming the Great World House critically engages with Martin Luther King Jr.'s concept of the world house over half a century since his untimely death. The authors included here represent various, diverse backgrounds and fields of study. They contend that King's vision and moral voice are timeless and as compelling today as in his own time. While the world King lived in and traveled was quite different in many respects from our own, the world still embodies many of the challenges he faced and those of his generation.

We have not yet witnessed the demise of the triple evils, and in fact newer and more pernicious forms of domination and oppression abound worldwide. Over sixty years following the African American freedom struggle of the twentieth century, we still face a world of vast inequalities. Disparities in housing, health care, education, and other sectors of American life persist. In spite of the two-term election of an African American president and some instances of black individual progress, the vast majority of African Americans and other people of color in the United States lag far behind. Institutional and systemic injustices are found in every area of American society, most notably in law enforcement and the criminal justice system. Income and wealth disparities deepen, and the gap widens between the haves and the have-nots.

On a worldwide scale, poverty persists amid rapid technological advancements and economic globalization in the twenty-first century. New forms of violence and extremism manifest in multiple modalities, ranging from the interpersonal to the intergroup and international. Ethnic, religious, and sectarian extremism expand along with new modes of terrorism, genocide, and crimes against the elderly and women and children. Instances of human trafficking and exploitation are growing, and armed conflict and nuclear escalation and destruction remain ever-present dangers threatening humanity. Considering these twenty-first-century evils, this volume urgently considers how King's ideas and values might be best understood and appropriated worldwide today and for future generations.

Part 1, "Creative Living in the World House: The Vision of Martin Luther King Jr. in Context," examines King's vision in historical context. In chapter 1, Victor Anderson, an ethicist and philosopher, and Teresa Delgado, a systematic theologian, build on the introduction with specific attention to King's world house as a moral vision forged on the basis of a theoretical framework that is well established in the larger disciplines of moral philosophy and theology.

In chapter 2, historian Larry O. Rivers focuses on racism as a barrier to human community and explores King's theistic personalism as it framed his vision of world community. Rivers traces King's conceptualization of the moral problem of racism from his formative years through adulthood, taking into account its impact on the physical and spiritual lives of humans as a whole. He concludes that King's world vision constitutes a tragic and enduring reminder that neither people of color nor whites can ever be safe in the face of white supremacy.

Chapter 3 focuses on the persistence of poverty as an economic injustice, and it notes that one of the striking features of King's social justice discourse and praxis in the last years of his life was its marked shift toward a pragmatic and structural emphasis. Here Gary S. Selby, a specialist in communications and ministerial formation (training in the fundamentals of Christian ministry), analyzes King's speeches from 1967 to 1968, in which he observes a shift in rhetorical strategies to accommodate changes occurring in the civil rights movement. Selby shows that King was able to advocate for political action in the American context while also remaining true to the vision of the great world house.

In chapter 4, Rufus Burrow Jr., a theological social ethicist, examines King's "nonviolent absolutism" in the context of the philosophy of personalism. He traces the evolution of King's views on nonviolence from his early childhood years through adulthood and contends that King rejected any measure of violence in the world house, on grounds that it was unethical and inconsistent with his theological and philosophical beliefs. King's theology of resistance is addressed here, as are the influences of his family, church, community, and strong personalist sources.

In chapter 5, historians Crystal A. deGregory and Lewis V. Baldwin acknowledge that King lived in a gendered world where separate domains for men and women were well-established constraints to women's full participation in society. This chapter explores King's sexism and how it both shaped and hindered his world house vision. Attention is devoted to the impact of King's upbringing on his emergent attitudes towards women and prescribed gender roles. From that point, the focus shifts to King's ambivalent and dualistic relationship with women activists with whom he had contact in the civil rights movement, as well as to his interactions with other women he encountered around the world. The authors argue that King's failure to sufficiently address women's issues and struggles cross-culturally and to denounce sexism was one of the greatest limitations of his world house vision.

Part 2, "Surviving in the Contemporary World House: The Enduring Threats," takes up current social justice issues and problems in the United States and the world, with much attention to King and how he might serve as an enduring resource for addressing such concerns. In chapter 6, ethicist Walter E. Fluker examines the relationship between King's world house vision and the notion of global citizenship as a critique of both the racialized house of the United States and the U.S. crusade to dominate struggling countries around the globe. Fluker explores King's query as to where we go from here and his admonition to blacks and other marginalized groups that their claims and practices toward self-liberation must extend beyond geopolitical boundaries and capitalist interests. Fluker argues that the notion of a post-racial society is a "foil for a nuanced and not-so-nuanced racialism" that results in eroding structural inequalities and encroachments on civil and human rights. In reflecting on King's great world house, Fluker concludes that this is a timely historical moment to revisit King's global vision as part of our recommitment to the ongoing project of democracy around the world.

In chapter 7, Nimi Wariboko, a social and economic ethicist and globalization theorist, probes the rising significance of class differences in the realization of the peaceful world house. He considers King's historical construction of the world house in the antiracism and antipoverty struggles as fundamentally expressed through the "axiom of equality" that guided his thought. Wariboko explores the rising significance of classism in the global economy and how the pernicious logic of the "axiom of inequality" has informed and shaped national and global distributions of the world's resources. He concludes with recommendations on how King's great world house vision might enable the creation of a new economic order in which resources are distributed fairly.

In chapter 8, Mary E. King, an authority in peace and conflict studies, ponders the significance of King's world house vision for contemporary campaigns and movements for nonviolence in the United States and around the globe. She contends that the turbulence in America and violence around the world call for a serious reconsideration of King's vision of the beloved community. This vision, along with the 1948 Declaration of Human Rights, provides an important framework for widening and deepening self-reliant campaigns and movements of nonviolent civil resistance. She holds that King's conviction regarding a universal order of justice, as expressed though the natural law tradition, should be a basis for supporting and improving grassroots campaigns and a vital source for uniting those campaigns to effectuate tangible social change globally.

Chapter 9 is framed around a question: is Martin Luther King Jr.'s world house vision still meaningful or relevant for women and LGBTQ people who confront the current moral perplexities surrounding sexism, sexual ethics, and the broader issues of human sexuality? The social ethicist Amy E. Steele and historians Vicki L. Crawford and Lewis V. Baldwin consider this in the context of King's moral and theological formulations of the world house, which are rooted in the ethical norms of love, justice, and community. King, they argue, demands that we consider the ethics and politics of patriarchal power and privilege, sexism, and homophobia. Are these right and morally defensible? Are they fair? Are they consistent with the highest democratic or egalitarian ideals? Are they in the best interest of the world house?

The implications of King's vision of the great world house for millennial activists involved in local and transnational struggles are explored in chapter 10. Michael B. McCormack, a professor of pan-African studies based in the United States, and Althea Legal-Miller, a highly regarded scholar in American studies from the UK, collaborate to consider how sociocultural exchanges between young activists might draw upon, contest, and/or reimagine King's vision in the continuing struggle for a stronger and better humanity. Here Black Lives Matter crusades in the United States and the UK provide a kind of case study for exploring such issues.

Finally, in part 3, "Envisioning, Pursuing, and Shaping the Future World House: Where Do We Go from Here?," the authors look ahead and envisage King's concept of the great world house for the twenty-first century. Chapter 11, by Hak Joon Lee, a Christian ethicist and public theologian, engages with current approaches to global ethics as it examines King's theology, ethics, and ministerial practices as the basis for a twenty-first-century global ethics. Lee discusses King's global ethics in terms of four categories—vision, values (norms), virtues, and practices—while seeking the implications for our current global political and economic circumstances. Lee argues that King continues to make a unique contribution to scholarly discussions and practices through his carefully conceived vision of the world house.

In the book's final essay, chapter 12, Lewis V. Baldwin, an authority on religious and cultural history, treats King as a symbol of a globalized rights culture and explores the imaginative potential of his vision for future generations. He maintains that King's strong and persistent efforts to bring the world house vision to fruition in his own lifetime will continue to resonate across the globe, and that his ideas and insights will continue to inform facets of the globalized rights culture. Baldwin pays considerable attention to how the world currently honors King and to King's legacy of ideas and social praxis and what this potentially means for future generations, particularly as they deal with the enduring problems of bigotry, intolerance, injustice, and oppression. The chapter concludes that King's ideas are useful for a reshaping of the processes of globalization and that he will remain a powerful and refreshing voice for rethinking issues around global justice and the advancement of democracy, freedom, and human rights in the years to come.

Generally speaking, this book reclaims King's significance as a globalist who never separated his people's struggle in the United States from that larger crusade for the liberation and empowerment of oppressed peoples everywhere. Thus, he continues to inform our sense of what it means to be truly human and ethical in an increasingly pluralistic, disturbingly tribalistic, and rapidly changing world.

NOTES

The epigraph is from Martin Luther King Jr., *The Trumpet of Conscience* (San Francisco: Harper & Row, 1967), 50.

1. Several important books have focused significantly on King's global consciousness and contributions as a world leader. See Lewis V. Baldwin, *Toward the Beloved Community: Martin Luther King, Jr. and South Africa* (Cleveland: Pilgrim Press, 1995); Lewis V. Baldwin and Paul Dekar, eds., *"In an Inescapable Network of Mutuality": Martin Luther King, Jr. and the Globalization of an Ethical Ideal* (Eugene, Ore.: Cascade Books, 2013); and Hak Joon Lee, *The Great World House: Martin Luther King, Jr., and Global Ethics* (Cleveland: Pilgrim Press, 2011).

2. Martin Luther King Jr., *Where Do We Go from Here: Chaos or Community?* (Boston: Beacon Press, 1967; rpt., 1968, 2010), 167–91. See also King, *Trumpet of Conscience*, 31.

3. King, *Where Do We Go from Here?*, 167.

4. Ibid., 201. It should be noted here and in other quotations cited throughout this volume that King's language reflected a gender-biased use of masculine nouns and pronouns when generically referencing both women and men. The implications of King's use of sexist language along with his views on women and relationships with women leaders and activists have been the subject for analysis by several authors, including Linda T. Wynn, "Beyond Patriarchy: The Meaning of Martin Luther King, Jr. for the Women of the World," in Baldwin and Dekar, *"In an Inescapable Network of Mutuality,"* chap. 3. See also chapter 5 in this volume, Crystal A. deGregory and Lewis V. Baldwin, "Sexism in the World House."

5. For background on King's formative years, see Martin Luther King Jr., *The Autobiography of Martin Luther King, Jr.*, edited by Clayborne Carson (New York: Warner Books, 1998), 1–16. King was largely influenced by both his father and mother, who resisted segregation and maintained a sense of dignity throughout their lives. Martin Luther King Sr. was the prominent pastor of Atlanta's Ebenezer Baptist Church, following his father-in-law, Adam Daniel Williams. King Sr. was also among Atlanta's black leadership circle that challenged Jim Crow through the NAACP, the Atlanta Negro Voters League, and other civic associations.

6. See the Morehouse College Martin Luther King Jr. (MLK) Collection, series 5: Educational Materials, Robert W. Woodruff Library, Atlanta. The series includes seminal documents from King's years at Morehouse College and Crozer Seminary.

7. See, for example, Martin Luther King Jr., "Mental and Spiritual Slavery," an unpublished sermon outline based on James Russell Lowell's poem "A Stanza on Freedom." For King's use of these and a range of other sources, see W. Jason Miller, *Origins of the Dream: Hughes's Poetry and King's Rhetoric* (Gainesville: University Press of Florida, 2015); Carolyn Calloway-Thomas and John L. Lucaites, eds., *Martin Luther King, Jr., and the Sermonic Power*

of Public Discourse (Tuscaloosa: University of Alabama Press, 1993); and Jonathan Rieder, *The Word of the Lord Is upon Me: The Righteous Performance of Martin Luther King, Jr.* (Cambridge, Mass.: Belknap Press of Harvard University Press, 2008).

8. See Randal Maurice Jelks, *Benjamin E. Mays, Schoolmaster of the Movement: A Biography* (Chapel Hill: University of North Carolina Press, 2012), which traces the profound impact of Mays on the education of leaders of the black church and a generation of educators, activists, and policy makers. Jelks documents the deep influence of Mays on King, who called Mays "one of the great influences on my life." King, *Autobiography of Martin Luther King, Jr.*, 16.

9. In his studies of King's theological social ethics, Rufus Burrow traces King's personalist ideas to his family background and black southern community values. Formal study of personalism while at Crozer and Boston University enabled King to "draw out the deeper implications of the meaning of human dignity, the need for self-love and respect for others." Burrow concludes that this formal study of personalism "contributed much to King's overall theological and philosophical development." Rufus Burrow Jr., *Martin Luther King, Jr., and the Theology of Resistance* (Jefferson, N.C.: McFarland, 2015), 19. See also Rufus Burrow Jr., *God and Human Dignity: The Personalism, Theology, and Ethics of Martin Luther King, Jr.* (Notre Dame: University of Notre Dame Press, 2006), and Rufus Burrow Jr., *Extremist for Love: Martin Luther King, Jr., Man of Ideas and Nonviolent Social Action* (Minneapolis: Fortress Press, 2014).

10. Burrow, *Martin Luther King, Jr. and the Theology of Resistance*, 5.

11. Martin Luther King Jr., *The Papers of Martin Luther King, Jr.*, vol. 6, *Advocate of the Social Gospel, September 1948–March 1963*, edited by Clayborne Carson, Susan Carson, Susan Englander, Troy Jackson, and Gerald L. Smith (Berkeley: University of California Press, 2007), 86.

12. Morehouse College MLK Collection, series 2: Writings by Martin Luther King Jr.

13. King, *Autobiography of Martin Luther King, Jr.*, 23–24.

14. Ibid., 36.

15. Coretta Scott King, *My Life with Martin Luther King, Jr.*, rev. ed. (New York: Henry Holt, 1993), 142–43.

16. Martin Luther King Jr., "Statement Regarding the Legitimacy of the Struggle in Montgomery, Alabama," May 4, 1956, Martin Luther King Jr. Papers, Howard Gottlieb Archival Research Center, Mugar Memorial Library, Boston University, Boston.

17. Lewis V. Baldwin, *There Is a Balm in Gilead: The Cultural Roots of Martin Luther King, Jr.* (Minneapolis: Fortress Press, 1991), 4–5, 323; and Adam Fairclough, "The Southern Christian Leadership Conference and the Second Reconstruction, 1957–1973," *The Southern Atlantic Quarterly*, Vol. 8, no. 2 (Spring, 1981): 178.

18. Martin Luther King Jr., *The Papers of Martin Luther King, Jr.*, vol. 6, 183.

19. Martin Luther King Jr., *A Testament of Hope: The Essential Writings and Speeches of Martin Luther King, Jr.*, edited by James Melvin Washington (New York: HarperCollins Publishers, 1986), 25, 30; Martin Luther King, Jr., *The Papers of Martin Luther King, Jr.*, vol. 5, *Threshold of a New Decade, January 1959–December 1960*, edited by Clayborne Carson, Tenisha Armstrong, Susan Carson, Adrienne Clay, and Kieran Taylor (Berkeley: University of California Press, 2005), 304; and William D. Watley, *Roots of Resistance: The Nonviolent Ethic of Martin Luther King, Jr.* (Valley Forge, Pa.: Judson Press, 1985), 101.

20. See Lewis V. Baldwin's definitive study of King and his influence on and connections in South Africa in Baldwin, *Toward the Beloved Community*, 1–185.

21. Martin Luther King Jr., "The Quest for Peace and Justice," Morehouse MLK Collection, series 2.

22. Ibid.

23. Ibid.

24. Martin Luther King Jr., *Testament of Hope*, 241.

25. George W. Shepard Jr., "Who Killed Martin Luther King's Dream?," *Africa Today* 15, no. 2 (April/May, 1968): 2.

26. Martin Luther King Jr., "Doubts and Certainties Link: Transcript of an Interview," London, UK, Martin Luther King Jr. Papers, Library and Archives of the Martin Luther King Jr. Center for Nonviolent Social Change, Atlanta.

27. Martin Luther King Jr., *Why We Can't Wait* (New York: New American Library, 1963), 77.

28. Ronald Sunderland and Earl Shelp describe King as "an American pastor who cared deeply about the soul of his nation." One might argue that King, in a larger sense, was also a pastor to the world—one who was equally committed to the redemption of the soul of the world. The eighteenth-century English Evangelist and revivalist John Wesley (1703–91) often said that the world was his parish. This was no less true for King but for different reasons, of course. See Earl E. Shelp and Ronald H. Sunderland, eds., *The Pastor as Prophet* (New York: Pilgrim Press, 1985), 15.

PART I
CREATIVE LIVING IN THE GREAT WORLD HOUSE
THE VISION OF MARTIN LUTHER KING JR. IN CONTEXT— WHERE WE WERE THEN

CHAPTER 1
FOR THE BEAUTY OF THE WORLD
VISION AND MORAL ORDER IN
MARTIN LUTHER KING JR.'S WORLD HOUSE

VICTOR ANDERSON AND TERESA DELGADO

Your vision will become clear only when you can look into your own
heart. Who looks outside, dreams; who looks inside, awakes.
CARL JUNG, *Letters*, volume 1

Frequently there appear on the stage of history individuals who have the insight to
look beyond the inadequacies of the old order and see the necessity for the new.
These are the persons with a sort of divine discontent. They realize that the world
as it is is far from the world that ought to be. They never confuse the "isness" of
an old order with the "oughtness" of a new order. And so in every age and every
generation there are those persons who have envisioned some new order.
MARTIN LUTHER KING JR., "THE VISION OF A WORLD MADE NEW"

This chapter explores Martin Luther King Jr.'s moral philosophy of nonviolent
resistance through the lens of what moral philosophers describe as disposi-
tional ethics. Here we explore King's moral disposition, which is his ethical orientation toward reality and the world. Ethics is not only about moral norms,
principles, styles of reasoning, critical judgments, and accounts of goods and
ends. However, King's moral philosophy has much to do with how he came to
see the world inhabited by all. It reflects his moral attitude and his basic moral
orientation toward the world and humans who inhabit it and interact with it not
always carefully or with the health of the planet in mind. King's moral philosophy literally comes to terms with how he saw the world, social reality, and possibilities for worlds to come. Powers of seeing, of insight, are a characteristic aspect of prophetic moral visionaries such as King.

In the first section of this chapter, we describe King's moral view as stereoscopic. To see stereoscopically is to see through binoculars. It is to see the world
and social reality clearly, in three dimensions. In the second section, we discuss King's pilgrimage to India in 1959 to see Mohandas Gandhi's influence
there. King would come to see India as light in the darkness, and Gandhi and

India would be moral compasses guiding his vision of the world house. In the third section, we track King's return to the United States and his enthusiastic and deep commitment to nonviolent resistance as the means toward ordering the world house even as he faced great challenges to his vision and disappointments. The chapter concludes with a critical assessment of King's vision of the world house in light of twenty-first-century social realities.

To See More Clearly:
Moral Vision through Stereoscopic Lenses

"In each of us," Martin Luther King Jr. says, "there are two basic faculties, the ethical and the aesthetic, our sense of duty and our sense of beauty."[1] Together they form stereoscopic lenses for King's moral attitude and orientation toward the world. To clarify what we mean by "stereoscopic," a familiar example might be helpful. In a typical eye examination one is asked to read a chart of letters on a distant wall, scaled from largest on top to smallest at bottom. One is then asked to view the chart through different lenses, with one eye open and the other shielded. Next one views the chart through various lenses to find the lens that provides the greatest clarity on the smallest letters on the chart. This procedure is repeated with the other eye. The goal is to eventually see and read the letters as clearly and distinctly as possible with both eyes open, stereoscopically.

Stereoscopic sight simultaneously brings into focus two angles of vision, thus producing a richly defined three-dimensional perspective on the world and reality. Moral philosophers have too often regarded the ethical and the aesthetic as two separate spheres to be observed one at a time, as if with one eye open and the other closed. Ethics, however, is more than deliberating over courses of action to take or what one's duty requires when confronted with dilemmas. Ethics also presents us with competing aesthetic pictures or visions of the world: alternative visions of what comprise good, cooperative communities, planetary flourishing, and human fulfillment. This wide moral scope that includes aesthetics fills out King's moral vision of the world house.

Further, as King understood so well, one's moral vision of the world must take into view human desires, conflicting purposes, and subjectivity that motivate social relations and politics. These aspects of human personality support ethical senses of duty, responsibility, obligation, and vision. Further, moral aspirations and expectations are also affected by our experiences and by how we see the world. For instance, we experience life in part as subjects being acted upon by circumstances, such that sometimes our aspirations are thwarted despite our best intentions. To be sure, human survival and prospects we hold for planetary equilibrium depend on our creative abilities that include not only cognition but also aesthetic sensibilities, which take account of human survival needs and capacities for seeing beauty, harmony, wonder, and mystery in the world. This powerful unity between thought and beauty is needed to address moral quandaries, with all of their ambiguities. We aspire for beauty and peace but experience ugliness and conflict, and our moral aspirations are constantly met by limits and feelings of inadequacy and sometimes futility. But we are not at the whims of fate. King was convinced of this, and it was the moral core of his stereoscopic vision of the world house. With both eyes open, despite seeing a world pervaded by human conflict and tragedy, he nevertheless envisioned a moral ordering of a common humanity living in peace.

King articulated his vision of moral order by asserting: "A widely separated family inherits a house in which they have to live together. This is our common inheritance. This is the great new problem of mankind. We have inherited a large house, a great 'world house' in which we have to live together." From one angle of vision, King saw a dysfunctional family living in a perpetual state of war. From another view, he saw moments of mutuality and creative exchange that modeled the actualization of peaceful community, diverse peoples that had "learned to live with each other in peace."[2] For King, post-independence India provided a moral case study and included both strife and creative actualization.

Moral visionaries like King offer stereoscopic perspectives on the world, a world of violence and strife but a world too in which enlightened people sometimes act in ways that foster peace and justice, that empower mutually transformative understanding, appreciation, and cooperation. To shut off such possibilities was a mistake, King believed, and this was his criticism of revolutionary members of the Black Power movement. The world is vast, and the word "world" is not necessarily limited to being synonymous with our home, the earth. Religious philosopher Victor Anderson metaphysically describes the world as "fluid, dynamic, processive, and exhibit[ing] the possibilities of tragedy and irony in human experience. In its concrete actuality and transcendent potentiality," the world discloses "the paradoxical, rhythmic push and pull of formation and deformation, life and death, and emergent galaxies and collapsing universes."[3] The world then is an expansive whole that even extends to interstellar and intergalactic relations.

King was well aware of the ways that science and technology were making inroads into space exploration. With an air of enchantment he wrote: "Physical science will carve new highways through the stratosphere. In a few years astronauts and cosmonauts will probably walk comfortably across the uncertain pathways of the moon." He was dazzled by human creativity in physical science and medicine and its potential for curing cancer and heart disease, and by technology, automation, and cybernation, all making "for working-people to have undreamed-of amounts of leisure time."[4]

For King, human creative intelligence and inventiveness were aspects of the beauty of the world house. With one eye he regarded "all this [as] a dazzling picture of the furniture, the workshop, the spacious rooms, the new decorations and the architectural pattern of the large world house in which we are living." Yet with the other eye he saw that this same creativity and inventiveness were misused and misdirected toward destructive ends: "One hundred years ago military men had not yet developed the terrifying weapons of warfare that we know today—not the bomber, an airborne fortress raining down death; not napalm, that burner of all things and flesh in its path."[5]

Inasmuch as King acknowledged evil in the world, he also stereoscopically saw a bigger picture, one that included ethical and aesthetic values necessary for moral order. He deeply perceived the world's ambiguities and complexity. When King was a student at Crozer Theological Seminary in Chester, Pennsylvania, in the late 1940s and early 1950s, his moral disposition was developing and critically informing his vision of the world and moral reality. Discussing Edgar Brightman's *Philosophy of Religion* and its treatment of human value and personality, King concluded: "If courage and meaning are imparted to life by a short {look} into the future, how much more dignity, hope, and perspective arise from the faith that every life capable of purposive development is eternal. Immortality symbolizes the intrinsic value of the individual person, the intrinsic value of shared, cooperative living, and the goodness of God."[6] King affirmed here a vision of human worth from the perspective of the goodness of God.

In another paper, titled "Religion's Answer to the Problem of Evil," King turned his eye to the world's dark side: "At the heart of all high religion there is the conviction that there is behind the universe an ultimate power which is perfectly good. In other words, the theist says: the power that is behind all things is good. But on every hand the facts of life seem to contradict such a faith. Nature is often cruel. 'Nearly all the things which men are hanged or imprisoned for doing to one another,' says John Stuart Mill, 'are nature's everyday performances. Nature kills, burns, starves, freezes, poisons.' Not only that, but the world seems positively immoral."[7] Later in the paper, young King concluded: "Evil is a reality. No one can make light of disease, slavery, war, or famine. It might be true that God is in heaven, but all is not right with the world, and only the superficial optimist who refuses to face the realities of life fails to see this patent fact."[8] King was no superficial optimist. He saw clearly in Mill's theodical contentions a dark truth about the world even as he clearly saw the tendency toward beauty, personality, and goodness in the world. Given the paradoxical character of the world, King maintained simply, "There is evil as well as value."[9]

This is a core insight into King's moral vision of the world house. On June 4, 1957, King addressed YMCA and YWCA student members at the University of California, Berkeley, and explained his moral philosophy of nonviolent direct action. He was keenly aware that his philosophy and its moral norms of agape and justice were not likely to win over black radicals and young people skeptical of religion and religious morality. He did not and could not presume any rhetorical advantage for his vision among these students, even as he tried to explain the ways in which agape was compatible with robust social activism and nonviolent direct action compatible with the demands of social justice. He was face to face with students who could not accept what he took for granted, namely that agape and justice are the only sure foundations undergirding the beauty of the world. King said to the students.

> I am quite aware of the fact that there are persons who believe firmly in nonviolence who do not believe in a personal God, but I think every person who believes in nonviolent resistance believes somehow that the universe in some form is on the side of justice. That there is something unfolding in the universe whether one speaks of it as an unconscious process, or whether one speaks of it as some unmoved mover, or whether someone speaks of it as a personal God. There is something in the universe that unfolds for justice and so in Montgomery we felt somehow that as we struggled we had cosmic companionship. And this was one of the things that kept the people together, the belief that the universe is on the side of justice.[10]

King's stereoscopic vision of the world house is based on an all-pervasive confidence that the universe is measured by a moral arc bending toward justice and ordered by agape.

Two years after this speech, from February 3 to March 10, 1959, King made a pilgrimage to India. It proved to be a life-changing experience for him and his travel companions (wife Coretta Scott King and Montgomery Improvement Association colleague Lawrence Reddick).[11] He had studied the philosophy of Mohandas Gandhi, had deployed Gandhi's nonviolent direct action as means of social change in Montgomery, and had defended it before skeptics, and now he was taking a pilgrimage to post-independence India to see Gandhi's influence for himself. India proved to be a determinant moral case study and validation of King's moral philosophy of nonviolent resistance.

India: A Light Shining in Darkness

With King recovering from a near-fatal stabbing in Harlem, and shortly after the Montgomery bus boycott had come to a successful conclusion (the city passed an ordinance authorizing black passengers to sit anywhere they chose), friends urged: "Why don't you go to India and see for yourself what the Mahatma, whom you so admire, has wrought?"[12] The visit forever enlarged King's perspective on the African American struggle for freedom and civil rights and fed his global vision of a crowded and diverse humanity living in peace. Young King had come to India with a mind already somewhat swayed: "For a long time I had wanted to take a trip to India. Even as a child, the entire Orient held a strange fascination for me—the elephants, the tigers, the temples, the snake charmers, and all the other storybook characters."[13] Edward Said describes such Orientalism as a "virtual European invention." Since antiquity, he says, the East has been "a place of romance, exotic beings, haunting memories and landscapes, remarkable experiences." It is also the site of "Europe's greatest and richest and oldest colonies, the source of its civilizations and languages, its cultural contestations, and one of its deepest and most recurring images of the Other."[14]

It would be an overstatement to say that King's India visit changed his views of the exotic Orient. But it is fair to say that it reshaped his vision of India, making it a more moral and spiritual one. His account mentions no elephants, tigers, or snake charmers. He certainly visited temples and shrines, but their aura fades along with the storybook characters of Rudyard Kipling's *The Jungle Book*, replaced by visions of crowded humanity living together in relative peace. These dominate page after page of his account, following conversations with Richard Wright in Paris on the way to India, on the French attitude toward "the Negro question," while dining on "the best French cooking."[15]

King's account exudes a heightened sense of celebrity, with recognition at grand receptions, generous Indian hospitality, and long talks with national, civic, and spiritual leaders, including Vinoba Bhave, the sainted leader of the Bhoodan movement. He seems to have enjoyed the spectacle and some of the attention of being a celebrity, but the latter appears at times to have been nearly overwhelming. King would write: "Since our pictures were in the newspaper very often it was not unusual for us to be recognized by crowds in public places and on public conveyances. Occasionally I would take a morning walk in the large cities, and out of the most unexpected places someone would emerge and ask: 'Are you Martin Luther King?'"[16]

King would recall "hundreds of invitations," "the opportunity to share our views with thousands of Indian people," "endless conversations at numerous discussion sessions," and speaking to "university groups and public meetings all over India." He would surmise, "Because of the keen interest that the Indian people have in the race problem these meetings were usually packed." With every encounter, King would recollect, he had sensed mutuality and kinship: "We were looked upon as brothers, with the color of our skins as something of an asset. But the strongest bond of fraternity was the common cause of minority and colonial peoples in America, Africa, and Asia struggling to throw off racism and imperialism."[17]

King's meeting with Bhave proved to have a lasting impact on the formation of his moral vision of the world house. Bhave's Bhoodan movement started in 1951 with his travels by foot all over India, on a mission to initiate voluntary land redistribution from India's wealthy landowners to people of small villages throughout India, from which sustainable cooperative economic developments among India's landless poor could prosper.[18] The Bhoodan land reform movement struck a chord with King. With excitement, he wrote, "The Indians have already achieved greater results than we Americans would ever expect. For example, millions of acres of land have been given up by rich landlords and additional millions of acres have been given up to cooperative management by small farmers. . . . India is a tremendous force for peace and nonviolence, at home and abroad."[19]

King's vision of the moral ordering of the world house had a basis in reality. Nearly a decade after this encounter with Bhave, King would assert: "A genuine program on the part of the wealthy nations to make prosperity a reality for the poor nations will in the final analysis enlarge the prosperity of all. One of the best proofs that reality hinges on moral foundations is the fact that when men and governments work devotedly for the good of others, they achieve their own enrichment in the process."[20]

Given King's disposition to see reality stereoscopically, it is not surprising that he saw more than mutuality and beloved community in India. One eye was focused fully on the plight of India's poor, but even then he saw hopeful signs:

> Everywhere we went we saw crowded humanity—on the roads, in the city streets and squares, even in the villages. Most of the people were poor and poorly dressed. In the city of Bombay, for example, over a half million people—mostly unattached, unemployed, or partially employed males—slept out of doors every night. Great ills flowed from the poverty of India but strangely there was relatively little crime. This was another concrete manifestation of the wonderful spiritual quality of the Indian people. They were poor, jammed together, and half-starved, but they did not take it out on each other.[21]

India's caste system, however, was repugnant to King, as was the plight of the Dalits, or Untouchables, specifically. King witnessed not only poverty and over-crowding but also discrimination in employment, housing, and education. King and his companions felt grief for the Dalits but also a sense of social solidarity.

In a sermon preached on July 4, 1965, some years after his first encounter with the Dalits, King would reflect on this experience. In his sermon, King would describe having given an address in India at a school where the principal introduced him as "a fellow untouchable from the United States of America." King would recall:

> For a moment I was a bit shocked and peeved that I would be referred to as an untouchable. . . . I started thinking about the fact: twenty million of my brothers and sisters were still smothering in an airtight cage of poverty in an affluent society. I started thinking about the fact: these twenty million brothers and sisters were still by and large housed in rat-infested, unendurable slums in the big cities of our nation, still attending inadequate schools faced with improper recreational facilities. And I said to myself, "Yes, I am an untouchable, and every Negro in the United States of America is an untouchable."[22]

In King's view, however, the government of India was at work to assure the civil rights of the Dalits, and in this he saw repentance and acts of atonement. While such efforts would never pan out the way King hoped, he bemoaned that India was far ahead of the United States in rectifying discrimination, and he contended: "From the prime minster down to the village councilmen, everybody declared publicly that untouchability is wrong. But in the United States some of our highest officials declined to render a moral judgment on segregation, and some from the South publicly boasted of their determination to maintain segregation. That would be unthinkable in India."[23] King's judgment was over-optimistic, however, and he would subsequently acknowledge the limits of legislative intervention and how deeply caste was embedded in Indian cultural norms, undergirded by religious authority and socioeconomic privilege. Still King would note, "Although discrimination has not yet been eliminated in India . . . , it is a crime to practice discrimination against an untouchable."[24]

Before leaving India, with its crowded humanity living in mass poverty and its outcastes stationed to a life of starvation, disease, illiteracy, murder, rape, prostitution, and in some cases bonded servitude, King joined his wife Coretta and his other travel companion as they retreated to the shores of Cape Comorin.[25] They went there perhaps to rediscover some of the beauty of India after seeing its ugly side. King described the cape as the place where the "mass of India ends" and "the vast rolling waters of the oceans" begin. Sitting on a rock looking out into the sea, enthralled by its immensity and listening to "oceanic music," they watched as the sun sank into the ocean in the west while the moon rose in the east. "The radiant light of the rising moon shone supreme," King later recalled. And he reflected:

> God has the light that can shine through all the darkness. We have experiences when the light of day vanishes, leaving us in some dark and desolate midnight— moments when our highest hopes are turned into shambles of despair or when we are victims of some tragic injustice and some terrible exploitation. During such moments our spirits are almost overcome by gloom and despair, and we feel that there is no light anywhere. But ever and again, we look toward the east and discover that there is another light which shines even in the darkness, and "the spear of frustration" is transformed "into a shaft of light."[26]

King and his companions returned to the United States on March 18, 1959. He may have gone on his pilgrimage with childlike excitement, anticipating the wonders and adventures that the Orient would provide, but he arrived back in the United States "more convinced than ever before that nonviolent resistance was the most potent weapon available to oppressed people in their struggle for freedom." "It was a marvelous thing to see the amazing results of a nonviolent campaign," he reported. "I returned to America with a greater determination to achieve freedom for my people through nonviolent means. As a result of my visit to India, my understanding of nonviolence became greater and my commitment deeper."[27]

Without a Vision and Moral Order We Perish

Nine years passed. It was 1968. Notwithstanding some legislative and judicial civil rights gains in the United States, King's own light shining in the darkness seemed to have dimmed somewhat under the canopy of pervasive disappointments. The exhilarating insight and the commitment King felt upon returning to the United States from India was being tested by a slew of struggles and assaults. Racial segregation, the jailing and murdering of civil rights activists, the bombing of black homes and churches (including the killing of four girls in Birmingham), the raging war in Vietnam, mass poverty, slum housing, and rioting across the country: together these overshadowed hard-won legislative and judicial achievements. Violence appeared to be the norm, making King's vision of a peaceful great world house an even harder sale to many black students and organizers whose earlier skepticism had by then hardened into cynicism. The explosion of violence concomitant with the rise of the Black Power movement

personally and ambiguously affected King more than anything else he encountered. Even as he empathized with the movement's exasperation and resentment over the gradual pace in legislative racial reform and perpetual assaults
on the dignity of black humanity, he recoiled against its philosophical nihilism
as he saw it.

The light in the east shining in darkness had provided King a life-changing,
beautiful vision of the great world house and a greater commitment to build its
foundation by nonviolent means and with the moral norms of agape and justice. The Black Power movement, in King's estimation, sorely challenged the
vision, the means, and the norms. While interracial civil rights campaigns had
been successful, leading to the landmark Voting Rights Act of 1965, this tack
was challenged by the competing vision of increasingly militant Black Power,
marching under its own banner and to a different drumbeat.

The Black Power movement strained King's moral disposition. While he understood the political aims of the movement—advancing a robust consciousness of black pride, self-empowerment, and economic autonomy by any means
deemed necessary for achieving revolutionary outcomes—King derisively considered its ideology divisive, politically impotent, and a dead end. He decried
the moral disposition of Black Power leaders, sensing nihilism fueled by black
frustrations, rage, and disenfranchisement: "Black Power is a nihilistic philosophy born out of the conviction that the Negro can't win. It is, at bottom, the view
that American society is so hopelessly corrupt and enmeshed in evil that there
is no possibility of salvation from within."[28]

This sense of hopelessness that King perceived in the Black Power movement led him to critique its roots: the failures and limits of liberal legislative
reforms, malaise among white compatriots marching and campaigning with
blacks in freedom movements, and the insurgent white backlash throughout the South. Some of King's sternest critiques were aimed at the black middle class, which, he charged, had succumbed to the sin of forgetfulness. He declared: "Many middle-class Negroes have forgotten their roots and are more
concerned about 'conspicuous consumption' than about the cause of justice."
He went on to condemn their moral apathy as "shameful ingratitude," and he
accused middle-class blacks of sitting "in some serene and passionless realm of
isolation, untouched and unmoved by the agonies and struggles of their underprivileged brothers." "This kind of selfish detachment," he added, "has caused
the masses of Negroes to feel alienated not only from white society but also
from the Negro middle class. They feel that the average middle-class Negro has
no concern for their plight."[29]

King himself had been subject to this critique in 1966, when he and members of his Southern Christian Leadership Conference were in Chicago waging a housing campaign and meeting with residents and local gang leaders in the Lawndale community of the city's West Side. Looking back on those experiences, King judged that discontent among the residents and gang leaders rendered them bitter and "uncertain about the efficacy of nonviolent direct action as a strategy for improving their living conditions." King became a target in venting their bitterness and frustration, and his moral lens turned inward. His sense of inadequacy and futility are evident in these words from his last book:

> In all the speaking that I have done in the United States before varied audiences, including some hostile whites, the only time that I have been booed was one night in a Chicago mass meeting by some young members of the Black Power movement. I went home that night with an ugly feeling. Selfishly I thought of my sufferings and sacrifices over the last twelve years. Why would they boo one so close to them? But as I lay awake thinking, I finally came to myself, and I could not for the life of me have less than patience and understanding for those young people. For twelve years I, and others like me, had held out radiant promises of progress. I had preached to them about my dream. I had lectured to them about the not too distant day when they would have freedom, "all, here and now." I had urged them to have faith in America and in white society. Their hopes had soared. They were now booing because they felt that we were unable to deliver on our promises. They were booing because we had urged them to have faith in people who had too often proved to be unfaithful. They were now hostile because they were watching the dream that they had so readily accepted turn into a frustrating nightmare.[30]

Against the nightmarish U.S. social realties of the 1960s, the aura of King's revelatory light shining in the darkness appears to have been almost extinguished and with it a beautiful vision of a great world house at peace. Almost! King's paradoxical dictum persists: "There is evil as well as value."[31]

King's book *Where Do We Go from Here?* is a powerful moral critique of the light of reform and the darkness of despair in the world house. As a young student at Crozer, King was clear-sighted enough to see that evil is a reality and "only the superficial optimist who refuses to face the realities of life fails to see this patent fact."[32] In 1967, writing *Where Do We Go from Here?*, King insisted, "The Negro's disappointment is real and a part of the daily menu of our lives." He continued: "The only healthy answer lies in one's honest recognition of disappointment even as he still clings to hope, one's acceptance of finite disappointment even while clinging to infinite hope." This infinite hope requires an infinite vision and moral ordering of the world house inhabited by all. With a sense of moral urgency, King warned: "The large house in which we live demands that we transform this worldwide neighborhood into a worldwide brotherhood. Together we must learn to live as brothers or together we will be forced to perish as fools."[33]

Vision and Moral Order in the World House

Seeing through stereoscopic moral lenses, Martin Luther King Jr. did not discount the harsh realities of the social ills persistent in the United States any more than he discounted the plight of India's Dalits. Still, marshalling evidence, he persisted on the validity of his vision of the world as a house of peace. He recounted legislative reforms dismantling the hold of Jim Crow segregation in transportation, business and commerce, and education, and culminating in the monumental Voting Rights Act of 1965, and he noted President Lyndon Johnson's Great Society initiatives. To King, these were hard-won gains wrought by nonviolent means in campaigns from Montgomery to Selma, campaigns based on norms of agape and justice. They were also a rearranging of the old furnishings of the world house.

Challenging the moral strength of King's vision was the malaise of white compatriots and the black middle class. Earlier, at the beginning of the Montgomery movement, King had cautioned: "The danger facing the American Negro is that because of . . . astounding advances he will become complacent and feel that the overall problem is solved. . . . We must not become so complacent that we forget the struggles of other minorities. We must unite with oppressed minorities throughout the world."[34] Simultaneous challenges came from competing revolutionary moral visionaries within the Black Power movement and from hopelessness and rage among young blacks, who turned to riotous violence as a consequence of promises and dreams deferred.

King's recognition that "there is evil as well as value" brought into sharp focus that the ethical and the aesthetic both demanded attention. Obligation mattered, and cooperation was necessary. For humans' highest ideals to be actualized in the world house, King wrote, "we have to live together—black and white, Easterner and Westerner, Gentile and Jew, Catholic and Protestant, Muslim and Hindu—a family unduly separated in ideas, culture and interest, who because we can never again live apart, must learn somehow to live with each other in peace."[35]

Fifty years have passed since the publication of *Where Do We Go from Here?*, and one is tempted to repeat the adage, "As much as things change, they remain the same." What parallels strike contemporary readers of King's book! As during King's time, there have been reforms, and there has been backlash. In the United States, the past fifty years have witnessed strengthened and expanded civil rights through laws covering discrimination based on race, gender, and sexuality, and judicial affirmation of same-sex marriage, even while women's reproductive rights have been under increased attack. The same five decades have been an era of technological and scientific advances unimaginable in King's day. Through economic globalization, the future validated King's assertion: "All inhabitants of the globe are now neighbors. This worldwide neighborhood has been brought into being largely as a result of the modern scientific and technological revolutions."[36] Taken for granted is King's insistence that all are interdependent and that all life is interrelated—but the vision is mostly militaristic and economically competitive, not one of mutual assistance and harmony.

And we are not saved, as Derrick Bell has noted. Twenty years after the publication of King's last book, announcing his vision of a great world house, Bell would write:

> Jeremiah's lament that "we are not saved" echoes down through the ages and gives appropriate voice to present concerns of those who, flushed with the enthusiasm generated by the Supreme Court's 1954 holding that segregated public schools are unconstitutional, pledged publicly that the progeny of America's slaves would at last be "Free by 1963," the centennial of the Emancipation Proclamation. That pledge became the motto for the National Association for the Advancement of Colored People's 1959 convention in New York City, where were gathered, in jubilant euphoria, veterans of racial bias and society's hostility who believed that they had finally, and permanently, achieved the reform of the laws that had been for centuries vehicles for the oppression of black men, women, and children. Not even the most skeptical at that convention could have foreseen that, less than three decades later, that achievement would be so eroded as to bring us once again into fateful and frightful coincidence with Jeremiah's lament. With the realization that the salvation of racial equality has eluded us again, questions arise from the ashes of our expectations.[37]

In the midst of these changes and the rearrangement of the furnishings in the world house, there are renewed efforts to place the furniture back where it was, under the rationale that the reasons for rearrangement are no longer valid. The 2013 U.S. Supreme Court case *Shelby County v. Holder* ruled in a 5–4 decision that a central component of the 1965 Voting Rights Act was unconstitutional and no longer applicable as it had been when the law was enacted.[38] The dissenting opinion, articulated by Justice Ruth Bader Ginsberg, noted that gutting this key provision of the Voting Rights Act was akin to "throwing away your umbrella in a rainstorm because you're not getting wet." Not surprisingly, 53 percent of the states implicated in the ruling acted immediately to instate or reinstate voting restrictions that disproportionately disenfranchised poor people of color, precisely the communities the act was envisioned to protect. Gerrymandering, redistricting, cutting voting hours, eliminating same-day registration, moving polling places without significant advance notice to locations out of the reach of public transportation, eliminating constable positions held by persons of color: these are but a few examples of the measures enacted post-*Shelby* to move the furniture of the world house back to arrangements more reminiscent of the plantation house.

Still, King's vision entailed worldwide "brotherhood" and was not limited to voting rights, the African American community, or the United States. His experience of India's crowded humanity informed that vision and the war in Vietnam sharpened it. King's April 4, 1967, speech from New York City's Riverside Church, "Beyond Vietnam," delivered exactly one year prior to his assassination, focused that vision on the giant triplets racism, materialism, and militarism and challenged listeners to understand that the world house would never be a place of refuge and peace if its inhabitants were constantly pitted against each other. King urged: "If we will only make the right choice, we will be able to transform this pending cosmic elegy into a creative psalm of peace. If we will make the right choice, we will be able to transform the jangling discords of our world into a beautiful symphony of brotherhood."[39]

The spaces of crowded humanity that exploded with grief and fury in the United States after King's assassination in April 1968—Detroit, Newark, Baltimore, New York, Washington, and Pittsburgh—have become fifty years later the crowded spaces of gentrification. The result is less a beautiful symphony of human kinship and more a discordant pushing of poor people to the outskirts of cities that have housed them for decades. A similar phenomenon is occurring around the world, in Thailand, the Philippines, and Vietnam, where wealthy developers and the tourists their properties attract have premier access to prized coastal lands, pushing the poor to areas not supported by basic infrastructure.[40] And Puerto Rico, a colony of the United States that experienced devastating hurricanes in September 2017, is now struggling to maintain its population from another mass out-migration sparked by economic ruin, while venture and disaster capitalists are all too eager to "rescue" the island for personal profit.[41] What part of King's world house are we left to salvage when its legacy has morphed into a question of who gets to live in the upper quarters and who is relegated to the basement, where such hierarchies are not always delineated in black and white?

King's vision of the world house did not account for the land itself—the planet—upon which that house would be built. Rachel Carson's *Silent Spring* (1962) waged a searing critique of the damage inflicted by chemical pesticides on the ecosystem, and King's compatriot Cesar Chavez would take up that cause twenty-six years later in a thirty-six-day fast, but the moral order and vision of the world house did not extend past the front door.[42] As much as King was enthralled by the cosmos, marked by his experiences in India, and fascinated with the technological advancements evident in space exploration, his vision was refracted by the anthropocentrism of Christian theology that, up to that point, had framed salvation in exclusively human terms.

While King's razor-sharp analysis articulated the intersections of racism, materialism, and militarism, his stereoscopic view was not panoramic enough to see how all of these converged upon the planet itself. We now know how closely race, poverty, war, and environmental degradation are intertwined. A King contemporary and fellow peace and civil rights activist, Trappist monk Thomas Merton, was beginning to deepen his own awareness, an earth consciousness, most notably in his "Letters to a White Liberal" (1963), around the same time that he was inspired by and in communication with King.[43] Perhaps more direct engagement between these two moral visionaries would have broadened King's view of the world house. Indeed, such a retreat was planned for late April 1968, but King died before that could take place.[44]

Audre Lorde's classic essay "The Master's Tools Will Never Dismantle the Master's House" questioned white feminists at the time, asking: "What does it mean when the tools of a racist patriarchy are used to examine the fruits of that same patriarchy? It means that only the most narrow parameters of change are possible and allowable."[45] Should a similar question be asked in relation to King's vision of the great world house, where an anthropocentric Christian understanding of justice and beauty are embedded in both its foundation and frame? Is King's vision of the great world house too limited and narrow in view of what the world, indeed the cosmos, needs at this time? Are justice and beauty and a peaceful world house only possible after the current house is razed and a new one is constructed?

The work of contemplative activists who refuse to perpetuate the dualism and anthropocentric hierarchies of Christian tradition force those committed to King's world house legacy to broaden the aperture of his vision. Eco-womanist voices like that of Melanie L. Harris invite new and exciting possibilities for engaging human-earth consciousness that extend an ecumenical dialogue of a kind that was so much a part of King's own theological development.[46] The ethical and the aesthetic are ecumenically intertwined and, as King wrote, "caught in an inescapable network of mutuality, tied in a single garment of destiny." That mutuality must be recognized as encompassing the entire planet if it is to be true to the spirit in which those words were penned from a Birmingham, Alabama, jail in 1963.[47]

King's words, spoken exactly one year before his death, serve as a poignant reminder necessary for any appraisal of the vision and moral order of the world house: "[L]et us rededicate ourselves to the long and bitter, but beautiful, struggle for a new world."[48] Justice and beauty—the ethical and the aesthetic—are often privileged points of reference for King's world house legacy. "There is evil and there is value," and it is the struggle against evil and the search for value that focus and sharpen a stereoscopic vision of the world house. Rededication to this struggle, in our time as distinct from King's, is needed for a stereoscopic vision of justice and beauty to emerge and a new kind of world house to be imagined and constructed. Without sustained and faithful rededication, the vision of the world house is but a faded blueprint, and without a new vision the structure will not accommodate its inhabitants or cohere with the environment on which it is built.

NOTES

The epigraphs are from Carl Jung, BrainyQuote, https://www.brainyquote.com/; and Martin Luther King Jr., "The Vision of a World Made New," in *The Papers of Martin Luther King, Jr.*, vol. 6, *Advocate of the Social Gospel, September 1948–March 1963*, edited by Clayborne Carson, Susan Carson, Susan Englander, Troy Jackson, and Gerald L. Smith (Berkeley: University of California Press, 2007), 182.

1. Martin Luther King Jr., "Pharisee and Publican," unpublished sermon, Ebenezer Baptist Church, Atlanta, October 9, 1966, King Papers, Library and Archives of the Martin Luther King Center for Nonviolent Social Change, Atlanta.

2. Martin Luther King Jr., *Where Do We Go from Here: Chaos or Community?* (Boston: Beacon Press, 1967; rpt., 1968, 2010), 167.

3. Victor Anderson, *Pragmatic Theology: Negotiating the Intersections of an American Philosophy of Religion and Public Theology* (Albany: State University of New York Press, 1998), 111.

4. Martin Luther King Jr., *Where Do We Go from Here?*, 168–69.

5. Ibid., 168.

6. Martin Luther King Jr., "A Comparison and Impression of Religion Drawn from Dr. Brightman's Book, Entitled *A Philosophy of Religion*," in Martin Luther King Jr., *The Papers of Martin Luther King, Jr.*, vol. 1, *Called to Serve, January 1929–June 1951*, edited by Clayborne Carson, Ralph E. Luker, Penny A. Russell, and Louis R. Harlan (Berkeley: University of California Press, 1992), 414. French brackets in original.

7. Martin Luther King Jr., "Religion's Answer to the Problem of Evil," in *Papers of Martin Luther King, Jr.*, vol. 1, 416.

8. Ibid., 417.

9. Martin Luther King Jr., "A Conception and Impression of Religion Drawn from Dr. Brightman's Book, Entitled *A Philosophy of Religion*," in ibid., 414.

10. Martin Luther King Jr., "The Power of Nonviolence (1957)," in *A Testament of Hope: The Essential Writings and Speeches of Martin Luther King, Jr.*, edited by James M. Washington (New York: HarperCollins, 1986), 13–14.

11. The Montgomery Improvement Association was formed December 5, 1955, by black clergy and community leaders in Montgomery, Alabama.

12. Martin Luther King Jr., *The Autobiography of Martin Luther King, Jr.*, edited by Clayborne Carson (New York: Warner Books, 1998), 121. For King stabbing, see ibid., 117–20.

13. Ibid., 121.

14. Edward Said, "Orientalism (1978)," in *The Edward Said Reader*, edited by Mustafa Bayoumi and Andrew Rubin (New York: Vintage, 2000), 67–68.

15. King, *Autobiography of Martin Luther King, Jr.*, 122.

16. Ibid., 123.

17. Ibid.

18. "Biography—Vinoba Bhave, a Missionary for the Mother Earth," n.d., http://vinobabhave.org/index.php/biography.

19. King, *Autobiography of Martin Luther King, Jr.*, 126.

20. Martin Luther King Jr., *Where Do We Go from Here?*, 180.

21. King, *Autobiography of Martin Luther King, Jr.*, 124–25.

22. Ibid., 131.

23. Ibid., 133.

24. Ibid.

25. Conditions for Dalits have not changed much nearly half a century later. See Hillary Mayell, "India's 'Untouchables' Face Violence, Discrimination," *National Geographic*, June 2, 2003, https://news.nationalgeographic.com/news/2003/06/indias -untouchables-face-violence-discrimination.

26. King, *Autobiography of Martin Luther King, Jr.*, 127–128.

27. Ibid., 134.

28. Martin Luther King Jr., *Where Do We Go from Here?*, 36–37, 44.

29. Ibid., 131–32.

30. Martin Luther King Jr., *Where Do We Go from Here?*, 45.

31. King, *Papers of Martin Luther King, Jr.*, vol. 1, 414.

32. Martin Luther King Jr., "Religion's Answer to the Problem of Evil," in *Papers of Martin Luther King, Jr.*, vol. 1, 417.

33. Martin Luther King Jr., *Where Do We Go from Here?*, 46, 171.

34. Martin Luther King Jr., "The Peril of Superficial Optimism in Race Relations," in *The Papers of Martin Luther King, Jr.*, vol. 6, *Advocate of the Social Gospel, September 1948–March 1963*, edited by Clayborne Carson, Susan Carson, Susan Englander, Troy Jackson, and Gerald L. Smith (Berkeley: University of California Press, 2007), 215.

35. Martin Luther King Jr., *Where Do We Go from Here?*, 167.

36. Ibid., 167–68.

37. Derrick Bell, *And We Are Not Saved: The Elusive Quest for Racial Justice* (New York: Basic Books, 1987), 3.

38. John Schwartz, "Between the Lines of the Voting Rights Act Opinion," *New York Times*, June 25, 2013. For more analysis of the court ruling, see Myrna Pérez and Vishal

Agraharkar, "If Section 5 Falls: New Voting Implications," Brennan Center for Justice, June 12, 2013, http://www.brennancenter.org/publication/if-section-5-falls-new -voting-implications.

39. Martin Luther King Jr., "Beyond Vietnam," in *A Call to Conscience: The Landmark Speeches of Dr. Martin Luther King, Jr.*, edited by Clayborne Carson and Kris Shepard (New York, Warner, 2001), 163–64.

40. Peter Penz, Jay Drydyk, and Pablo S. Bose, *Displacement by Development: Ethics, Rights and Responsibilities* (New York: Cambridge University Press, 2011); Erhard Berner, "Poverty Alleviation and the Eviction of the Poorest: Towards Urban Land Reform in the Philippines," *International Journal of Urban and Regional Research* 24, no. 3 (June 28, 2008): 536–53; Rowland Atkinson and Gary Bridge, *Gentrification in a Global Context: The New Urban Colonialism* (London: Routledge, 2005).

41. Simon Davis-Cohen, "Meet the Legal Theorists behind the Financial Takeover of Puerto Rico," *Nation*, October 30, 2017, https://www.thenation.com/article/meet-the -legal-theorists-behind-the-financial-takeover-of-puerto-rico. For extensive treatment of gentrification and the population swap in Puerto Rico, see Franz Strasser, "Puerto Rico's Population Swap: The Middle Class for Millionaires," *BBC News*, May 5, 2015, https:// puertoricosyllabus.com/huyendo-fleeing-crisis/gentrification-and-puerto-ricos-new -millionaires.

42. Rachel Carson, *Silent Spring* (New York: Houghton Mifflin, 1962); Jacques E. Levy, *Cesar Chavez: Autobiography of La Causa* (New York: W. W. Norton, 1975).

43. Monica Weis, *The Environmental Vision of Thomas Merton*, Culture of the Land (Lexington: University Press of Kentucky, 2011).

44. Patricia Lafevere, "Merton and King: Spiritual Brothers Who Never Had a Chance to Meet," *National Catholic Reporter*, April 4, 2018, https://www.ncronline.org/. Merton died suddenly in December 1968.

45. Audre Lorde, *Sister Outsider: Essays and Speeches* (Berkeley: Crossing Press, 2007), 110–14.

46. Melanie L. Harris. *Ecowomanism: African American Women and Earth-Honoring Faiths* (Maryknoll, N.Y.: Orbis, 2017).

47. See Martin Luther King Jr., *Why We Can't Wait* (New York: New American Library, 1963), 77.

48. Martin Luther King Jr., *Testament of Hope*, 243.

CHAPTER 2
THE SCOURGE OF THE COLOR BAR
RACISM AS A BARRIER TO HUMAN COMMUNITY

LARRY O. RIVERS

Racism is total estrangement. It separates not only bodies, but minds and spirits.
Inevitably it descends to inflicting spiritual or physical homicide upon the out-group.
MARTIN LUTHER KING JR., *Where Do We Go from Here?*

Too often at the level of individual action there seems to be no urgency for
implementation of the Christian ethic. Our generation demands of us not only
a spirit that voids superficial distinctions among men but a faith in collective
action to remove the social manifestations of superficial distinctions.
JAMES HUDSON, "Brotherhood in Christ"

On November 7, 1956, the lion's roar of the British Empire quieted to a whimper in Africa. Bowing to international pressure, the United Kingdom reluctantly stopped bombing the peninsular home of Mount Sinai, where Abrahamic religions say Moses received God's commandments.[1] Far across the Atlantic Ocean, in the southern Confederacy's former capital city, news of the Suez Crisis cease-fire seemed to confirm Martin Luther King Jr.'s faith that God's moral laws would prevail. Six days later, journalists around the world flooded him with requests for a comment on the U.S. Supreme Court's decision upholding a district court ruling that racial segregation in public transportation systems was unconstitutional—a victory for the eleven-month-old Montgomery bus boycott.[2] While King perceived both the high court's action and the halt of Britain's advance in Egypt as triumphs against racism, during television and newspaper interviews he carefully refrained from revealing his opposition to imperialistic conquests. Instead, he preferred to cast the battle against Jim Crow as simply an extension of U.S. efforts to spread democratic, equalitarian principles.[3] Nonetheless, before listeners he knew shared his anticolonial sentiments, King decried American and European exploitation of people of color throughout the globe with a directness that most reporters would not record for another nine years.[4]

For instance, in a sermon delivered to his parishioners at Montgomery's Dexter Avenue Baptist Church months later, on April 7, 1957, King argued that the British forces' attempt to take over the Suez Canal had failed in part because "they were fighting more than Egypt. They were attacking world opinion, they were fighting the whole Asian-African bloc." Observing how Britain's invasion of Egypt enraged that community of nations, one the United States wanted to court as an ally against the Soviet Union, he observed that the White House had marshaled its economic might to impel America's closest global partner to abandon its military venture. This underscored King's belief that the Asian-African bloc, newly empowered with leverage as a consequence of the Cold War, "is the bloc that now thinks and moves and determines the course of the history of the world."[5] Significantly, he viewed the British Empire's decline—hastened by the Suez humiliation that had followed India's independence—as illustrating the sort of repercussion that awaited nations that violated God's moral laws. Here King built upon points from his December 6, 1956, address at Howard University. Western civilization, led by the United States, he had insisted, perpetuated colonialism rooted in a white supremacist outlook. This made it, King believed, a "prodigal son" that had to be called home to redemption and atonement, lest it be crushed by the corrective force of universal moral laws. "I can hear a voice crying out through the distance of time saying, 'Western civilization you've strayed away to the far country of colonialism and imperialism, you have taken one billion six hundred million colored people of the world and exploited them and dominated them and crushed them,'" he preached, "'but western civilization, if you will rise up and come back home I'll take you in and make this a better world.'"[6]

Moral force underscored all. Britain, one of Western civilization's greatest powers, was a prodigal son that had refused to come home before its imbalance with the objective moral order surpassed the tipping point. This objective moral order, King believed, comprised a system of moral laws God had set in place along with the objective physical order that included the law of gravity.[7] "God has injected a principle in this universe," King explained to his Dexter Avenue Baptist flock. "God has said that all men must respect the dignity and worth of all human personality, 'And if you don't do that, I will take charge.'"[8] The minister's next words anticipated his future warning to the United States about its arrogance on the world stage.[9] "It seems this morning that I can hear God speaking," he expressed. "I can hear him speaking throughout the universe, saying, 'Be still, and know that I am God.' And if you don't stop, if you don't straighten up, if you don't stop exploiting people, I'm going to rise up and break the backbone of your power. And your power will be no more!' And the power of Great

Britain is no more." Referencing the British boast that "the sun never sets on our great Empire," King said that things had changed: "The sun hardly rises on the British Empire. Because it was based on exploitation. Because the God of the universe eventually takes a stand."[10]

King's December 1956 message to his Montgomery congregation that Sunday combined personalistic philosophy with prophetic interpretation. As a theistic personalist, Martin Luther King Jr. viewed existence as a community of interdependent human persons, self-conscious beings endowed with the capacity to reason and think morally, within God—the supreme person.[11] Racism, in his eyes, existed as a human-made division that stood in conflict with the system of moral laws God had established. This nefarious social edifice hindered the Lord's children from living as brothers and sisters in the manner that God intended. Thus, King's ministry confronted racism as part of its mission to challenge obstacles that impeded social facts from aligning with spiritual realities.[12] Globally, King saw imperialism—especially in its cultural and neocolonial forms—and apartheid as white supremacist structures that threatened the world house.

"My parents would always tell me that I should not hate the white man"

The roots of King's conceptualization of racism as an internationally corrosive social vice arose from his upbringing. As a child in Atlanta, he adopted what theologian Rufus Burrow Jr. terms a "homespun personalism."[13] This evolution began when his parents, Alberta Williams King and Martin Luther King Sr., introduced him to the *imago Dei* principle by teaching him that he, like all other human beings, was created in God's image.[14] All humans—regardless of skin color—were God's children. This meant there was no spiritually sound justification for racism anywhere in God's creation. Sermons and Sunday school lessons at Atlanta's Ebenezer Baptist Church, where his father pastored, reinforced the principles stressed during family discussions. King recalled: "My parents would always tell me that I should not hate the white man, but that it was my duty as a Christian to love him." Love for one's self and others, his parents added, meant using moral means to contest affronts against one's own sacred worth. He remembered his father's unyielding—but nonviolent—opposition to racial segregation through regular individual acts of resistance as well as his leadership in the Atlanta branch of the National Association for the Advancement of Colored People. "With this heritage, it is not surprising that I also learned to abhor segregation," King remarked, "considering it both rationally inexplicable and morally unjustifiable."[15]

Within the King household, the steadfast belief in universal human brotherhood merged with a parallel emphasis on exploring and learning about the world, in part through interacting with people from across the globe. In 1934, King Sr. and a group of ministers from various parts of the United States embarked to the Fifth Baptist World Congress, scheduled for August 4–10 in Germany. En route to the meeting they visited France, Italy, Tunisia, Libya, Egypt, and Palestine.[16] Finally, at the convention in Berlin's Kaiser-Damm Hall, King Sr. fellowshipped with seven thousand Baptists from Germany and more than thirty-two hundred others representing sixty additional countries.[17] He later recalled "praying, hoping, feeling that we could take back home, some of us, a new sense of how peace was to be accomplished among men."[18] This prefaced his son's future call for "true intergroup, interpersonal living."[19] Further, his visit to the region from which Protestantism had emerged influenced King Sr.'s ultimate decision to change his name and his eldest son's name from Michael King to Martin Luther King.[20] But Daddy King, as friends called him, also recounted how the ominous presence of Adolf Hitler's Nazi Party surrounded the interracial religious gathering, as "the militaristic march of jackboots continued beneath unfurling flags with swastikas emblazoned on them."[21] King Sr. remained resolute in keeping the light of hope that he witnessed during that convention burning bright amid the terror of the Third Reich. Five years later, in 1939, he chaired the local arrangements committee for the Sixth Baptist World Congress, which met in Atlanta.[22] Additionally King Sr. regularly read the African American–owned *Atlanta Daily World* and maintained a friendship with its long-time editor and publisher, Cornelius Adolphus Scott.[23] The *Atlanta Daily World* editions found in the King home throughout young Martin's childhood in the 1930s and 1940s featured articles on Mohandas K. Gandhi's nonviolent resistance campaigns against British colonial rule in India, Gandhi's criticism of European "exploitation of Africa," coverage of "German prejudice against Jews," African opposition to the Nazi government's efforts to regain control of its former colonies on the continent, post–World War II movements to avert the restoration of French and Dutch colonialism in Asia, and apartheid in South Africa.[24]

"Jesus Christ was not a white man"

A physician's handbag holds instruments such as a stethoscope, thermometer, and reflex hammer. A theologian's conceptual tool kit contains theoretical examination lenses and a social prescription pad for spiritual illnesses, but as King Jr. opened his in the late 1950s he found its contents inadequate for diagnosing, let alone treating, racism in "the world house."[25] His writings in 1957 reflected his growing self-awareness of this problem. That April he returned to his Dexter pulpit after an extended trek through Ghana, Nigeria, Italy, Switzerland, France, and the United Kingdom. Upon King's reentry into the United States, he attended a screening of *The Ten Commandments* in New York City.[26] While lauding the film for its riveting depiction of the Hebrew Exodus from pharaoh's bondage, he hinted at how the casting of white actors as ancient Egyptians reinforced the common misperception that Egypt was not part of Africa. "There are many familiar names associated with Africa that you would probably remember, and there are some countries in Africa that many people never realize," King said. "For instance, Egypt is in Africa."[27] King once more addressed race in the Judeo-Christian heritage in an edition of his "Advice for Living" column, published months later in *Ebony* magazine. A reader asked: "Why did God make Jesus white, when the majority of peoples in the world are non-white?" King, beginning with a disclaimer that "the color of Jesus' skin is of little or no consequence," asserted that Christ "would have been no more significant if His skin had been black. He is no less significant because His skin was white."[28] *Ebony* later published a letter from a respondent "disturbed" by King's answer. "I believe, as you do, that skin color 'shouldn't be' important," the reader stated. "But I don't believe Jesus was white. What is the basis for your assumption that he was?" No response from King ever appeared in the periodical.[29]

One might have heard clanging sounds from King rummaging through his theological tool kit and finding no instrument sufficient for answering the reader's question. Protestant doctrine and personalistic principles did not provide help, nor did liberal theology. Early in life, King had gravitated toward theological liberalism, and he would later recall, "At the age of thirteen, I shocked my Sunday school class by denying the bodily resurrection of Jesus."[30] After being formally trained in liberal theology in seminary and graduate school, he still stood firm in his rejection of biblical literalism and, for that matter, biblical infallibility.[31] Yet he apparently found it easier to dismiss dogma in the church led by his evangelical pastor father than to explain why he had passively accepted the idea that Jesus was white. During 1940, the year King turned eleven, sociologist E. Franklin Frazier published a study of the "personality development" of black youth in which one of his questions to children had been, "Is God a White Man?" Historians Edward J. Blum and Paul Harvey report that "what Frazier heard troubled him. Black youth bought into the great lie of white supremacy—that God and Jesus were white. . . . To Frazier, a belief in a white Jesus led to low self-esteem and poor group image, a point psychologists Kenneth and Mamie Clark made through their now-famous doll tests."[32] Frazier believed that black churches bore part of the blame, and he wrote: "The religious ideology of the Negro church tends to perpetuate such notions as a white God and white angels, conceptions which tend toward the disparagement of things black."[33] Three years after the Clarks' doll test had helped decide the 1954 *Brown v. Board of Education* case, King faced the question of whether he had demonstrated an internalized "preference for the white doll" when asked about Jesus's race.[34] Thereafter he began rethinking the image of the white Jesus he had accepted as fact.

By 1968 King had finally declared publicly that "Jesus Christ was not a white man."[35] This followed a period of reengagement with theologian Howard Thurman's 1949 *Jesus and the Disinherited* and an embrace of Black Power's call for "an audacious appreciation" of the black presence in world history.[36] Thurman argued that segregation used the symbolism of God "imaged as an elderly, benign white man," angels as "blonds and brunets," a red Satan, and black imps to rationalize race-based caste systems as "normal," "correct," "moral," and "religious." Thurman wrote: "The implications of such a view are simply fantastic in the intensity of their tragedy. Doomed on earth to a fixed and unremitting status of inferiority, of which segregation is symbolic, and at the same time cut off from the hope that the Creator intended it otherwise, those who are thus victimized are stripped of all social protection. It is vicious and thoroughly despicable to rationalize this position. . . . Under such circumstances, there is but a step from being despised to despising oneself."[37] King's change of thinking on Jesus's color also reflected how Black Power had challenged him to reexamine his assumptions. Describing Black Power as a "psychological call to manhood," he noted that "the job of arousing manhood within a people that had been taught for so many centuries that they were nobody is not easy. Even semantics have conspired to make that which is black seem ugly and degrading." King then pointed to how "in Roget's *Thesaurus* there are some 120 synonyms for blackness and at least sixty of them are offensive," including "devil." He contrasted that with the "some 134 synonyms for whiteness and all are favorable."[38]

No book within the then-emergent Black Power literature would have a greater influence than *The Autobiography of Malcolm X*, first published in 1965. It included Malcolm's recollection of a tense exchange between him, while a prisoner in Boston's Charlestown State Prison around 1952, and a visiting white seminary student from Harvard University. During a Bible class the seminarian had led, Malcolm had successfully prodded this student to concede that "Jesus was brown." Malcolm remembered, "In all of the years since, I have never met an intelligent white man who would try to insist that Jesus was white."[39] King's interest in Malcolm's life is well documented. Alex Haley, who assisted Malcolm in writing the autobiography, traveled to Atlanta in 1964 to interview King for *Playboy*. King "was privately intrigued to hear little-known things about Malcolm X I told him," Haley remarked in the epilogue to Malcolm's autobiography.[40] Following Malcolm's assassination in 1965, King offered a public statement that demonstrated to historian of religion Lewis V. Baldwin that he possessed "a broad knowledge of Malcolm's rise from poverty and crime to leadership in the Nation of Islam."[41] In the statement, King referred to how Malcolm's knowledge of the sexual abuse his grandmother had endured and the lynching of his father had helped fuel a "quest for meaning."[42] "Martin probably read Malcolm's interview with Alex Haley, which appeared in the May 1963 issue of *Playboy*," Baldwin asserted. "His deep knowledge of the Muslim leader's life history could not have resulted solely from watching the 1959 CBS documentary *The Hate That Hate Produced*. Malcolm's autobiography had not yet appeared in published form."[43] While it remains unclear whether King ever read *The Autobiography of Malcolm X*, the book was available to him in the period immediately following Malcolm's death, from February 1965 on. It is therefore possible that Malcolm's comments on Jesus's color had an effect on him.

Over time, King had come to see the concept of a white Jesus as a historically inaccurate idea that was regularly used to buttress racist worldviews. White privilege had shaped the Western world's predominant memory of Christ's color, often manifesting itself through cultural imperialism. As art historian Bernard Smith wrote, "Cultural imperialism is the imposition of the culture of an imperial power upon the culture of other peoples."[44] King did not use the term "cultural imperialism" in his final book, *Where Do We Go from Here? Chaos or Community*. But he described the sentiments that drove such conquests when he observed, "The Western arrogance of feeling that it has everything to teach others and nothing to learn from them is not just."[45] He did not go so far, though, as to state that Jesus was black.[46] Nor do King's well-known and most widely circulated writings contain criticism of artists whose works depicted Jesus as white. Here King might have applied the thesis from Reinhold Niebuhr's *Moral Man and Immoral Society*, which in King's summary "reminded us [that] groups tend to be more immoral than individuals."[47] Individual artists might have had innocent intentions when they drew, painted, molded, or theatrically presented Jesus as a white man. Art, after all, rejects the limitations of empiricism in its search for truth. King did not recant his previous praise of Leonardo da Vinci as a "great painter" who created a "beautiful picture" in *The Last Supper*.[48] Additionally, he did not express regrets for attending a special 1965 screening of George Stevens's film "*The Greatest Story Ever Told*" that served as a fund-raising event for his Southern Christian Leadership Conference. The movie showed Simon of Cyrene, played by Sidney Poitier, helping Jesus, played by a white actor in Max von Sydow, carry the cross.[49] One who does not believe Jesus was white might nevertheless find both spiritual sincerity and aesthetic allure in those works as well as Michelangelo Buonarroti's *The Last Judgment*, Diego Velázquez's *Christ Crucified*, Paul Landowski's *Christ the Redeemer* statue in Rio de Janeiro, and Salvador Dalí's *Christ of Saint John of the Cross*. Still, while King did not condemn those individual artists, he saw the symbolism of a white Jesus being weaponized at the group level to further racist ends both inside the United States and across the globe.

White supremacist Christology, King suggested, deified the supposed color of Jesus's skin. To King, this was not just theologically unsound, it also constituted blasphemy. Quoting one of his longtime role models, social ethicist George Kelsey, in *Where Do We Go from Here?*, King wrote: "Racism is a faith. It is a form of idolatry." Kelsey had explained that racism raised "a human factor," whiteness, "to the level of the ultimate," or God.[50] "Whiteness" as an object of sacred devotion and "blackness" as a mark of inferiority were obstacles to true community, King argued: "An individual has value because he has value to God. Whenever this is recognized, 'whiteness' and 'blackness' pass away as determinants in a relationship and 'son' and 'brother' are substituted." In the pages that followed, he denounced specific pseudoscientific and religious justifications for racism that had long hindered this reconciliation process, including the Teutonic origins theory, "head-size theory," and the claim "that the Negro was inferior by nature because of Noah's curse upon the children of Ham." The use of the Bible to portray God as a racial oppressor rather than a liberator particularly hurt and angered King. This rampant sacrilege, like a virus, had invaded the bloodstream of Christianity in Western civilization and sickened the entire body. "The greatest blasphemy of the whole ugly process was that the white man ended up making God his partner in the exploitation of the Negro," King wrote. "What greater heresy has religion known? Ethical Christianity vanished and the moral nerve of religion was atrophied. This terrible distortion sullied the essential nature of Christianity."[51]

The distinction King drew between "ethical Christianity" and the heretical "distortion" that sanctioned racism paralleled Howard Thurman's differentiation "between Christianity and the religion of Jesus." While in India in 1935, on a "pilgrimage of friendship" at the invitation of the World Student Christian Federation, Thurman detailed this to an Indian man who had called him "a traitor to all the darker peoples of the earth" for representing a religion used to justify the oppression of African Americans. Thurman explained that "the religion of Jesus projected a creative solution to the pressing problem of survival for the minority, of which He was a part in the Greco-Roman world. When Christianity became an imperial and world religion, it marched under banners other than that of the teacher and prophet of Galilee."[52] Like Thurman, King did not define the religion of Jesus dogmatically; he defined it ethically. King's Christianity was not based on confessing the belief that Jesus was a deity; rather, it was anchored in a commitment to the agape Jesus exemplified. "Agape is the highest form of love," King said. "It's completely unselfish. It seeks nothing in return."[53] This stood at the foundation of King's argument that Mohandas Gandhi was not only a Christian but, further, the foremost exemplar of Christianity in modern history. In 1959, following a visit to India during which King and his wife met a number of the late Gandhi's disciples and family members, King preached to his Dexter Avenue Baptist Church congregation: "Here was a man [Gandhi] who was not a Christian in terms of being a member of the Christian church but who was a Christian. And it is one of the strange ironies of the modern world that the greatest Christian of the twentieth century was not a member of the Christian church."[54] To reach those in the audience who did not share his theological liberalism, King grounded his premise in John 10:16, in which he quoted Jesus as saying, "I have other sheep, which are not of this fold." King continued: "I think this is what Jesus would say if he were living today concerning this passage, that 'I have people who are following me who've never joined the Christian church as an institution.'"[55]

King had not finished. Even more audaciously, he added: "And the second thing is, that this man [Gandhi] took the message of Jesus Christ and was able to do even greater works than Jesus did in his lifetime. Jesus himself predicted this: 'Ye shall do even greater work' [John 14:12]."[56] This expounded upon points King had made in his 1958 *Stride toward Freedom: The Montgomery Story.* There he had written: "Gandhi was probably the first person in history to lift the love ethic of Jesus above mere interaction between individuals to a powerful and effective social force on a large scale." The translation of that love ethic into what Gandhi had termed the "science of nonviolence" demonstrated, according to King, how "Christ furnished the spirit and the motivation while Gandhi furnished the method."[57] So even during a time in the late 1950s in which King still might have believed that Jesus had been white, he also held that a man of color had done "greater works than Jesus did" as part of battling racism. That work was now a light of hope in one of the most dangerous eras the world had ever experienced. "History has shown that, like a virulent disease germ, racism can grow and destroy nations," King wrote in *Where Do We Go from Here?* He quoted anthropologist Ruth Benedict in stating: "Since racism is based on the dogma 'that the hope of civilization depends upon eliminating some races and keeping others pure,' its ultimate logic is genocide. Hitler, in his mad and ruthless attempt to exterminate the Jews, carried the logic of racism to its ultimate tragic conclusions."[58] The German dictator's use of industrial technology to implement that hate-filled vision showed how in the twentieth century, more than any other previous period of history, racism posed an existential threat to civilization. Nuclear weapons, first developed by the United States with the intention of being deployed against the Nazi military, now were proliferating throughout a world in which racism still thrived.[59] "The choice today is no longer between violence and nonviolence," King insisted. "It is either nonviolence or nonexistence."[60] The emergence of Gandhi's scientific discipline of satyagraha, or love-force, from the soil of the love ethic tilled by Jesus and others revealed how the objective moral order was moving to counterbalance the presence of weapons of mass destruction.[61]

With an understanding of the religion of Jesus that emphasized the love ethic and rejected dogma, King wanted no part of the form of Christian evangelism that divided the world into the "saved" who accepted doctrine such as the divinity of Christ versus the "heathens" who did not. During his 1935 visit to India, Howard Thurman had informed his skeptical questioner that he did not "come to make converts to Christianity."[62] Echoing this aversion to missionary work that viewed anyone who did not identify as Christian as "lost," King declared: "Christianity should be a crusade not against infidels but against injustice."[63] This admonition struck at the core of the paternalistic "civilizing argument" that had depicted slavery and empire building as "Christian" causes. Shouting Jesus's name, churches had praised the mass "conversion" of black slaves in the American colonies during the eighteenth century's Great Awakening, evangelism throughout the so-called "dark continent" of Africa in the nineteenth century, and the U.S. expansionist conquests throughout South America and the Caribbean in the twentieth century (sometimes under the rubric "white man's burden," from the Kipling poem) as serving God's so-called purpose of reshaping "savages" into morally upstanding, industrious people.[64]

Throughout his ministry, King consistently opposed such racist interpretations of Jesus's call to "go and make disciples of all nations" (Matthew 28:19). He spoke against the stereotype of a "godless," "primitive" Africa that had needed to be saved by "Christian" Western civilization. For example, in a 1958 *Ebony* "Advice for Living" column, King argued against viewing African tribal faiths as completely detached from the God recognized by the Abrahamic tradition. "I believe that God reveals Himself in all religions," he wrote.[65] As King expounded upon this premise, his words paralleled the standpoint of theologian Benjamin E. Mays, one of his role models, who had concluded that Christianity owed much of its foundational structure to "the essential elements of Pagan religions."[66] Christianity, King said, "is the synthesis of the best in all religions. In this sense Christianity is more valid than the tribal religions practiced by our African ancestors. This does not mean that these tribal religions are totally devoid of truth. It simply means that Christianity, while flowing through the stream of history has incorporated the truths of all other religions and brought them together into a meaningful and coherent system."[67] And contrary to the claim that most African societies had been backward and full of "black cannibals and ignorant primitives" until their contact with Western nations, King pointed out how white-led foreign governments had actually destabilized the continent's states and stolen vast amounts of their wealth.[68] "For more than two hundred years before the Declaration of Independence, Africa had been raped and plundered by Britain and Europe, her native kingdoms disorganized, and her people and rulers demoralized," King wrote in *Where Do We Go from Here?*[69]

"Here we see racism in its more sophisticated form"

Although King lamented Christianity's role in Western empire building across Africa, Asia, and Latin America, he had faith that the machinery behind those racist invasions could be reconfigured for God's work. Identifying colonialism and imperialism as "the old order," he observed in 1954 that "one of the tragedies of the Church was that it became allied to the old order."[70] Ten years later, in a 1964 address to the European Baptist Assembly, King outlined the steps for the church's institutional redemption and atonement. They began with confessing the sins committed. Referring to the belief that the West was God's anointed vessel to Christianize the world, King advised: "We now realize that much of this was based on an unbiblical theology and that in our own enthusiasm to bring the world to Christ we allowed our faith in Christ and our faith in Western culture and technology to become interchanged."[71] Then, acknowledging that Christian missions provided charity, education, and medical services, he declared that these gifts were insufficient for making amends. "In a mass technological society, it is not enough to send missionary baskets. It is not enough to build schools and hospitals," King said. Similar to his support of the National Urban League's proposal for a domestic Marshall Plan to lift the "handicapped multitudes" of the United States, King called for multibillion-dollar spending to assist the countries that Western powers had exploited. "If millions are to be fed, clothed and housed, the resources of nations must be put to the task," King argued. "Mammoth programs of area development, comparable to the Marshall Plan, which aided in the rebuilding of Europe, must be developed to aid Africa and Asia." He declared that "Christians must encourage, yea demand" such action, concluding, "This is the road evangelism must take in these times."[72] With this change in priorities, the religious bodies that had perpetuated "unbiblical" and racist cultural imperialism in God's name could be redeemed and reborn into standard-bearers for an ethical Christianity that would revolutionize human relations.

Writing three years later in *Where Do We Go from Here?*, King added more details to the new plan that he challenged Christian churches to champion. "The wealthy nations of the world must promptly initiate a massive, sustained Marshall Plan for Asia, Africa and South America," King said. "If they would allocate just 2 percent of their gross national product annually for a period of ten or twenty years for the development of the underdeveloped nations, mankind would go a long way toward conquering the ancient enemy, poverty." Those "wealthy nations," he specified, were "America, Britain, Russia, Canada, and Australia, and those of Western Europe." King emphasized that money needed to be given based on "a moral obligation" and not merely used as bait to hook vulnerable countries into exploitive arrangements with former colonizers: "The aid program that I am suggesting must not be used by the wealthy nations as a surreptitious means to control the poor nations." King wrote, "Such an approach would lead to a new form of paternalism and a neocolonialism which no self-respecting nation could accept."[73]

The reference to neocolonialism appeared to build upon former Ghanaian prime minister Kwame Nkrumah's definition of the term. On March 6, 1957, King and his wife were Nkrumah's guests in Ghana during the ceremony celebrating the country's independence from British rule.[74] King, upon his return to the United States, continued to study Nkrumah's work, including his autobiography.[75] In 1966, the year the prime minister was ousted by a coup d'état, Nkrumah had published *Neo-Colonialism: The Last Stage of Imperialism*. "The essence of neo-colonialism is that the State which is subject to it is, in theory, independent and has all the outward trappings of international sovereignty," he wrote. "In reality its economic system and thus political policy is directed from outside." Nkrumah called neocolonialism "the worst form of imperialism" and stated that its result "is that foreign capital is used for the exploitation rather than for the development of the less-developed parts of the world."[76] King used similarly critical language against neocolonialism in *Where Do We Go from Here?* when he described it as "racism in its more sophisticated form." He drew a direct link between U.S. neocolonial intervention throughout Latin America and the intense disdain for Americans throughout that part of world. "Everywhere in Latin America one finds a tremendous resentment of the United States, and that resentment is always strongest among the poorer and darker peoples of the continent," he observed.[77]

That resentment, King believed, extended from Latin American awareness of his home country's hypocrisy. The nation preached liberty but, in practice, prioritized expansionist ends such as military alliances, trade agreements, access to raw materials, and control of waterways over human freedom. The Panama Canal was a daily reminder. It stood on territory the United States had acquired by undermining Colombian sovereignty and then developed at the cost of as many as fifteen thousand worker deaths, mainly of black West Indians killed by disease and industrial accidents.[78] Under U.S. neocolonialism, repressive undemocratic governments reigned throughout much of South America and the Caribbean. François "Papa Doc" Duvalier in Haiti and Anastasio Somoza in Nicaragua were among the dictators who ruled with U.S. support in 1967.[79] U.S.-backed military juntas also governed states such as Argentina, Brazil, and Ecuador.[80] "The decisions affecting the lives of South Americans are ostensibly made by their government, but there are almost no legitimate democracies alive in the whole continent," King wrote. "The other governments are dominated by huge and exploitive cartels that rob Latin America of her resources while turning over a small rebate to a few members of a corrupt aristocracy, which in turn invests not in its own country for its own people's welfare but in the banks of Switzerland and the playgrounds of the world." The disaffected men and women in those countries, unsurprisingly, were angry at the United States for its role in perpetuating this inequitable profiteering. "The life and destiny of Latin America are in the hands of United States corporations," King concluded. This unjust situation, in King's view, only served to add more and more people to the millions who already harbored animosity toward the United States. He said: "The Bible and the annals of history are replete with tragic stories of one brother robbing another of his birthright and thereby insuring generations of strife and enmity. We can hardly escape such a judgment in Latin America, any more than we have been able to escape the harvest of hate sown in Vietnam by a century of French exploitation."[81]

South Africa's "Policy of Organized Racism"

In 1948, a nineteen-year-old Martin Luther King Jr. graduated from Morehouse College with a bachelor of arts in sociology, President Harry Truman ordered the desegregation of the U.S. military, an assassin's bullet took Gandhi's life, and South Africa—where Gandhi had lived for twenty-one years—saw the ascent of apartheid.[82] The *Atlanta Daily World* denounced what it called "South African Jim Crow." One of its numerous articles on the topic included a 1952 wire story that described how South Africa was "executing a policy of apartheid, extreme racial segregation, with the purpose of keeping native Africans, Indians, colored persons of mixed blood, and whites separate from one another." The same report detailed a major development in the South African city of Phoenix, Natal, home of a settlement that Gandhi had founded. It said that Gandhi's second-oldest son, Manilal, "was following in the footsteps of his late father" by fasting in support of the African National Congress call for nationwide demonstrations against the discriminatory system.[83] King had recently initiated his first in-depth scholarly study of Gandhi in 1950 as a student at Crozer Theological Seminary in Pennsylvania. Gandhi's "experiments with truth," which had begun in South Africa, fascinated him.[84] Five years later, given an international platform thanks to the Montgomery bus boycott, King labored to mobilize worldwide political and economic pressure for apartheid's abolishment.

Nonviolent action methods can be grouped into three categories. Political theorist Gene Sharp terms them "protest and persuasion," noncooperation, and intervention.[85] Examples of King deploying "protest and persuasion" tactics against apartheid date back to at least 1957. During that year he was a signatory for the "Declaration of Conscience," produced by the pacifist American Committee on Africa (ACOA). The document stated: "The South African Government has relentlessly over the past few years extended its policy of organized racism—apartheid. 156 leaders who have peacefully sought a just society for all, black and white, are now charged with treason and involved in court action."[86] One of those defendants was Nelson Mandela, who had been arrested on December 5, 1956, the first anniversary of the start of the Montgomery bus boycott.[87] In response, the declaration called for a day of protest against South African apartheid on December 10, 1957, Human Rights Day.[88] As the U.S. vice-chairman of the effort, King urged clerics, scholars, and heads of state across the world to endorse the declaration, and he proved key in persuading 123 such individuals to sign.[89] Subsequently, as an extension of his work on the Declaration of Conscience, King helped garner about 150 signatures from academic, religious, political, and social movement leaders across the globe in support of the 1962 "Appeal for Action against Apartheid." King jointly released this ACOA statement with Albert John Lutuli, president of the African National Congress (ANC), who was the 1960 recipient of the Nobel Peace Prize.[90] The Appeal for Action transcended the nonviolent protest calls of the Declaration of Conscience by proposing nonviolent noncooperation, or withdrawal of participation in an unjust system's operations. For economic noncooperation, it recommended disinvestment in South Africa and a boycott against the country's products. Then, for political noncooperation, it advocated economic sanctions by individual governments and a United Nations "resolution calling for isolation of South Africa."[91]

International action was essential, King posited, because black South Africans had little freedom to effect nonviolent change on their own. Like Gandhi, King believed there was always a nonviolent solution to conflict. But, whereas African Americans had successfully elicited repeated federal enforcement of their First Amendment rights to peacefully assemble and petition "for a redress of grievances," with U.S. troops and the National Guard sent to escort demonstrators during a number of protests—the police state of South Africa regularly treated even nonviolent dissent as treason. "In South Africa even the mildest form of non-violent resistance meets with years of imprisonment, and the leaders over many years have been restricted and silenced and imprisoned," King said. "We can understand how in that situation people feel so desperate that they turned to other methods, such as sabotage."[92] Thus, men and women of conscience in countries that permitted nonviolent organizing had to bear the cross for their South African neighbors and push for their respective national governments to intervene. The sanctions King wanted against the apartheid regime would be no less severe than the U.S., British, and Dutch embargo against Japan decades earlier. Enacted in 1941, it had taken away 75 percent of Japan's foreign trade and 90 percent of its oil imports, leaving the industrialized country with oil reserves that would only sustain it for eighteen months at most.[93] Calling attention to how the United States, especially, kept the repressive South African state vibrant with "forty million dollars in loans through our most distinguished banking and financial institutions," mineral purchases, providing "a sugar quota," "maintaining three tracking stations there," and supplying refined uranium to its nuclear reactor, King said his home country and its allies had enough leverage to force apartheid's elimination.[94] "If the United Kingdom and the United States decided tomorrow morning not to buy South African goods, not to buy South African gold, to put an embargo on oil; if our investors and capitalists would withdraw their support for that racial tyranny, then apartheid would be brought an end," King said.[95]

Paralleling Ruth Benedict's argument that racism's "ultimate logic is genocide," King saw the apartheid regime as following the same path as the Third Reich. "The South African Government to make the white supreme has had to reach into the past and revive the nightmarish ideology and practices of Nazism," he said. "We are witnessing a recrudescence of that barbarism which murdered more humans than any war in history." Countries such as the United States, United Kingdom, and France—already guilty of helping to "prop up the

economy of South Africa" despite the Soviet Union's publicly announced openness to a boycott—would be partially culpable if a deadly pogrom occurred in
South Africa.[96] And if democratic countries regularly ignored or condoned human rights violations by their trade partners in the post–World War II age, then
the civilization-threatening violence of racism could swell, spread, and desta-
bilize nuclear-armed nations. "In a world living under the appalling shadow of
nuclear weapons do we not recognize the need to perfect the use of economic
pressures? Why is trade regarded by all nations and ideologies as sacred?," King
asked during a speech on South African independence.[97] His confidante Harry
Belafonte later recalled that "midway through the Civil Rights Movement," despite its progress in achieving desegregation, King had lamented: "I have come
to believe that we are integrating into a burning house." When Belafonte had
asked, "What should we do?," King had replied, "I guess we're just going to have
to become firemen."[98] Looking across the globe, King also saw the world house
ablaze from the fire of racism. Economic sanctions could be the powerful waters that extinguished those flames. There was no reason to just "confine an international boycott to South Africa," he said. "Rhodesia has earned a place as a
target, as has Portugal, colonial master of Angola and Mozambique. The time
has come for an international alliance of peoples of all nations against racism."[99]

Racism inevitably devolved into violence, and King saw violence as a barrier to human community.[100] These connections appeared to be on King's mind
when, on the last day of his life, he told his brother, Alfred Daniel King, that
he planned to deliver a sermon entitled, "Why America May Go to Hell."[101] In
1961, King had explained to *Ebony*: "I do not believe in hell as a place of a literal
burning fire. Hell, to me, is a condition of being out of fellowship with God. It is
man's refusal to accept the Grace of God."[102] The United States, Western civilization's primary power, continued to permit racism to drive a wedge between
it and God. Its neocolonialism and support of apartheid made that gap wider
each day. Western nations were now at a crossroads. Like the prodigal son, they
could select the path home or stray further from grace. If they chose the latter,
the decision might finally tip Western civilization's center of mass in the moral
universe toward a fall from which it could not recover. "If Western Civilization
does not now respond constructively to the challenge to banish racism, some
future historian will have to say that a great civilization died because it lacked
the soul and commitment to make justice a reality for all men," King wrote in his
final book.[103] To have a future, the Western world, he concluded, would have to
repent and then be reborn not as an empire but as a genuine community that
accepted the truth that all humanity had worth. Life anew was the answer, and
love was the way.

NOTES

The epigraphs are from Martin Luther King Jr., *Where Do We Go From Here? Chaos or Community* (Boston: Beacon Press, 1967; rpt., 1968, 2010), 74; James Hudson, "Brotherhood in Christ," intended for publication in *Young Adult Quarterly*, September 27, 1953, James Hudson Papers, Carrie Meek–James M. Eaton Sr. Southeastern Regional Black Archives Research Center and Museum, Florida A&M University, Tallahassee. James Hudson was a personalist philosopher, civil rights activist, and university chaplain. See Larry O. Rivers, "'A New Social Awakening': James Hudson, Florida A&M University's Religious Life Program, and the 1956 Tallahassee Bus Boycott," *Florida Historical Quarterly* 95 (Winter 2017): 325–55.

1. Scott Lucas, ed., *Britain and Suez: The Lion's Last Roar* (Manchester, UK: Manchester University Press, 1996), xii.

2. Martin Luther King Jr., *The Autobiography of Martin Luther King, Jr.*, edited by Clayborne Carson (New York: Warner, 1998), 93–94.

3. Thomas F. Jackson, *From Civil Rights to Human Rights: Martin Luther King, Jr., and the Struggle for Economic Justice* (Philadelphia: University of Pennsylvania Press, 2007), 68.

4. Ibid., 1–5, 218–370.

5. Martin Luther King Jr., "The Birth of a New Nation," *The Papers of Martin Luther King, Jr.*, vol. 4, *Symbol of the Movement, January 1957–December 1958*, edited by Clayborne Carson, Susan Carson, Adrienne Clay, Virginia Shadron, and Kieran Taylor (Berkeley: University of California Press, 2000), 165.

6. Martin Luther King Jr., "Remember Who You Are!", December 6, 1956, series 2, sub-series 2.2, Martin Luther King Jr. Collection, Morehouse College, Robert W. Woodruff Library, Atlanta University Center, Atlanta.

7. For example, in 1957 Martin Luther King Jr. said: "There are moral laws of the universe just as abiding as the physical laws, and when we disobey these moral laws we suffer tragic consequences." See Martin Luther King Jr., "Advice for Living," October 1957, in *Papers of Martin Luther King, Jr.*, vol. 4, 280.

8. Martin Luther King Jr., "Birth of a New Nation," 165.

9. See Martin Luther King Jr., "Why I Am Opposed to the War in Vietnam," April 4, 1967, speech, Riverside Church, New York City, excerpt in Orlando Bagwell and W. Noland Walker, directors, *Citizen King* (Alexandria, Va.: PBS Home Video, 2004), DVD.

10. Martin Luther King Jr., "Birth of a New Nation," 165–66.

11. On the personalistic definition of persons (or personality), see Edgar Sheffield Brightman, *Personality and Religion* (New York: Abingdon Press, 1934). For a description of theistic personalism, see Rufus Burrow Jr., *Personalism: A Critical Introduction* (St. Louis: Chalice Press, 1999), 72–76.

12. Andre C. Willis, "Why Martin Luther King Jr. Stands Alone," *Root*, January 18, 2010, https://www.theroot.com/why-martin-luther-king-jr-stands-alone-1790878338.

13. Rufus Burrow Jr., "Martin Luther King, Jr. and the Objective Moral Order: Some Ethical Implications," *Encounter* 61 (Spring 2000): 221–23.

14. Ibid., 221–22. On *imago Dei*, see Richard Wayne Wills Sr., *Martin Luther King Jr. and the Image of God* (New York: Oxford University Press 2009).

15. King, *Autobiography of Martin Luther King, Jr.*, 5, 7.

16. Martin Luther King Sr., *Daddy King: An Autobiography*, with Clayton Riley (New York: William Morrow, 1980; rpt., 2017), 88; and "Baptist Alliance to Meet in Berlin," *New York Times*, November 23, 1933.

17. Martin Luther King Sr., *Daddy King*, 88; and "Religion: Baptists in Berlin," *Time*, August 13, 1934.

18. Martin Luther King Sr., *Daddy King*, 88.

19. Martin Luther King Jr., "Keep Moving from This Mountain," in *The Papers of Martin Luther King, Jr.*, vol. 5, *Threshold of a New Decade, January 1959–December 1960*, edited by Clayborne Carson, Susan Carson, Susan Englander, Troy Jackson, and Gerald L. Smith (Berkeley: University of California Press, 2005), 418.

20. Martin Luther King Sr., *Daddy King*, 88.

21. Ibid., 88.

22. Martin Luther King Jr., *The Papers of Martin Luther King, Jr.*, vol. 1, *Called to Serve, January 1929–June 1951*, edited by Clayborne Carson, Ralph E. Luker, Penny A. Russell, and Louis R. Harlan (Berkeley: University of California Press 1992), 80.

23. Martin Luther King Sr., *Daddy King*, 102, 106, 109, 145–46. See also Eric Pace, "C. A. Scott, 92, Voice of Blacks as Publisher of Atlanta World," *New York Times*, May 11, 2000.

24. "Gandhi's Plan to Starve Self Not New as Political Weapon," *Atlanta Daily World*, September 20, 1932; "Strikes Grip India as Gandhi Begins 'Fast,'" *Atlanta Daily World*, March 6, 1939; "Gandhi Declares India Will Not Help to Exploit Africa," *Atlanta Daily World*, February 17, 1940; "Gandhi Calls for Uprising in Freedom Move for India," *Atlanta Daily World*, August 8, 1942; "New Riots Flare in India as Gandhi Remains in Jail," *Atlanta Daily World*, August 15, 1942; "German Prejudice against Jews Reaches Peak," *Atlanta Daily World*, September 12, 1936; "NAACP Chief Flays German Dictator, Hitler," *Atlanta Daily World*, September 26, 1936; "African Colonies Don't Want Rule of Germany," *Atlanta Daily World*, May 17, 1937; "Hitler's African Colonial Demands Stir Cape Town," *Atlanta Daily World*, December 11, 1937; "Claims African Natives Will Resist Transfer of Formerly Owned Colonies to Germany," *Atlanta Daily World*, March 22, 1938; "See Removal of Jews to Africa as Impossibility; Nazis React," *Atlanta Daily World*, November 22, 1938; D. A. A. Chari, "Asiatics Fight Colonialism Return," *Atlanta Daily World*, April 24, 1947; Lawrence C. Burr, "Dutch Seek to Restore Colonialism In Asia," *Atlanta Daily World*, September 19, 1947; "General Smuts—of All People—Defends Africans," *Atlanta Daily World*, October 8, 1948.

25. The term "conceptual tool" refers to a component of a larger "conceptual framework" or conceptual tool kit. In the definition of Sharon F. Rallis and Gretchen B. Rossman, "a conceptual framework is a structure that organizes the currents of thought that provide focus and direction to an inquiry. It is the organization of ideas . . . that will guide the project. Framework = organization or structure. Conceptual = concerning thoughts, ideas, perceptions, or theories." Sharon F. Rallis and Gretchen B. Rossman, *The Research Journey: Introduction to Inquiry* (New York: Guilford Press, 2012), 88–89.

26. Clayborne Carson, ed., *The Martin Luther King, Jr. Encyclopedia* (Westport, Conn.: Greenwood, 2008), 114; and Martin Luther King Jr., "Birth of a Nation," 155.

27. Martin Luther King Jr., "Birth of a New Nation," 155.

28. Martin Luther King Jr., "Advice for Living," October 1957, 279–80.

29. Ibid., 280. For another discussion of this topic, see Ibram X. Kendi, *Stamped from the Beginning: The Definitive History of Racist Ideas in America* (New York: Nation Books, 2016), 368.

30. King, *Autobiography of Martin Luther King, Jr.*, 6.

31. For example, in his October 1957 "Advice for Living" column, King had answered a question about "Paul's statements on obeying duly-constituted authorities, Romans 13:1–7," with a response that implicitly denied biblical infallibility. Martin Luther King Jr., "Advice for Living," October 1957, 280–81. See also Lee E. Dirks, "'The Essence Is Love':

The Theology of Martin Luther King, Jr.," *National Observer*, December 30, 1963. On liberal theology, see Gary Dorrien, *The Making of American Liberal Theology: Idealism, Realism, and Modernity, 1900-1950* (Louisville: Westminster John Knox Press, 2003), 1.

32. Edward J. Blum and Paul Harvey, *The Color of Christ: The Son of God and the Saga of Race in America* (Chapel Hill: University of North Carolina Press, 2012), 182.

33. E. Franklin Frazier quoted in ibid.

34. Kenneth B. Clark, *Prejudice and Your Child* (Middleton, Conn.: Wesleyan University Press, 1988), 22-23. As psychologists, Kenneth and Mamie Clark examined the "racial preferences" of black children by asking them a set of questions that requested them to choose between a brown and a white doll. They reported that "the majority of these Negro children at each age indicated an unmistakable preference for the white doll and a rejection of the brown doll."

35. Martin Luther King Jr. quoted in Lewis V. Baldwin, *The Voice of Conscience: The Church in the Mind of Martin Luther King, Jr.* (New York: Oxford University Press, 2010) 319n28; and Lewis V. Baldwin, "Of Their Spiritual Strivings: Malcolm and Martin on Religion and Freedom," in Lewis V. Baldwin and Amiri YaSin Al-Hadid, *Between Cross and Crescent: Christian and Muslim Perspectives on Malcolm and Martin* (Gainesville: University Press of Florida, 2002), 98, 382n48. In both books, Baldwin cites an unpublished speech by Martin Luther King Jr. entitled "An Address to the Ministers' Leadership Training Program," February 19-23, 1968, Library and Archives of the Martin Luther King Jr. Center for Nonviolent Change, Atlanta.

36. Lerone Bennett Jr., *What Manner of Man: A Biography of Martin Luther King*, 8th rev. ed. (Chicago: Johnson Publishing, 1992), 74-75; Howard Thurman, *With Head and Heart: The Autobiography of Howard Thurman* (New York: Harcourt Brace Jovanovich, 1979), 254-55; and King, *Autobiography of Martin Luther King, Jr.*, 326.

37. Howard Thurman, *Jesus and the Disinherited* (New York: Abingdon Press, 1949), 43-44. See also Blum and Harvey, *Color of Christ*, 182.

38. Martin Luther King Jr., "Where Do We Go from Here?," in *A Testament of Hope: The Essential Writings and Speeches of Martin Luther King, Jr.*, edited by James M. Washington (New York: HarperCollins, 1986), 245, 579. In the address, King referred to observations Ossie Davis made on the connection between language and racism. See Ossie Davis, *Life Lit by Some Large Vision: Selected Speeches and Writings* (New York: Atria Books, 2006), 9-18.

39. Malcolm X, with Alex Haley, *The Autobiography of Malcolm X* (New York: Grove Press, 1965), 191.

40. Alex Haley, "Epilogue," in ibid., 403. See also Robert Jefferson Norrell, *Alex Haley and the Books that Changed a Nation* (New York: St. Martin's Press, 2015), 82-83.

41. Lewis V. Baldwin, "Reluctant Admiration: What Malcolm and Martin Thought about Each Other," in Baldwin and Al-Hadid, *Between Cross and Crescent*, 313.

42. Martin Luther King Jr. quoted in Baldwin and Al-Hadid, *Between Cross and Crescent*, 314, 424n101. Baldwin cited an unpublished statement by Martin Luther King Jr. entitled "People to People: The Nightmare of Violence," February 26, 1965, Library and Archives of the Martin Luther King Jr. Center for Nonviolent Social Change, Atlanta.

43. Baldwin, "Reluctant Admiration," 424n101.

44. Bernard Smith, *Modernism's History: A Study in Twentieth-Century Art and Ideas* (Sydney, Australia: University of New South Wales Press, 1998), 305.

45. Martin Luther King Jr., *Where Do We Go From Here: Chaos or Community?* (Boston: Beacon Press, 1967), 199.

46. Baldwin, "Of Their Spiritual Strivings," 98.

47. King, *Autobiography of Martin Luther King, Jr.*, 191. See also Reinhold Niebuhr, *Moral Man and Immoral Society: A Study in Ethics and Politics* (New York: Charles Scribner's Sons, 1932).

48. Martin Luther King Jr., "Facing Life's Inescapables," in *The Papers of Martin Luther King, Jr.*, vol. 6, *Advocate of the Social Gospel, September 1948–March 1963*, edited by Clayborne Carson, Susan Carson, Susan Englander, Troy Jackson, and Gerald L. Smith (Berkeley: University of California Press 2007), 89.

49. Aram Goudsouzian, *Sidney Poitier: Man, Actor, Icon* (Chapel Hill: University of North Carolina Press, 2004), 231–32.

50. George Kelsey quoted in J. Deotis Roberts, *Bonhoeffer and King: Speaking Truth to Power* (Louisville: Westminster John Knox Press, 2005), 44; and Martin Luther King Jr., *Where Do We Go from Here?*, 73.

51. Martin Luther King Jr., *Where Do We Go from Here?*, 75–79, 102–3.

52. Thurman, *With Head and Heart*, 113–14.

53. Dirks, "Essence Is Love," 1, 12; and Martin Luther King, Jr., *Testament of Hope*, 8, 13, 19–20.

54. Martin Luther King Jr., "Palm Sunday Sermon on Mohandas K. Gandhi," in *Papers of Martin Luther King, Jr.*, vol. 5, 147–48. On King's 1959 visit to India, see Martin Luther King Jr., "My Trip to the Land of Gandhi," in *Testament of Hope*, 23–30; and Carson, *Martin Luther King, Jr., Encyclopedia*, 144–46.

55. King, "Palm Sunday Sermon on Mohandas K. Gandhi," 146–47.

56. Ibid., 148.

57. Martin Luther King Jr., *Stride toward Freedom: The Montgomery Story* (New York: Harper & Row, 1958), 72, 84–85, 97. On the "science of nonviolence," see Mohandas K. Gandhi's description in *Harijan*, February 22, 1942, in Krishna Kripalani, ed., *All Men Are Brothers: Autobiographical Reflections* (New York: Columbia University Press, 1958), 83–84.

58. Martin Luther King Jr., *Where Do We Go from Here?*, 74.

59. Michael Bess, *Choices under Fire: Moral Dimensions of World War II* (New York: Vintage Books, 2008), 242–43.

60. Martin Luther King Jr., "Pilgrimage to Nonviolence," in *Papers of Martin Luther King, Jr.*, vol. 5, 424.

61. On satyagraha, Gandhi wrote: "I have also called it Love-force or Soul-force." M. K. Gandhi, *Non-Violent Resistance (Satyagraha)* (New York: Schocken Books, 1951), 6.

62. Thurman, *With Head and Heart*, 114.

63. Martin Luther King Jr. quoted in Lewis V. Baldwin and Paul R. Dekar, "Becoming 'a Single Neighborhood': Martin Luther King, Jr. on the 'White' and 'Colored' Worlds," in Lewis V. Baldwin and Paul R. Dekar, eds., *"In an Inescapable Network of Mutuality": Martin Luther King, Jr. and the Globalization of an Ethical Ideal* (Eugene, Ore.: Cascade Books, 2013), 31n22. Baldwin and Dekar cite a statement from Martin Luther King Jr. and Wyatt Tee Walker to Mr. John Collins and the Student Interracial Ministry Committee, New York City, March 29, 1961, Library and Archives of the Martin Luther King Jr. Center for Nonviolent Social Change.

64. Albert J. Raboteau, *Canaan Land: A Religious History of African Americans* (New York: Oxford University Press, 2001), 16–17; David L. Edwards, *Christianity: The First Two Thousand Years* (London, UK: Continuum, 1998), 530–42; Albert J. Raboteau, *A Fire in the Bones: Reflections on African-American Religious History* (Boston: Beacon Press, 1995), 42–51; Lara Putnam, *Radical Moves: Caribbean Migrants and the Politics of Race in the Jazz Age* (Chapel Hill:

University of North Carolina, 2013), 56; Emily Rosenberg, *Spreading the American Dream: American Economic and Cultural Expansion, 1890-1945* (New York: Hill and Wang, 1982), 8, 41–48.

65. Martin Luther King Jr., "Advice for Living," September 1958, in *Papers of Martin Luther King, Jr.*, vol. 4, 471–72.

66. Benjamin E. Mays quoted in Randal Maurice Jelks, *Benjamin Elijah Mays, Schoolmaster of the Movement: A Biography* (Chapel Hill: University of North Carolina Press, 2012), 90. Jelks cites Benjamin E. Mays, "Pagan Survival in Christianity" (MA thesis, University of Chicago Divinity School, 1925).

67. Martin Luther King Jr., "Advice for Living," September 1958, in *Papers of Martin Luther King, Jr.*, vol. 4, 471–72.

68. "Africa has been depicted for more than a century as the home of black cannibals and ignorant primitives. Despite volumes of facts contradicting this picture, the stereotype persists in books, motion pictures, and other media of communication." See Martin Luther King Jr., "Let My People Go," in *"In a Single Garment of Destiny": A Global Vision of Justice*, edited by Lewis V. Baldwin (Boston: Beacon Press, 2012), 39.

69. Martin Luther King Jr., *Where Do We Go From Here?*, 75.

70. Martin Luther King Jr., "The Vision of a World Made New," in *"In a Single Garment of Destiny,"* 7–8.

71. Martin Luther King Jr., "Revolution and Redemption," in *"In a Single Garment of Destiny,"* 3, 16.

72. Ibid., 3, 16, 20.

73. Martin Luther King Jr., *Where Do We Go from Here?*, 189.

74. Carson, *Martin Luther King, Jr., Encyclopedia*, 255.

75. Martin Luther King Jr., "Birth of a New Nation," 162.

76. Kwame Nkrumah, *Neo-Colonialism: The Last Stage of Imperialism* (New York: International Publishers, 1966), x–xi.

77. Martin Luther King Jr., *Where Do We Go from Here?*, 185.

78. Julie Greene, *The Canal Builders: Making America's Empire at the Panama Canal* (New York: Penguin Books, 2009), 21, 132.

79. Frank J. Coppa, ed., *Encyclopedia of Modern Dictators: From Napoleon to the Present* (New York: Peter Lang, 2006), 83–87, 283–86.

80. William Michael Schmidli, *The Fate of Freedom Elsewhere: Human Rights and U.S. Cold War Policy toward Argentina* (Ithaca, N.Y.: Cornell University Press, 2013), 41–42; Thomas E. Skidmore, *The Politics of Military Rule in Brazil, 1964-1985* (New York: Oxford University Press, 1988), 192; and Vijay Prashad, *The Darker Nations: A People's History of the Third World* (New York: New Press, 2007), 106, 140–43.

81. Martin Luther King Jr., *Where Do We Go from Here?*, 185.

82. King, *Autobiography of Martin Luther King, Jr.*, 13, 16; Carson, *Martin Luther King, Jr., Encyclopedia*, 15, 109–10, 338.

83. "Young Gandhi Begins Fast Against S. African Jim Crow," *Atlanta Daily World*, March 13, 1952.

84. Larry O. Rivers, "'Militant Reconciling Love': Howard University's Rankin Network and Martin Luther King, Jr.," *Journal of African American History* 99, no. 3 (Summer 2014): 239. See also Mohandas K. Gandhi, *An Autobiography, or, The Story of My Experiments with Truth* (1927; repr., Boston: Beacon Press, 1993).

85. Gene Sharp, *The Politics of Nonviolent Action*, pt. 2, *The Methods of Nonviolent Action*, Extending Horizons Books (Boston: Porter Sargent, 1973), xi–xviii.

86. Eleanor Roosevelt, James A. Pike, and Martin Luther King Jr., "Declaration of Conscience," American Committee on Africa, in Martin Luther King Jr., "*In a Single Garment of Destiny*," 30.

87. Nelson Mandela and Mandla Langa, *Dare Not Linger: The Presidential Years* (New York: Farrar, Straus and Giroux, 2017), 317.

88. Roosevelt, Pike, and King, "Declaration of Conscience," 31.

89. Baldwin, introduction to part 2, Martin Luther King Jr., "*In a Single Garment of Destiny*," 25.

90. Ibid., 25–26.

91. Martin Luther King Jr. and Albert John Luthuli [Lutuli], "Appeal for Action against Apartheid," American Committee on Africa, in Martin Luther King Jr., "*In a Single Garment of Destiny*," 33–35; and Sharp, *Politics of Nonviolent Action*, pt. 2, xiii–xv, 183–84.

92. Martin Luther King Jr., "South African Independence," in "*In a Single Garment of Destiny*," 36–37.

93. Bess, *Choices under Fire*, 52.

94. Martin Luther King Jr., "Let My People Go," in "*In a Single Garment of Destiny*," 41.

95. Martin Luther King Jr., "South African Independence," 37.

96. Martin Luther King Jr., "Let My People Go," 40–41.

97. Martin Luther King Jr., "South African Independence," 37.

98. "Dr. Martin Luther King Jr: 'I Fear I Am Integrating My People into a Burning House,'" *New York Amsterdam News*, January 12, 2017; Stephen Kendrick and Paul Kendrick, "King's Determined Final Days Still Hold a Lesson for Us All," *Atlanta Journal-Constitution*, April 8, 2018.

99. Martin Luther King Jr., "Let My People Go," 42.

100. Wills, *Martin Luther King Jr. and the Image of God*, 142.

101. Earl Caldwell, "Mrs. King to March in Husband's Place in Memphis Today," *New York Times*, April 8, 1968; Richard L. Lyons, "Pope, Other World Figures Join in Tributes to Dr. King," *Washington Post*, April 8, 1968.

102. Martin Luther King Jr., "What Happened to Hell?," in *Papers of Martin Luther King, Jr.*, vol. 6, 411. Coretta Scott King reported that the sermon her husband had planned to deliver, "Why America May Go to Hell," was preached at Atlanta's Ebenezer Baptist Church "that next Sunday" by King's brother A. D. See Coretta Scott King, *My Life with Martin Luther King, Jr.*, rev. ed. (New York: Henry Holt, 1993), 292.

103. Martin Luther King Jr., *Where Do We Go From Here?*, 186–87.

CHAPTER 3
FOR THE LEAST OF THESE
THE SCANDAL OF POVERTY IN THE WORLD HOUSE

GARY S. SELBY

Our loyalties must become ecumenical rather than sectional. Our loyalties must
transcend our race, our tribe, our class, and our nation; and this means we must
develop a world perspective. . . . Now the judgment of God is upon us, and we must
either learn to live together as brothers or we are all going to perish together as fools.
MARTIN LUTHER KING JR., *The Trumpet of Conscience*

No man is an island, entire of itself; every man is a piece of the continent, a part of
the main. . . . Any man's death diminishes me, because I am involved in mankind.
And therefore never send to know for whom the bell tolls; it tolls for thee.
JOHN DONNE, *Devotions upon Emergent Occasions Together with Death's Duel*

"No individual or nation can be great if it does not have a concern for 'the least
of these.'"[1] With these words, spoken in his 1964 Nobel lecture at the University
in Oslo, Norway, Martin Luther King Jr. called the world to open its eyes to the
plight of those who languished in poverty. Quoting the words of Jesus in Matthew 25, he challenged the wealthy of the world to acknowledge the "image of
God" in their fellow human beings and to be outraged at the sight of people
hungry or "victimized with starvation and ill health when we have the means
to help them." In his sermon "Remaining Awake through a Great Revolution,"
given at the Washington National Cathedral on March 31, 1968, just days prior to
his assassination, King similarly challenged his own nation: "If ye do it unto the
least of these, my brethren, ye do it unto me."[2]

King drew, of course, from Jesus's parable of the sheep and the goats in
which God, the judge, explains the basis for separating the saved from the
damned—a judgment that rests entirely on their treatment of the poor and vulnerable. These familiar words of Jesus would have seemed unremarkable on
the lips of an ordained minister and would have added religious authority to his
call for compassion to the poor. But as I will argue, those phrases "my brethren"
and "ye do it unto me" also pointed to the fundamental way King saw the world
and to the central persuasive strategy he would use to call for the elimination of

global poverty—for a world in which all persons were deeply and inextricably bound to one another. Unbeknown to the righteous in the parable, when they served the poor stranger, they were serving fellow members of the human family. When the wicked ignored those in poverty, they were in fact ignoring God.

More broadly, this citation also signals the shift that King's organizational and rhetorical energies underwent in the final years of his life to more of a focus on global poverty, reflecting his growing conviction that entrenched, structural poverty was a deeper and more pressing obstacle to human flourishing than even legalized segregation. In calling for action, however, King faced the challenge of demonstrating why poverty mattered to the rest of society, why all should feel an urgency to respond to the plight of poor people. In this essay I argue that King met this challenge by drawing on what was then becoming a dominant theme of both academic and popular culture, that of systems theory. Although this sense of an interrelated world had always been present in his discourse, I show that, at the same time he was turning to poverty as his emphasis, the deep interconnectedness of all of life became one of his most pervasive rhetorical motifs. King repeatedly situated his hearers within a complex, rhetorical web of economic, social, and spiritual systems in which the well-being of one was integrally tied to the well-being of all. This symbolic construction of reality, I conclude, provided the basis for his call to alleviate poverty worldwide and also undergirded his prophetic warnings about the consequences that would come if society ignored this dire threat to its own welfare.

King's Turn toward Global Poverty

Although King had always recognized the plight of the poor in the United States, in the final two years of his life he made global poverty the central focus of his attention and energy, a shift that was clearly evident in his public oratory. In the first decade of the civil rights movement, King had focused far more on eliminating racial segregation in the nation's public transportation, businesses, schools, and other public spaces, and overturning the systematic exclusion of blacks from political life, in the belief that those changes would inevitably improve their economic situation.

By late 1966, however, that emphasis changed, as King became increasingly convinced that systemic poverty, resulting from deeply entrenched social and economic structures, was the true obstacle to flourishing, rather than merely legalized segregation.[3] This shift can be accounted for by several factors. On the one hand, King felt a strong resonance with the social democratic political and economic systems that he found in Scandinavia, an orientation reflected in comments he made when he traveled to Sweden in 1964, en route to receive the Nobel Peace Prize in Norway. Upon his arrival at the Stockholm airport, King spoke of the world's need to "learn from Sweden's democratic socialist traditions," which had enabled that country to "overcome so many of the problems of poverty, housing, unemployment, and medical care for . . . [their] people— problems that still plague far-more affluent and powerful nations."[4] After his return to the United States, he praised the way Sweden had demonstrated "in her life and politics a recognition of the interrelatedness of mankind." Truly, King exclaimed, they justified the conviction reflected in John Donne's "immortal words, that, 'No man is an island entire of itself; every man is a piece of the continent, a part of the main.'"[5]

As Paul Le Blanc and Michael Yates have shown, King's turn to global poverty also reflected the influence of such figures as A. Philip Randolph and Bayard Rustin, who represented an "activist wing of the civil rights movement" with a socialist orientation that favored a "socially owned and democratically controlled economy, one in which production would be for the benefit of all."[6] Their vision called for eliminating poverty, achieving full employment, and providing health care and education to all citizens "as a matter of right," and especially they sought a political coalition that would link "the goal of racial justice for African Americans with the goal of economic justice for all Americans."[7]

By his own account, King's embrace of this view was also hastened by several personal experiences that profoundly affected him. In August 1965 he toured the ravaged Watts community in Los Angeles and was "awed by the physical devastation of the area," writes historian David Garrow. Garrow writes that King told Bayard Rustin and Bernard Lee that

> his visit to Watts had brought home to him more than ever the material and spiritual desolation that shattered the lives of the millions of black citizens trapped in America's ghettos. "I'll never forget the discussion we had with King that night," Rustin recalled. "He was absolutely undone, and he looked at me and said, 'You know, Bayard, I worked to get these people the right to eat hamburgers, and now I've got to do something . . . to help them get the money to buy it.'"

King's experience in Watts, Garrow concludes, convinced him of what Rustin had been arguing for the previous two years, namely "that the most serious issues facing the movement were economic problems of class rather than race." That night, Garrow quotes Rustin as saying, "I think it was the first time he really understood."[8]

As 1966 unfolded, King's transition continued as he became increasingly convinced that the anger and frustration he was seeing in black communities resulted from the grinding poverty that blacks faced, especially in the ghettos of America's cities. In a speech he gave a year later, on August 31, 1967, King told of his own disheartening encounter with that anger at a rally for open housing in Chicago, when he was booed by some of the "angry young men of our movement."[9] Although he initially reacted with defensiveness, he came to realize that what he was seeing was the "bewildering frustration and corroding bitterness" that come from being trapped in poverty.[10]

By late 1966, then, King had determined that he would focus on poverty and economic justice, an emphasis that would extend to *all* the poor, black and white. As he put it in a document prepared for the press in October 1966, "America's greatest problem and contradiction is that it harbors 35 million poor at a time when its resources are so vast that the existence of poverty is an anachronism." A month later he told an audience in Washington, D.C., "We need civil rights legislation"—like Lyndon Johnson's fair-housing proposal, Garrow notes—"but that isn't enough." From that point, Garrow writes, the movement would tackle "basic class issues between the privileged and the underprivileged." This shift to combating poverty marked the genesis of the "Poor People's Campaign," a vision of which King shared with several aides at a Southern Christian Leadership Conference staff retreat in May the following year: "We ought to come in mule carts, in old trucks, any kind of transportation people can get their hands on. People ought to come to Washington, sit down if necessary in the middle of the street and say, 'We are here; we are poor; we don't have any money; you have made us this way; you keep us down this way; and we've come to stay until you do something about it.'"[11] From this point on, the problem of poverty became the focus of his work.

Reflecting this shift, eliminating poverty now became a central theme in King's speeches and sermons. For example, in "Why Jesus Called a Man a Fool," delivered at Mount Pisgah Missionary Baptist Church in Chicago on August 27, 1967, he decried the "tragic fact that the vast majority of Negroes in our country find themselves perishing on a lonely island of poverty in the midst of a vast ocean of material prosperity." He added: "One hundred and four years later, fifty percent of the Negro families of our country are forced to live in substandard housing conditions, most of whom do not have wall-to-wall carpets; many of them are forced to live with wall-to-wall rats and roaches."[12] In his famous "Beyond Vietnam" address, he spoke of how the Vietnam War had drawn the nation's attention away from the problem of poverty: "I knew that America would never invest the necessary funds or energies in rehabilitation of its poor so long as adventures like Vietnam continued to draw men and skills and money like some demonic, destructive suction tube. So I was increasingly compelled to see the war as an enemy of the poor and to attack it as such."[13]

King called attention not only to poverty in the United States but also to the plight of poor people worldwide. Just four days before his assassination, on March 31, 1968, he echoed the language of his Nobel lecture: "We are challenged to rid our nation and the world of poverty. Like a monstrous octopus, poverty spreads its nagging, prehensile tentacles into hamlets and villages all over our world. Two-thirds of the people of the world go to bed hungry tonight. They are ill-housed; they are ill-nourished; they are shabbily clad. I've seen it in Latin America; I've seen it in Africa; I've seen this poverty in Asia."[14] Addressing poverty would be the dominant motif of King's rhetoric from this point on.

If he had any hope of reaching his hearers, however, King needed them to feel a sense of urgency and alarm toward global poverty. He needed, in Aristotle's words, to bring the suffering of the poor "before the eyes," which he did with his vivid descriptions of the "wrinkled stomachs of millions of God's children all over the world at night," of "God's children" in Calcutta whom he saw "sleeping on the sidewalks at night," and of the mother in Harlem who described having to stay awake at night "to keep the rats and roaches from getting to the children."[15] But King also needed to create a sense of connection on the part of an audience with those who were suffering, since, as Aristotle noted in his discussion of compassion, "it is when the sufferings of others are close to us that they excite our pity." For King, this may have presented a formidable challenge, since the homeless people of India or even poor people in U.S. ghettos could seem so distant from the experiences of comfortable middle-class people. Exacerbating that challenge was what Nancy Christie and Michael Gauvreau identify as the "postwar cultural and social mores" that enshrined individualistic values of "freedom, choice, and individual happiness."[16] In the face of these obstacles, King needed to demonstrate not only that this grinding poverty existed but also that it should matter to the rest of society, that it was connected to their own lives and futures. For this crucial element of his task in persuading, King drew on the growing prevalence of systems theory as a framework for seeing the world.

A World of Connections

Few intellectual and cultural shifts in the past century have been more important for contemporary thinkers, in fields ranging from business, organizational development, and psychology to science and mathematics, than the turn toward systems theory as a fundamental way of understanding the world. This turn is frequently traced to the work of philosopher Ludwig von Bertalanffy, whose writings on systems theory began to appear in the mid-1950s but were drawn together in a pathbreaking volume published in 1968 under the title *General System Theory*. By the time of that book's publication, Bertalanffy pointed out, "systems" had become among the culture's most "current notions and fashionable catchwords" and a perspective that permeated "all fields of science" as well as "popular thinking, jargon, and mass media."[17]

As a basic mathematical expression, Bertalanffy defined a system as a "set of elements standing in interrelations. Interrelations means that elements, p, stand in relations, R, so that the behavior of an element p in R is different from its behavior in another relation, R'."[18] The key to this formulation was the interconnection of individual elements within the system, which turned the focus from those individual elements themselves to the configuration of relationships between them. In a simplified illustration, we might imagine a group of people among whom a ball of yarn has been thrown, person to person, until each member of the group is holding a piece of the yarn, creating a taut web of yarn connecting them. If one person gives a slight shake of the yarn, the action will be felt by everyone in the system. If one member of the system takes a step forward or backward or drops his or her piece of yarn, then the position of everyone else in the circle changes. As this example demonstrates, systems theory "embodied an alternative approach to the standard reductionistic/mechanistic approach in which both the natural and social world, especially the world of living organisms, is investigated and explicated with respect to the chaotic, atomistic elements and events, which are isolated from one another and their environmental context."[19] In other words, no longer would we see phenomena in terms of simple causation but rather as embedded within complex webs of interconnectedness.

The impact of this paradigm shift on widely diverse fields of study and practice would be difficult to overstate, but two examples will suffice. As one example, in psychotherapy, many family therapists now began to focus not so much on the individual with presenting symptoms but rather on the interaction within the systems and subsystems of which that person was a member. Changing a dysfunctional behavior pattern now meant that the therapist joined and somehow disrupted or reconfigured this larger system since, as Arlene Vetere noted, "when the structure of the relational group changes, the position of the members in the group changes," which, in turn, leads to different forms of communication and behavior among the system's members.[20] This might take the form of something as simple as rearranging the seating configuration of family members in the therapy setting, a change that can lead to different communication patterns, emotions, and eventually, altered patterns of behavior. A second example concerns the application of the same perspective to organizational systems, as in Peter Senge's best-selling book *The Fifth Discipline*, which challenges managers to shift their focus from "personalities and events" to the "underlying structures which shape individual actions and create the conditions where types of events become likely." Senge concentrated on "small, well-focused actions" with the potential for "significant, enduring improvements" in the organization, in the same way that turning a ship's "trim tab . . . makes it easier to turn the rudder, which, then, makes it easier to turn the ship."[21]

The turn to systems theory provided a powerful means for explaining why things and people and even larger entities like organizations behave as they do and, more importantly, a mode for strategically intervening in order to bring about systemic change since, again, when the position of one element in the system changes, the entire configuration changes. King clearly recognized this and at times used systems theory to explain or advance policies to mitigate the grip of structural poverty. For example, he responded to the common myth attributing unemployment to "a want of industrious habits and moral fiber" by asserting that the "operation of our economic system" had, in fact, "thrust people into idleness" and bound them "in constant or frequent unemployment against their will." He argued that a guaranteed national income would ripple out into other elements of the system: "The poor, transformed into purchasers, will do a great deal on their own to alter housing decay," and a "host of positive psychological changes inevitably will result from widespread economic security." In this way, King used systems theory to demand that society do more than simply "help the discouraged beggars in life's marketplace" and that people face the fact that "an edifice which produces beggars needs restructuring."[22]

But King did far more than simply draw on systems theory to diagnose or propose strategic interventions for global poverty. He used the language of systems to create a rhetorical frame through which he invited his hearers to see themselves and their world. Using the systems paradigm, he symbolically placed hearers within an interconnected world in which their well-being was integrally linked to the well-being of everyone—especially poor people.

Poverty within a Systems Frame

From the earliest days of the civil right movement, King made connections between local protests and what he posited as a worldwide movement. In his "Death of Evil on the Seashore" sermon, for example, originally delivered in July

1955, six months before the Montgomery bus boycott had even begun, he identified the U.S. Supreme Court's historic 1954 *Brown v. Board of Education* decision
as a global "victory of the forces of freedom and justice." The "colored people" of
the world, he asserted, had "won their freedom from the Egypt of colonialism
and are now free to move toward the promised land of economic security and
cultural development."[23] But for the most part his focus in the early years was
local in scope, encouraging protesters in their efforts to overturn discrimination
in the nation's political and economic practices, especially in the South. His references to a global movement for freedom served primarily to legitimate and
encourage local protests.

In the final period of his life, however, at the same time he began to emphasize domestic and global poverty, King's rhetoric underwent a fundamental
shift marked by a thematic focus on the world as a complex system. Running
through many of the speeches from this period is a clear stress on the interconnectedness of all things. This turn to a systems perspective becomes evident
when we compare King's earlier 1964 Nobel lecture, in which he identified the
three great evils of contemporary society as poverty, racism, and war, to the later
version of that same content in his "world house" essay.[24] In the earlier address,
we see a hint of this interconnectedness in his claim that "equality with whites"
would be irrelevant "in a society under the spell of terror and a world doomed
to destruction," and when he called the world to embrace loyalties that were
"ecumenical rather than sectional."[25] But although he recognized that each of
these evils was "inextricably bound to the other," King seemed for the most part
to treat them as a *series* of problems, almost as if they were separate issues to be
tackled one after the other. In the "world house" essay, by contrast, they became
deeply intertwined. The "racist government of South Africa" he now depicted
as the product of the "economic policies of the United States and Great Britain."
Conversely, he claimed that the exploitative neocolonial practices of U.S. corporations in Latin America now represented "racism in its more sophisticated
form." Technological progress, which gave us "wonder drugs" to cure diseases,
was now connected to the production of "the terrifying weapons of warfare that
we know today"—including nuclear weapons, of course, but also "the bomber,
an airborne fortress raining down death," and "napalm, that burner of all things
and flesh in its path."[26] Rather than being separate issues, economics, racism,
and war were now deeply intertwined, drawn together within a rhetorical depiction of the world that situated individual persons within a complex, interlocking web.

In some cases, this interconnectedness took the form of simple references
to obvious global economic interdependence evidenced in the average U.S. cit-

izen's use of products from all over the world. One passage that appears in his later speeches on poverty invites hearers to consider a typical morning routine:

> Maybe you haven't ever thought about it, but you can't leave home in the morning without being dependent on most of the world. You get up in the morning, and you go to the bathroom and you reach over for a sponge, and that's even given to you by a Pacific Islander. You reach over for a towel, and that's given to you by a Turk. You reach down to pick up your soap, and that's given to you by a Frenchman. Then after dressing, you rush to the kitchen and you decide this morning that you want to drink a little coffee; that's poured in your cup by a South American. Or maybe this morning you prefer tea; that's poured in your cup by a Chinese. Or maybe you want cocoa this morning; that's poured in your cup by a West African. Then you reach over to get your toast, and that's given to you at the hands of an English-speaking farmer, not to mention the baker. Before you finish eating breakfast in the morning you are dependent on more than half of the world.[77]

Such was the nature of our interconnected world that one could not even "leave home in the morning without being dependent on most of the world."[28]

King also sought to show the way economic structures were interwoven with racism, poverty, and war. He linked the current plight of impoverished blacks in the United States to historical systems of white privilege in the nation's history, as when he noted how the federal government "gave away millions of acres of land in the West and the Midwest" in order to undergird "white peasants from Europe with an economic floor," building "land-grant colleges to teach them how to farm" and providing "federal agents to further their expertise in farming" as well as "low interest rates so that they could mechanize their farms"—programs sustained by the "very people who tell Negroes that they must lift themselves up by their own bootstraps."[29] As noted above, in the "world house" essay, he argued that U.S. and British economic policies had played a crucial role in sustaining the system of apartheid in South Africa and that U.S. corporations had conspired to exploit Latin American countries in a way that kept them mired in poverty. Those economic policies, in turn, were linked to racist attitudes toward persons of color throughout the world. He also showed how technological "progress" was tied to the ever more horrific forms of weaponry being used in Vietnam, a war whose effects also rippled out in consequences for the poor by leading to the evisceration of new programs to help poor people, black and white, and by drawing "men and skills and money like some demonic, destructive suction tube," even as it "strengthened the military-industrial complex."[30] The effects of the war also rippled out in other ways, "devastating the hopes of the poor at home" who were "sending their sons and brothers and their husbands to fight and to die in extraordinarily high proportions relative to the rest of the population."[31]

As these examples show, King grounded this theme of systemic interconnection in empirical realities that would have been undeniable to his hearers. His illustration of how one might use products from all over the world before even leaving home in the morning appealed to daily lived experiences that all would have recognized but perhaps never considered. Similarly, when he spoke of dazzling advances resulting from the "modern scientific and technological revolutions"—Edison's "incandescent lamp to bring light to many dark places of the earth, . . . wonder drugs to end many dread plagues and diseases, . . . skyscraping buildings to kiss the stars, and . . . gargantuan bridges to span the waters"[32]—he tapped into the widely shared sense that his hearers were witnessing an era of technological progress. As William H. Young and Nancy K. Young write: "Laboratories routinely announced major discoveries that would impact many areas of American life: a cure for polio, space exploration, miniaturization, the introduction of the computer, and color television." It was an era when "science and technology would lead everyone to a better life."[33] Few could deny King's claim that this "modern . . . scientific ingenuity . . . had been able to dwarf distance and place time in chains" and that "jet planes have compressed into minutes distances that once took weeks and even months." The irresistible conclusion of "all this" was that "our world is a neighborhood."[34]

But what is striking about the way he embedded this systemic framework within his antipoverty rhetoric was how it linked these empirical signs of interconnectedness to what we might call metaphysical forms of interconnectedness, forms he had occasionally alluded to in his earlier civil rights movement addresses. The world's economic systems had become intertwined with moral and spiritual ones. He posited a linkage between what he called the "inner" and "outer" parts of human experience. His Nobel lecture, again, hinted at this connection when he asserted that every person "lives in two realms, the internal and the external."[35] The inner, spiritual realm of human existence is the realm of "art, literature, morals, and religion," whereas the outer is that of "devices, techniques, mechanisms, and instrumentalities by means of which we live." Implied in this dualism is an assumption that humans flourish when these two realms of the "human system" are held in a healthy but delicate balance, and in this view contemporary society's malady was the result of disorder between the physical and spiritual realms. Science, King said, had wrought wonders, and no one wished to "turn back the clock of scientific progress."[36] What was needed, rather, was for "our moral lag" to "be redeemed. When scientific power outruns moral power, we end up with guided missiles and misguided men." Or as his Nobel lecture put it, "Enlarged material powers spell enlarged peril if there is not proportionate growth of the soul. When the 'without' of man's nature subjugates the 'within,' dark storm clouds begin to form in the world."[37]

King also advanced this metaphysical systemic construction of reality in his frequent references to what he called a "global revolution" against poverty and oppression. In some cases, he grounded his claims about the global revolution in the empirical realities of technological and economic interconnectedness, as when he spoke of the "coming of the automobile, the upheavals of two world wars, [and] the Great Depression" as "forces conjoined to cause . . . Negro masses all over . . . to re-evaluate themselves."[38] In other words, technological progress was inevitably tied to aspirations for spiritual progress. His "Remaining Awake through a Great Revolution" address similarly linked the "technological revolution" to a "human rights revolution, with the freedom explosion that is taking place all over the world." And in his "world house" essay, King explicitly argued that the "marvels of Western technology" had whetted "the aspirations and appetites of the world," so that the poor of the world would no longer stand to be "locked out of the earthly kingdom of wealth, health and happiness."[39]

This interweaving of empirical and metaphysical systems supported a theme that had been present in King's rhetoric from the earliest days of the movement, a theme that attributed this global revolution to a worldwide zeitgeist. He repeatedly declared: "Consciously or unconsciously, he [the African American] has been caught up by the spirit of the times, and with his black brothers of Africa and his brown and yellow brothers in Asia, South America, and the Caribbean, the United States Negro is moving with a great sense of urgency toward the promised land of racial justice."[40] Similarly, King's "Beyond Vietnam" address, pervaded by themes of systemic linkage between poverty, economics, and war, claimed that an upheaval was sweeping across this interconnected world: "All over the globe men are revolting against old systems of exploitation and oppression, and out of the wounds of a frail world, new systems of justice and equality are being born. The shiftless and barefoot people of the land are rising up as never before. The people who sat in darkness have seen a great light."[41] His "three evils" address highlighted the "rising expectations" of oppressed peoples "the world over." "The deep rumblings that we hear today, the rumbling of discontent," King said, represented the "thunder of disinherited masses rising from dungeons of oppression to the bright hills of freedom. All over the world like a fever, freedom is spreading in the widest liberation movement in history."[42] In this way, King asserted that just as all people are bound together in systems of economic and technological interdependence, they are also inescapably part of a metaphysical system, forced to reckon with a world in which the oppressed and marginalized now claimed their full dignity and rights as persons.

By far the clearest metaphysical dimension of this systemic perspective, however, was King's claim that the world—indeed the entire cosmos—was linked in a spiritual and even a theological system of interconnectedness, rooted in the very intention and design of God. In his Southern Methodist University address of March 1966, he argued that "black supremacy" was as dangerous as "white supremacy" because God was interested not simply in freedom for blacks but also in the "freedom of the whole human race and the creation of society where all men will live together as brothers."[43] As he said in his "Christmas Sermon on Peace" in December 1967: "We are all caught up in an inescapable network of mutuality, tied into a single garment of destiny. . . . Whatever affects one directly, affects all indirectly," for such is the "interrelated structure of reality."[44] In his "Beyond Vietnam" sermon, King spoke of the "force which all of the great religions have seen as the supreme unifying principle of life," which was love, the "key that unlocks the door which leads to ultimate reality."[45] And in one of his most fully developed examples of this theological interconnectedness, in his "Remaining Awake through a Great Revolution" speech of March 1968, King echoed his language from the Christmas sermon, this time tying it to God's vision: "For some strange reason, I can never be what I ought to be until you are what you ought to be. And you can never be what you ought to be until I am what I ought to be. This is the way God's universe is made; this is the way it is structured."[46] It was precisely in just such an interconnected theological universe that the actions taken on behalf of "the least of these, my brethren," could be offered to God.

In the construction of this symbolic world of interconnectedness we see King's strategy for meeting the demands of his rhetorical situation and indeed his genius as a visionary leader. Whereas, for most, systems theory was a tool for diagnosing and intervening within family or organizational systems, for King it was a resource for creating an entire symbolic world. The veracity of his depiction of that world, moreover, was self-confirming because it was based in realities of economic interconnectedness that were tangible and objective in people's experience, as in his example of how one might encounter a long list of products from all over the world before even leaving the house in the morning. The way that King interwove those empirical demonstrations of interconnection with the spiritual and metaphysical dimensions of this systemic cosmos created the sense that his hearers truly were members of one family living in God's "world house."[47]

For King, then, the language of systems theory functioned as what communication scholars have called a "rhetorical frame"—that is, a symbolic conceptual and emotional lens or schema through which people could view their world. Communications scholar Jim Kuypers defines rhetorical frames as "central organizing ideas" that function "to define problems, diagnose causes, make moral judgments, and suggest remedies," providing "interpretive cues for otherwise neutral facts." In the same way that a camera filter shapes our perception of the scene before us, rhetors construct frames in order to shape their audiences' perceptual and emotional responses to the "reality" they encounter. So a Ku Klux Klan march framed in terms of "free speech" is met with greater tolerance than when it is framed as a "public disturbance."[48] Trade conflicts framed as "wars" elicit support for protectionist trade policies, as opposed to simply navigating a "two-way street."[49] In the early days of the AIDS epidemic, people supported proposals for mandatory HIV testing when they were framed as a public health issue as opposed to a threat to civil liberty.[50] These and many other similar studies emphasize the potency of rhetorical frames to shape how we think and feel about ourselves, others, and the world. King drew on that power by persistently invoking a systems frame to place his hearers symbolically within a fundamentally interconnected world. In its earlier usage, that sense of interconnectedness helped to lend a sense of legitimacy to the struggle for civil rights by placing it within a worldwide zeitgeist. As King shifted to a greater focus on global poverty, that interconnectedness, now pervasive in his rhetoric and bolstered by his references to the empirical realities of global economic systems, supported his call for eliminating global poverty in several ways.

First, by situating hearers within this interconnected world, this "world house," King sought to evoke the kind of empathy that is foundational to compassion. King knew that his audience would only feel that emotion toward the suffering of those with whom they felt a personal connection, and his pervasive use of the language of systems provided that logic of connection. Among the most poignant moments of empathy was a passage from the "Beyond Vietnam" sermon that linked U.S. military force to the impoverishment of Vietnamese peasants. King asked of these North Vietnamese citizens, "What must they think of the United States of America," when "our bombs now pummel the land, and our mines endanger the waterways"?:

> They watch as we poison their water, as we kill a million acres of their crops. They must weep as the bulldozers roar through their areas preparing to destroy the precious trees. They wander into hospitals with at least twenty casualties from American firepower for one Vietcong-inflicted injury. So far we may have killed a

million of them, mostly children. They wander into the towns and see thousands of the children, homeless, without clothes, running in packs on the streets like animals. They see the children degraded by our soldiers as they beg for food.[51]

King called his hearers to the true measure of compassion, which was the ability to see even "the enemy's point of view." But, as noted above, King also brought the images of those who suffered in poverty elsewhere in the world "before the eyes" of his hearers when he spoke of how "God's children" suffered from "wrinkled stomachs" or slept "on the sidewalks at night" or kept vigil over their children to protect them from "rats and roaches."[52] Viewed within the framework of the "world house," this suffering was now being experienced by persons with whom his hearers were irrevocably connected.

Second, King's persistent use of systems language provided the symbolic framework in which he could highlight both the scandal of poverty and the obligation to take action toward its elimination. In an individualistic society, poverty is simply the by-product of unbridled self-interest, and in a fragmented, disconnected world no one is under obligation to seek the well-being of any other. But in an interconnected world, poverty is unconscionable. Only in an interconnected world could King exclaim that "there are forty million poor people here [in the United States]" and expect a reaction of outrage.[53] Only in an interconnected world could he decry that "the well-off and the secure have . . . become indifferent and oblivious to the poverty and deprivation in their midst."[54] Only in an interconnected world could he expect his hearers to recoil from the irony that "we spend in America millions of dollars a day to store surplus food," food that could be stored "free of charge—in the wrinkled stomachs of millions of God's children who go to bed hungry at night."[55] In other words, as his hearers came to see their world through the rhetorical frame of interconnectedness, they would feel the sense of scandal when confronted with the reality of global poverty.

That frame, moreover, provided the logic for his frequent calls to action on behalf of the poor. At times King appealed to pragmatism and necessity, as when he asserted that "the universe is so structured that things go awry if men are not diligent in their cultivation of the other-regarding dimension. 'I' cannot reach fulfillment without 'thou.'"[56] But more often he presented what he thought of as self-evident moral imperatives, as when he urged, "We must devote at least as much to our children's education and the health of the poor as we do to the care of our automobiles and the building of beautiful, impressive hotels." He added: "All the wealthy nations—America, Britain, Russia, Canada, Australia, and those of Western Europe—must see it as a moral obligation to provide capital and

technical assistance to the underdeveloped areas."[57] In each case, the imperative "we must" was simply a logical extension of the fact that we live in an interconnected world. Indeed, it was precisely for this reason, he said in his "Beyond
Vietnam" address, that it was, for him, even a "necessary task to speak for those
who have been designated as our enemies."[58] Viewed from a systems perspective, he had no choice but to ask what it must be like for them to witness the U.S.
war machine destroying their lands and plunging them into poverty.

But this systems framework also provided the logical basis for King's prophetic warnings of what would come if the world ignored the plight of the poor.
He warned that when a civilization loses the appropriate balance between "machines and computers" and "profit motives and property rights" and inherently valuable humans, that civilization risks foundering "in the face of moral
bankruptcy," just as easily as it might founder "through financial bankruptcy."[59]
King noted how the technology that linked disparate peoples of the world more
closely together than ever before had also whetted the appetites of those who
had been "locked out of the earthly kingdom of wealth, health, and happiness,"
warning that they would either "share in the blessings of the world" or "organize
and overthrow those structures or governments that stand in their way."[60] In his
SMU speech, he spoke ominously about the threat of poverty: "There is nothing more dangerous than to build a society with a large segment of people who
have no stake in it, who feel they have nothing to do. These are the people who
will riot." Later in the speech he put it more tersely, "The hour is late and the
crux of destiny is kicking out. We must act before it is too late."[61] Again, in a fragmented world, these warnings made no sense. But undergirded by the logic of
interconnectedness, the suffering, distress, and anger of the poor people of the
world threatened the entire globe. The world ignored them at its peril.

The King Legacy and the Continuing Trends
toward Global Interconnectedness

When Martin Luther King Jr. began to turn his focus and energy more toward
the plight of poor people worldwide, he faced the acute challenge of evoking a
sense of urgency and obligation among those who were well-off—who perhaps
felt secure in their own prosperity—toward those who were shut out from the
prosperity of the modern, technical age. In this essay, I have argued that he responded to this challenge by drawing on the language of systems theory to construct a rhetorical frame through which his hearers could see themselves and
their world. They existed within an inescapable web of connection that linked
their lives to every other living thing and to the very life of God. In this symbolic

world, the welfare of each person was inextricably linked to the welfare of every other. Indeed, as I have shown, this theme of interconnectedness was a central motif throughout the speeches and sermons of King's final years. It provided the underlying logic for his call to empathy, for his challenge to the wealthy of the world to take action to end poverty, and for his prophetic warning about the fate of the world if they did not. To the degree that his hearers adopted this systemic perspective, they would have no choice but to act.

Given his historical and cultural context, King's call to embrace the reality of global interconnectedness was bold for his time. As noted above, he spoke at a moment when U.S. culture was becoming increasingly individualistic, focusing far more on personal freedom and happiness than on any sense of obligation for the welfare of the world. But King spoke at the height of the Cold War, which pitted East against West and which, with the Cuban Missile Crisis in 1962, had brought the world to the brink of nuclear war. His vision also prophetically challenged powerful economic interests that had much to lose if it ever became reality. It is not surprising, then, as Paul Le Blanc and Michael Yates observe, that King's call for economic justice, or a radical redistribution of economic resources, was met by "a well-financed and steady (and soon accelerating) conservative onslaught that culminated in the right-wing triumph of the Reagan-Bush years." The "crises of the twenty-first century's first two decades," Le Blanc and Yates conclude, "cannot be separated from these defeats."[62]

Indeed, in the years since King's death, the trends toward interconnection that he identified have only increased. As a result of continued global urbanization, sociologist James Hunter observes, "The majority of people in the world now live in and around cities," while advances in the technology of transportation have not only made travel easier but also drastically increased "the mix of cultures regionally and internally."[63] King pointed to the expanding reach of global communication some twenty-five years before the Internet would link people in real time from all over the world. Since then the stunning growth of communication technologies facilitating "the massive flow of information" have made it "impossible to avoid the plurality of cultures." The result, Hunter claims, is that the average person is exposed to a diversity of culture and ethnicity "more frequently and more intensely than ever before in human history." We have also come to realize the same kind of interconnectedness that King emphasized in the science of climate change, where barely detectable shifts in climate patterns have been shown to systematically affect "century-scale biological trajectories and ultimately the persistence of species."[64] Clearly, King spoke with an acute prescience in his warning that "we cannot ignore the larger world house in which we are also dwellers."[65]

At the same time, we are seeing the rise of nativism across the world, conjoined with virulent anti-immigrant sentiments. We find ourselves in a period marked by partisan tribalism in our political and social life. We see a decline in social trust, especially across political and ethnic lines, as people respond with increasing suspicion and animosity toward those who are different from them or with whom they disagree. And even our communication technology, as philosopher Matthew Crawford notes, has only accentuated the rise of the radically autonomous, unencumbered self as the cultural vision of personhood, driving us more and more into "the world inside our heads."[66] In the face of all of this, we hear Dr. King's voice calling us back to loyalties that transcend race, tribe, class, and nation, or to a world perspective: "No individual can live alone; no nation can live alone. . . . Now the judgment of God is upon us, and we must either learn to live together as [sisters and] brothers or we are all going to perish together as fools."[67] If there were ever a time when we needed to rise to his challenge, that time is now.

NOTES

The epigraphs are from Martin Luther King Jr., *The Trumpet of Conscience* (San Francisco: Harper & Row, 1967), 68; and John Donne, *Devotions upon Emergent Occasions, Together with Death's Duel* (Ann Arbor: Ann Arbor Paperbacks, 1959), http://www.gutenberg.org/files/23772/23772-h/23772-h.htm.

1. Martin Luther King Jr., "The Quest for Peace and Justice," Nobel lecture, Oslo, Norway, December 11, 1964, https://www.nobelprize.org/nobel_prizes/peace/laureates/1964/king-lecture.html.

2. Martin Luther King, Jr., "Remaining Awake through a Great Revolution," sermon, National Cathedral, Washington, D.C., March 31, 1968, Martin Luther King, Jr. Research and Education Institute, Stanford University, https://kinginstitute.stanford.edu/king-papers/publications/knock-midnight-inspiration-great-sermons-reverend-martin-luther-king-jr-10.

3. David J. Garrow, *Bearing the Cross: Martin Luther King, Jr., and the Southern Christian Leadership Conference* (New York: William Morrow, 1986), 439.

4. Martin Luther King Jr., "Press Statement Delivered at Stockholm Airport Arrival," unpublished, December 12, 1964, Library and Archives of the Martin Luther King Jr. Center for Nonviolent Social Change, Atlanta.

5. "King's Europe Tour Gigantic Success," *Southern Christian Leadership Conference Newsletter*, 3, no. 2 (March–April 1966), 1, 6; and "Dr. King Thanks Sweden," ibid., 2.

6. Paul Le Blanc and Michael Yates, *A Freedom Budget for All Americans: Recapturing the Promise of the Civil Rights Movement in the Struggle for Economic Justice Today* (New York: Monthly Review Press, 2013), 19, 21.

7. Ibid., 9–10.

8. Garrow, *Bearing the Cross*, 439.

9. Ibid., 527; Martin Luther King Jr., *Where Do We Go from Here: Chaos or Community?* (Boston: Beacon Press, 1967; rpt., 1968, 2010), 45; and Martin Luther King Jr., "The Three

Evils of Society," speech, Chicago, August 31, 1967, transcribed by the author from a recording available online, https://www.youtube.com/watch?v=j8d-IYSM-08.

10. Martin Luther King Jr., "Three Evils of Society."

11. Quoted in Garrow, *Bearing the Cross*, 533, 535–36.

12. Martin Luther King Jr., "Why Jesus Called a Man a Fool," sermon, Mount Pisgah Missionary Baptist Church, Chicago, August 27, 1967, Martin Luther King, Jr. Research and Education Institute, Stanford University, https://kinginstitute.stanford.edu/king -papers/documents/why-jesus-called-man-fool-sermon-delivered-mount-pisgah -missionary-baptist; and Clayborne Carson and Peter Holloran, eds., *A Knock at Midnight: Inspiration from the Great Sermons of Reverend Martin Luther King, Jr.* (New York: Warner, 1998), 145.

13. Martin Luther King Jr., "Beyond Vietnam," speech, Riverside Church, New York City, April 4, 1967, Martin Luther King, Jr. Research and Education Institute, Stanford University, https://kinginstitute.stanford.edu/king-papers/documents/beyond -vietnam; and Martin Luther King Jr., *A Call to Conscience: The Landmark Speeches of Dr. Martin Luther King, Jr.*, edited by Clayborne Carson and Kris Shepard (New York: Warner, 2001), 142.

14. Martin Luther King Jr., "Remaining Awake through a Great Revolution," in Carson and Holloran, eds., *Knock at Midnight*, 212.

15. Aristotle, *The Art of Rhetoric*, Penguin Classics (New York: Penguin Books, 1991), 2.8, 162–64; and Martin Luther King Jr., "Remaining Awake through a Great Revolution," 212–14.

16. See Nancy Christie and Michael Gauvreau, *The Sixties and Beyond: Dechristianization in North America and Western Europe, 1945–2000* (Toronto: University of Toronto Press, 2013), 7.

17. Ludwig von Bertalanffy, *General System Theory: Foundations, Development, Applications*, rev. ed. (New York: George Braziller, 1968), xvii, 3.

18. Ibid., 55–56.

19. Francisco Miranda, *Systems Theory: Perspectives, Applications and Developments* (New York: Nova Publishers, 2014), 2.

20. Arlene Vetere, "Structural Family Therapy," *Child Psychology and Psychiatry Review*, 6, no. 3 (2001): 133–34.

21. Peter M. Senge, *The Fifth Discipline: The Art and Practice of the Learning Organization* (New York: Doubleday, 1990), 42–43, 64.

22. Martin Luther King Jr., "Where Do We Go From Here?," address to the Southern Christian Leadership Convention, Atlanta, August 16, 1967, Martin Luther King, Jr. Research and Education Institute, Stanford University, https://kinginstitute.stanford.edu /king-papers/documents/where-do-we-go-here-address-delivered-eleventh-annual -sclc-convention.

23. Martin Luther King Jr., "Death of Evil upon the Seashore," sermon, Montgomery, Alabama, July 21, 1955, sermon box, folder 174, Coretta Scott King Collection, Library and Archives of the Martin Luther King Jr. Center for Nonviolent Social Change, Atlanta.

24. Martin Luther King Jr., *Where Do We Go From Here?*, 167–91.

25. Martin Luther King Jr., "Quest for Peace and Justice"; and Martin Luther King Jr., *Where Do We Go from Here?*, 167, 177.

26. Martin Luther King Jr., *Where Do We Go from Here?*, 168, 173–86.

27. Carson and Holloran, eds., *Knock at Midnight*, 151–52; Martin Luther King Jr., *Where*

Do We Go from Here?, 181; Martin Luther King Jr., *Trumpet of Conscience*, 69–70; and Martin Luther King Jr., *Strength to Love* (1963; repr., Philadelphia: Fortress Press, 1981), 69–70.

28. Martin Luther King Jr., *Trumpet of Conscience*, 69.

29. Martin Luther King Jr., "Remaining Awake through a Great Revolution," 211.

30. Martin Luther King Jr., *Call to Conscience*, 142; and Martin Luther King, "Remaining Awake through a Great Revolution," 219.

31. Martin Luther King Jr., "Beyond Vietnam"; and Martin Luther King Jr., *Call to Conscience*, 142–43.

32. Martin Luther King Jr., *Where Do We Go from Here?*, 168.

33. William H. Young and Nancy K. Young, *The 1950s: American Popular Culture through History* (Westport, Conn.: Greenwood, 2004), xii.

34. Martin Luther King Jr., "Remaining Awake through a Great Revolution," 207; and Martin Luther King Jr., *Testament of Hope*, 209.

35. Martin Luther King Jr., "Quest for Peace and Justice."

36. Martin Luther King Jr., "Three Evils of Society."

37. King, "Quest for Peace and Justice"; and King, "Nobel Lecture," 2–4.

38. Martin Luther King Jr., "Speech at Southern Methodist University," Dallas, March 17, 1966, https://www.smu.edu/AboutSMU/MLK#transcript.

39. Martin Luther King Jr., *Where Do We Go from Here?*, 176.

40. King, *Where Do We Go from Here?*, 170. As John Ansbro points out, King used almost identical language to describe this emerging consciousness, which reflected his study of Hegelian philosophy, as early as his 1959 farewell address at Dexter Avenue Baptist Church in Montgomery. See John J. Ansbro, *Martin Luther King, Jr: Nonviolent Strategies and Tactics for Social Change* (New York: Madison Books, 2000), 126–27. Similar language appears in Martin Luther King Jr., "Letter from the Birmingham Jail," Martin Luther King, Jr. Research and Education Institute, http://okra.stanford.edu/transcription /document_images/undecided/630416-019.pdf.

41. Martin Luther King Jr., "Beyond Vietnam"; and Martin Luther King Jr., *Call to Conscience*, 159–60.

42. Martin Luther King Jr., "Three Evils of Society."

43. Martin Luther King Jr., "Speech at Southern Methodist University"; and Martin Luther King Jr., *Testament of Hope*, 215.

44. Martin Luther King Jr., *Trumpet of Conscience*, 69–70.

45. Martin Luther King Jr., "Beyond Vietnam"; Martin Luther King Jr., *Call to Conscience*, 161; and Martin Luther King Jr., *Where Do We Go from Here?*, 190–91.

46. King, "Remaining Awake through a Great Revolution," 208. An earlier version of this claim can be found in King's "Letter from a Birmingham Jail" (1963), where he responds to the charge of being an "outside agitator." See Martin Luther King Jr., *Why We Can't Wait* (New York: New American Library, 1963), 77.

47. King, *Where Do We Go from Here?*, 167–68.

48. Jim A. Kuypers, "Framing Analysis," in *The Art of Rhetorical Criticism* (Boston: Allyn & Bacon, 2004), 186–87.

49. Shani Robins and Richard E. Mayer, "The Metaphor Framing Effect: Metaphorical Reasoning about Text-Based Dilemmas," *Discourse Processes* 30 (2000): 57–86.

50. Kuypers, "Framing Analysis," 186.

51. Martin Luther King Jr., "Beyond Vietnam"; and Martin Luther King Jr., *Call to Conscience*, 146–50.

52. Martin Luther King Jr., "Remaining Awake through a Great Revolution," 212–13; and Martin Luther King Jr., *Testament of Hope*, 272–73.

53. Martin Luther King Jr., "Where Do We Go From Here?" (address to the SCLC convention).

54. Martin Luther King Jr., *Where Do We Go from Here?*, 178.

55. Martin Luther King Jr., "Remaining Awake through a Great Revolution," 213.

56. Martin Luther King Jr., *Where Do We Go from Here?*, 180.

57. Martin Luther King Jr., "Three Evils of Society"; and Martin Luther King Jr., *Where Do We Go from Here?*, 178.

58. Martin Luther King Jr., "Beyond Vietnam"; and Martin Luther King Jr., *Call to Conscience*, 142, 146, 152.

59. Martin Luther King Jr., "Three Evils of Society"; and Martin Luther King Jr., *Where Do We Go from Here?*, 186.

60. Martin Luther King Jr., *Where Do We Go from Here?*, 176.

61. Martin Luther King Jr., "Speech at Southern Methodist University"; and Martin Luther King Jr., *Trumpet of Conscience*, 50.

62. LeBlanc and Yates, *Freedom Budget for All Americans*, 10.

63. James D. Hunter, *To Change the World: The Irony, Tragedy, and Possibility of Christianity in the Late Modern World* (New York: Oxford University Press, 2010), 200–201.

64. Camille Parmesan and Gary Yohe, "A Globally Coherent Fingerprint of Climate Change Impacts across Natural Systems," *Nature*, January 2, 2003, 41.

65. Martin Luther King Jr., *Where Do We Go from Here?*, 167.

66. See Matthew B. Crawford, *The World beyond Your Head: On Becoming an Individual in an Age of Distraction* (New York: Farrar, Straus, and Giroux, 2010), 16–27.

67. Martin Luther King Jr., "Remaining Awake through a Great Revolution," 207.

CHAPTER 4
LIVING BY THE SWORD
THE HAUNTING SPECTACLE OF VIOLENCE AND HUMAN DESTRUCTION

RUFUS BURROW JR.

If we assume that life is worth living and that man has a right
to survive, then we must find an alternative to war.
MARTIN LUTHER KING JR., *Where Do We Go from Here?*

We as a Council [South African Council of Churches] deplore all forms of violence. . . .
We deplore structural and legalized violence that maintains an unjust socio-
political dispensation, and the violence of those who would overthrow the State.
DESMOND TUTU, *Hope and Suffering*

Martin Luther King Jr. was in theory and practice a nonviolent absolutist, one who rejected the use of the sword of violence on any level, for any reason, anywhere in the world house. Convinced that humanity's choice is ultimately between what he termed "nonviolent coexistence or violent coannihilation," he even opposed violence as a self-defensive weapon or as a means of defending family, group, or nation. King never advocated violence as a personal or social ethic, and he denounced war as a sure path to tragic self-destruction. He understood but wholeheartedly disagreed with those who felt forced to resort to the instruments of violence because all other methods had been tried and failed. The global King was not simply a nonviolent pragmatist. Rather, for him, nonviolence was the only acceptable method in a world he believed to be founded on morality and sustained by a personal and loving creator God.

Because King was not merely the quintessential social activist but also a man of ideas and ideals, it is important to examine his nonviolent absolutism through the lens of his philosophy of personalism. Three personalist doctrines undergird the discussion in this chapter: God as personal, the inviolable sacredness of human beings, and the conviction that the universe is social and is grounded on morality. Any one of these may be put forth as a reasonable explanation for King's nonviolent absolutism in the world house. For example, he asserted that it was out of his commitment to the sacredness of persons that he felt compelled to reject the war in Vietnam.[1] Taken together, these doctrines provide a convincing theological-philosophical foundation for King's stance on nonviolence as a way of life. I will give brief attention to the first two but focus on the third doctrine.

This chapter examines the evolution of King's nonviolent absolutism and his consistent adherence to it on all levels. Were there signs in his childhood that suggested possible leanings in this direction? What were some contributions of his formal education from college through doctoral studies? Did he ever own and use guns? How did he respond to personal acts of violence against him? At what points did he embrace nonviolence as both a personal and social ethic? What exactly was his stance on violence and war in the waning months of his life? To what extent did he support the internationalization of nonviolence?[2] These are a few of the questions that guide the ensuing discussion.

The boy King seemed to prefer words, ideas, and ideals as the best means of solving conflict, rather than appealing to violence. Numerous people from his childhood, not least his parents, help to enlighten us regarding his attitude toward violence and pacifism. Were there basic teachings in the home and church that contributed to this?

King's Earliest Attitude toward Violence and Nonviolence

The mature Martin Luther King Jr. was always speaking and writing about the sacredness and interrelatedness of persons. He was already a staunch believer in the preciousness of human beings long before he studied the works of the great personalists in seminary and during his doctoral studies. As a child he learned about his own sacredness when, after the parents of his white boyhood friends forbade them to play together because they were of different races, his mother placed him on her lap and told him what virtually every loving black mother has had to tell her children—namely, that he was as good as anybody and that he was never to allow anyone to convince him otherwise. Both of King's parents and his maternal grandmother were committed to instilling in him and his siblings a strong sense of self and "somebodiness" as well as the value of acknowledging and respecting the humanity and the dignity of others. These teachings, along with the conviction that God is personal and loving, were the bases of what I have called King's homespun personalism.[3] In addition, these early teachings likely had much to do with his attitude toward violence when he was a child. By the time he formally studied personalism, he was already committed to its fundamental principles, as a result of his family and black church upbringing.

No one is born a nonviolent absolutist. The curious person cannot help wondering whether the boy King exhibited evidence of leaning in the direction of nonviolent absolutism. What do we learn about this from King himself, his parents, neighborhood adults, and his boyhood companions? Was there consistency in their recollections?

Indicators show that from the time he was a child, Martin Luther King Jr. typically sought to avoid violence. This is not to say that he was born a Gandhian or nonviolent absolutist. He was not. But it is significant that King as a young boy apparently had a preference for avoiding violent responses to violence done to him. This shows just how deeply embedded and enduring was his disdain for violence. It also dispels the idea that he only began to entertain the nonviolent approach to solving conflict after he read and pondered Henry David Thoreau's famous essay on civil disobedience in a philosophy class under Samuel Williams at Morehouse College. It is true, however, that looking back, King pointed to the reading of Thoreau's essay as his first academic introduction to nonviolence.[4] He was fascinated by Thoreau's idea of noncooperation with an evil social system. The effect the essay had on him might well have had something to do with how he had viewed or reacted to violence when he was a child as well as his mature stance on the issue as an adult.

There was a time when some were inclined to believe that King was born a Gandhian. Fortunately, this myth was early identified, evaluated, and rejected. As Lerone Bennett Jr. claimed, "Gandhis are not born; they invent themselves."[5] Bennett therefore argued against trying to locate in King an embryonic Gandhi and believed it necessary to examine the totality of his experience in the South and as a son of a strong black religious family in order to determine the factors that made Gandhi's ideas appealing to him.

King's father, Martin Luther King Sr., had a volatile temper and reportedly got physical with a ministerial colleague who failed to repay a debt to him.[6] Moreover, when Martin Jr. decided to disobey an injunction not to march in Birmingham, risking being jailed, his father—perhaps out of parental fear for his safety—passionately remarked: "Well, you didn't get this nonviolence from me. You must have got it from your Mama."[7] Clearly, the elder King was not a nonviolent ideologue, although later in life he acknowledged having developed a strong appreciation for his son's nonviolent absolutism.[8] Martin Luther King Jr.'s mother and maternal grandmother, on the other hand, were representatives of a gentler spirit and were predisposed to nonviolence. Perhaps more than anyone else, his mother shaped his sense of morality by instilling in him three things: the sense of the strict Baptist moral code that stressed the importance of personal morality, such as avoiding drinking, smoking, dancing, and premarital sex; the sense that he was somebody; and the sense of the power and duty of Christian love. The latter two were central influences throughout King's adult life and were fundamental to the development of his nonviolent absolutism.

David L. Lewis, another early King biographer, believed that Bennett's claim that Gandhis are not born was too strong and that it was truer to say that Gandhis are indeed born, "but they develop their traits over a period of years."[9] This stance is actually quite similar to Bennett's. Both men have rightly thought it necessary to examine King's development from childhood to try to determine whether there were factors that contributed to his disdain for violence and his later attraction to Gandhi's ideas.

Lawrence D. Reddick, King's first biographer, asserts that King had an aversion to violence that went back to his childhood. In his 1959 *Crusader without Violence*, he acknowledges that King playfully wrestled and tussled with his friends but says he never liked fighting and would only fight as a last resort. This version of the boy King leaves one wondering whether his seeming antipathy to violence was a conscious decision, as Reddick seems to suggest when he says: "This was a personal and individual reaction, for both his father and brother were stout counter-attackers. His mother and sister were normally nonviolent . . . but even they felt that, if somebody hits you first, you have the right— perhaps obligation—to hit back."[10] Reddick later would try to make the case for what he saw as the boy King's repugnance to violence, noting that he did not fight back when beaten up by the school bully, he did not resist when beaten up by a boy with whom he had a disagreement over who had arrived first at the turnstile in a grocery store, and, while waiting for his mother to return to the store where they had been shopping, he did not retaliate after being slapped by a white woman who claimed that he had earlier stepped on her foot.[11] In such cases, King said and did nothing in his own defense. Looking back years later, he claimed that in part he did not retaliate because "it was part of my native structure—that is, that I have never been one to hit back."[12] As another example of King's pacifist leanings, Reddick claims that when Daddy King commanded his children to chastise each other by striking hands, arms, or buttocks, Martin refused to hit either of his siblings but willfully received their blows. Reddick concludes from these incidents that "the nonviolent tendency must have been quite pronounced" in King and that his "withdrawal from violence was not cowardice or timidity."[13] Reddick's stance supports those who believe that the boy King had an "impulse toward nonviolence as a personal way of life."

King's mother gave an account of his childhood that is similar to Reddick's. The year before she was fatally wounded by Marcus Wayne Chenault at a Sun-

day worship service in 1974 at the Ebenezer Baptist Church where her husband
was senior minister, Mrs. King made a tape recording of herself recalling her
son's life from birth to age twelve.[14] She described King as a relatively normal,
outgoing boy who sometimes engaged in mischief and was occasionally involved in incidents that left minor cuts and bruises on his body, such as when
he was struck on two different occasions by a car as he rode his bicycle in the
street. A couple of things stood out for Mrs. King regarding her son's behavior in
comparison to other boys. First, she asserted that he did not ask for or have a desire to play with toy guns, as most little boys did. He apparently did not want to
even pretend to shoot or be shot at by toy guns. Interestingly, in the early weeks
of the Montgomery bus boycott, before he was instructed by Bayard Rustin and
later Glenn Smiley, both active in the Fellowship of Reconciliation (FOR), King
felt compelled to own a pistol to protect himself and his young family. The sher-
iff's department denied him a permit, and after conversations with his wife he
decided against gun ownership, later recalling that he was actually more afraid
with the gun in the house.[15]

Second, Mrs. King asserted that her son did not get into fights, a claim that
is similar to Reddick's and to King's claim that he had "never been one to hit
back," an assertion that is quite different from what some of his boyhood friends
remembered. According to these, King was known to challenge and to accept
challenges of opponents to "go to the grass," a phrase his circle of peers said he
invented whenever disagreements could not be settled with words. King was
said by some to be as quick to launch or accept a challenge to "go to the grass"
as his peers.[16] However, there is no indication that he was ever one who picked
fights or sought to bully others. He defended himself through fighting when
the need arose, but he was not known to start fights. This sounds more credible than the view that he did not get into fights at all as a young boy and that
this somehow proves that he grew up with an inclination toward nonviolence,
rather than violence, as a personal ethic. In addition, inasmuch as King was not
troubled by "going to the grass," but generally preferred to avoid fighting and
to use words and reason to settle conflicts, shows that he had elements of both
parents in him: the calmness and cool-headedness of his mother and the passion and assertiveness of his father. This combination of traits would serve him
well throughout his civil rights ministry.

Although King's father would remember him as being generally sensitive
and disposed to negotiating his way out of difficult situations, he also recalled
the time when Martin Jr. cracked his younger brother, A. D., over the head with
a telephone when he persisted in pestering their sister Willie Christine. This

left A. D. "dazed and wobbly on his feet."[17] So while the boy King might well have been inclined to avoid violence whenever he could, he at times resorted to self-defensive violence or the violent defense of another. He was therefore quite normal, rather than extraordinary, in this regard. This is a stark reminder that the boy King was nowhere close to his later stance on nonviolence as a way of life. He was a long way from being "Alabama's Gandhi," as Baltimore's *Afro-American* called him, and was at best a nonviolent pragmatist.[18]

King's fascination with language and love for words was known to many during those very early years. Observing his father and other gifted black ministers and their ability to arrange words in order to dazzle and even dominate their audiences, six-year-old Martin Jr. told his mother that he was going to get him some big words someday. "The idea of using words as weapons of defense and offense was thus early implanted and seems to have grown in King as naturally as a flower," Bennett writes.[19] More often than not, the youngster relied on words and at times silence rather than his fists.

Philip Lenud, King's boyhood friend, Morehouse classmate, and roommate at Boston University in the early 1950s, told Lewis V. Baldwin that King was "just a born pacifist," although we have seen that not all of his childhood peers remembered him this way.[20] Regardless, King's thought and stance on the global significance of nonviolence evolved during his student years at Morehouse College, Crozer Theological Seminary, and Boston University. King reflected that his reading of Thoreau's essay on civil disobedience at Morehouse left him impressed by the doctrine and practice of noncooperation with an unjust system. By his own account, this was his first intellectual contact with the theory of nonviolent resistance as a means of addressing war and other social evils. The mature King rejected Thoreau's openness to the destruction of the political system, which did not exclude anarchism and violence, as in his defense of the abolitionist John Brown's raid on the military armory at Harper's Ferry in an attempt to free enslaved blacks in 1859.[21] However, the principle of noncooperation would always play a central role in King's theory and practice of nonviolent resistance.

Although King did not study Gandhi at Morehouse, he was informed about his nonviolent campaigns through reading the black-owned *Atlanta Daily World* (to which his parents subscribed while he was in high school and college), which often featured articles about struggles for justice and independence in other parts of the world. Moreover, since Morehouse president Benjamin E. Mays visited with Gandhi in 1936 and asked him to explain his doctrine and practice of nonviolence, King and his classmates surely heard about this during weekly presidential chapel talks. By the time King graduated from Morehouse, he had some sense of the global importance of nonviolence.

When King entered Crozer Theological Seminary and made the conscious decision to seek a sound theological foundation for his "already substantial" social conscience and to search for a viable method to address social evils, he did not forget Thoreau's essay. While at Crozer, he heard a talk by visiting lecturer and well-known pacifist A. J. Muste of the FOR. Although "deeply moved" by Muste's lecture—and despite spirited dialogue with him during the question-and-answer period that followed, King was not convinced of the validity and practicability of Muste's absolute pacifism. It simply made no sense to young King at that time to reject war as a national policy under all circumstances. Instead, King, as most Crozer students, believed that while war could never serve as a positive good, it might well serve as a negative good, such as preventing the development and spread of an evil force like that of Hitler.

Later, during his second year at Crozer, King heard Howard University president Mordecai W. Johnson's talk at the Philadelphia Fellowship House on Gandhi's doctrine of nonviolent resistance as a method for social change. He characterized Johnson's presentation as so "profound and electrifying" that he was compelled to purchase several books on Gandhi and his philosophy. King said that for the first time he could see the relevance of Jesus's love ethic for more than individual relationships. "Love for Gandhi was a potent instrument for social and collective transformation," King concluded, and he naturally saw a connection between Gandhian philosophy and the New Testament's Sermon on the Mount.[22] Undoubtedly the connection became clearer as King studied Gandhi in a psychology of religion course with Crozer's professor George W. Davis. Gandhi, on whom King chose to write a research paper, was one of several important religious personalities King studied.

It is significant that Davis was the teacher who introduced King to the philosophy of personalism as advocated by Edgar S. Brightman of Boston University. As noted above, personalism maintains that reality is a society of interacting selves and persons summoned into existence by a supreme person as its creative center. Because the universe is believed to be social and grounded on morality, this provides a strong basis for King's nonviolent absolutism in an international context. Although King received a strong introduction to personalist philosophy at Crozer, he studied it systematically at Boston University. By the time his formal academic studies were completed, he had a strong philosophical foundation for his belief in the absolute sacredness and interrelatedness of persons throughout the world house. Without a doubt, one who holds such a belief will inevitably find violence against sacred, interdependent beings to be problematic.

While a statesman, King was also a leader who possessed intelligence, courage, character, integrity, and loyalty. In this regard, he was without question what Walter Earl Fluker and other leadership scholars view as an ethical leader, always putting the interests of the people before his own.[23] In addition, as a personalist and internationalist, King had a clear sense of the interrelated structure of reality and the world, and he would live by the conviction that no group or nation can live in isolation. King would come to see that individuals, groups, and nations are interactive and interrelated, such that what affects one affects all others, whether directly or indirectly. He would also conclude that peace on earth would be possible only if people consciously and consistently strive to transcend loyalty to self, race, ethnic group, and nation. Thus, an international perspective needs to be developed. This point of view was already expanding for King when he enrolled at Crozer.[24] To be sure, one must be concerned, he felt, about self and one's own group and nation. In other words, there is nothing wrong with a healthy sense of nationalism. King understood and accepted this even in his early years, but he rejected the worst forms of nationalism, such as those types that are "perverted into chauvinism and isolationism."[25] His point was that one must recognize that the interdependent structure of the world requires the development of an international outlook and concern for the welfare of the entire world house. One is not only a member of a particular group and nation but also a world citizen inextricably bound to every other person and affected in some way by whatever happens everywhere in the world.

King would ultimately become the quintessential theologian of nonviolent resistance. Indeed, by his second year at Crozer, he was already writing and praying for "a warless world," a theme that he would continue to stress throughout his ministry.[26] Later, he persistently proclaimed that he was "maladjusted to the madness of militarism and the self-defeating effects of physical violence."[27] Inasmuch as there are indicators that this was King's position when he enrolled in seminary, it must also be the case that he held this view to some degree while he was a student at Morehouse. While a sociology major at Morehouse, he regularly browsed through the *Atlanta Daily World*, which frequently included articles on freedom struggles in Africa, Asia, and elsewhere in the world, and consequently developed an early awareness of and concern about violence and war.[28] It was during King's first year in seminary that he began writing about the need for "world brotherhood" and "world cooperation" and insisted on the need to recognize that "all humanity is so interwoven in a single process that whatever affects the man in Russia also affects the man in America."[29]

On Violence as a Violation of Human Personhood

Violence is commonly defined as the use of physical force that is intended to cause bodily harm or even death.[30] For our purpose, consonant with King's thought, violence needs to be defined more broadly, so that it may be seen as that which is a violation of human personhood. Because of King's high estimate of the worth and sacredness of human beings, this broader definition is consistent with his thought, since to violate a human being in any way is to subject a person to violence. Therefore, the fact that persons are subjected to injustice means that they are victims of violence, since injustice demeans and dehumanizes. King, echoing Gandhi, contended that "the presence of injustice in society is already the presence of violence."[31] Consequently, violence is not always accompanied by lethal force or physical injury, but it is always a violation of human personhood. The name-calling endured by nonviolent demonstrators was for King as much an act of violence as spitting in their faces, hitting them with rocks and bottles or baseball bats, turning high-powered water hoses on them, or siccing dogs on them. Hatred and thinking ill of others were also considered by King to be acts of violating human personhood. As for himself, King asserted that he had seen and been on the receiving end of too much hatred to want to hate. He had seen it too often in the faces of southern sheriffs, Citizens' Council members, and Klansmen. Thus, he concluded that hatred was just "too great a burden to bear."[32]

King was certain that whenever blacks were denied educational opportunities and jobs for which they qualified, they were victims of violence. Having to pay higher prices for a poorer quality of goods, including "higher rent for equivalent housing than [is] charged in the white areas of the city," were also deemed by King to be instances of violence against blacks.[33] When he thought about the poverty he witnessed on the streets of Calcutta during his trip to India in 1959, he saw this as violence being done to massive numbers of human beings. He drew the same conclusion when he read about the treatment of Jews in Russia and apartheid and massive poverty among black South Africans. He concluded similarly when he reflected that many of the problems experienced by Latin America and its massive poor population had their roots in the United States.[34] Violence, according to King, is denying people human rights and basic necessities of life such as food, shelter, health care, and education. Consequently, he considered no form of violence, external or internal, however subtle or covert, to be acceptable or justifiable.

There is no question that King was convinced that violence is much more than a social and political issue or even a psychological problem, for that matter. In the deepest sense, it is a moral and theological problem. It is a question of the dignity and sacredness of human beings and God's unending love for them. This makes it a moral and theological problem of the first magnitude. Nothing, in King's estimation, was more important to God than the well-being and survival of human beings.

Much influenced by the anthropology and social ethics of Reinhold Niebuhr, King surely understood the stance of those who argued that violence may at times be justifiable. Indeed, he did not hesitate to acknowledge that it could not be expected that blacks would respond nonviolently to everything that society did to them. He tried very hard to understand the decision of Black Power youths to turn to retaliatory violence.[35] Moreover, reflecting on the struggle against apartheid, King even said that he could understand how black South Africans could feel desperate and turn to violence after they had been subjected to decades of brutal repression despite their nonviolent protests.[36] Indeed, King was much disturbed by the Sharpeville massacre in that country on March 21, 1960, when police killed 69 and wounded 180 young people who were demonstrating nonviolently against "pass laws." Many of the youths were shot in the back. After Claude Barnett, head of the Associated Negro Press, asked King to send a letter with his reflections on the massacre, King responded:

> The recent mass murder of Africans engaged in {the} peaceful protest against restrictive laws is a tragic and shameful expression of man's inhumanity to man. Such barbaric and uncivilized acts are shocking to all men of goodwill. This tragic massacre by police troops in South Africa should arouse the conscience of the whole world. This tragic occurrence in South Africa should also serve as a warning signal to the United States where peaceful demonstrations are also being conducted by student groups.[37]

Convinced that the entire universe is held securely in God's hands, King was certain that the days of segregation and injustice in the world house were numbered. It was therefore natural for him to declare that "all of the lands of Africa will be free one day."[38]

When pressed on the practicality or impracticality of violent revolution, King conceded that the violence of nations has sometimes led to immediate victory but that this victory has been temporary. "Violence often brings about momentary results," he wrote. "Nations have frequently won their independence in battle. But . . . in spite of temporary victories, violence never brings permanent peace."[39] Of course, at some point it will be instructive to determine just how permanent have been the victories of nonviolence, both in the United States and in other countries.

King's Responses to Physical Violence against Himself

The adult King was violently attacked numerous times. What exactly were his responses? How and why did he respond as he did, and what does this tell us about how serious he was about rejecting violence and insisting on nonviolence? What do his responses tell us about his commitment to nonviolence as a personal ethic or way of life?

During his years as a public figure and civil rights leader, King was not just a nonviolent ideologue. He literally lived the nonviolent faith, and this was nowhere more evident than when he was attacked physically during the civil rights movement. Earlier, we saw evidence that as a young boy King sometimes responded to acts of violence against him or his beloved sister with violence in return. This, of course, was long before he read Thoreau's essay in college, read and studied Gandhi in seminary, was instructed on the practice of strategic and organized nonviolence by Rustin and Smiley in Montgomery, and thought deeply about the meaning of nonviolence as a personal and social ethic and what it could mean for national and international freedom struggles. At any rate, King suffered several attacks upon his person, four of which stand out. In Harlem in 1958, while autographing copies of his first book, *Stride toward Freedom: The Montgomery Story*, he was stabbed in the chest with a sharp letter opener by Izola Ware Curry, a black woman diagnosed as demented. In 1963 and 1965, he sustained violent physical attacks in Birmingham and Selma, Alabama, respectively. In August 1966, while leading a nonviolent march on Chicago's southwest side, King was struck on the right side of his head with a brick, which dropped him to his knees. A knife was also thrown at him, but it missed its target and landed instead in the shoulder of an unsuspecting onlooker. On later reflection, King reported, "I've been in many demonstrations all across the South, but I can say that I have never seen, even in Mississippi, mobs as hostile and as hate-filled as in Chicago."[40] Even so, King never retaliated in any way against his attackers. The calmness and strength of resolve he displayed when confronted with each and every instance of physical and verbal violence visited upon him is significant, because his responses communicated to witnesses the depth of his commitment to nonviolence as a way of life. His responses also buttressed his thoughts about the need for peaceful means in maintaining relations between individuals, groups, and nations. Since the lesson from each violent attack King faced was essentially the same, namely, the redemptive nature of suffering through expressed, organized nonviolence, only one such case is discussed at length here.[41]

At the first integrated Southern Christian Leadership Conference (SCLC) con-

vention in Birmingham in 1963, King was making closing announcements when
Roy James, a member of the American Nazi Party, casually emerged from the
audience, ascended the steps to the stage, and began violently pummeling him
in the face, head, and back. James delivered several powerful blows that staggered and disoriented King before the audience realized he was being attacked.
Septima Poinsette Clark, who developed the Citizenship Schools for the SCLC,
was present and witnessed the attack. Clark was awestruck by King's response.
She watched him receive the heavy blows, while offering no defense. In the process, King reportedly had a certain look on his face, a "transcendent calm," as
Taylor Branch put it. It was a look that Clark and others said emblazoned itself
in their memory. Clark said that what she witnessed that day convinced her of
King's nonviolent absolutism, that he was wedded to and would live nonviolence for the rest of his life. Branch recalled Clark's reaction: "King dropped his
hands 'like a newborn baby,' she said, and from then on she never doubted that
his nonviolence was more than the heat of his oratory or . . . instincts."[42] From
that day forward, Clark was convinced that nonviolence was the real deal for
King. She marveled at his reaction to the brutal attack. She concluded that King
was absolutely devoted to nonviolence and determined that he would not live
violently or support violence on any level, anywhere in the world. In what King
believed to be a fundamentally social and value-fused world created and sustained by God, only nonviolent means were acceptable for resolving conflict.
But we might ask: What does personalist doctrine contribute to his nonviolent
absolutism and its significance for the world house? Did King see nonviolent
absolutism as essential for nondemocratic countries such as Hitler's Germany,
war-torn Vietnam, and the apartheid regime in predemocratic South Africa?

In part, King was willing and able to withstand violent attacks and to respond to them nonviolently because of his sense that such sacrifices were part
of a larger divine plan to prepare him for a greater work in the Deep South, the
rest of the nation, and indeed the world house. He drew this conclusion after reflecting on the stabbing he suffered in Harlem. It was, as historian Stephen B.
Oates puts it, a lesson in "personal redemption through suffering," a lesson that
King carried forward and consistently applied.[43] Yet King saw the broader social implications of incidents of violence perpetrated against an individual such
as himself. He saw that a climate so thoroughly infused with "hatred and bitterness" inevitably bursts forth with devastating violence on a massive scale. In
any event, each time King was physically attacked he afterward harbored no resentment toward the attacker and preferred that the authorities provide the as-
sailant with help instead of prosecution.

Nonviolence in a Universe Founded on Morality

Martin Luther King Jr. was an unwavering personalist. He unashamedly asserted that personalism—the philosophy that God is "a personal being of boundless power and infinite love" and human beings are inestimably sacred—was his "basic philosophical position."[44] Through this philosophy he found metaphysical grounding for his belief in a personal God, his conviction that every person possesses intrinsic and inviolable dignity by virtue of relatedness to God, his sense that freedom is fundamental to what it means to be human, and his conviction that reality is social and the universe is founded on morality. As previously shown, each of these convictions grounded King's nonviolent absolutism, and taken together they help explain his unrelenting adherence to it as he put forth his vision for the great world house.

For the theistic personalist like King, each individual is blessed with infinite and inherent value because of relatedness to God and by virtue of the image of God invested in him or her. King agreed with his personalist forebears at Boston University that every person derives from "divine parentage and divine destiny, and has, therefore, an inextinguishable claim to our reverence." Consequently, the individual must never be sacrificed for impersonal objects, all of which exist for persons and not the other way around. For example, the individual does not exist for the state or to serve the state. So precious is the person that she "may never be regarded as fuel for warming society."[45] The individual is not a means to someone else's ends. King believed that until people and nations truly acknowledge and respect the dignity of persons and the image of God in them, we will engage in violence and fight wars.[46]

Human beings are utterly sacred, according to King, too precious and valuable in the eyes of God to be killed as a result of gang violence, in Saturday night brawls, and on the world's battlefields.[47] King was adamant that every person is made for and belongs to God.[48] No human being has the right to violate that which belongs to and is loved by God, and to kill a person is a form of theft.[49] That is, to take a human life is to take that which belongs only to God. This is why violence and war were so problematic for King.

King learned from personalism that reality and its many entities, not least human beings, are social and interdependent and cannot be self-actualized in isolation from each other.[50] This is why he so often said that what affects one person or group directly affects all others in some way. Because we are sisters and brothers, one who harms others also harms oneself, all of humanity, and God. King believed that we are bound together in the bundle of life.[51] What we do locally affects what we do nationally and even internationally. Echoing the words of Benjamin E. Mays, King often said as much: "It really boils down to this: that all life is interrelated. We are all caught in an inescapable network of mutuality, tied into a single garment of destiny. Whatever affects one directly, affects all indirectly. We are made to live together because of the interrelated structure of reality."[52] Put another way, King believed that reality is social and thoroughly interactive. Accordingly, we cannot separate violence in the United States from violence in Germany, Vietnam, South Africa, Latin America, or any other place in the world house. The struggle for justice in the United States or anywhere is always part of the larger world struggle for justice, since justice is indivisible. Without doubt, King agreed with the view of the South Vietnamese Buddhist monk Thich Nhat Hanh, whom he met at a press conference in Chicago in 1966 and who advocated both nonviolence and neutrality regarding the Vietnam War. When we harm other human beings we harm ourselves, Nhat Hanh wrote, since "the fate of each individual is inextricably linked to the fate of the whole human race."[53]

In "A Christmas Sermon on Peace," delivered in 1967 in Atlanta, King posited that if there is to be peace on earth and goodwill to all, it will be necessary for us to finally come to terms with "the ultimate morality of the universe, and believe that all reality hinges on moral foundations."[54] This means that things must be done in a certain way, and that greed, lies, violence, and war cannot have the last word. God and the universe are on the side of justice and right and therefore are friendly toward the achievement of good in the world.[55] In the value-fused universe, good will ultimately emerge, triumphant. Also, in such a universe, one who struggles against injustice and evil is assured of cosmic companionship. Further, the sword of violence has no place in a world that is occupied by infinitely valuable beings created in the image of a personal and loving God, because, among other things, violence disrupts the rhythm and flow of things in the moral universe. This is why King called for the internationalization of nonviolence.

International Influence and the Significance of Nonviolence

Reference was made above to Martin Luther King Jr.'s reaction to the Sharpeville massacre in South Africa in March 1960, when nearly one hundred black youth were mercilessly killed by police, many while running away, and almost two hundred more wounded while marching nonviolently against pass laws. King offered a vigorous and passionate response to the massacre and a stirring indictment of the entire system of apartheid. This is an important reminder that early in his civil rights ministry, King was not only keenly aware of the problem of violence on an international scale but also did not hesitate to publicly denounce it. Indeed, his critique of the Sharpeville massacre was among his strongest and earliest statements against violence and for absolute nonviolence abroad.

As also noted above, during his academic studies King grappled with the problem of war between nations. He was unquestionably against war but could not subscribe to the absolute pacifist stance of A. J. Muste, and he concluded that while war could accomplish no positive good, it was indeed a negative good or necessary evil, especially in halting the growth, development, and spread of evil social forces such as Nazism and Fascism.[56] After the successful outcome of the Montgomery bus boycott in 1956 and after King's experiences in Ghana in 1957 and India in 1959, which enlightened him about the global potential of nonviolence, a decisive shift occurred in his thinking. He then concluded that because of the destructive potential of modern weapons and bombs, there was no longer a possibility of war serving as even a negative good or necessary evil in the world house. No nation could win a war. "The choice is no longer between violence and nonviolence," King asserted. "It is either nonviolence or nonexistence."[57] King could see that war has devastating effects in the worldwide neighborhood. Further, if human beings are truly precious, if life is truly worth living, and if human beings deserve to survive, then an alternative to war must be found.

King periodically wrote and spoke against war throughout the 1950s and the early 1960s. He issued his first public statement on the Vietnam War while answering questions by the press following an address at Howard University on March 2, 1965, asserting that the war was "accomplishing nothing."[58] By 1967, he had become the most eloquent and passionate voice against war in general and the Vietnam War in particular. He agreed with his good friend Rabbi Abraham Joshua Heschel that "to speak about God and remain silent on Vietnam is blasphemous."[59] In "The Casualties of the War in Vietnam," an address to the Nation Institute in Los Angeles, February 25, 1967, King enumerated and discussed six casualties of the war: the Charter of the United Nations, the principle of self-determination, the Great Society (President Lyndon Johnson's domestic program), the humility of the United States, the principle of dissent, and the prospect of humankind's survival. He was deeply pained by the human casualties, especially the bombing and burning of children with napalm. But there were other catastrophic casualties: principles and values. These, King maintained, "are ultimately more harmful because they are self-perpetuating." If principles and values do not recover, physical casualties will proliferate.[60] Less than two months later, in his address "Beyond Vietnam: A Time to Break Silence," delivered at Riverside Church in New York City on April 4, 1967, precisely one year before he was assassinated, King expressed a number of reasons for his opposition to the war in Vietnam, not least because it was siphoning funds from social programs, particularly the Great Society initiatives. King argued that as long as the buildup of troops continued in Vietnam, as long as money and resources kept being spent on the war, the United States would not invest the necessary and sufficient resources to meet the needs of the nation's poor people. He knew that the war undercut spending for these programs.[61] This led King to conclude, more generally with Thich Nhat Hanh, that war is the enemy of all human beings, regardless of religious affiliation.[62] More specifically, King believed that the war in Vietnam was the enemy of blacks and the poor and that it decimated their hopes. In addition, he saw that poor and black sons, brothers, fathers, and husbands were being sent in massive numbers "to fight and die in extraordinarily high proportions relative to the rest of the population."[63] Black and white boys who were not permitted to live together on the same block and attend the same schools and churches in U.S. cities were being forced to kill and die together in Vietnam, ostensibly for the liberation of others.

As a child of God, King proudly asserted that he was the brother of the suffering poor in the United States and Vietnam. In addressing the Vietnam War at Riverside Church, King concluded that the solution to war, poverty, and racism was to be found in a "genuine revolution of values [that] means in the final analysis that our loyalties must become ecumenical rather than sectional." "Every nation," he declared, "must . . . develop an overriding loyalty to mankind as a whole in order to preserve the best in their individual societies."[64] In other words, one's neighborly concern must transcend race, tribe, and nation to include the entirety of the world house.

In "Showdown for Nonviolence," published in *Look* magazine nearly two weeks after he was assassinated and representative of his most mature thinking about nonviolence, King declared that he was "committed to nonviolence absolutely." He went on to say: "I'm just not going to kill anybody, whether it's in Vietnam or here."[65] King would continue to preach and teach nonviolence even if he were the only one doing so, even if it failed in this country or abroad. He would not break his vow to nonviolence but would be faithful to it until he died. Nonviolence was, for him, the only way forward. It is important to remember this, since some may be inclined to believe that near the end of his life King was tiring of nonviolence. I will return to this important point.

Unquestionably, Martin Luther King's was a theology of absolute nonviolent resistance. He believed that God intends for human beings to live together peacefully, civilly, and respectfully as sisters and brothers. The careful examiner of King's ideas and social activism can only conclude that despite his periodic personal moral shortcomings, he persistently sought to be faithful to what he believed to be God's will, especially as it pertained to the eradication of all forms of violence in the world house.

A nonviolent absolutist or purist like Gandhi and Thich Nhat Hanh, King refused absolutely to resort to self-defense, defense of loved ones, or defense of nations using any but nonviolent methods. For such a one, there is no situation in which violence is an acceptable or justifiable response.[66] This was also the view of Nhat Hanh, who asserted, "No act of killing can be justified."[67] As described above, the nonviolent absolutist is wedded irrevocably to nonviolence, a point that King stressed emphatically at the SCLC staff retreat in Frogmore, South Carolina, in November 1967. He told his staff: "I have taken a vow. I Martin Luther King, take thee, nonviolence, to be my wedded wife, for better or for worse, for richer or for poorer, in sickness and in health, till death do us part."[68] The only acceptable sword for the King disciple, then, is the sword of love, and love is at the center of nonviolence. King's rationale for this stance was based on his understanding of the Christian gospel and his theological and philosophical personalism. He was convinced that while the gospel of Jesus Christ requires that evil be resisted, it rejects violence and requires nonviolent resistance instead.

We have seen how King responded to violence and war generally and the war in Vietnam in particular. Reflecting on Adolf Hitler's efforts to exterminate the Jews, King said that he would have joined the Jews in opposition. This raises the question: what would likely have happened had the Jews organized mass nonviolent demonstrations against the likes of Adolf Hitler?

King's Response to Hitlerism and Its Assault on the World House

During his conversation with the students and faculty at the Inter-American University in Puerto Rico in 1962, King reflected on whether nonviolence could work in a nondemocratic nation like Adolf Hitler's Germany. Could an organized mass nonviolent movement against Nazism have been successful? King told his audience that there was no empirical evidence to prove that nonviolence could not work in such "extremely difficult" situations.[69] And then, similar to Gandhi and other nonviolent absolutists, he said: "I would only say that there was never any organized mass nonviolent movement against Hitler." To his credit, King proceeded to say: "This is speculation, naturally. I cannot say, because it's impossible to know." King would have been on solid ground had he stopped here, but unfortunately he did not. Instead, he said, like Gandhi and like Walter Wink many years later: "I think this is a real possibility that if there had been an organized nonviolent movement and a nonviolent movement resisting the inhuman and brutal and vicious methods being used by Hitler, *the casualty list may have been less*."[70] In contrast, Jewish theologians such as Martin Buber and Jewish thinkers such as Hayim Greenberg insisted that any such efforts by German Jews would have led to their being mowed down or immediately marched off en masse to the death camps.[71]

Not surprisingly, King saw Hitler as "a misguided individual" who led a nation and caused "the destruction of many individuals."[72] In more specific terms, Hitler was for him a thuggish, ruthless, murderous dictator who coldly and calculatingly took advantage of people who feared knowledge, thinking, and change. Hitler's followers, in King's estimation, were softheaded people all too willing to follow Hitler's dictates. According to King, dictators like Hitler "have led men to acts of barbarity and terror that are unthinkable in civilized society." Hitler himself realized that softheadedness was so prevalent among his followers that he declared: "I use emotions for the many and reserve reason for the few." In *Mein Kampf*, he asserted, anticipating President Donald J. Trump: "By means of shrewd lies, unremittingly repeated, it is possible to make people believe that heaven is hell—and hell heaven. . . . The greater the lie, the more readily it will be believed."[73]

King held that throughout human history, dictators like Hitler and other presumed world leaders publicly called for peace while rejecting that which might have made peace possible. Describing Hitler as one of many megalomaniacs in history, King said: "He sent his blitzkrieg-bent legions blazing across Europe, bringing havoc and holocaust in his wake. There is grave irony in the fact that Hitler could come forth, following nakedly aggressive expansionist theories, and do it all in the name of peace."[74]

King said that he would have "aided and comforted" the Jews and would have joined them in protest against Hitler had he lived in Germany and *possessed his attitude of absolute nonviolence*.[75] King would not, under any circumstance, at any level—local, regional, national, or international—respond to violence with violence. This is essentially what he told *Redbook* magazine in November 1964. And this is precisely the point at which his stance on the internationalization of nonviolence meets strong headwinds. For example, although King posited that nonviolence was the best method in the struggle against apartheid in South Africa, it is also known that South African leaders such as Albert Lutuli, Desmond Tutu, and Allan Boesak rejected the idea that nonviolence is the only acceptable or justifiable method in every context.[76] Although these leaders had a predilection for nonviolence and never advocated or publicly supported the violence of the military wing of the African National Congress (ANC), they were quick to say that some situations are so horrific that violence—though highly undesirable— might be justifiable.[77] We will see below that some Buddhist monks held a similar view regarding the war in Vietnam. In this regard, they were, along with the South African leaders, more in line with French philosopher Jean-Paul Sartre, who argued that violence should not be rejected on principle, lest one risk becoming an accomplice.[78]

Challenges to Nonviolence on the World Stage

During his "Beyond Vietnam" address at Riverside Church in April 1967, Martin Luther King Jr. declared that there would be future Vietnams in "Guatemala and Peru," "Thailand and Cambodia," "Mozambique and South Africa," and other so-called Third World countries if U.S. foreign policy continued to focus on the investments and other interests of large corporations rather than the interests and needs of the poor.[79] This deepened his pain and disappointment with the United States all the more. Furthermore, he was aware that in many freedom struggles around the world, Christians and other religious people were having a difficult time consistently resorting to nonviolence or had given up on it altogether. Reflecting specifically on Latin America, quite likely with the Colombian revolutionary priest Camilo Torres in mind, he commented:

> In Latin America . . . national reform movements have almost despaired of nonviolent methods; many young men, even many priests, have joined guerrilla movements in the hills. So many of Latin America's problems have roots in the United States of America that we need to form a solid, united movement, nonviolently conceived and carried through, so that pressure can be brought to bear on the capital and government power structures concerned, from both sides of the problem at once. I think that may be the only hope for a nonviolent solution in Latin America today; and one of the most powerful expressions of nonviolence may come out of that international coalition of socially aware forces, operating outside governmental frameworks.[80]

Still King remained absolutely devoted to nonviolence and called for the internationalization of nonviolent movements for social change. This was consistent with his acceptance of personalism's principles of the interrelated structure of reality and the idea that the universe is value fused. His absolute commitment to nonviolence was also consistent with his view that every person is sacred and precious to God and should be treated accordingly.

At the same time, King was enough of a realist to know that the United States and other countries were a long way from the "planetization" of nonviolent movements for justice.[81] Similarly, like Gandhi he was certain that even on the individual level it is highly unlikely that there will ever be more than a "creative minority" of nonviolent absolutists, people who are "unswervingly committed to the nonviolent way."[82] Most only use nonviolent resistance pragmatically or tactically but are not willing to discipline their lives by it.[83]

Not at all optimistic that most countries would work toward absolutizing nonviolence in their relations with each other, King was encouraged to know that nonviolence was being put to good use in places like South Africa under the leadership of ANC leader Lutuli. He challenged the nations of the world to work cooperatively to "bring an end through all types of non-violent means to the apartheid policies of South Africa."[84] In addition, he recalled his visit to Ghana in 1957 for independence celebrations and was heartened by Prime Minister Kwame Nkrumah's statement that he had read and pondered Gandhi's writings and believed that his method of nonviolence could be workable in Ghana.[85]

Toward More Militant and Creative Nonviolent Methods

A nonviolent absolutist, Martin Luther King Jr. could see by the mid-1960s that nonviolence was not having transformative effects in the North. This led him to conclude that it was necessary for nonviolent methods to be reassessed and adapted to specific situations and also vital that the methods be more creative and militant. "More militant" does not mean that he ever came to seriously consider substituting violence for nonviolence. Rather, he believed that more radical methods of nonviolence, such as mass civil disobedience and nonviolent sabotage, might be necessary. This was in part because of the refusal of the U.S. Congress to legislate laws guaranteeing freedom and equality for all.[86]

When the decision was made to launch the movement in the North, and also when King began thinking more deeply about the enduring racism in Congress and its refusal to act, King's realism kicked in. He surmised that the impact of nonviolent demonstrations used in the South would be slight in the North— if noticed at all. "In the South," he argued, "a march was a social earthquake; in the North, it is a faint, brief exclamation of protest." The nonviolent actions used in the North had to "mature to a new level to correspond to heightened black impatience and stiffened white resistance. This higher level is mass civil disobedience."[87] King's planned mass civil disobedience project known as the Poor People's Campaign was designed to so disrupt the halls of Congress and the federal government that they would essentially be shut down until the legislative and executive branches listened to and gave substantive responses to the demands of the thousands of poor people who would be camped out in Washington, D.C. This hoped-for scenario was striking and clearly indicative of King's awareness of the need for more creative and radical methods of nonviolence.

That King was aware of the need to adapt and radicalize nonviolence in the United States also suggests his openness to the same thing occurring internationally. This is implied in his insistence that nonviolence needed to be internationalized. When he suggested that nonviolent resistance was the most appropriate and effective basis for effecting change, whether it was in Hitler's Germany, in Vietnam, in South Africa, or in Latin America, he did not arrogantly believe that the exact methods had to be the same as those used in the United States—only that they should be nonviolent.

King was moved deeply by Thich Nhat Hanh's commitment to absolute nonviolence during the war in Vietnam. He agreed with Nhat Hanh's assertion that "warfare respects no man, woman or child, whether he be Catholic, Protestant or Buddhist."[88] But there are also the practices of self-immolation and fasting unto death adopted by Nhat Hanh's kindred monks and laywomen as a radical addition to their nonviolent protest against the war in Vietnam. I have often wondered whether King might have considered adding one or both of these practices.

Without question these practices of self-immolation and extreme hunger strikes contradict King's doctrine of the sacredness of persons and his stance against all forms of violence. However, King himself acknowledged that extreme situations require extreme solutions.[89] Just how far would he have been willing to go? I would have to say that he clearly was not willing to go as far as self-immolation and fasting unto death. These violate human life, yet many Buddhists see it as the ultimate sacrifice for the common good.

I know of no writing in which King seriously considered adapting his nonviolent activism to include self-immolation or fasting unto death. However, in a letter from Thich Nhat Hanh in 1965, he was made aware that some Buddhist monks, including Thich Quang Duc and thirty-six other monks and laywomen, had self-immolated as part of their witness and nonviolent protest against the war in Vietnam. At that time, King had not yet been as publicly vocal against the war as he would be subsequently. In addition, he opposed self-immolation primarily because he saw it as a form of suicide and thus a contradiction to his doctrines of love, the sacredness of persons, and nonviolence. Nhat Hanh's letter sought to call attention to the suffering of the Vietnamese in a universal language. He explained why Vietnamese monks and laywomen took up self-immolation in protesting the war and urged King to more consistently and openly voice his opposition to the war. The letter was powerful, stating: "The self-burning of Vietnamese Buddhist monks in 1963 is somehow difficult for the Western Christian conscience to understand. The press spoke then of suicide, but in the essence, it is not. It is not even a protest. What the monks said in the letters they left before burning themselves aimed only at alarming, at moving the hearts of the oppressors, and at calling the attention of the world to the suffering endured by the Vietnamese." In bringing more clarity to the issue, Nhat Hanh wrote:

> The Vietnamese monk, by burning himself, says with all his strength and determination that he can endure the greatest sufferings to protect his people. *The importance is not to take one's life, but to burn*. What he really aims at is the expression of his will and determination, not death. To express will by burning oneself, therefore, is not to commit an act of destruction but to perform an act of construction, i.e., to suffer and die for the sake of one's people. . . . I am sure that since you have been engaged in one of the hardest struggles for equality and human rights, you are among those who understand fully, and who share with all their hearts, the indescribable suffering of the Vietnamese people. The world's greatest humanists would not remain silent. You yourself cannot remain silent. You cannot be silent since you have already been in action and you are in action because, in you, God is in action, too.[90]

The most important point for the monks was not the taking of their life, but a willingness to endure the most excruciating pain and suffering to protect the lives of others. Nevertheless, King did not include self-immolation as part of his nonviolent strategy and did not support its use in Vietnam. Nhat Hanh, Thich Quang Duc, and other Buddhist monks, declared that self-immolation—even if supported by the best, most positive motivation—is a tragic and extreme act that should be avoided if at all possible. They reasoned, however, that some things are so horrible and destructive of human life that something as radical as offering one's body through self-immolation "as a torch of compassion to dissipate darkness and ignorance, is the only possible recourse."[91] Unlike Nhat Hanh and Quang Duc in Vietnam, and unlike Lutuli, Tutu, and Boesak in South Africa, King was adamant that violence can never be justified, even if one can understand appeals to its use.

It is no secret that King grew tired and impatient with the results of nonviolence in the last couple of years of his life, but there is no evidence that he ever gave serious thought to reneging on his vow of absolute nonviolence. For King, there was no place whatever for violence, a point that he made unequivocally clear many times. "Occasionally in life one develops a conviction so precious and meaningful that he will stand on it till the end," he said. "This is what I have found in nonviolence."[92] By the last months of his life he was still an unrelenting nonviolent absolutist. Today King is no longer here to suggest how creative and radical methods of nonviolence need to be in today's world, but we are.

Martin Luther King Jr. did not hesitate to declare that whether anyone stood with him or not, he would stand as the lone advocate and defender of nonviolence if necessary. To the very end, he dreamed of the day when people would see that one who lives by the sword will die by the sword, and when "war will come to an end, [and] men will beat their swords into plowshares and their spears into pruning hooks, and [when] nations will no longer rise up against nations, neither will they study war anymore." He dreamed of the day when "the lamb and the lion will lie down together and every man will sit under his own vine and fig tree and none shall be afraid."[93] He dreamed of the day when people will understand that our only choice is between "nonviolent coexistence or violent coannihilation."[94]

NOTES

The epigraphs are from Martin Luther King Jr., *Where Do We Go from Here: Chaos or Community?* (Boston: Beacon Press, 1967; rept., 1968, 2010), 183; Desmond Tutu, *Hope and Suffering: Sermons and Speeches* (Grand Rapids, Mich.: Eerdmans, 1984), 181.

1. Martin Luther King Jr., *The Wisdom of Martin Luther King in His Own Words* (New York: Lancer Books, 1968), 47.

2. Because King did not use the term "globalization" but tended to use words such as "internationalize," "internationalization," and "planetize," I use King's terms here, since the focus of this part of the book is on the historical King, or King in context. However, the term "globalization" was in use during the 1960s and was familiar to King. See Lewis V. Baldwin's discussion of this in "Living in the 'World House,'" in Baldwin and Paul R. Dekar, eds., *"In An Inescapable Network of Mutuality": Martin Luther King Jr. and the Globalization of an Ethical Ideal* (Eugene, Ore.: Cascade Books, 2013), 6.

3. See Rufus Burrow Jr., *Martin Luther King Jr. for Armchair Theologians* (Louisville: Westminster John Knox Press, 2009), 57–60; Rufus Burrow Jr., *God and Human Dignity: The Personalism, Theology, and Ethics of Martin Luther King Jr.* (Notre Dame: Notre Dame Press, 2006), 5, 6, 8, 77, 79; and Rufus Burrow Jr., *Martin Luther King Jr. and the Theology of Resistance* (Jefferson, N.C.: McFarland, 2015), 10, and chapter 5, "The King Type of Personalism."

4. Martin Luther King Jr., *Stride toward Freedom: The Montgomery Story* (N.Y.: Harper & Row, 1958), 91.

5. Lerone Bennett Jr., *What Manner of Man: A Biography of Martin Luther King Jr.*, 8th rev. ed. (Chicago: Johnson Publishing, 1976), 21.

6. See Lewis V. Baldwin, *There Is a Balm in Gilead: The Cultural Roots of Martin Luther King Jr.* (Minneapolis: Fortress, 1991), 124. This was reported to Baldwin during his interview with King's boyhood friend, Philip Lenud, April 7, 1987.

7. Quoted in Taylor Branch, *Parting the Waters: America in the King Years 1954-63* (New York: Simon & Schuster, 1988), 730.

8. Martin Luther King Sr., with Clayton Riley, *Daddy King: An Autobiography*, (New York: William Morrow, 1980), 208.

9. David L. Lewis, *King: A Critical Biography* (New York: Praeger, 1970), 13.

10. Lawrence D. Reddick, *Crusader without Violence: A Biography of Martin Luther King Jr.* (New York: Harper, 1959), 59.

11. Ibid., 59–60.

12. Martin Luther King Jr., *The Autobiography of Martin Luther King, Jr.*, edited by Clayborne Carson (New York: Warner, 1998), 9.

13. Reddick, *Crusader without Violence*, 60.

14. All references to this recording: Frederick L. Downing, *To See the Promised Land: The Faith Pilgrimage of Martin Luther King Jr.* (Macon: Mercer University Press, 1986), 41–45, citing Mrs. Alberta King, "Dr. Martin Luther King, Jr.: Birth to Twelve Years Old by His Mother," Ebenezer Baptist Church, January 18, 1973, recording, King Papers, Library and Archives of the Martin Luther King Jr. Center for Nonviolent Social Change, Atlanta.

15. Martin Luther King Jr., *Autobiography of Martin Luther King, Jr.*, 82.

16. Bennett, *What Manner of Man*, 21.

17. Martin Luther King Sr., *Daddy King*, 127.

18. "Alabama's Gandhi" cited in Martin Luther King Jr., *The Papers of Martin Luther King Jr.*, vol. 3, *Birth of a New Age, December 1955–December 1956* (Berkeley: University of California Press, 1997), 20.

19. Bennett, *What Manner of Man*, 17.

20. Baldwin, *There Is a Balm in Gilead*, 40.

21. John J. Ansbro, *Martin Luther King, Jr.: The Making of a Mind* (Maryknoll, N.Y.: Orbis Books, 1982), 112–14; and Martin Luther King Jr., *Autobiography of Martin Luther King, Jr.*, 14, 24, 54.

22. Martin Luther King Jr., *Autobiography of Martin Luther King, Jr.*, 24.

23. See Walter Earl Fluker, *Ethical Leadership: The Quest for Character, Civility, and Community* (Minneapolis: Fortress, 2009).

24. As one of numerous examples in King's early writings and statements on the subject, see Martin Luther King Jr., *The Papers of Martin Luther King, Jr.*, vol. 6, *Advocate of the Social Gospel, September 1948–March 1963*, edited by Clayborne Carson, Susan Carson, Susan Englander, Troy Jackson, and Gerald L. Smith (Berkeley: University of California Press, 2007), 112. Here King said in 1951 that the survival of civilization was dependent on movement from narrow tribalism and nationalism "to the wide horizon of world cooperation." He also stressed the need for "an international ethical code," claiming further that "this is truly what Mr. [Wendell] Wilkie called 'one world,' and we can readily make an addition to that phrase by saying, one world or none." King was still in seminary at this time.

25. King, *Papers of Martin Luther King, Jr.*, vol. 6, 133.

26. Ibid., 88.

27. Ibid., 327.

28. Crystal A. deGregory and Lewis V. Baldwin reference this point about the influence of the *Atlanta Daily World* on the early shaping of King's perspective on worldwide freedom struggles in note 5 of chapter 5 of this book. See also Martin Luther King Jr., *The Papers of Martin Luther King, Jr.*, vol. 1, *Called to Serve, January 1929–June 1951*, edited by Clayborne Carson, Ralph E. Luker, Penny A. Russell, and Louis R. Harlan (Berkeley: University of California Press, 1992), 105, 161.

29. King, *Papers of Martin Luther King, Jr.*, vol. 6, 112.

30. Robert L. Holmes, *On War and Morality* (Princeton: Princeton University Press, 1989), 32.

31. King, *The Papers of Martin Luther King, Jr.*, vol. 5, *Threshold of a New Decade, January 1959–December 1960*, edited by Clayborne Carson, Tenisha Armstrong, Susan Carson, Adrienne Clay, and Kieran Taylor (Berkeley: University of California Press, 2005), 546; Martin Luther King Jr., *The Papers of Martin Luther King, Jr.*, vol. 7, *To Save the Soul of America, January 1961–August 1962*, edited by Clayborne Carson and Tenisha Armstrong (Berkeley: University of California Press, 2014), 576. Gandhi said: "An unjust law is itself a species of violence." See M. K. Gandhi, *Non-Violence in Peace and War*, vol. 1 (Ahmedabad: Javajivan Press, 1942), 144.

32. Martin Luther King Jr., *A Testament of Hope: The Essential Writings and Speeches of Martin Luther King Jr.*, edited by James M. Washington (New York: Harper & Row, 1986), 256.

33. Ibid., 327.

34. Martin Luther King Jr., *The Trumpet of Conscience* (New York: Harper & Row, 1968), 63.

35. King, *Where Do we Go from Here?*, 21, 45.

36. Martin Luther King Jr., "South African Independence," in *"In a Single Garment of Destiny": A Global Vision of Justice*, edited by Lewis V. Baldwin (Boston: Beacon Press, 2012), 36.

37. King, *Papers of Martin Luther King, Jr.*, vol. 5, 399–400.

38. Ibid., 175.

39. King, *Papers of Martin Luther King, Jr.*, vol. 6, 464.

40. Martin Luther King Jr., *Autobiography of Martin Luther King, Jr.*, 305.

41. Dorothy Cotton, SCLC director of education, wrote about a similar incident (witnessed by her and others) that occurred on January 22, 1965, as they were checking in at the Albert Hotel during the Selma, Alabama, voters' rights campaign. See Dorothy Cotton, *If Your Back's Not Bent: The Role of the Citizenship Education Program in the Civil Rights Movement* (New York: Atria Books, 2012), 234.

42. Branch, *Parting the Waters*, 654. Clark recalled that when men in the audience came up to counterattack James, "King put up his hand and said, 'No, we mustn't fight back. We have to pray for him.'" See Septima Clark, *Septima Clark and the Civil Rights Movement: Ready from Within*, edited by Cynthia Stokes Brown (Trenton, N.J.: Africa World Press, 1990), 73.

43. See Stephen B. Oates, *Let the Trumpet Sound: The Life of Martin Luther King, Jr.* (New York: Harper & Row, 1982), 140.

44. King , *Papers of Martin Luther King, Jr.*, vol. 6, 325; Martin Luther King Jr., *Stride toward Freedom*, 100.

45. Borden P. Bowne, *The Principles of Ethics* (New York: Harper & Brothers, 1892), 199, 203.

46. Martin Luther King Jr., *Trumpet of Conscience*, 72.

47. Martin Luther King Jr., *Where Do We Go From Here?*, 64, 125; King, *Papers of Martin Luther King, Jr.*, vol. 7, 480.

48. King, *Papers of Martin Luther King, Jr.*, vol. 6, 156.

49. Thich Nhat Hanh argues that the taking of life in general, and I would say the taking of human life in particular, "is a form of stealing," and that "stealing, in the forms of exploitation, social injustice, and oppression, is an act of killing." See Thich Nhat Hanh, *Living Buddha, Living Christ* (New York: Riverhead Books, 1995), 94.

50. Borden P. Bowne, *Theism* (1887; repr., New York: American Book Company, 1902), 57.

51. See 1 Samuel 25:29, and Martin Luther King Jr., *Trumpet of Conscience*, 69.

52. Martin Luther King Jr., *Trumpet of Conscience*, 69. In his baccalaureate sermon at Bucknell University in 1954, Mays said: "The destiny of each man is tied up with the destiny of another. We are so interlaced and interwoven that what affects one touches all. We are all bound together in one great humanity." Mays, "His Goodness Was Not Enough," in *Dr. Benjamin E. Mays Speaks: Representative Speeches of a Great American Orator*, edited by Freddie C. Colston (Lanham, Md.: University Press of America, 2002), 211. King failed to attribute the statement to Mays.

53. Thich Nhat Hanh, *Love in Action: Writings on Nonviolent Social Change* (Berkeley: Parallax Press, 1993), 39, 120.

54. Martin Luther King Jr., *Trumpet of Conscience*, 75.

55. King, *Papers of Martin Luther King, Jr.*, vol. 6, 116, 288.

56. Martin Luther King Jr., *Stride toward Freedom*, 95.

57. Ibid., 224.

58. Quoted in David J. Garrow, *Bearing the Cross: Martin Luther King Jr., and the Southern Christian Leadership Conference* (New York: William Morrow, 1986), 394, citing Paul A. Schuette, "King Preaches on Non-Violence at Police-Guarded Howard Hall," *Washington Post*, March 3, 1965.

59. Abraham J. Heschel, "The Moral Outrage of Vietnam," in Robert McAfee Brown, Abraham Joshua Heschel, and Michael Novak, *Vietnam: Crisis of Conscience* (New York: Herder and Herder, 1967), 49.

60. Martin Luther King Jr., "The Casualties of the War in Vietnam," Nation Institute, Los Angeles, February 25, 1967, http://www.aavw.org/special_features/speeches _speech_king02.html.

61. Martin Luther King Jr., *Testament of Hope*, 233.

62. See Lewis V. Baldwin, *The Voice of Conscience: The Church in the Mind of Martin Luther King Jr.* (New York: Oxford, 2010), 212.

63. Martin Luther King Jr., *Testament of Hope*, 233.

64. Ibid., 242.

65. Martin Luther King Jr., "Showdown for Nonviolence," in *Testament of Hope*, 69. First published in *Look*, April 16, 1968, 23–25.

66. This is different from the nonviolent stance of Albert Lutuli, Desmond Tutu, and Allan Boesak, all of whom believed that there are violent situations (e.g., the apartheid regime in South Africa) in which retaliatory violence may be justifiable.

67. Nhat Hanh, *Living Buddha, Living Christ*, 91.

68. Martin Luther King Jr., "The State of the Movement," unpublished address, SCLC Staff Retreat, Frogmore, South Carolina, November 28, 1967, King Papers, Library and Archives of the Martin Luther King Jr. Center for Nonviolent Social Change, Atlanta.

69. King, *Papers of Martin Luther King, Jr.*, vol. 7, 403. It is instructive to note that Walter Wink observed that there was considerable evidence that nonviolence worked when used against the Nazis in Bulgaria, Denmark, Norway, Sweden, and elsewhere in Europe. See Walter Wink, *The Powers That Be: Theology for a New Millennium* (New York: Doubleday, 1998), 151–53. In addition, Thich Nhat Hanh contends that a number of tactics, not least fasting (even unto death), the use of art, culture, and literature, resignations from professorships and political appointments, and self-immolation were used by nuns, monks, and laity in nonviolent resistance against the Vietnam War. He acknowledged that these

tactics were not successful in the general understanding of the term. Rather, he said, "The success of a nonviolent struggle can be measured only in terms of the love and nonviolence attained, not whether a political victory was achieved." See Nhat Hanh, *Love in Action*, 47.

70. King, *Papers of Martin Luther King, Jr.*, vol. 7, 403 (my italics). For Wink, see Wink, *Powers That Be*, 151–53.

71. See Martin Buber, "Gandhi, the Jews and Zionism: Martin Buber's Open Letter to Gandhi Regarding Palestine (February 24, 1939)," Jewish Virtual Library, http://www .jewishvirtuallibrary.org/letter-from-martin-buber-to-gandhi; and Hayim Greenberg, "We Are Treated as Subhumans—We Are Asked to be Superhuman," in Gandhi, *Non-violence in Peace and War*, vol. 1, 464.

72. Martin Luther King Jr., "Greatest Hope for World Peace," in "*In a Single Garment of Destiny*," 148.

73. Quoted in Martin Luther King Jr., *Testament of Hope*, 493.

74. King, *Where Do We Go from Here?*, 182.

75. King, *Papers of Martin Luther King, Jr.*, vol. 7, 201, 537, 595. My italics.

76. Martin Luther King Jr., *Trumpet of Conscience*, 63.

77. See Albert Lutuli, "On the Rivonia Trial," in Gerald J. Pillay, ed., *Voices of Liberation*, vol. 1, *Albert Lutuli* (Pretoria: HSRC Publishers, 1993), 152; Tutu, *Hope and Suffering*, 81; Desmond Tutu, "The South African Problem and Black Protest," in *Crying in the Wilderness: The Struggle for Justice in South Africa*, edited by John Webster (Grand Rapids, Mich.: Eerdmans, 1982), 41–42; John Allen, *Rabble Rouser for Peace: The Authorized Biography of Desmond Tutu* (New York: Free Press, 2006), 172; and Allan Boesak, *Black and Reformed: Apartheid, Liberation and the Calvinist Tradition* (Maryknoll, N.Y.: Orbis, 1984), 49.

78. See Robert C. Solomon, *Introducing the Existentialists: Imaginary Interviews with Sartre, Heidegger, and Camus* (Indianapolis: Backett Publishing, 1981).

79. Martin Luther King Jr., "Beyond Vietnam," in Clayborne Carson and Kris Shepard, *A Call to Conscience* (New York: Warner, 2001), 156.

80. Martin Luther King Jr., *Trumpet of Conscience*, 63. Camilo Torres joined the Army of National Liberation and was killed in an exchange of gunfire with Colombian soldiers on February 15, 1966. See Torres, *Revolutionary Priest: The Complete Writings and Messages of Camilo Torres*, edited by John Gerassi (New York: Vintage, 1971), 30–31.

81. Martin Luther King Jr., *Trumpet of Conscience*, 64. King felt this way despite his view of "the United Nations as a gesture in the direction of nonviolence on a world scale." See Martin Luther King Jr., *Where Do We Go from Here?*, 184.

82. Martin Luther King Jr., *Stride toward Freedom*, 218.

83. Martin Luther King Jr., *Why We Can't Wait*, 61–64.

84. Martin Luther King Jr., "Facing the Challenge of a New Age," valedictory address, June 20, 1965, University of the West Indies, Mona, Jamaica, Martin Luther King Jr. Papers, Library and Archives of the Martin Luther King Jr. Center for Nonviolent Social Change, Atlanta.

85. King, *Papers of Martin Luther King, Jr.*, vol. 5, 127.

86. King, *Trumpet of Conscience*, 15.

87. Ibid., 14, 15.

88. Quoted in Baldwin, *Voice of Conscience*, 212.

89. King, *Autobiography of Martin Luther King, Jr.*, 234.

90. Thich Nhat Hanh, From a Buddhist Monk to Martin Luther King, Jr., letter, June 1, 1965, *Dialogue* (Saigon), June 1965, reprinted in *Liberation*, December 18–19, 1965 (my italics).

91. Quoted in Katia Buffetrille, "Self-Immolation in Tibet: Some Reflections on an Unfolding History," *Revue d'Etudes Tibétaines*, no. 25 (December 2012), 2.

92. King, *Autobiography of Martin Luther King, Jr.*, 331.

93. Martin Luther King Jr., *Trumpet of Conscience*, 77.

94. Martin Luther King Jr., "Casualties of the War in Vietnam," 4.

CHAPTER 5
SEXISM IN THE WORLD HOUSE
WOMEN AND THE GLOBAL VISION OF
MARTIN LUTHER KING JR.

CRYSTAL A. DEGREGORY AND LEWIS V. BALDWIN

His-or-her is a careful distinction peculiar to our time, and Dr. King
died before a movement emerged to include the existence of
women in every thought pretending to be profound.
JUNE JORDAN, "How Shall We Know His Name?"

Women must be respected as human beings and not be treated as mere means.
MARTIN LUTHER KING JR., "The Crisis in the Modern Family"

Martin Luther King Jr.'s vision for the future course of humankind was a powerful and pervasive theme in his sermons, speeches, interviews, and writings.
He thought increasingly in terms of a great "world house," in which a "widely
separated" human family is compelled inevitably to choose between the polar
opposites of justice and injustice and freedom and unfreedom. King declared
unequivocally that equality between the different racial groups in the United
States would "not solve the problems of either whites or Negroes" if it meant
"equality in a world society stricken by poverty and in a universe doomed to extinction by war."[1] However, the clarity, vitality, and integrity of this vision was
significantly undermined by King's inability to see beyond his own sexism, by
his failure to show affinity with the women's cause worldwide, and by his refusal to identify sexism as another "grave problem" that prevented humankind
from "living creatively" in the world house.[2]

   This chapter explores King's sexist and chauvinist tendencies and how they
informed his global vision and his efforts to translate that vision into practical
reality. Beginning with the premise that King's lifelong belief in separate gender
roles was the determinative factor in his attitude toward women and his relationships with women, the discussion then turns to the ways in which his experiences with women in the civil rights movement in the United States mirrored
his attitude toward women and the human rights crusade worldwide. We exam-

ine some of King's most provocative public statements about women, consider his dealings with female activists, admirers, and supporters around the globe, and address his absence of attention to sexism and the overall status of women in his articulation of his world house vision and efforts to bring it to fruition. While acknowledging King's amazing capacity for logical, sequential thought around most issues of a moral and sociopolitical nature, the chapter concludes that King's failure to sufficiently address women's issues and struggles cross-culturally reflected unresolved tensions in his personality and thought and was perhaps the most glaring limitation of his world vision.

Divided Humanity: Separate Domains for Men and Women

Martin Luther King Jr. was born into a family that encouraged a concern for the struggles of the oppressed worldwide. His parents, Martin Sr. and Alberta Williams King, who occasionally traveled abroad in the 1930s and 1940s, were known to express their great displeasure and frustration with the corroding effects of racism, colonialism, and poverty throughout Africa, and with a world in which white men established empires on the backs of peoples of color. Inspired by this family tradition, King, at age fifteen, in a high school speech entitled, "The Negro and the Constitution" (1944), addressed not only the resonating irony of a nation claiming freedom while oppressing its black citizens but also America's moral responsibility in a world in which the true flowering of democracy was consistently frustrated and denied.[3] However, this early interest in the liberation and empowerment of the oppressed did not extend to women and the global structures that subjugated them in terms of power and status. King was taught very early, by word and example, that men should be the heads of households and that men and women had different spheres of activity in the family and at virtually every other level of society. These ideas were first filtered largely through familial and church life.[4] Then they were reinforced as King studied at Morehouse College, Crozer Theological Seminary, and Boston University, despite his exposure to personalism, which affirmed the dignity and worth of all humans and the social nature of human existence, and despite his growing realization that oppressed people worldwide were increasingly revolting against systems and conditions that kept them down.[5] Apparently, it never occurred to young King at that time, understandably, that sexism was as much a social evil as racism, classism, and colonialism, and that it too had to be resisted with unwavering determination and a fierce sense of urgency. In large part, because of the prevalence of patriarchy, gender inequality was almost never a topic of serious discussion in classrooms in the forties and fifties, and King, like all too many men and women in that period, was simply ill prepared, from the standpoint of sheer discernment more so than conscience, to take sexism seriously as an international problem.

Greater sensitivity to a range of women's issues came gradually, as King moved deeper and deeper into a romantic relationship with Coretta Scott, the Alabama native he met in 1952 while both were studying in Boston. King was at Boston University and Coretta at the New England Conservatory of Music, and the two soon discovered in each other a certain beauty of stature, mind, and spirit. However, King's tendency to subscribe to traditional gender roles and to view women stereotypically must have been evident to Coretta from the beginning of their courtship, when he said that "every Napoleon has his Waterloo, and you are my Waterloo," but she seems not to have been annoyed and to have said nothing.[6] King professed in their very first conversation that Coretta had every quality he wanted in a wife—namely, intelligence, personality, character, and beauty. But in response to Coretta asking about his amazing popularity with girls, he declared: "You know women are hero-worshippers." On another occasion, King, after eating Coretta's home-cooked soul food for the first time, assured her that she "had passed the test."[7] Coretta, who was well aware of her worth, did not typically take offense and never seriously challenged King's propensity for chauvinistic quips and teasing during that time. This is difficult to explain in view of her own mounting interest in the struggles of women of different socioeconomic classes everywhere. Her "spirit of independence" and "strong hope" about "serving humanity" were already well established among family and friends, and she had enrolled at Antioch College in the fall of 1945 because it offered "equivalent opportunities to both men and women" and was "among the first to appoint a woman to its faculty and its Board of Trustees." Although Coretta encountered incidents of racism and sexism at Antioch, the emphasis there on "giving service to humankind" as a whole captivated her, and she began to think of how "politics and the use of government," in addition to a career in music, might be put to the task of freeing men and women from various forms of oppression.[8] Coretta also joined and worked with the Antioch chapter of the National Association for the Advancement of Colored People, the college's Race Relations Committee and Civil Liberties Committee, and also its Quaker peace groups.[9] Clearly, she was more concerned than King about gender inequality and more convinced that sexism, like racism and war, had to be totally eliminated in the interest of a better humanity and world. The couple, after marrying in June 1953, continued to express a shared commitment to improving the quality of life for the disadvantaged and marginalized, but there was no common vision in those days of the status of women globally, and there was no shared sense of the pressing need for a world devoid of sexism. In fact, King made it clear early on that he wanted a wife who could adjust to black church culture in the American South, which meant submitting to the politics of gender identity, male authority, subordination of women, and separate gender roles.[10] Strangely, Coretta offered no serious resistance to such an arrangement in the 1950s and 1960s, even as her husband emerged as a voice and source of authority and inspiration for oppressed peoples around the globe.[11]

Still, King and his wife became great conversation partners over time, and, in spite of his sexist and chauvinistic tendencies, he learned much from his exchanges with her about women's issues and larger concerns regarding human rights and freedom.[12] But King never embraced the idea of Coretta taking on an active, public leadership role, certainly not in the freedom struggle. He spoke of the two-parent family as the ideal in any enlightened and vital culture, with husband and wife working in an equal partnership.[13] But he remained wedded to the common, age-old view that women are naturally better homemakers than men, especially from the standpoint of household chores and as trainers, nurturers, and molders of children.[14] In a Mother's Day sermon, delivered in May 1963, King declared that every mother has "a basic responsibility to instill within . . . the minds and in the hearts . . . of her children certain eternal and abiding principles of the universe," without which "we are all doomed for destruction." Here he had in mind "the world perspective," "a desire to achieve excellence in his or her field of endeavor," "a principle . . . that causes . . . a child to maintain a keen sensitivity where the social evils (i.e., war, poverty and economic injustice, and racial injustice) of our day are involved," "a respect for personhood" or "all human personality," and "a God consciousness."[15] In yet another Mother's Day sermon, preached in May 1966, three years later, King explained that "A mother who knows nothing about love is not a true mother," and that "it is the responsibility of a good mother" to "instill the heightening, majestic, and lofty meaning of love into her children." That responsibility, King added, also involved inculcating "a kind of healthy, rational, and even moral self-love," an unselfish, altruistic concern for "other selves," and "a deep and abiding love for the Almighty God whose purpose changeth not."[16] King's exaltation of both womanhood and motherhood here, as elsewhere, was unmistakable, despite his sexism and uncritical acceptance of the gender hierarchy sanctioned in black churches and widely practiced at every level of black life and culture.

Although King thought in terms of the distinct functions of female and male, he was never quite as rigid as his father, Martin Luther King Sr., who subscribed unwaveringly to the old Victorian ideals of the female who nurtures and instructs her children and the stern male who heads the household as a firm disciplinarian. The younger King, due largely to the influence of Coretta, became a bit more flexible in his thinking over time and certainly more open, at least in principle, to the view that "women are just as intelligent and capable as men" and that they too "should hold positions of authority and influence."[17] This had become quite evident by April 1954, when King became the pastor of Dexter Avenue Baptist Church in Montgomery, Alabama. It is highly conceivable that Coretta, who often helped her husband prepare his sermons, was the primary source behind the powerful statement King made against male supremacy at Dexter Avenue Baptist in May 1955. In a sermon titled "The Crisis of the Modern Family," the young pastor, who had not yet been catapulted to leadership in the city's bus boycott, boldly declared: "Men must accept the fact that the day has passed when the man can stand over the wife with an iron rod asserting his authority as 'boss.' This does not mean that women no longer respect masculinity, i.e., strong, dynamic manliness; women will always respect that. But it does mean that the day has passed when women will be trampled over and treated as some slave subject to the dictates of a despotic husband."[18] At the risk of gross overstatement, King went on to assert: "One of the greatest contributions that Christianity has made to the world is that of lifting the status of womanhood from that of an insignificant child-bearer to a position of dignity and honor and respect. Women must be respected as human beings and not be treated as mere means. Strictly speaking, there is no boss in the home; it is no lord-servant relationship. The family should be a cooperative enterprise [where] all members are working together for a common goal."[19]

To further illustrate his point about male supremacy and Christianity's elevation of "the status of womanhood," King occasionally quoted Galatians 3:28: "There is neither Jew nor Greek, there is neither slave nor free, there is neither male nor female; for you are all one in Christ Jesus."[20] By quoting the Apostle Paul in this manner, King was seemingly suggesting that for those who are baptized in the name and spirit of Jesus Christ, gender distinctions have been transcended, but this never led him to categorically reject patriarchy and the idea of separate gender roles. While he persistently spoke of the essential oneness of humanity as a matter of principle, based largely on his reading of scripture and personalism, this was not borne out by his attitude and actions toward women in the freedom movement and in the larger society and world.

King's assault on male dominance in the home and society, in "The Crisis of the Modern Family," seemed quite legitimate, well intentioned, and somewhat surprising, especially for that time, but it also reflected a stunning disregard for Christianity's long history of subordinating, marginalizing, and victimizing women. The record shows that King was not oblivious to that history, and this makes his claims about the Christian faith and its tradition of bestowing "dignity and honor and respect" upon women, especially at a time when women were rejected as pastors and barred from pulpits worldwide, all the more perplexing. Moreover, if King meant to suggest that Christianity was far more advanced in its treatment of women than other world religions, he would have been hard-pressed to come up with solid evidence for such a position. Clearly, his claims in this regard constituted additional evidence that he was blinded by his own sexism and thus unable or unwilling to come to terms with the history of human oppression based on gender. Such claims also revealed the lingering, vacillating tendencies, or what Coretta King called "a real ambivalence," in King's personality and thinking.[21]

The same might be said of King's views about respecting and treating women "as human beings" and "not as mere means" to an end. While stressing this as a matter of principle, King undermined the principle by his tendency to view women as sex objects and by repeatedly turning to women other than his wife for sexual gratification. Although his extramarital affairs involved choices made by consenting adults and never indicated the full measure of his character, they nonetheless revealed an attitude toward women that had long been condoned and even sanctioned under the structures of patriarchy. Evidently, King found it difficult and perhaps even impossible at times to maintain consistency between his lofty proclamations about the sanctity and nobility of "womanhood" and "motherhood" and his behavior toward women in his private and public life.[22] He was never really able to overcome such paradoxical tendencies, and this would figure prominently in his failure to envision and embrace a strategy by which men and women might strive together equally toward human freedom.[23] "His sexism softened somewhat eventually," writes religion professor Cheryl A. Kirk-Duggan, "but not to the extent of his historical ancestors [and boyhood idols] who supported women's rights—Frederick Douglass and W. E. B. Du Bois."[24]

King's sexism and chauvinism expose him as a product of his time and culture, and he, like most of his male contemporaries, could never rise above that. This does not excuse him or justify his words and actions in this regard, but it offers an explanation. In all fairness, it might be said that King did not appear to be as committed to female subordination and marginalization as most men in the 1950s and 1960s, and he was certainly not misogynistic. Unlike most ministers and lay persons in black churches in those times, for example, King was in favor of ordaining women into the ministry, had no problem with women preachers and with women ascending the pulpit in Christian congregations, never hesitated to use the title "Reverend" when referring to women ministers, and approved of women speaking and acting in the public sphere in the interest of universal human rights and freedom.[25] King's liberal theological education was undoubtedly the key here, especially his exposure to personalism, or personal idealism, which taught him that he could never be what he "ought to be" until his "brothers and sisters" were "what they ought to be."[26] But this outlook, when considered in light of King's failure to seriously address patriarchy, sexism, and misogyny, revealed shortcomings and tensions in his ethical personalism and his moral vision, and certainly deficiencies in his worldview.[27]

Women's Rights and Human Rights: King and the Female Sphere of Activity

The Montgomery bus boycott in 1955–56 was Martin Luther King Jr.'s first effort at sustained, organized social action, and he understood early on that this was not merely local but part of a national struggle for civil rights and a larger international quest for human rights.[28] In May 1956, King asserted that "the people of the Third World are now rising up, and at many points I feel that this movement in Montgomery is a part of this overall movement in the world in which oppressed people are revolting against the imperialism and colonialism that have too long existed."[29] He felt essentially the same about other freedom struggles he led throughout the South and in places like Washington, D.C., and Chicago, and he appreciated the contributions of black women as nurturers, cultural communicators, and grassroots organizers, although he never addressed gender-based exclusion in the leadership ranks of the movement.[30] He understood that "oppressed people" included men and women, but he was not thinking during those times of patriarchy, sexism, and the worldwide oppression of women as problems that should be specifically defined, seriously addressed, and ultimately eradicated. This simply did not and would not occur on any significant level, even as King increasingly studied the vast landscape of humanity and advanced his obligations as a civil rights and human rights activist over time.

King's concern for the oppressed of all lands increasingly evolved throughout the 1950s and 1960s, as he benefited more and more, particularly at the level of ideas, from considerable travel, observation, study, and reflection.[31] His appearance at the independence celebration of Ghana in March 1957, at the invitation of Prime Minister Kwame Nkrumah, apparently afforded opportunities for serious discussions not only about "the worldwide implications and repercussions" of that particular event but also about connecting southern Jim Crow to European colonialism and apartheid in South Africa.[32] But the low status of women and the violation of their human rights across the globe were not seriously entertained.[33] This would have caught the attention of Coretta, who accompanied her husband on the trip to Ghana and was always interested in the challenges confronting women cross-culturally. She later recalled how they felt after witnessing the plight of servants in Ghana, some of whom were undoubtedly women, who received "only twenty-eight cents a day" to "bring us breakfast" and "perform other such duties." Sensitive to how these servants "had been trained to bow, almost to cringe," King, according to Coretta, "was extremely upset" by their "decreased" and "demoralized" stature and by "the servile attitude to which their suffering had brought them," but experiences of this nature never diminished King's tendency to completely overlook the oppression of women when addressing global problems and the greatest internal and external barriers to human community.

Consideration of the Kings' travels and contacts in India, in February and March 1959, removes any possible lingering doubt about whether or not this was the case. In his essay "My Trip to the Land of Gandhi," King recounts that "Coretta was particularly interested in the women of India," but he and his friend Lawrence D. Reddick, who accompanied them on the tour, were clearly more interested in the activities of Mohandas K. Gandhi and the history of India's government. In explaining their different interests, King writes: "The three of us made up a sort of three-headed team with six eyes and six ears for looking and listening."[34] In any case, the Kings quickly learned, much to their surprise, that "Indian women held much higher positions than women back home" in the United States, as Coretta would later recall. They discovered, as they moved through the larger cities of Delhi, Calcutta, Madras, and Bombay, that women served in Parliament and that a woman was a justice in India's high courts. The Kings dined at Prime Minister Jawaharlal Nehru's residence in New Delhi with the prime minister himself, his daughter Indira Gandhi, and Lady Mountbatten, the wife of the last viceroy of India. Although Coretta was favorably impressed with the high status of some Indian women and thought of the time when women might secure similar positions of power and influence in America, her husband seemed uninterested and unmoved. In "My Trip to the Land of Gandhi," he repeatedly refers to Prime Minister Nehru by name, and he mentions the grinding poverty, the caste system, and the dreadful conditions endured by Dalits, but his lack of any attention to women's concerns is telling.[35] Evidently King, who was accustomed to women acting in supporting roles for men in the civil rights movement, missed another opportunity to get a better sense of the unique perspectives, gifts, and talents that women might bring to leadership in any enlightened society.[36]

There is nothing tangible in that period that indicates that King might eventually become a proponent of women's liberation. Convinced that men should be the leading figures in any successful struggle for human rights and freedom, he never really embraced the amazing potential of women as leaders and as creative agents of change. This largely explains his response to Deolinda Rodrigues, a young activist in Angola, who wrote him for concrete suggestions about any course she and her people might take in their independence struggle against the Portuguese in 1959. King wrote back: "I would say . . . that the first step toward rectifying the situation is to develop real leadership in your country. Some one person or some few persons must stand as a symbol for your independence movement. As soon as your symbol is set up it is not difficult to get people to follow, and the more the oppressor seeks to stop and defeat the symbol, the more it solidifies the movement. It would be a wonderful thing to return to your country with this idea in mind."[37]

Interestingly enough, King did not challenge Rodrigues to take on the mantle of leadership herself, nor did he offer any thoughts about the capacity of freedom-loving women like her to do so. King related differently in the 1950s to young African males, some of whom he was helping to groom, through scholarship aid from Montgomery's Dexter Avenue Baptist Church, for leadership once African countries ridded themselves of the structures of colonialism. Regarding leadership in movements for freedom and justice anywhere in the world, King was prone to be more encouraging to men than to women. His reactions to the South African government's brutal treatment of black female and male leaders in the early 1960s vividly illustrate the point. In May 1962, Adelaide Tambo, the wife of the exiled African National Congress (ANC) leader Oliver Tambo, contacted King after South Africa's ruling elite deported Elizabeth Mafekeng and banned Lillian Ngoyi, Florence Matomela, Florence Mkhize, and others in the ANC's Women's League, asking him to use his influence to draw attention to their plight, but King apparently offered no public response.[38] In contrast, when King spoke on South African apartheid in London in December 1964, he praised the leadership and nonviolent tactics of the ANC's Albert J. Lutuli (sometimes spelled "Luthuli") and mentioned Nelson Mandela, Robert Sobukwe, and others who were "wasting away in Robben Island Prison" but again said nothing about the persecution of Adelaide Tambo and other courageous women who were also risking their lives and livelihood daily under the banner of organizations such as the Women's League and the Federation of South African Women.[39] King's silence is especially notable in view of his growing moral leadership globally at that time, and it is remarkable too since he always appeared quite intentional about not segregating his moral concerns.[40] Perhaps most importantly, King's failure to speak out publicly and forcefully occurred during a time when the status and treatment of black South African women had become a metaphor for the more general abuse of power at virtually every level of governmental and institutional life on the world stage.

Despite King's abysmal failure to question and challenge male domination in the United States or cross-culturally, he knew nonetheless that liberation causes around the world could not be won without women. He worked or associated with women on a number of initiatives designed to advance the struggles for freedom and independence in Africa. Sensitive to the bonds and obligations between people of African descent everywhere, King joined Eleanor Roosevelt in July 1957 in promoting, under the auspices of the American Committee on Africa (ACOA), the "Declaration of Conscience," a document proclaiming "December 10, 1957, Human Rights Day, as a Day of Protest against the organized inhumanity of the South African government and its *apartheid* policies." Roosevelt served as the international chair of this campaign, which included Bishop James A. Pike as U.S. chair and King as U.S. vice-chair.[41] The declaration bore the signatures of 123 world leaders, some of whom were female dignitaries, and groups like the World Assembly of Youth in Paris, the National Union of Students in India, and the Danish Youth Council, which included female members, also supported the effort.[42] King lavishly praised Eleanor Roosevelt for her efforts on behalf of the declaration and for her larger "commitment to the great issues of our time," and he predicted that she would "remain a symbol of world leadership." "Her extensive travels in the interest of humanity," King added, "made her at home in Bangkok as well as Birmingham, Beirut as well as Boston."[43]

About three years later, in April 1960, King united with Eleanor Roosevelt, Lillian Smith, and a large group of other female and male activists, under the banner of Americans for Democratic Action (ADA), in urging that "the U.S. Ambassador to South Africa be recalled to Washington for consultation, and that American purchases of gold from South Africa be suspended during his time of consultation here."[44] Female support across the globe was equally significant when King and the South African leader Albert Lutuli collaborated in 1962 in cosponsoring the ACOA's Appeal for Action against Apartheid, which was "in the nature of a follow-up" to the Declaration of Conscience.[45] During that period, King also joined Dorothy I. Height and several male civil rights activists in forming the American Negro Leadership Conference on Africa (ANLCA), an organization that related black Americans with Africa and its multitude of problems.[46] Through both the ACOA and the ANLCA, King associated with women in the mid- and late 1960s in supporting the anti-apartheid crusade and anticolonial struggles throughout Africa. Of special significance was his appearance with the famous South African folksinger Miriam Makeba, who introduced the world to Xhosa and Zulu music, at Hunter College in New York in December 1965. On that occasion, King spoke at length on the evils of both South African apartheid and European colonialism, an address that blended well with the freedom songs rendered by Makeba.[47]

King was genuinely moved by the suffering of women under the yoke of colonialism. For example, he lamented the devastating impact of U.S. bombs on South Vietnamese women, and he said as much and more in a major address at Riverside Church in New York in April 1967.[48] Still, it is impossible to assess the impact of such inhumane acts on his attitude toward females in general. Although King was highly impressed with Eleanor Roosevelt's work in the global human rights field and viewed her as a bright interlude in the dismal history of humankind, any growth on his part with regard to women's issues during those years was due first and foremost to the influence of his wife.[49] Coretta King's interest in women's issues, evident as early as her college years, significantly increased through her work with the Women's International League for Peace and Freedom (WILPF), an organization that grew out of the Women's Peace Party.[50] Coretta joined WILPF soon after it was formed and participated actively in its "international effort to influence the atomic-test-ban talks" taking place in Geneva, Switzerland, in March 1962.[51] Dr. King eagerly supported and was apparently inspired and informed by her efforts with WILPF, and at the very least her witness further convinced him that women had something to offer in terms of a meaningful and constructive way forward in the quest for world peace and community.[52] He spoke at the fiftieth anniversary of WILPF in October 1965, undoubtedly at the encouragement of his wife. In his address, he praised the "past deeds" of towering figures like Jane Addams and Emily Balch, Nobel Peace Prize recipients, and he declared, "Few organizations have so distinguished themselves over so long a time and in so great a cause as the peace and freedom of this chaotic world of ours." "Your endeavors," King added, "constitute impressive milestones marking man's trek along the rugged roadway to peace." Although King challenged the women present to continue their diplomacy, efforts toward international peace, and the larger quest for a humanitarian and communitarian ideal, which were in line with his vision of a world house, he said nothing about the problems of sexism, patriarchy, and misogyny.[53] Seemingly, he had not come to realize that the maltreatment and subordination of women persisted as a monumental and enduring threat to the ideal world he sought to bring into being, namely *the beloved community* on a grand scale.

The World House without Women:
Chaos or Community?

In his address at the fiftieth anniversary of the Women's International League for Peace and Freedom, Martin Luther King Jr. shared his eagerness "to enter into a new world which is now possible given the forces of goodwill striding toward freedom and peace." He had in mind "a planetary order" guided by a spirit of "international concord." He went on to clarify his vision, insisting, "A world of peace, then, would be a system of international life which facilitates tranquil, wholesome and harmonious inter-state affairs, a world order which favors 'life, liberty and the pursuit of happiness for all.'" And then King alluded to the great world house that humankind had inherited, in which people are compelled "to live together" in peace in spite of differences in nationality, race and ethnicity, religion, ideas, culture, and interests. But King's frequent use of words like "men," "mankind," and "brothers" to the neglect of more gender-inclusive language, and the absence of any reflection at all on the low status and condition of women worldwide, clearly revealed not only the limitations of his vision but also the conflicted man that lurked inside him—the man who envisioned a world free of injustice and oppression while, at the same time, having adjusted to a global social order that was wholly unsympathetic to gender equality.[54] King's appearance before WILPF in 1965 afforded perhaps the greatest opportunity he had had up to that point to address sexism in a forum that included women from various parts of the world, and, considering Coretta's growing influence on him, it is still perplexing that he refused to do so.

In 1967, two years later, King issued his most extensive and penetrating commentary on the "great world house" up to that point, devoting an entire chapter to the subject in what would be the last book he authored.[55] He challenged humankind on the moral imperative to rid the world of racism, poverty, and war, which he considered the greatest external barriers to the full realization of a peaceful world house. But why didn't King see sexism as one of those barriers? A number of answers are provided here, taking into account the time and context in which King thought and functioned.

King was obviously a victim of his own sexist tendencies, perhaps even unconsciously, and this figured prominently in his failure to treat sexism as both a colossal evil and a tremendous obstacle to international peace and community. He often noted how prejudice blinds the visions of men, not realizing that, when it came to the subordination and marginalization of women, he was in effect making a statement about himself. King was somewhat uncomfortable around assertive women, as evidenced by his attitude and behavior toward females in the SCLC, the Student Nonviolent Coordinating Committee (SNCC), the Mississippi Freedom Democratic Party, and the National Welfare Rights Organization, and he was apparently comfortable with structures that relegated women to the margins of the independence struggles in parts of Africa, Asia, and Latin America.[56] Sexism prevented King from seeing that in a world that clamored for strong, competent, and effective leadership at all societal levels, women would not forever be satisfied to serve merely as secretaries, teachers, administrative assistants, and homemakers and in other supportive roles for men. He seemed not equipped or perhaps unwilling to understand that females were an enormous resource for the continuing enrichment of his own understanding of human rights, that their input could improve the discussion of issues pertaining to justice and equality of opportunity, and that they were capable of offering a powerful alternative model for what constitutes both quality leadership and the great world house.[57] A product of a history and culture steeped in patriarchy, King never saw the wisdom in putting more females in high positions of power, a development absolutely essential to the elimination of male authority, the subservience of women, and rigidly separate gender roles.

Unresolved tensions in King's own personality and thought played perhaps a greater role than has previously been acknowledged in his refusal to seriously address sexism as a perennial existential threat to the world house.[58] He frequently said that America is "something of a schizophrenic personality, tragically divided against herself," mainly because "we have proudly professed the principles of democracy" on the one hand while sadly practicing "the very antithesis of those principles" on the other.[59] Ironically, that same logic applied to the dichotomy or paradox within King, who extolled the vision and virtues of a world house without injustice and oppression while practicing sexism and refusing to specifically address the oppression of women on grounds of gender, race, and class. Further explanation of this kind of conflicted personality and way of thinking is offered by King himself, who spoke to the issue of the paradoxical or dialectical nature of humanity, or to good and evil as both being natural tendencies in the human spirit.[60] He explained that every human being amounts to "two selves" or "two personalities," and he spoke more specifically in terms of "the higher" or "good self" and "the lower" or "evil self." "The great burden of life," he concluded, is "to always keep that higher self in command," but this is something that is not always possible, in part due to the potential of sin and evil at every level of human existence. In other words, every human life is a study in contradictions. King's "best self" or "higher self" was committed to the full actualization of "the great world house," but his "worst self " or "lower self" embraced practices that were antithetical to that vision.[61] There was always a bit of mixed messaging when King spoke boldly and consistently of the dignity and worth of all human personality, of the essential social nature of human existence, of the interrelated structure of all life and reality, and of living creatively in the world house, while simultaneously remaining silent on sexism and the violation of the human rights of women.[62]

The well-established or deeply entrenched gender hierarchy in the black church and at other levels of black society and culture in the 1950s and 1960s also contributed in some measure to King's inability to view sexism as a major problem in the world house. Black society in that period seemed irredeemably patriarchal, and the masses of men and women, even in congregations, fully expected females to operate in the private realm of homemaking and child-rearing responsibilities while males dominated the leadership roles in the church and in the larger public arena.[63] King adjusted uncritically to this model of gender roles in the church and in the movement, despite his call for all freedom-loving people to always be "maladjusted" in the face of inequality and injustice, and he was actually encouraged to do so by men and women. The social and cultural pressure King faced daily in this regard simply proved too much for him to resist, let alone overcome. Thus, he was not prepared, morally and intellectually, to advocate for a more "group-centered" leadership model that included the full participation of men and women in freedom struggles at home and abroad.[64]

Of equal significance is the fact that the women closest to King during the civil rights movement never really pressed him on the issues of gender inequality, let alone the place of women in the great world house. There was apparently no real pressure from his wife, his mother, his sister Christine, and other female members of his family. Females like Ella Baker, Septima Clark, and Dorothy Cotton of the SCLC, and Diane Nash of SNCC knew that King was sexist and a male chauvinist and that his perspective on women around the globe had much to be desired, but they never confronted him or made this shortcoming a topic of serious discussion.[65] Baker occasionally downplayed gender issues, and Clark admitted that "in those days I didn't criticize Dr. King, other than asking him not to lead all the marches."[66] Molly Martindale and other women activists in the West Side Christian Parish, who helped organize the Chicago Freedom Movement in 1965–66, in which King and his SCLC participated, held meetings in which they raised questions about "the disrespect they felt from other staff members—both black men and white women"—but King and his attitude and actions were never specifically targeted for extensive and serious critique.[67] Numerous considerations possibly accounted for this reluctance to challenge King's male chauvinist and sexist behavior. First, black women, including those

most active in the freedom movement, generally believed at that time that racism, not gender discrimination and inequality, constituted the greatest source
of the oppression of their people. Second, they understood the need for black
unity in the struggle against white supremacist policies and practices that had
national and even international implications and repercussions. Finally, there
was the justifiable fear that the white power structure might exploit gender issues to distort the agenda and goals of the civil rights cause and to ultimately
destroy the movement itself.[68] Such considerations, though understandable, do
not excuse King's sexism or the silence of his female associates and their failure
to seriously and consistently address the issue. In both cases, the problem most
likely resulted from a failure to see that sexism was as much a threat to the world
house as racism, poverty, and war and that all had to be eliminated as a precondition for the full realization of that higher human and ethical ideal.[69]

King was assassinated before he could benefit, in terms of his thinking and
human rights activism, from the second wave of feminism and the women's
rights movement, and this too helps explain the absence of any attention on his
part to sexism in the world house. King died in April 1968, at the very time that
movement was blossoming and gaining momentum, a development that extended through the 1970s and beyond.[70] Thus, any further explanation for his
lack of attention to sexism in the world house must be left largely to the processes of history. But, given King's capacity for growth and maturation around
issues that had moral, spiritual, and sociopolitical significance, especially when
confronted with rational and moral argument, there is reason to believe that he
would eventually have reexamined and perhaps even altered his attitude regarding women and their condition for the better. It would not have been impossible for him to seriously think through the cultures of widespread sexism
globally and to eventually embrace gender equality as a universal value. This is
what happened in the case of female activists such as Septima Clark and Diane
Nash. Both later hinted that they would never have tolerated the sexism of King
and other males in the movement if they had had earlier exposure to the wom-
en's movement.[71] Even so, it is to King's credit that, despite his own sexism and
male chauvinism, he and the crusade he led for freedom, justice, and human
dignity contributed substantially, as John J. Ansbro contends, "to the direction
and momentum of the Feminist Movement."[72] Septima Clark, Dorothy Cotton,
Coretta Scott King, and other women who worked closely with King in the civil
rights cause have conceded as much and more, and so have scholars such as
Katie G. Cannon, Cheryl Kirk-Duggan, and Cheryl J. Sanders, who are equally
forceful in criticizing King for his failure to seriously address the need for wom-
en's liberation. What a splendid affirmation of the King legacy that King's name

is being widely evoked today by leading figures in the annual Women's March, and also by women in the Black Lives Matter, Me Too, and March for Our Lives movements.

NOTES

The epigraphs are from June Jordan, "How Shall We Know His Name? The Legacy of Martin Luther King, Jr.—20 Years On," *Christianity and Crisis*, May 18, 1987, 193; and Martin Luther King Jr., *The Papers of Martin Luther King, Jr.*, vol. 6, *Advocate of the Social Gospel, September 1948–March 1963*, edited by Clayborne Carson, Susan Carson, Susan Englander, Troy Jackson, and Gerald L. Smith (Berkeley: University of California Press, 2007), 212.

1. Martin Luther King Jr., *Where Do We Go from Here: Chaos or Community?* (Boston: Beacon Press, 1967; rpt., 1968, 2010), 167, 191; and Martin Luther King Jr., "Address at the 50th Anniversary of the Women's International League for Peace and Freedom," Philadelphia, October 15, 1965, Martin Luther King Jr. Papers, Library and Archives of the Martin Luther King Jr. Center for Nonviolent Social Change, Atlanta (King Papers).

2. Although King occasionally used terms like "human beings" or "the human family" when referring to people throughout the world collectively, he was mostly apt to speak of "mankind" or "a world-wide brotherhood," which were in more common usage in the 1950s and 1960s. See King, *Where Do We Go from Here?*, 167, 171–72, 181–86, 191; and King, "Address at the 50th Anniversary of the Women's International League for Peace and Freedom."

3. Michael Long, based on a careful reading of this speech, suggests that King had something of an international perspective as early as his high school years. See Michael G. Long, *Against Us, but for Us: Martin Luther King, Jr. and the State* (Macon, Ga.: Mercer University Press, 2002), 6n17. See also Lewis V. Baldwin, *Toward the Beloved Community: Martin Luther King, Jr. and South Africa* (Cleveland: Pilgrim Press, 1995), 8–9; Martin Luther King Jr., *"In a Single Garment of Destiny": A Global Vision of Justice*, edited by Lewis V. Baldwin (Boston: Beacon Press, 2012), xix; and Martin Luther King Jr., *The Papers of Martin Luther King, Jr.*, vol. 1, *Called to Serve, January 1929–June 1951*, edited by Clayborne Carson, Ralph E. Luker, Penny A. Russell, and Louis R. Harlan (Berkeley: University of California Press, 1992), 109–10.

4. The King household was clearly father centered. See King, *Papers of Martin Luther King, Jr.*, vol. 1, 29, 107; Martin Luther King Sr., *Daddy King: An Autobiography*, with Clayton Riley (New York: William Morrow, 1980), 130–31; Christine King Farris, *Through It All: Reflections on My Life, My Family, and My Faith* (New York: Atria Books, 2009), 10; Martin Luther King Jr., *The Autobiography of Martin Luther King, Jr.*, edited by Clayborne Carson (New York: Warner, 1998), 4–5; Lawrence D. Reddick, *Crusader without Violence: A Biography of Martin Luther King, Jr.* (New York: Harper, 1959), 51; and Coretta Scott King, *My Life with Martin Luther King, Jr.*, rev. ed. (New York: Henry Holt, 1993; 1st ed. published in 1969), 87–88.

5. King, *Papers of Martin Luther King, Jr.*, vol. 1, 211–25, 294–326; King, *Papers of Martin Luther King, Jr.*, vol. 6, 105–6, 146–50; and King, *Autobiography of Martin Luther King, Jr.*, 23. Much of King's earliest perspective on freedom movements around the globe was shaped by the *Atlanta Daily World*, which was "the first black-owned daily newspaper in the United States." This paper was launched in Atlanta by W. A. Scott in 1928. It was headquartered on Auburn Avenue, not far from the King home, and the Kings were among its first and most avid readers. Martin Luther King Jr. grew up reading the paper, which

carried commentaries on Mohandas Gandhi and anticolonial struggles throughout Asia and Africa in the 1930s and 1940s. While a student at Crozer and Boston University, King routinely asked his parents to send the newspaper to him, and occasionally it featured articles about him or made references to him. See King, *Papers of Martin Luther King, Jr.*, vol. 1, 26, 161; Martin Luther King, Jr., *The Papers of Martin Luther King, Jr.*, vol. 2, *Rediscovering Precious Values, July 1951–November 1955*, edited by Clayborne Carson, Ralph E. Luker, Penny A. Russell, Peter Holloran, and Louis R. Harlan (Berkeley: University of California Press, 1994), 225.

6. Coretta Scott King, "Meeting Martin" (video clip), in "Coretta Scott King: National Visionary," National Visionary Leadership Project, http://www.visionaryproject.org/kingcorettascott.

7. Ibid.; Coretta Scott King, *My Life with Martin Luther King, Jr.*, 53, 55, 64–65; and Coretta Scott King, "Address at the National Conference on Civil Rights," Fisk University, Nashville, Tennessee, April 5, 1986, unpublished notes in the personal collection of Lewis V. Baldwin.

8. Edythe Scott Bagley, *Desert Rose: The Life and Legacy of Coretta Scott King*, with Joe Hilley (Tuscaloosa: University of Alabama Press, 2012), 72–73; Coretta Scott King, *My Life with Martin Luther King, Jr.*, 48; Coretta Scott King, *My Life, My Love, My Legacy*, with Barbara Reynolds (New York: Henry Holt, 2017), 23–26; and Octavia Vivian, *Coretta: The Story of Coretta Scott King* commemorative ed. (Minneapolis: Fortress, 2006), 33–35.

9. Angela Shelf Medearis, *Dare to Dream: Coretta Scott King and the Civil Rights Movement* (New York: Puffin Books, 1994), 16; and Coretta Scott King, *My Life with Martin Luther King, Jr.*, 193.

10. Coretta Scott King, *My Life with Martin Luther King, Jr.*, 58.

11. This is clear from a reading of an earlier edition of Coretta King's book, where she speaks of the traditional role of the wife as "an adjustment I had to make" and says "this is one of the most important roles I can play." See ibid., 1969 ed., 27, 83, 103–4, 109, 179; and Lewis V. Baldwin, *Behind the Public Veil: The Humanness of Martin Luther King, Jr.* (Minneapolis: Fortress, 2016), 91n106.

12. Coretta Scott King, *My Life with Martin Luther King, Jr.*, 193, 284–85.

13. Here King had in mind the immediate or nuclear family model, consisting of a father, a mother, and children, which he called "the main educational agency of mankind." See Martin Luther King Jr., "The Dignity of Family Life," unpublished speech, Abbott House, Westchester County, New York, October 29, 1965, KCLA: 1; Martin Luther King Jr., "The Negro Family," unpublished address, University of Chicago, Chicago, Illinois, January 27, 1966, KCLA: 2; and Lewis V. Baldwin, *There is a Balm in Gilead: The Cultural Roots of Martin Luther King, Jr.* (Minneapolis: Fortress, 1991), 91–158.

14. King biographer Lawrence Reddick, who was one of his close friends, reported that King felt that "biologically and aesthetically women are more suitable than men for keeping house. And for the children, there is no substitute for an attentive mother." Reddick, *Crusader without Violence*, 5. See also David J. Garrow, *Bearing the Cross: Martin Luther King, Jr., and the Southern Christian Leadership Conference* (New York: William Morrow, 1986), 375–76; and Traci C. West, "Gendered Legacies of Martin Luther King, Jr.," *Theology Today* 65, no. 1 (April 2008): 41–48.

15. Martin Luther King Jr., "What a Mother Should Tell Her Child," sermon, Ebenezer Baptist Church, Atlanta, Georgia, May 12, 1963, Martin Luther King Jr. Papers (King Papers), Library and Archives of the Martin Luther King Jr. Center for Nonviolent Social Change, Atlanta.

16. Martin Luther King Jr., "Training Your Child in Love," sermon, Ebenezer Baptist Church, Atlanta, Georgia, May 8, 1966, King Papers; and King, *The Autobiography of Martin Luther King, Jr.*, 3–4. In some of his speeches, King noted that "family life not only educates in general but its quality ultimately determines the individual's capacity to love." Apparently he was speaking from personal experience while growing up in Atlanta. See King, "Negro Family"; and King, *Papers of Martin Luther King, Jr.*, vol. 1, 360.

17. Coretta Scott King, *My Life with Martin Luther King, Jr.*, 57–58; and Coretta Scott King, *My Life, My Love, My Legacy*, 51, 97.

18. When teasing his wife, King sometimes made statements that seemed to undermine this assertion. According to Coretta, he would say: "I want my wife to respect me as the head of the family. I *am* the head of the family." Coretta continued: "We laughed together at that slightly pompous speech, and he backed down. 'Of course, I don't really mean that', he said. 'I think marriage should be a shared relationship.'" While King was known to tease his wife around the question of gender roles, one might conclude that he was not really joking on such occasions—that he perhaps was unconsciously conveying what he actually felt deep within the recesses of his own mind and heart. See King, *Papers of Martin Luther King, Jr.*, vol. 6, 212; Coretta Scott King, *My Life, My Love, My Legacy*, 54; and Coretta Scott King, *My Life with Martin Luther King, Jr.*, 88.

19. King, *Papers of Martin Luther King, Jr.*, vol. 6, 212; Coretta Scott King, *My Life with Martin Luther King, Jr.*, 88; and Reddick, *Crusader without Violence*, 5–8.

20. Note that King made this point while using the word "men" as inclusive of all humanity, male and female. See Martin Luther King Jr., *The Papers of Martin Luther King, Jr.: Symbol of the Movement*, vol. 4, *January 1957–December 1958*, edited by Clayborne Carson, Susan Carson, Adrienne Clay, Virginia Shadron, and Kieran Taylor (Berkeley: University of California Press, 2000), 124; Martin Luther King Jr., *The Papers of Martin Luther King, Jr.*, vol. 3, *Birth of a New Age, December 1955–December 1956*, edited by Clayborne Carson, Stewart Burns, Susan Carson, Peter Holloran, and Dana L. H. Powell (Berkeley: University of California Press, 1997), 278–79, 417; and Martin Luther King Jr., *The Trumpet of Conscience* (San Francisco: Harper & Row, 1967), 72.

21. Coretta Scott King, *My Life with Martin Luther King, Jr.*, 57.

22. Septima Clark, *Ready from Within: Septima Clark and the Civil Rights Movement*, edited by Cynthia Stokes Brown (Trenton, N.J.: Africa World Press, 1990), 78–79; Georgia Davis Powers, *I Shared the Dream: The Pride, Passion, and Politics of the First Black Woman Senator from Kentucky* (Far Hills, N.J.: New Horizon Press, 1995), 145–49, 185–86; Ralph David Abernathy, *And the Walls Came Tumbling Down: An Autobiography* (New York: Harper & Row, 1989), 434–36, 470–75; Clayborne Carson, *Martin's Dream: My Journey and the Legacy of Martin Luther King, Jr.—A Memoir* (New York: Palgrave Macmillan, 2013), 117–18; Garrow, *Bearing the Cross*, 374–76; and Baldwin, *Behind the Public Veil*, 95–101. For fuller treatment of King's infidelity and what this reflected concerning his attitude toward women in general, see Rufus Burrow Jr., "Ruminating about Martin Luther King Jr. and Sex," in Lewis V. Baldwin and Rufus Burrow Jr., eds., *The Domestication of Martin Luther King, Jr.: Clarence B. Jones, Right-Wing Conservatism, and the Manipulation of the King Legacy* (Eugene, Ore.: Cascade, 2013), 120–40.

23. King himself spoke in dramatic terms concerning such paradoxical tendencies, noting that "each of us is something of a schizophrenic personality. We're split and divided against ourselves. And there is something of a civil war going on within all of our lives. There is a recalcitrant South of our soul revolting against the North of our soul.

There is this continual struggle within the very structure of every individual life." King went on to declare, in terms that are clearly applicable to any serious discussion of his attitude toward women: "There is something within all of us that causes us to cry out with Ovid, the Latin poet, 'I see and approve the better things of life, but the evil things I do.'" See Clayborne Carson and Peter Holloran, eds., *A Knock at Midnight: Inspiration from the Great Sermons of Reverend Martin Luther King, Jr.* (New York: Warner, 1998), 45–46.

24. Cheryl A. Kirk-Duggan, *Refiner's Fire: A Religious Engagement with Violence* (Minneapolis: Fortress Press, 2001), 90.

25. See the comments of the Reverend Willie Barrow, a black female preacher who worked alongside King on civil rights in places like Chicago, in "'I Remember Martin': People Close to the Civil Rights Leader Recall a Down to-Earth and Humorous Man," *Ebony*, April 1984, 34. King's position on the ordination of women was shared in an interview with this author: Ralph David Abernathy, interview by Lewis V. Baldwin, West Hunter Baptist Church, Atlanta, March 17, 1987.

26. King, "What a Mother Should Tell Her Child," 8. At other points, in his writings, King stated this principle in terms of what he called "the other-regarding dimension," which insists that "'I' cannot reach fulfillment without 'thou.' The self cannot be self without other selves. Self-concern without other-concern is like a tributary that has no outward flow to the ocean." At first glance, such a perspective seemingly has clear implications for the struggle against all forms of injustice and oppression, including sexism and the subjugation of women. King, *Where Do We Go from Here?*, 180–81, 186. See also King, *Trumpet of Conscience*, 69–70. Here King skillfully uses the "basic fact of the interrelated structure of all reality" to make essentially the same point about humanity.

27. For this insight, I am indebted to Rufus Burrow, *God and Human Dignity: The Personalism, Theology, and Ethics of Martin Luther King, Jr.* (Notre Dame, Ind.: Notre Dame Press, 2006), 8, 10–15.

28. See William D. Watley, *Roots of Resistance: The Nonviolent Ethic of Martin Luther King, Jr.* (Valley Forge, Pa.: Judson Press, 1985), 63.

29. Martin Luther King Jr., "Statement Regarding the Legitimacy of the Struggle in Montgomery, Alabama," May 4, 1956, King Papers.

30. King was never apt to ignore the activities of black women when highlighting the civil rights movement as an extension of a larger global struggle for freedom, justice, and human dignity. He included Rosa Parks among those pioneers in Montgomery who started "a movement whose lofty echoes would be heard all around the world," and in another statement he hinted at the evils of both sexism and racism in noting that Parks was saying "by her presence that 'it is wrong for a woman to have to give up her seat to a man merely because his skin is white and her skin is black.'" King commended Rebecca Dixon, another protester in Montgomery, for standing "in the glow of the world's bright tomorrows" and predicted that the four innocent little girls who died in Birmingham's Sixteenth Street Baptist Church "will long be remembered by the world as some of the most noble and courageous soldiers that the world has known." Small wonder that King donated a significant portion of the $54,000 he received in Nobel Peace Prize money to the National Council of Negro Women in December 1964. But "King and SCLC assumed," according to Cheryl A. Kirk-Duggan, "the Men Led, [and failed to note] Women Organized." Kirk-Duggan, *Refiner's Fire*, 90 (Kirk-Duggan's brackets). See also Martin Luther King, "President's Address," second anniversary of the Montgomery Bus Protest, Montgomery Improvement Association, Montgomery, Alabama, December 5,

1957, King Papers; Martin Luther King Jr., "East or West—God's Children," speech, Berlin, Germany, September 13, 1964, King Papers; Martin Luther King Jr., *The Papers of Martin Luther King, Jr.*, vol. 5, *Threshold of a New Decade, January 1959–December 1960*, edited by Clayborne Carson, Tenisha Armstrong, Susan Carson, Adrienne Clay, and Kieran Taylor (Berkeley: University of California Press, 2005), 407–8; Martin Luther King Jr., "Statement for the Press," Sheraton-Atlantic Hotel, New York City, December 4, 1964, King Papers; Martin Luther King Jr., "Statement to the Press," December 17, 1964, King Papers.

31. Baldwin, *Toward the Beloved Community*, 4; and Martin Luther King Jr. to Mr. Enoch Dumas, January 11, 1960, King Papers.

32. Kwame Nkrumah, Invitation to Martin Luther King, Jr. on the Occasion of the Independence Ceremonies in Ghana, March 1957, King Papers; King, *Papers of Martin Luther King, Jr.*, vol. 4, 145–48; Coretta Scott King, *My Life with Martin Luther King, Jr.*, 142–46; Coretta Scott King, *My Life, My Love, My Legacy*, 76–77; "Conversation in Ghana," *Christian Century*, April 10, 1957: 446–47; and Martin Luther King Jr. to Dr. Kwame Nkrumah, April 17, 1959, King Papers.

33. King was interviewed at length during Ghana's independence celebration by Etta Moten Barnett, an actress, singer, and radio personality from Texas, but apparently the struggles of women in Africa and other parts of the world never came up. See King, *Papers of Martin Luther King, Jr.*, vol. 4, 145–48.

34. Martin Luther King Jr., *A Testament of Hope: The Essential Writings and Speeches of Martin Luther King, Jr.*, edited by James M. Washington (San Francisco: HarperCollins, 1986), 23–24; and Coretta Scott King, *My Life with Martin Luther King, Jr.*, 142–45,

35. Coretta Scott King, *My Life, My Love, My Legacy*, 79–82; Martin Luther King Jr., *Testament of Hope*, 23–30; Coretta Scott King, *My Life with Martin Luther King, Jr.*, 160–64; and King, *Papers of Martin Luther King, Jr.*, vol. 5, 5, 130n1.

36. Although King rejected in principle W. E. B. Du Bois's "talented tenth" idea because it "was a tactic for an aristocratic elite" that offered "no role for the whole people," he seemingly contradicted that by affirming, endorsing, and fully embodying the charismatic male leadership model while not pushing for strong female leadership in the civil rights movement and in the larger crusade for human rights worldwide. See Martin Luther King Jr., *Why We Can't Wait* (New York: New American Library, 1963), 33.

37. King, *Papers of Martin Luther King, Jr.*, vol. 5, 250–51, 345–46nn1–2.

38. No response from King to Tambo has been found. See Martin Luther King Jr., *The Papers of Martin Luther King, Jr.*, vol. 7, *To Save the Soul of America, January 1961–August 1962*, edited by Clayborne Carson and Tenisha Armstrong (Berkeley: University of California Press, 2014), 462–63.

39. Martin Luther King Jr., *"In a Single Garment of Destiny,"* 36–37.

40. Martin Luther King Jr., "The Other America," address, Local 1199 Salute to Freedom, Hunter College, New York City, March 10, 1968, King Papers.

41. The ACOA was formed by self-proclaimed pacifists in New York in 1951. It was initially called Americans for South African Resistance but became the American Committee on Africa in 1953. King's work with the organization began soon after his appearance at the independence celebration in Ghana. See Eleanor Roosevelt, James A. Pike, and Martin Luther King Jr. to Friends and Supporters of the ACOA, July 1957, American Committee on Africa Collection, Amistad Center, Tulane University, New Orleans; John Hughes, "South Africa Retorts to Racial Critics," *Christian Science Monitor*, December 13, 1957; Baldwin, *Toward the Beloved Community*, 15–16; and Martin Luther King Jr., *"In a Single Garment of Destiny,"* 30–32.

42. Paul W. Ward, "Liberals Bid U.S. Censure South Africa: A.D.A. Petition Urges Envoy's Recall, Halt in Gold-Buying," *Baltimore Sun*, April 17, 1960; "The ACOA Reports on the 'Declaration of Conscience,'" January 9, 1958, Martin Luther King Jr. Papers, Howard Gottlieb Archival Research Center, Mugar Memorial Library, Boston University, Boston; and Baldwin, *Toward the Beloved Community*, 15-18.

43. Martin Luther King Jr., "Epitaph for a First Lady: Eleanor Roosevelt," unpublished, November 24, 1962, King Papers; King, *Papers of Martin Luther King, Jr.*, vol. 3, 420-21; and King, *Papers of Martin Luther King, Jr.*, vol. 5, 516-17.

44. See Americans for Democratic Action press release, Washington, D.C., April 17, 1960, ACOA Collection, Amistad Center, Tulane University, New Orleans. King called Smith "an outstanding personality of the world," and he insisted to her, "I am always inspired by your great spirit." See Martin Luther King Jr. to Lillian Smith, April 3, 1962, King Papers; Martin Luther King Jr. to Lillian Smith, June 14, 1962, King Papers; King, *Papers of Martin Luther King, Jr.*, vol. 3, 273-74; King, *Papers of Martin Luther King, Jr.*, vol. 4, 465; and King, *Papers of Martin Luther King, Jr.*, vol. 7, 474.

45. Martin Luther King Jr., *"In a Single Garment of Destiny*," 33-35; Baldwin, *Toward the Beloved Community*, 36-38; George M. Houser to Martin Luther King Jr., February 6, 1962, American Committee on Africa Collection, Amistad Center, Tulane University, New Orleans; "Appeal for Action against Apartheid," sponsored by Martin Luther King Jr. and Albert J. Luthuli, 1962, King Papers.

46. Under the auspices of the ACOA, the ANLCA was organized in New York by King of the SCLC, Dorothy Height (National Council of Negro Women), Roy Wilkins (NAACP), Whitney Young (National Urban League), A. Philip Randolph (Brotherhood of Sleeping Car Porters), and James Farmer (Congress of Racial Equality). See George M. Houser, *No One Can Stop the Rain: Glimpses of Africa's Liberation Struggle* (New York: Pilgrim Press, 1989), 266; Martin Luther King Jr. to Mr. Theodore E. Brown, April 1, 1963, King Papers; and Baldwin, *Toward the Beloved Community*, 38-40.

47. Baldwin, *Toward the Beloved Community*, 48, 211n92.

48. See King's address, "A Time to Break Silence," in King, *Testament of Hope*, 231, 236.

49. On the occasion of Eleanor Roosevelt's death in November 1962, King called her "a many-sided humanitarian" and "world citizen," and she occasionally came to mind when he thought of human rights concerns worldwide. See King, "Epitaph for a First Lady," 2-3.

50. "Even in my college days," wrote Coretta King, "I had taken an active interest in promoting world peace through the Quaker peace groups at Antioch." Coretta Scott King, *My Life with Martin Luther King, Jr.*, 193. See also Coretta Scott King, *My Life, My Love, My Legacy*, 23-24. The Woman's Peace Party was started in 1915 by Jane Addams, Marian Cripps, and Margaret E. Dungan. WILPF, an offshoot of this organization, was formed in 1961 by Bella Abzug and Dagmar Wilson. See Coretta Scott King, *My Life, My Love, My Legacy*, 97.

51. Edythe Scott Bagley, Coretta's sister, says that "Coretta was ahead of Martin" on world peace "and kept up a consistent presence" in the WILPF. Bagley, *Desert Rose*, 201-2. See also Coretta Scott King, *My Life, My Love, My Legacy*, 97-98; and Coretta Scott King, *My Life with Martin Luther King, Jr.*, 193-95, 284-85.

52. Edythe Scott Bagley says that "although Coretta was a chief sounding board" for her husband's "ideas and a promoter of his involvement in the Civil Rights Movement," she did not have a great "influence over his thought." King himself suggested otherwise, noting, "I think at many points she educated me." "I wish I could say, to satisfy my mas-

culine ego, that I led her down this path," King continued, "but I must say that we went down together." Bagley, *Desert Rose*, 201–2, 204–5; Coretta Scott King, *My Life with Martin Luther King, Jr.*, 193–95, 284–85; Coretta Scott King, *My Life, My Love, My Legacy*, 97–98; and *Martin Luther King, Jr.: A Personal Portrait* (Goldsboro, N.C.: Michaelis Tapes, 1987), VHS.

53. King, "Address at the 50th Anniversary of the Women's International League for Peace and Freedom."

54. Ibid.

55. Martin Luther King Jr., *Where Do We Go from Here?*, 167–91.

56. See Paula Giddings, *When and Where I Enter: The Impact of Black Women on Race and Sex in America* (New York: William Morrow, 1984), 312–13; Barbara Ransby, *Ella Baker and the Black Freedom Movement: A Radical Democratic Vision* (Chapel Hill: University of North Carolina Press, 2003), 4, 10, 35, 171–74; Clark, *Ready from Within*, 77–79; and Jordan, "How Shall We Know His Name?," 193.

57. Delores S. Williams, "Between Hagar and Jezebel: A Womanist Assessment of Martin Luther King, Jr.'s Beloved Community," lecture in commemoration and celebration of the life and legacy of Dr. Martin Luther King Jr., videotaped lecture, All Faith Chapel, Vanderbilt University Divinity School, Nashville, January 13, 1997, Vanderbilt Divinity School Library.

58. Kenneth L. Smith has stressed that "there were unresolved tensions" in King's thought "up to the time of his assassination," which makes it impossible to show "a genuine religious synthesis in King's faith, thought, and praxis." This apparently has some meaning when related to King's relations with women. See Kenneth L. Smith, forward to Baldwin, *Toward the Beloved Community*, x.

59. See King's speech "The American Dream" in Martin Luther King Jr., *Testament of Hope*, 208–9.

60. Here King was drawing on his reading of great thinkers such as Plato, the Apostle Paul, Thomas Carlyle, and Reinhold Niebuhr. See John J. Ansbro, *Martin Luther King, Jr.: The Making of a Mind* (Maryknoll, N.Y.: Orbis Books, 1982), 90–92; and Kenneth L. Smith and Ira G. Zepp Jr., *Search for the Beloved Community: The Thinking of Martin Luther King, Jr.* (Valley Forge, Pa.: Judson, 1974), 73–83.

61. See King, *Papers of Martin Luther King, Jr.*, vol. 6, 95–97; and Martin Luther King Jr., "The Prodigal Son," sermon, Ebenezer Baptist Church, Atlanta, Georgia, September 4, 1966, King Papers. Lewis V. Baldwin has drawn on King's logic regarding "two selves" or "two personalities" in explaining King's tendencies toward infidelity and adulterous behavior, which also figured into his view of women in general. Septima Clark, who worked closely with King in the SCLC, said that King "would have to see that women are more than sex symbols." See Baldwin, *Behind the Public Veil*, 98–99; and Clark, *Ready from Within*, 79.

62. Martin Luther King Jr., *Where Do We Go from Here?*, 123, 181; Martin Luther King Jr., *Trumpet of Conscience*, 68–70; and Martin Luther King Jr., "Facing the Challenge of a New Age," speech, Booker T. Washington High School Gymnasium, Rocky Mount, North Carolina, November 27, 1962, King Papers.

63. Septima Clark noted: "But in those days, of course, in the black church men were always in charge." Clark, *Ready from Within*, 78. See also Lynne Olson, *Freedom's Daughters: The Unsung Heroines of the Civil Rights Movement from 1830 to 1970* (New York: Scribner, 2001), 142–45. This chapter has benefited from Crystal deGregory's thoughts on the "great man theory" and how it impacted the civil rights movement and its charismatic leadership.

See also Lewis V. Baldwin and Paul R. Dekar, eds. *"In an Inescapable Network of Mutuality":* *Martin Luther King, Jr. and the Globalization of an Ethical Ideal* (Eugene, Ore.: Cascade Books, 2013), 255–56; and Lewis V. Baldwin and Amiri YaSin Al-Hadid, *Between Cross and Crescent: Christian and Muslim Views on Malcolm and Martin* (Gainesville: University Press of Florida, 2002), 184–93.

64. This "group-centered" leadership model was what King appeared to support in principle but not in practice when it came to the civil rights movement in particular and freedom struggles in general. Women like Ella Baker and Fannie Lou Hamer, who spoke of "group centered leadership" and "a partnership between men and women," respectively, were far more advanced than King in this respect. See Vicki L. Crawford, Jacqueline A. Rouse, Barbara Woods, Broadus Butler, Marymal Dryden, and Melissa Walker, eds., *Women in the Civil Rights Movement: Trailblazers and Torchbearers, 1941–1965* (Brooklyn: Carlson Publishing, 1990), 51, 53, 61, 213; and Martin Luther King Jr., *Why We Can't Wait*, 33.

65. Bagley, *Desert Rose*, 204–5; Clark, *Ready from Within*, 77–79; Olson, *Freedom's Daughters*, 145; Garrow, *Bearing the Cross*, 376; Adam Fairclough, *To Redeem the Soul of America: The Southern Christian Leadership Conference and Martin Luther King, Jr.* (Athens: University of Georgia Press, 1987), 49–50; and Rosetta E. Ross, *Witnessing and Testifying: Black Women, Religion, and Civil Rights* (Minneapolis: Fortress, 2003), 191.

66. See Bettye Collier-Thomas and V. P. Franklin, eds., *Sisters in the Struggle: African American Women in the Civil Rights–Black Power Movement* (New York: New York University Press, 2001), 52; and Clark, *Ready from Within*, 78.

67. Mary Lou Finley, Bernard LaFayette Jr., James R. Ralph Jr., and Pam Smith, eds., *The Chicago Freedom Movement: Martin Luther King, Jr. and Civil Rights Activism in the North* (Lexington: University Press of Kentucky, 2016), 352–65.

68. Baldwin and Al-Hadid, *Between Cross and Crescent*, 182, 397nn67–68. Gloria Joseph and Jill Lewis write, "Even when black women started complaining about their roles in the Civil Rights Movement organizations, their complaints were directed mainly at their roles within the groups themselves." See Gloria I. Joseph and Jill Lewis, *Common Differences: Conflicts in Black and White Feminist Perspectives* (Boston: South End Press, 1981), 110.

69. See James H. Cone, *Martin and Malcolm and America: A Dream or a Nightmare* (Maryknoll, N.Y.: Orbis, 1991), 273–74; and Manning Marable, "Along the Color Line: 'Developing Black Leaders,'" *National Baptist Union-Review* 92, no. 15 December 1988, 6.

70. Jordan, "How Shall We Know His Name?," 193.

71. Septima Clark also thinks that King would have grown significantly in his attitude toward women and women's issues. See Clark, *Ready from Within*, 78–79. See also Olson, *Freedom's Daughters*, 188.

72. Ansbro, *Martin Luther King, Jr.*, xv.

PART II
SURVIVING IN THE CONTEMPORARY WORLD HOUSE
THE ENDURING THREATS—
WHERE WE ARE NOW

CHAPTER 6
PLENTY GOOD ROOM
MARTIN LUTHER KING JR.'S VISION OF THE WORLD HOUSE AND THE ETHICAL QUESTION OF GLOBAL LEADERSHIP

WALTER E. FLUKER

There's plenty good room,
Plenty good room, plenty good room
Plenty good room in my Father's Kingdom
Plenty good room, plenty good room
Choose your seat and sit down
AFRICAN AMERICAN SPIRITUAL

There is no need to fight for food and land. Science has provided
us with adequate means of survival and transportation, which
make it possible to enjoy the fullness of this great earth.
MARTIN LUTHER KING JR., *Where Do We Go from Here?*

These words of the old Negro spiritual above frame the contours of the discussion in this chapter. In the midst of bondage, and living in a world too crowded to grant them citizenship rights and the dignity of full humanity, "black and unknown bards of long ago" envisioned a world in which there was "plenty good room."[1] The old spiritual by that title expresses the deep dignity and self-respect that these enslaved Africans knew to be theirs, despite the annihilation of space and the reordering of time for the body.[2] The emphatic assertion that there is "plenty good room" is both an imaginative conjuring of sequestered space and a demand for the reconfiguration of time and memory that rests in a return to the *imago Dei* creation.[3] According to Charles H. Long, the spirituals resituated "the problematic [of race] within the structures of inwardness as the locus for a new rhythm of time" and thus represented the appropriation of a mythos that provided meaning and affirmation of human dignity to an otherwise hopeless existence.[4] Martin Luther King Jr.'s vision of the world house is rooted in this long-standing tradition of African American religion and culture that is based on the fundamental belief that all persons have inherent worth and dignity as acts of divine creation and are therefore bound by the moral obligation to create and share space with others. From his earliest public addresses at Holt Street Baptist Church in Montgomery until his last public words in Memphis, Tennessee, King saw the struggles of oppressed peoples around the world as inextricably bound to the struggle for democratic space among African Americans in the United States.[5]

During his last year, as his vision of the search for the beloved community matured, King asked the difficult but necessary question: "Where do we go from here?" His question was a signal to African Americans and other marginalized groups that their liberative claims and practices would need to extend beyond the restricted boundaries of U.S. geopolitical and capitalist interests. His query also interrogated the promised land of freedom and opportunity and the precarity of ghostly nondemocratic performances in neoliberal constructions of race, religion, and the culture of violence and death that persist today.[6] I refer here to the ways in which the specter of postracialism was but a foil for the ways in which the democratic ideal of "the radical egalitarian hypothesis" has masqueraded—and continues to masquerade—as a shape-shifting national imaginary of a nonracial, colorblind society while the economic, political, and social situation of the poor of all colors and creeds progressively deteriorate.[7]

In this chapter I will use the guiding metaphor of "plenty good room" to examine the relationship between King's quest for democratic space and his vision of the world house. I will explore ways in which these conjoined ideas can provide a critique of the racialized house of U.S. territorialism and global crusades of domination.[8] Finally, I will address existential and ethical questions regarding the meaning of "democratic space" and its compatibility with the notion of "global citizenship."

The Shape of Democratic Space

Indian physician Shah Alam Khan has written: "Democratic space is an unwritten permission to think. A fundamental consideration and respect granted by a state to its subjects to raise a voice of dissent and disagree. It is this democratic space which forms the basis of a vibrant democracy."[9] For Martin Luther King Jr., democratic space likewise had to do with the right to dissent, but he believed that the right to dissent has its basis in dignity, the respect afforded to others simply because of shared humanity. The idea of creating and sharing democratic space based on human dignity was deeply rooted in his religious and philosophical convictions, which are best understood in the historical context of the struggle against racial oppression and domination in the United States and among colonized peoples of the world.[10] King's quest for the actualization of dignity and freedom within ostensible democracy was simultaneously a quest for plenty good room. For him, the praxis of creating democratic space grows out of a history of resisting chattel slavery, Jim Crow, segregation, and the terror of the lynching rope. Therefore, while his concept of dignity has roots in Enlightenment thinkers like Immanuel Kant and Charles Montesquieu and in American patriots like Thomas Jefferson and John Adams, one cannot assume that democratic space for King was the same as it was for them. Gaining democratic space, for King, meant claiming both the right and the moral duty to dissent based on the inherent dignity and worth of the individual, and in his case the context was black suffering.[11] In practical political terms, for King, this was demonstrated through the rights to vote and to share public space with others, particularly white Americans, but he also had the larger global community in mind.[12]

Definitions of democratic space must avoid the totalizing diatribe by rising ideological conservative political movements (the language of rights based on the freedom to dissent, assemble, bear arms, and so on) without historical and ethical contextual analysis. One could plausibly argue for the right to drive a licensed motor vehicle, but if the vehicle is used in the assault and eventuating murder of pedestrians peacefully assembling, then that particular right is superseded by a more fundamental moral claim of the inherent worth and dignity of individuals and their freedom to peacefully protest without being attacked by a vehicle. Similarly, one could claim that the white supremacist marchers in Charlottesville certainly had the right to dissent but that it is morally indefensible to argue that they had the "right" to victimize, assault, and murder those who protested against their vitriol and violence. Equivocating rhetoric, such as was championed by the president of the United States, is ludicrous and threatens the norms and values of a democratic society, especially when it suggests that those who marched against historic monuments erected in the name of racism and white supremacy share equal blame for the violence that took the life of thirty-two-year-old Heather Heyer and injured at least nineteen others.

The recognition of human dignity and freedom, in the tradition represented by King, is an assertion of plenty good room in the United States. But with "America First" and "Let's make America great again" we are witnessing a reversal of time, a return to an ugly past where black, brown, and poor people in this country were assigned seats in what African American scholar Wahneema Lubiano calls "the house that race built."[13] Martin Luther King Jr. and the noble souls who forged the modern civil rights movement, like their ancestors, refused that arrangement, chose their own seats, and sat down in spite of the indignities hurled against them.

As we commemorate the life, death, and legacy of King, we need to return to that old spiritual and ask whether there is room for the hopeless, poor, and disenfranchised people around the world. Such a question is inescapable, since we hear the U.S. president disparage African nations as holes for defecation and deride our neighbors Haiti and Mexico. We witness huge tax cuts for global capitalists, the building of walls to keep others out, outright attacks on our fragile natural environment, mounting campaigns to destroy immigration policy (specifically Deferred Action for Childhood Arrivals), saber-rattling with Iran and North Korea, and terrorism in our schools and inner cities. King's notion of democratic space reminds us that there is plenty good room in our nation for a diverse society, what the late historian John Hope Franklin called "the land of room enough."[14] Inherent in King's work to expand democracy as an expression of human dignity and nondomination is the larger vision of a beloved community, which in his later years he referred to as the "world house." But first we must create space and focus on sharing in our "precious but precarious democratic experiment" here in the United States.[15]

King knew that sharing space with others with whom we have become accustomed is not hard, but to work to create space with those with whom we strongly disagree or who frighten us in their *otherness* is difficult and dangerous. Fear of otherness is not a justification for purging, injuring, or killing. Democracy at its best, for King, is a squabble, a contentious exchange of ideas, opinions, values, and practices within the context of civil relations. The practice of transformative civility was paramount in King's public conversations and actions throughout his career. But he and other practitioners of nonviolent resistance eschewed dysfunctional civility that masked deep-seated rage and hatred, sensing that this only perpetuated structural inequality and injustice. King's dignified civility was a subversive tool to expose hidden agendas of hatred and injustice and to create an environment of reason and truth-telling.[16] When we forget the importance of the transformative, subversive qualities of civility, we create conditions of alienation and spirals of violence that limit and destroy democratic possibilities. However we feel about building walls to keep others out, our greatest challenge is not keeping others out of our country but instead, as King thought, developing new and better ways of seeing and responding to our own interconnectedness—in the United States of America and throughout the world. This leads to the discourse and practice of global citizenship.

Global Citizenship and King's Ethical Vision of the World House

The subject of global citizenship, sometimes referred to as "cosmopolitanism," "planetary citizenship," and "citizenship beyond the nation-state," is a controversial concept, but the strongest resistance to the idea tends to come from those with strongly held views of a parochial patriotism and of statehood driven by group identity (nationalism) and assumptions of American moral superiority.[17] For instance, moral philosopher Martha Nussbaum thinks that narrow, myopic patriotism in our contemporary global context fails to serve the ideals of justice and equality that are indigenous to a democratic worldview. She locates her moral justification in "the very old idea of the cosmopolitan, the person whose allegiance is to the worldwide community of human beings." Nussbaum is in agreement with ancient Stoic philosophy that claimed that "local origins and group memberships" must be regulated by more inclusive global moral concerns of justice and the equality of all human beings.[18] To be "*kosmon polites*," or world citizens, does not mean that we abolish our local and national forms of government and create a world state. Rather, it means that we give our primary allegiance to reason and moral capacity and thereby to the contemporary solidaristic approaches represented by Amartya Sen, who addresses "our inescapably plural identities," and Kwame Anthony Appiah's notion of "cosmopolitanism."[19] Being a global citizen does not exclude local concerns. Rather, global citizens strive to be "glocal" in their perspectives, taking into account both local and global considerations, especially as they relate to the future of our lives on this planet and the nagging issues of poverty, race, and war that King identified as the triplets of evil.

Political theorist Benjamin R. Barber disagrees with what he sees as Nussbaum's "Kantian universalism" and "the thinness of cosmopolitanism" in its failure to grasp "the crucial humanizing role played by identity politics in the deracinating world of contracts, markets and legal personhood."[20] Scholar and law professor Amy Chua strikes a similar note relative to "tribal politics" rooted in "group instincts" of human beings, which become even more formidable as they are expressed among regional, religious, ethnic, and clan-based identities. Chua quotes a writer in the *Huffington Post* who responded to a Newt Gingrich comment in 2009, "I am not a citizen of the world," with the quip: "Mr. Gingrich, if you are not a citizen of the world, then stay the *eff* out of it."[21]

Global citizenship, as it is used in this discussion, refers to "a sense of belonging to a broader community and common humanity. It emphasizes political, economic, social and cultural interdependency and interconnectedness between the local, the national and the global."[22] The term "global citizenship" does not merely refer to legal rights; its significance lies in the united web of humanity and our moral interconnectedness and obligation to nature and the larger world society.[23] This view finds affinity with King's idea of the world house and his notion of democratic space.

King's perspective on the civil rights movement was always global, but during his later years his statements about Americans' connectedness with people around the globe were more pronounced. He believed that first there needed to be a reckoning with Western imperialism's own presuppositions about power. Before his tragic death in April 1968, King reminded Americans that we no longer live in a small house that race built but rather that we have inherited a world house. He asserted in clear and strident language that we must learn to live together as brothers and sisters or die apart as fools. He was acutely aware of the need for a broader interpretive framework for understanding what he perceived as a crucial passage in history.[24] Moreover, King suggested that the struggles of African Americans must be understood in light of a "shifting" of the West's basic outlooks and philosophocal presuppositions about power.[25] King argued:

> We have inherited a large house, a great "world house" in which we have to live together—black and white, Easterner and Westerner, Gentile and Jew, Catholic and Protestant, Moslem and Hindu—a family unduly separated in ideas, culture and interest, who, because we can never again live apart, must learn somehow to live together with each other in peace. However deeply American Negroes are caught in the struggle to be at last home in our homeland of the United States, we cannot ignore the larger world house in which we are also dwellers. Equality with whites will not solve the problems of either whites or Negroes if it means equality in a world society stricken by poverty and in a universe doomed to extinction by war.[26]

This understanding of the world house as a metaphor for expanding the boundaries of U.S. territorialism was linked to King's vision of democratic space. His concern, however, was to inscribe a new geography where the Atlantic nexus of Euro-American power no longer dominated through its geopolitical interests, or by what we now know as neoliberal constructions of capital around the globe. With respect to the ethical issues at stake, King saw how neoliberalism co-opts traditional norms and values—ideologically, structurally, and strategically—perpetuating what Peter Bloom calls "the ethical capitalist subject" that is based on permanent profit-maximizing individualism.[27] In his 1964 Nobel Peace Prize lecture, King presciently alluded to the increasing structural gulf between the haves and the have-nots as the basis for poverty around the globe:

> Like a monstrous octopus, [capitalism] projects its nagging, prehensile tentacles in lands and villages all over the world. Almost two-thirds of the peoples of the world go to bed hungry at night. They are undernourished, ill-housed, and shabbily clad. Many of them have no houses or beds to sleep in. Their only beds are the sidewalks of the cities and the dusty roads of the villages. Most of these poverty-stricken children of God have never seen a physician or a dentist. This

problem of poverty is not only seen in the class division between the highly developed industrial nations and the so-called underdeveloped nations; it is seen
in the great economic gaps within the rich nations themselves.[28]

Scholars like Joshua F. J. Inwood suggest that King's vision calls for an expanded
mapping of the world and that it encourages us to think of the beloved community as a kind of countergeography that extends boundaries beyond the nodes
of Africa and the Americas to include other colonized and exiled peoples of the
world. Inwood writes: "Viewing Dr. King's life and work through the prism of
an expanded transatlantic experience provides a framework for examining the
ways his work arose out of a particular geographical experience. The concept
of the expanded Black Atlantic provides a framework for looking at how Martin
Luther King Jr. advocated a complete re-creation of space and place through his
concept of the Beloved Community."[29]

For King, in order for democratic life to exist and flourish, it must be related
to a larger global moral order, which he called "a world perspective." In June
1961, at Lincoln University in Pennsylvania, in a speech entitled, "The American Dream," King stated: "First I think all of us must develop a world perspective if we are to survive. The American dream will not become a reality devoid of
the larger dream of a world of brotherhood and peace and good will. The world
in which we live is a world of geographical oneness and we are challenged now
to make it spiritually one."[30] Six years later, on December 24, 1967, King delivered his Christmas sermon in Ebenezer Baptist Church in Atlanta. It was the
fifth and final sermon of the 1967 Massey Lecture Series, broadcast by the Canadian Broadcasting Corporation and later published in *The Trumpet of Conscience*.
In it King echoed the same message of interconnectedness and of democracy
grounded in a moral and spiritual ecumenicity:

> Now let me suggest first that if we are to have peace on earth, our loyalties must
> become ecumenical rather than sectional. Our loyalties must transcend our race,
> our tribe, our class, and our nation; and this means we must develop a world per-
> spective. No individual can live alone; no nation can live alone, and as long as we
> try, the more we are going to have war in this world. Now the judgment of God is
> upon us, and we must either learn to live together as brothers or we are all going
> to perish together as fools.[31]

King's notion of the world house as expanding democratic space is both an opportunity and an appropriate ethical ideal for the new moment to which we
have been called by history. Christian ethicist Hak Joon Lee suggests: "The link
between a theory and the practice of global ethics is naturally formed when

global ethics is framed in the context of a global civil society and in relation to its various democratic movements, dynamics, and functions." According to Lee, King achieves this by including four ethical elements—vision, principles, virtues, and political practice—within the communal-political nexus, which are organically and dialectically related. Lee's first principle is the all-encompassing vision of the world house wherein all people are treated with dignity and people live in peace across human differences. The vision is both metaphysical and practical: metaphysical in that humans are essentially social—our fundamental desire is to belong, in communal solidarity with others; and practical because the world is shrinking and our interconnectedness is increasing. King's vision, therefore, is not a naïve fantasy but is instead grounded in experience that directs and inspires sustained social transformation and is justified through the efficacy of its impact. Second, the vision of the world house involves principles (values, moral rules) founded on the sanctity and solidarity of all human beings. "For King, these principles indicated the minimum requirements in approximating the great world house," Lee writes. Third, the vision involves virtue: "King recognized that the formation of cosmopolitan virtues and the practice of nonviolence are necessary to build the great world house. The great world house is a virtuous community, and nonviolent resistance builds virtuous citizens."[32] These three elements, Lee argues, lead to the fourth consideration, political practice, which emphasizes persuasion. Being convinced that knowledge alone is insufficient for bringing about change in political contests, King came to understand the power to effect change to structural evil, both in society and within the individual, through nonviolent resistance.

For the purposes of this essay, the world house is a vision that marshals these four elements and helps initiate and sustain their cultivation. It is also supported by them because there is an organic reciprocity between King's world house vision and his moral principles, virtues, and nonviolent political practice. Using this ethical framework, King's vision of the world house may also be an effective catalyst for new global movements because embedded in it are the twin notions of diasporas and exiles as suggested by Inwood. In an earlier work, I reference the ethical obligations of the world house that involve new and creative ways of communication and modeling global citizenship in exiles and diasporas among scattered and scattering peoples.[33] The existential and ethical issues at stake in this new moment, however, demand that we congregate, conjure, and conspire about the ways in which this possibility is actualized. Critical to this is the matter of equity and justice for poor people and people whose lives are in a perpetual state of exile and transition. The surge of economic globalization and neoliberalism has created a new form of capitalist inquisition, what

Amy Chua labels "a world on fire." Chua argues that the exportation of free market democracy breeds ethnic hatred and global instability and caters to a new
elite of "market-dominant minorities" who profit most from globalization.[34]
Toni Morrison speaks of this scattering in terms of a search for "home":

> The overweening, defining event of the modern world is the mass movement
> of raced populations, beginning with the largest forced transfer of people in the
> history of the world: slavery. The consequences of which transfer have deter-
> mined all the wars following it as well as the current ones being waged on ev-
> ery continent. The contemporary world's work has become policing, halting,
> forming policy regarding, and trying to administer the movement of people. Na-
> tionhood—the very definition of citizenship—is constantly being demarcated
> and redemarcated in response to exiles, refugees, *Gastarbeiter*, immigrants, mi-
> grations, the displaced, the fleeing, and the besieged. The anxiety of belonging is
> entombed within the central metaphors in the discourse on globalism, transna-
> tionalism, nationalism, the break up of federations, the rescheduling of alliances,
> and the fictions of sovereignty. Yet these figurations of nationhood and identity
> are frequently as raced themselves as the originating racial house that defined
> them. When they are not raced, they are . . . imaginary landscape, never inscape;
> Utopia, never home.[35]

Where might these exiles in search of home find the democratic spaces, the
new geography, the new world house of which King prophesied? It will not be
in their places of origin or national allegiance and loyalty. Rather, it will begin
with the acknowledgment that indeed the ground has shifted—and that a new
generation of leaders must emerge bearing the mantle of prophetic speech and
action that is King's enduring legacy. These new harbingers of peace must assume the new time and embody the new spaces wrought by a global citizenship
that seeks justice in a new global community of plenty good room. These new
leaders will be characterized by an appreciation and celebration of difference
and a healthy suspicion of models of democratic discourse that fail to do so.[36]
Moreover, democratic space for this new moment refers to the ongoing struggle
against the reconfiguration of space and the reordering of time for subjugated
bodies. This idea is represented in political philosopher Jacques Rancière's notion of policing as the rule that governs the body's appearing, "a configuration
of occupations and the properties of the spaces where these occupations are
distributed." Here the concern is with the demos—the people who are not accounted for in the configuration of power, those relegated to animal life, who
can make sounds (*phônê*) but cannot speak. Nonetheless, these bodies must
dare to speak, break, shift, and redefine the spaces they have been assigned.

And it is precisely because they dare to use speech (*logos*) that they reveal the process of equality, because only a free human can speak.[37] Beyond the facility of speech as a mark of rationality (rational communication), these leaders must demonstrate the human capacity for "affective experiences, occurrences in the world, or aesthetic events" that cannot be thought but are *embodied* and *experienced* in the sense of freedom and equality as profoundly imaginative and creative potentialities that point to newness, openness, expectation and hope.[38]

Lewis V. Baldwin provides a key to this search for "home." He argues that King's distinctive contribution to the idea of global citizenship is his deep commitment to justice, the same commitment that led him to condemn the United States for its "materialism, power and supremacy over other nations."[39] King called upon the United States, because of its unique democratic heritage and its great wealth and technology, to lead the way toward a new world order:

> I am convinced that if we are to get on the right side of the world revolution we as a nation must undergo a radical revolution of values. A true revolution of values will soon cause us to question the fairness and justice of many of our past and present policies. A true revolution of values will soon look uneasily on the glaring contrast between poverty and wealth. With righteous indignation, it will look across the seas and see individual capitalists of the West investing huge sums of money in Africa, Asia, and South America only to take the profits out with no concern for the social betterment of the countries, and say: "This is not just." It will look at our alliance with the landed gentry of Latin America and say: "This is not just." The Western arrogance of feeling that it has everything to teach others and nothing to learn from them is not just.[40]

When King called for an end to the war in Vietnam, he was raising the prospect of a movement among diasporic and exiled peoples of the earth. His call implied that African Americans' freedom, their human rights, and their religion are inextricably bound with the yearnings and hopes of oppressed people everywhere. He often reminded listeners, "Injustice anywhere is a threat to justice everywhere."[41] *Diasporas*, in King's view of a world house, is a shape-shifting metaphor that emerges and leads to identity that is not confined to narrow categories of religion and nation. *Diasporas*, in this sense, recognizes African Americans and other historically oppressed peoples as global citizens and allows them to engage in their struggles for justice and peace from a global perspective. Furthermore, diasporas afford a prophetic locus relative to the narrowly defined tropes of national loyalty and citizenship that are rooted in *dilemma* or what W. E. B. Du Bois called "double consciousness."[42] This tension between loyalty to race and loyalty to nation has in many respects prevented African

Americans from more fully approximating the ideal of the beloved community and global solidarity expressed in King's vision of the world house.[43]

This understanding of the radical nature of King's dream will make some people uneasy, especially those who are involved in transactional leadership that conducts "business as usual" and who suggest that we can govern by making deals with oligarchs and plutocrats. As we experience the utter pillage and plunder of our most cherished ideals of democracy, and the attendant ambiguities and concerns about our nation's future, Martin Luther King Jr.'s vision of the world house is no longer the distant imaginings of a utopian dreamer but may be the only viable option for peaceful coexistence in the United States and on this planet.[44]

Ethical Leadership and Global Citizenship Training for New Leaders

I have argued that the time has come to push beyond attachment to race-based language and metaphors of dilemma and exodus that have outlived their use, and to offer a global vision for black churches that will involve new ways to model citizenship in diasporas and exiles.[45] The primary aim of this argument is to explore new strategies to identify, recruit, educate, and train a new generation of leaders from black and other historically oppressed communities in global citizenship.[46] These emerging leaders, I argue, need tools to foster a sense of identity and human flourishing in a world where the porous boundaries of nation-states are giving way. With movements among youth in the United States against gun violence, protests against the murder of young black men and women, and calls for eco-justice, King's notion of democratic space provides opportunities for global citizenship training that is not limited by narrow, nostalgic, and exclusive visions of statehood. We need a new generation of leaders who are spiritually disciplined, intellectually astute, and morally anchored. Much like their predecessors in the civil rights movement, these new leaders will need courage to organize and sustain local and global campaigns for justice, keeping a mind always on compassion for "the least of these." We might take our cue from Hak Joon Lee's four ethical elements—vision, principles (or values), virtues, and political practices—in a spiraling dance of a sort that authors Don Edward Beck and Christopher C. Cowan call "spiral dynamics." This is a theory of leadership that takes seriously global paradigm shifts, the exploration of the science of mimetics, and change that creates a context for ways to understand genetic and cultural coding that are undefined by projects of linearity and hierarchal architectonics of race, ethnicity, gender, and sexual orientation.[47] The vision of the world house in an age of globalization, neoliberalism, and postmodernism, with its disrupted narratives of identity and otherness, is an excellent basis from which to assemble and reason together about local, national, and global futures.[48] The principles of justice, equality, and compassion for the poor, homeless, and forgotten—all part of King's global vision—are even more urgent today. Hard questions about violence are also global in nature, and we must see not only violence at home but also the violence manifested outside our borders by imperialist engagement, whether war or economic policies, that keep inequality and poverty firmly in place.

Where do we begin? A major task will be to rethink ways of engaging in civil discourse and action without falling into the very spiral of violence and death that we seek to overcome. Many young leaders are deeply aware that we are in the midst of a world culture of death: a death march against affordable health care, a death sentence to fair and compassionate immigration policy, the deathly effects of industrial toxins, war deaths—far more than just in combat, dead zones of urban battlefields, the sometimes deadly erection of barriers to immigrants, the death cages of prisons, the deadly spread of opioids (in the Rust Belt, old mill towns of New England, and Appalachia with its "hillbilly elegies"), the deathly "blood and soil" rallying cry of neo-Nazis, and the ideological death traps of Christian fantasia throughout the heartland.[49] How and where do brave and justice-seeking emerging leaders begin to create and share democratic space?

First, creating democratic space requires youthful movements for justice to allow for differences in perspectives and in ways in which we protest. The presidential election of 2016 was a wake-up call. It is clear that the election of Donald Trump demonstrated that a majority of white people voted based on racial identification, fears of terrorism, aversion to immigration, and economic concerns, and many who voted for Trump were poor white people.[50] Poor white people in the rural United States deserve to be heard just as much as poor people in cities, but we must learn to look, listen, and learn from one another without giving sway to the irrational, nonproductive fallacy of white privilege that breeds fear, misunderstanding, and violence. Nor should we allow concerns about gun control, gender diversity, sexual orientation, and disability to be mocked and cast aside as foul, profane, and un-American. The point is that in the project of creating and sharing democratic space, we cannot allow the things that divide us to prevent us from finding common ground in the world house. King's vision of the world house is needed now even more than it was in 1967, when he suggested that our choice is between community and chaos.

Although civility too is needed even more than in 1967, that need not be limited to simple etiquette. One can be civil, as I have suggested, and also be disruptive, subversive, and transformative. Perhaps better than any other leader of the twentieth century, King was able to forge civility into a subversive and transformative weapon in the struggle for equality and justice in the United States. Subversive civility allows us to "civilize political contestation" and "subvert complacent consensus" by providing those with different beliefs, values, and orientations with space to engage with others, perhaps even opponents, without dismissing or eliminating them.[51] King's distinctive contribution in this regard is the way in which he dialectically explored the options afforded him and used existing tensions "to spark a dialogue" through nonviolent acts of civility.[52] King called the participants in this process "transformed nonconformists," seeing them as primarily concerned with the disruption of "negative peace" as a way of bringing to the surface hidden tensions that create the conditions for creative understanding and new transformative possibilities.[53]

King's "Letter from Birmingham Jail" (1963) is an example of the uses of subversive, transformed civility.[54] It was written in response to a statement authored by eight white Alabama clergymen and titled "A Call for Unity." This statement denounced the methods of nonviolent direct action as "unwise" and "untimely" and called King an "extremist" and an "outsider."[55] King addressed his detractors respectfully yet condemned their moderate position as complicit with racism and exposed the moral and theological contradictions inherent in their claims. In doing so, he created democratic space where rational communication was possible, even if the intended recipients chose not to take it to heart. Moreover, he forced the clergy and citizens of Birmingham and throughout the nation to face their collusion with segregation and unjust voting practices. Youth activism by those involved in the March for Our Lives Campaign and Black Lives Matter today is a hopeful sign of a similar struggle for democratic space in the United States and around the world.[56]

Second, creating new spaces for others—immigrants, refugees in particular—means that we must see ourselves as intimately connected to peoples around the world no matter where they live and despite their differing circumstances. We have learned that what happens in the White House affects what happens in our house, that what happens downtown goes around town, that what happens in Afghanistan affects what happens in New York, and that what happens to our natural environment affects the future of human existence on this planet. Being the world's only real superpower entails the extraordinary capacity to destroy fragile relationships with nature, to demolish other nations and their cultures. While self-interest is a legitimate prerogative of any nation, we run the risk of forfeiting that right through aggression and dominance by military and economic co-optation. A more reasonable and potentially productive course of action is to listen deeply to the unpopular voices of people both within and beyond our society who seek diverse ways of understanding and who are willing to connect in spaces of strategic interest and mutuality. Building world consensus and creating unlikely partnerships with global neighbors who have criticized U.S. arrogance and avarice is hard to do, but we must give peace a chance. So much weighs on our willingness to find peaceful ways to address violent situations. During this fiftieth anniversary of King's assassination, when we commemorate the legacy of our nation's greatest peacemaker, we are continuing to send thousands of young men and women to fight against nations that most Americans cannot locate on a world map.

Much has changed since Martin Luther King Jr.'s prophetic statements about America and the world, yet so much remains the same. King not only spoke to the vision of a world house and what that would mean for U.S. self-identity and its suppositions about power, he was also an astute observer of culture. He strongly believed that there needed to be a revolution of values and priorities in order to make the shift necessitated by global connectedness. This revolution of values and priorities meant a basic restructuring of how we live together in community here and throughout the world—essentially, a restructuring of both our private and public lives. In many respects, King's call for a reprioritization of values on a national scale had everything to do with how we live our day-to-day lives in world community. For young leaders of educational, civic, and religious organizations, this most important issue needs careful deliberation.

Finally, King encouraged us to hope. The basis for his profound hope is found in the experience of inner transformation and in the crucible of struggle. In his 1967 "Christmas Sermon on Peace," he spoke of the disparity between his dream of 1963 and his personal nightmare that had evolved over the following four years: "Yes, I am personally the victim of deferred dreams, of blasted hopes, but in spite of that I close today by saying I still have a dream, because, you know, you can't give up in life. If you lose hope, somehow you lose that vitality that keeps life moving, you lose the courage to be, that quality that helps you go on in spite of all. And so today I still have a dream."[57]

As Americans witness the shifting grounds in our nation and abroad, we must ask new questions about the nature and scope of our long, arduous journey on these shores. What does this new season of struggle mean for us, for the United States, and for the world? Can we create democratic space for others? Is there indeed plenty good room for everybody? Can we all get along? Dare we hope, or must we conclude with those who say that we are at the end of history? King did not think we were at the end of history. To the contrary, he believed that what we were witnessing was a worldwide revolution challenging the very foundations of Western hegemony. In his last public words, he said that he was pleased to live during this chaotic and precarious age because beyond the despair and hopelessness that abounded, he believed that this was a great moment for the united struggles of people throughout the world. King declared:

> I know, somehow, that only when it is dark enough, can you see the stars. And I see God working in this period of the twentieth century in a way that men, in some strange way, are responding—something is happening in our world. The masses of the people are rising up. And wherever they are assembled today, whether they are in Johannesburg, South Africa; Nairobi, Kenya; Accra, Ghana; New York City; Atlanta, Georgia; Jackson, Mississippi; or Memphis, Tennessee— the cry is always the same—"We want to be free."[58]

Choose Your Seat and Sit Down!

During the spring of 2006, I traveled throughout South Africa lecturing on ethical leadership. One of my visits was to Durban. My hosts took me to Pietermaritzburg, the township famous for an incident early in the career of Mohandas Gandhi. In 1893 Gandhi arrived in Durban to serve as legal counsel to the merchant Dada Abdulla. Early in his employment, he was asked by Dada Abdulla to take a trip to Pretoria in the Transvaal. Traveling by train, Gandhi acquired a first-class ticket and had proceeded to his compartment when a railway official requested that he remove himself to the van compartment, since "coolies" and nonwhites were not permitted to sit in first-class compartments. When Gandhi protested and refused to comply, he was thrown violently off the train and his luggage tossed onto the platform. Gandhi stayed at the Pietermaritzburg station in the cold of that winter night and began to reflect on his "duty." Should he stay and fight for his "rights" or return to India? He stayed and chose a seat in the heart of South African politics but returned later to India where he challenged the hegemony of the Great British Empire—and the world has never been the same.[59] As I stood in the train station, which now has a memorial dedicated to Gandhi's courageous action, I reflected on a similar incident that involved an African American seamstress named Rosa Parks, who also had been told to give up her seat to a white passenger. But Rosa Parks, in a defiant act of courage, chose her seat and sat down, and when she sat, Martin Luther King Jr. stood up.[60]

On February 1, 1960, four students at the historically black North Carolina A&T State University—Joseph McNeil, Franklin McCain, Ezell Blair Jr. and David Richmond—decided there was plenty good room and chose their seats and sat down in the Woolworth's store in downtown Greensboro, North Carolina, despite statutes prohibiting black people from eating at that location. They were denied service, but that did not stop them. They sat in their seats until the store closed and returned the next day with sixteen more students. On the third day there were sixty students, and by the fourth day over three hundred people arrived and sat down. Their courageous actions gained momentum, and sit-ins spread throughout the South, and "the Greensboro Four," as they came to be called, were a catalyst for the formation of the Student Nonviolent Coordinating Committee, which changed the course of the civil rights movement. For those who are working for the creation of a better world, especially young activists who see their role as part of a new generation of "transformed nonconformists," Martin Luther King Jr. is still a model. He reminds us that the struggle for plenty good room requires revolutionary patience, irrepressible hope, and an insatiable desire to be free.

NOTES

The epigraphs are from *Songs of Zion*, Supplemental Worship Resources 12 (Nashville, Tenn.: Abingdon Press, 1981), 99; Martin Luther King Jr., *Where Do We Go from Here: Chaos or Community?* (Boston: Beacon Press, 1967; rpt., 1968, 2010), 181.

1. James Weldon Johnson, ed., "O Black and Unknown Bards," in *The Book of American Negro Poetry* (New York: Harcourt, Brace, 1922), 50–51.

2. For a fully developed argument along these lines, see Walter Earl Fluker, "The Politics of Conversion and the Civilization of Friday," in Quinton Dixie and Cornel West, eds., *The Courage to Hope: From Black Suffering to Human Redemption* (Boston: Beacon Press, 1999), 103–17. American theologian Willie James Jennings argues that Europeans acted as a divine council by performing "a deeply theological act that mirrored the identity and action of God in creating," in which they transitioned and reconfigured boundaries and confiscated indigenous territories as part of the domain of the project of whiteness. He adds: "Theorists and theories of race will not touch the ground until they reckon deeply with the foundations of racial imaginings in the deployment of an altered theological vision of creation. We must narrate not only the alteration of bodies but of space itself." Willie James Jennings, *The Christian Imagination: Theology and the Origins of Race* (New Haven, Conn.: Yale University Press, 2010), 60, 63.

3. Richard W. Wills Sr., *Martin Luther King, Jr., and the Image of God* (New York: Oxford University Press, 2009). See especially chapter 6, "Beloved Community," where Wills argues that beyond the creation of the phrase "beloved community," credited to American philosopher Josiah Royce and his successors, the concept for King was grounded in the *imago Dei*, which "provided the initial basis of the recognition of humanity's common dignity" (140).

4. Charles Long writes: "The slaves who lived both within and outside of history, created historical structures but having no power to determine the locus of their meaning found a spiritual locus outside the body of historical time in which to save their bodies and to give meaning to their communities. The spirituals were their myths, and as Ashis Nandy put it, the 'affirmation of ahistoricity is an affirmation of the dignity and auton-

omy of the non-modern, [non-Western] peoples.'" Charles H. Long, "Howard Thurman and the Meaning of Religion in America," in Mozella G. Mitchell, ed., *The Human Search: Howard Thurman and the Quest for Freedom, Proceedings of the Second Annual Thurman Convocation* (New York: Peter Lang, 1992), 141 (brackets in original).

5. See Martin Luther King Jr., "Address at the Initial Mass Meeting of the Montgomery Improvement Association," Holt Street Baptist Church, Montgomery, Alabama, December 5, 1955, Martin Luther King Jr. Papers, Library and Archives of the Martin Luther King Jr. Center for Nonviolent Social Change, Atlanta; Martin Luther King Jr., "I See the Promised Land (April 3, 1968)," in *A Testament of Hope: The Essential Writings of Martin Luther King, Jr.*, edited by James M. Washington (New York: HarperCollins, 1986), 280; and Lionel K. McPherson, "The Costs of Violence: Militarism, Geopolitics, and Accountability," in Tommie Shelby and Brandon M. Terry, eds., *To Shape a New World: Essays on the Political Philosophy of Martin Luther King, Jr.* (Cambridge, Mass.: Belknap Press of Harvard University, 2018), 253–66.

6. Judith Butler defines "precarity" as the "politically induced condition in which certain populations suffer from failing social and economic networks of support and become differentially exposed to injury, violence, and death." Judith Butler, *Frames of War: When Is Life Grievable?* (repr., New York: Verso, 2010), 20. See also Judith Butler, *Precarious Life: The Powers of Mourning and Violence* (New York: Verso, 2004), xvii, 2–6, 128–53.

7. For a more fully developed argument along these lines, see Walter Earl Fluker, *The Ground Has Shifted: The Future of the Black Church in Post-Racial America* (New York: New York University Press, 2016). See, for example, my argument that the "principle of non-racism in black churches and black communities is a radical egalitarian hypothesis that has been tested with uneven results from the earliest movements of independent black churches to the present, in every major war fought by the United States, and in every struggle for civil and human rights, including contemporary movements like Black Lives Matter. . . . African Americans' belief in the radical egalitarian hypothesis is like the belief in what William James calls the *religious hypothesis*: a *living, forced*, and *momentous option*" (23–24; emphasis in original).

8. Two books that share the title of this chapter are Lewis V. Baldwin, *Plenty Good Room: A Bible Study Based on African American Spirituals* (Nashville: Abingdon Press, 2002); and Marcia Y. Riggs, *Plenty Good Room: Women versus Male Power in the Black Church* (Eugene, Ore.: Wipf and Stock, 2008).

9. Shah Alam Khan, "Democratic Space—What Is That?," Countercurrents.org, June 3, 2009, http://www.countercurrents.org/khan030609.htm.

10. See Sarah Azaransky, *This Worldwide Struggle: Religion and the International Roots of the Civil Rights Movement* (New York: Oxford University Press, 2017), for treatment of Pauli Murray, Bayard Rustin, James Farmer, Juliette Dericotte, Howard Thurman, Benjamin Mays, William Stuart Nelson, and the vast network of intellectuals and activists engaged in laying the theological and moral framework for expanding democratic space in the United States through international exchanges and camaraderie. See also Gary Dorrien, *Breaking White Supremacy: Martin Luther King Jr. and the Black Social Gospel* (New Haven: Yale University Press, 2018).

11. Bernard Boxill, for instance, frames the question of freedom within "republican political thought" and the republican concept of freedom, which he takes to mean that every person should obey only his or her own will against the unfreedom of slavery or bondage of any form. Boxill asks us to think about King's notion of civil disobedi-

ence in light of the republican nondomination theory of freedom and underscores the importance of chattel slavery, particularly black slavery in the United States, for these debates. Bernard R. Boxill, "The Roots of Civil Disobedience in Republicanism and Slavery," in Shelby and Terry, eds., *To Shape a New World*, 58–77. In the same volume, Robert Gooding-Williams, "The Du Bois-Washington Debate and the Idea of Dignity" (19–34), looks at *Stride toward Freedom* and *Why We Can't Wait* to situate King within the debate between Du Bois and Booker T. Washington during the first phase of his civil rights movement leadership. Especially important in this discussion is the theme of dignity.

12. Derrick Darby understands King's defense of voting rights to be grounded in the concept of dignity, which has two forms in King's thought: 1) conduct in keeping with certain public norms, and 2) the capacity that provides every person with intrinsic moral value. Voting, Darby says, establishes the legitimacy for a legal system of rights and duties. The inhibiting of voting rights is, therefore, the refusal to acknowledge the inherent moral value of the disenfranchised. However, Darby, following King, suggests that black Americans can act collectively with dignity to demand equal treatment that they rightly deserve. Darby plays with the concept of dignity a little more toward the end of the essay to suggest that it can also be understood as a status conferred by granting the right to vote by a legal system. Therefore, voter suppression is a significant moral problem, he argues. Derrick Darby, "A Vindication of Voting Rights," in Shelby and Terry, eds., *To Shape a New World*, 161–83.

13. Wahneema Lubiano, ed., *The House that Race Built: Black Americans, U.S. Terrain* (New York: Pantheon, 1997), 1–300.

14. John Hope Franklin, "The Land of Room Enough," *Daedalus* 110, no. 2 (Spring 1981): 1–12.

15. Cornel West, quoted in Margaret Isa, "West Speaks on 'Black Love': African-Americans Must Resist Feelings of Hate, Despair," *Harvard Crimson*, October 30, 1992, http://www.thecrimson.com/article/1992/10/30/west-speaks-on-black-love-pblacks.

16. Walter Earl Fluker, *Ethical Leadership: The Quest for Character, Civility, and Community* (Minneapolis: Fortress Press, 2009), 87–90.

17. See Richard Bellamy, "Citizenship beyond the Nation State: The Case of Europe," in Noel O'Sullivan, ed., *Political Theory in Transition* (London: Routledge, 2000); Margaret E. Keck and Kathryn Sikkink, *Activists beyond Borders: Advocacy Networks in International Politics* (Ithaca, N.Y.: Cornell University Press, 1998); Kwame Anthony Appiah, "Education for Global Citizenship," in D. Coulter, John R. Wiens, and Gary D. Fenstermacher, eds., *Why Do We Educate? Renewing the Conversation*. vol. 1 (Oxford, UK: Blackwell Publishing, 2008), 107; and Hazel Henderson and Daisaku Ikeda, *Planetary Citizenship: Your Values, Beliefs and Actions Can Shape a Sustainable World* (Santa Monica, Calif.: Middleway Press, 2004).

18. Martha C. Nussbaum, "Patriotism and Cosmopolitanism," in *For Love of Country?*, new ed., edited by Joshua Cohen (Boston: Beacon Press, 2002), 6–7.

19. Amartya Sen, *Identity and Violence: The Illusion of Destiny*, Issues of Our Time (New York: W. W. Norton, 2006); and Kwame Anthony Appiah, *Cosmopolitanism: Ethics in a World of Strangers* (New York: W. W. Norton, 2007).

20. Benjamin R. Barber, "Constitutional Faith," in Nussbaum, *For Love of Country?*, 30–31.

21. Amy Chua, *Political Tribes: Group Instinct and the Fate of Nations* (New York: Penguin Press, 2018), 6, 180.

22. *Global Citizenship Education: Preparing Learners for the Challenges of the 21st Century*

(Paris, France: UNESCO, 2014), 14, http://unesdoc.unesco.org/images/0022/002277
/227729e.pdf. See also Fluker, *Ground Has Shifted*, 134.

23. Chernor Bah, chair of the Youth Advocacy Group of the Global Education First Initiative, writes: "As a citizen you get your rights through a passport/national paper. As a global citizen, it is guaranteed not by a State but through your humanity. This means you are also responsible to the rest of humanity and not the State alone." *Global Citizenship Education*, 14. According to Carlos Alberto Torres, director of the Paulo Freire Institute at the UCLA Graduate School of Education, "Global citizenship is marked by an understanding of global interconnectedness and a commitment to the collective good." Ibid.

24. Martin Luther King Jr., *Where Do We Go From Here?*, 167, 169, 171.

25. Martin Luther King Jr., "The Quest for Peace and Justice," Nobel lecture, 1964, https://www.nobelprize.org/nobel_prizes/peace/laureates/1964/king-lecture.html.

26. Martin Luther King Jr., *Where Do We Go From Here*, 167.

27. Peter Bloom, *The Ethics of Neoliberalism: The Business of Making Capitalism Moral* (London: Routledge, 2017), 19–35. For a historical and sociological review of the term of "neoliberalism" that critically interrogates its use to mean laissez-faire economics, see William Davies, "Neoliberalism: A Bibliographic Review," *Theory, Culture and Society* 31, nos. 7–8 (2014): 309–17. For a feminist/womanist perspective, see Keri Day, *Religious Resistance to Neoliberalism: Womanist and Black Feminist Perspectives* (New York: Palgrave MacMillan, 2015).

28. Martin Luther King Jr., "Quest for Peace and Justice"; and Martin Luther King Jr., *Where Do We Go from Here?*, 177.

29. Joshua F. J. Inwood, "Searching for the Promised Land: Examining Dr. Martin Luther King's Concept of the Beloved Community," *Antipode* 41, no. 3 (June 2009): 490–91.

30. Martin Luther King Jr., *Testament of Hope*, 209.

31. Martin Luther King Jr., *The Trumpet of Conscience* (New York: Harper and Row, 1967), 68.

32. Hak Joon Lee, "Toward the Great World House: Hans Küng and Martin Luther King Jr. on Global Ethics," *Journal of the Society of Christian Ethics* 29, no. 2 (Fall/Winter 2009), 97–119.

33. Fluker, *Ground Has Shifted*, 137–41, 165–96.

34. Amy Chua, *World on Fire: How Exporting Free Market Economy Breeds Ethnic Hatred and Global Instability* (New York: Doubleday, 2003), 9. Also quoted in Lewis V. Baldwin and Paul R. Dekar, eds., *"In An Inescapable Network of Mutuality": Martin Luther King, Jr. and the Globalization of an Ethical Ideal* (Eugene, Ore.: Cascade Books, 2013), 10.

35. Toni Morrison, "Home," in Lubiano, *House that Race Built*, 10–11.

36. Quoting Gayatri Spivak and Dipesh Chakravarty, Sarah Azaransky writes: "The intellectual traditions of Europe created 'categories, concepts, and genealogies' of political modernity including, but not limited to, social justice, citizenship, democracy, political sovereignty, scientific rationality, the public sphere, human rights and equality before the law." Sarah Azaransky, "Impossible, Inadequate, and Indispensable: What North American Christian Social Ethics Can Learn from Postcolonial Theory," *Journal of the Society of Christian Ethics* 37, no. 1 (2017): 49. See also Benjamin Isakhan, "Eurocentrism and the History of Democracy," *Politische Vierteljahresschrift* 51, 56–70.

37. Politics, on the other hand, is "an extremely determined activity antagonistic to policing: whatever breaks with the tangible configuration whereby parties and parts or lack of them are defined by a presupposition that, by definition, has no place in that con-

figuration—that of the part of those who have no part." Jacques Rancière, *Disagreement: Politics and Philosophy*, translated by Julie Rose (Minneapolis: University of Minnesota Press, 1999), 29–30.

38. Charles. E. Scott, "The Betrayal of Democratic Space," *Journal of Speculative Philosophy* 22, no. 4 (2008): 304. See also Jean Luc-Nancy, *The Experience of Freedom* (Stanford: Stanford University Press, 1993), xx.

39. See Baldwin and Dekar, "*In an Inescapable Network of Mutuality*," 9. Also quoted in Fluker, *Ground Has Shifted*, 151.

40. Martin Luther King Jr., *Trumpet of Conscience*, 32–33.

41. Martin Luther King Jr., *Testament of Hope*, 290.

42. W. E. B. Du Bois, *The Souls of Black Folk* (repr., New York: Millennium Publications, 2014), 5.

43. Peter J. Paris, *The Social Teaching of the Black Churches* (Minneapolis: Fortress Press, 2014, 1985), 27–56; and Fluker, *Ground Has Shifted*, 81.

44. Fluker, *Ground Has Shifted*, 154.

45. Ibid., 67–76.

46. See also Walter Earl Fluker, "Strategies and Resources for Ethical Leadership Education in the Twenty-First Century," in *Educating Ethical Leaders for the Twenty-First Century* (Eugene, Ore.: Cascade Books, 2013).

47. Don Edward Beck and Christopher C. Cowan, *Spiral Dynamics: Mastering Values, Leadership, and Change* (Malden, Mass.: Blackwell, 2006). See also Margaret J. Wheatley, *Leadership and the New Science: Discovering Order in a Chaotic World*, 3rd ed. (San Francisco: Berrett-Koehler, 2006).

48. According to Keri Day, "Assemblage theory rather than intersectionality is better poised to speak of *love* in political terms as an affective politics, which challenges neoliberal forms of protective disgust based on fear and hatred of difference." Day, *Religious Resistance*, 17. Day employs queer theorist Jasbir Puar's theory of assemblage and argues that Puar's theory "offers a groundbreaking analysis on the limits of intersectionality and how a 'theory of assemblage' might help ground an articulation of affective political communities. For Puar, a theory of assemblage suggests a different set of metaphors for identities within the social world such as mosaics, patchwork, heterogeneity, fluidity, and temporary configurations. Within this theory, there is not a fixed, stable ontology for the social world and its multiplicity of identities (as theories of intersectionality assume). Rather, identities (such as race, class, sexuality, gender) are complex, fluid configurations that can properly be characterized as discursive practices and expressions, which means that identities are social constructions generated by material and linguistic conditions rather than ontological assertions." Fluker, *Ground Has Shifted*, 260–61n57.

49. See J. D. Vance, *Hillbilly Elegy: A Memoir of a Family and Culture in Crisis* (New York: Harper and Row Paperbacks, 2018).

50. "How Groups Voted 2016," Roper Center, Cornell University, https://ropercenter .cornell.edu/polls/us-elections/how-groups-voted/groups-voted-2016.

51. Jeffrey C. Goldfarb, *Civility and Subversion* (New York: Cambridge University Press, 1998), 1.

52. Stephen L. Carter, *Civility: Manners, Morals and the Etiquette of Democracy* (New York: Basic Books, 1998), 29.

53. Fluker, *Ethical Leadership*, 88.

54. Martin Luther King Jr., "The Negro Is Your Brother" (aka "Letter from Birmingham

Jail"), *Atlantic Monthly*, August 1963, 78–88, https://www.theatlantic.com/magazine/archive/2018/02/letter-from-birmingham-jail/552461.

55. James H. Cone, *Martin and Malcolm and America: A Dream or a Nightmare* (Maryknoll, N.Y.: Orbis Books, 1991), 138.

56. "March for Our Lives Protests Planned for 800 Places across the World," *Guardian*, March 24, 2018; and Ishaan Tharoor, "Black Lives Matter Is a Global Cause," *Washington Post*, July 12, 2018.

57. Martin Luther King Jr., "A Christmas Sermon on Peace," in *Testament of Hope*, 257.

58. Martin Luther King Jr., "I See the Promised Land," 280.

59. See Vinay Lal, "Pietermaritzburg: The Beginning of Gandhi's Odyssey," https://web.archive.org/web/20160307131455/http://www.sscnet.ucla.edu/southasia/History/Gandhi/Pieter.html.

60. See Fluker, *Ethical Leadership*, 132–33.

CHAPTER 7
THE RISING SIGNIFICANCE OF CLASS
THE HAVES AND THE HAVE-NOTS
IN THE WORLD HOUSE

NIMI WARIBOKO

So it is obvious that if man is to redeem his spiritual and moral
"lag" he must go all out to bridge the social and economic gulf
between the "haves" and the "have nots" of the world.
MARTIN LUTHER KING JR., "Nobel Lecture"

A growing divide between the haves and the have-nots has left increasing
numbers in the Third World in dire poverty, living on less than a dollar a day.
JOSEPH E. STIGLITZ, *Globalization and Its Discontents*

Martin Luther King Jr.'s thought is often portrayed as limited to African American civil rights and nonviolence as a political strategy. To the contrary, he was also concerned with eradicating poverty and economic injustice not only in the United States but also all over the world.[1] "I never intend to adjust myself to the inequalities of an economic system which takes necessities from the masses to give luxuries to the classes," King said.[2] His metaphor of the "world house" in his writings captures his interest in economic freedom, and in eliminating economic unfreedom worldwide. The term "world house," interpreted as meaning the planetary household of God or the universal "site of human livelihood," speaks not only to the technical, neoclassical economic sense of the global economy as a configuration of households but also to the social-ethical sense of all the living relationships of human beings on earth. More importantly, "world house" denotes the world economy theologically conceived as the household of all God's children that mediates both their existence and their flourishing.[3]

The world house for King is arguably the *oikonomia tou theou* (economy of God), which is a community life and livelihood founded on mutuality and sharing, on the principle of providing for the flourishing of all humans. This kind of community and its basic principle is the *home base* of humans' sociopolitical existence and the ontological foundation of King's political and economic thought. "Home base" is also an evocative metonym for the axiom of equality that guides this thought. Deviations from this base amount to homelessness, which King describes in many ways and posits as the apt characterization of both American and global economic life. For instance, one of the ways King showed America's departure from the home of justice, equality, and care for all its citizens was by pointing, in his 1963 "I Have a Dream" speech, to the domestic exile of blacks as a manifestation of racial injustice: "Five score years ago, a great American, in whose symbolic shadow we stand today, signed the Emancipation Proclamation. This momentous decree came as a great beacon light of hope to millions of Negro slaves who had been seared in the flames of withering injustice. . . . One hundred years later, the Negro is still languished in the corners of American society and finds himself in exile in his own land."[4] Instead of experiencing America as a sweet home, a place governed by the axiom of equality, blacks encountered hell, a space where they were seared in the consuming fires of inequality.

King's phrase "inescapable network of mutuality" and his appeals to the rights of blacks and colored and poor people all over the world have as their presupposition a community or a common household.[5] His critique of U.S. society—a critique that always correlates America's socioeconomic problems to the liberal ideals of equality and justice and those of the Christian faith—points his audience to the brokenness of the nation's community and attenuation of commonly shared meanings. King's notion of the *beloved community* is both a call to and transformation of the primordial understanding of the integrity, mutuality, and siblinghood of God's *oikos*. These three moments or movements (primordial God's household; broken community; world house—beloved community; home to homelessness—uprootedness to home as a covenantal bond; creation, reconciliation, redemption) constitute the deep structure of the philosophy that undergirds King's economic ethics and political struggles. Thus, for King, the task of political praxis, liberatory thought, and all struggles for economic justice is to return contemporary human societies (or systems) to the home base—that is, to equality of access to human flourishing and ennobling livelihood, to the ethical commitment to God's household, the world house.[6]

King envisions this world house as a site of flourishing livelihood. It is created and sustained by one mutually habitable home—mutually interdependent, diverse humanity working together and fervently committed to peace, nonviolence, political and economic justice, equality of opportunity, and equal access of all persons to power and resources. For King, the world house is not only a dream of how human beings ought to live together and a praxis to be enacted and relentlessly performed, but it also acts as God's agent to democratize access to livelihood. The world house is a prophetic vision rooted in God as the power of being and in nonviolence as a way of life to transform the nightmarish world of discrimination, injustice, and poverty into that of a peaceful and prosperous household of God.

King's notion of home as encapsulated in the vibrant metaphor of the world house captures what economic theologian M. Douglas Meeks considers as the basic essence of Christian economic thought: access to the resources of life and God's righteousness in the context of universal, inclusive household. As Meeks puts it:

> To receive God's justice is to receive access to home. What is home? In Robert Frost's poem "The Death of the Hired Man," home is defined as "the place where, when you have to go there, they have to take you in." Poetic descriptions of "home" would suggest these characteristics. Home is where everyone knows your name. Home is where you can always count on being confronted, forgiven, loved, and cared for. Home is where there is always a place for you at the table. And finally, home is where you can count on sharing what is on the table. . . .
>
> To be part of a home or a household is to have access to life. The heart of justice is participation in God's economy or God's household. Unless the power of God's love creates household, justice will disintegrate into meaninglessness.[7]

This notion of a peaceful, friendly home, which served King as a tool for theological-ethical analysis and as a hermeneutic resource, will frame the logic and dynamics of the discourse in this chapter. This said, let me offer a quick summary of the architecture of the arguments ahead, demonstrating what corrections I intend to offer to the reception of King's ideas in economic ethics and how to extend the implications of King's legacy to poverty and economic injustice in the world today. King is known by almost every person in America to have fought against racial segregation. But what is not so widely known about him is that he expanded his campaign to encompass poverty and militarism (state violence and war). His antipoverty and antiwar struggles did not arise outside of racial segregation but were fundamental expressions of the axiom of equality that guided his whole thought and praxis. He saw racial siblinghood and work against poverty and war as integral in achieving concrete equality that could sustain a healthy global social fabric. Today, more than when King lived, rising income inequality and widening gaps between the rich and the poor pose enormous threats to the social fabric and the human dignity of all God's children. This chapter explores the rising significance of classism in the normal functioning of the global economy and how a pernicious logic, the axiom of inequality, has shaped and informed the global and national distribution of basic resources for human flourishing. It ends with suggestions on how King's world house vision, rooted as it is in the healthy axiom of equality, might help countries to create or undergird an inclusive and embracing economic community.

To unpack all this, I have divided this chapter into four sections: (1) King's philosophical conceptualization of home as a point of departure for the examination of racial discrimination, income inequality, and poverty; (2) homelessness as economic dislocation, showing how crippling inequality, poverty, racism, and militarism drive persons out of the home—the beloved community—as King defines it; (3) the vision of the world house, inclusive home for all God's children, to address homelessness and broken communities, and (4) concluding remarks.

Let me add that even as I attempt to explore the global implications of King's thought and legacy, I am careful to ensure that the tenor of my analysis, the philosophical perspective that undergirds it, and its overall ethos are rooted in and nourished by the African American tradition that provided the most powerful context for King's ideas. I have tried to immerse myself in the thought-world of King and African Americans in the 1950s and 1960s in order to craft an endogenous theoretical framework or to construct indigenous philosophical principles characteristic of their own most widespread interpretative lens. In this kind of exercise, one hopes to develop a philosophical framework that is not only a product of the black experience of the past but also robust enough for today's blacks to recognize themselves—and their experiences—in it. It is also my hope that if this framework (the imagery of home, homelessness, pluralistic beloved home) is able to encapsulate the important social dimensions of blacks as an oppressed group, it might also provide a powerful lens for economically oppressed, marginalized groups and mistreated classes around the world to interpret their own experiences and stories.

Thus, a particular-universal sensibility guides my economic-ethical interpretation of King's legacy and its import for today's world economic situation. I believe that any serious discussion of the implications of King's legacy in the twenty-first century must strive to have both a domestic and a worldwide focus. As Thomas F. Jackson argues, for King, "the domestic struggle against poverty and racism was part of a worldwide human rights movement" and a form of participation in "all out world war on poverty."[8] The *glocal*, tripartite framework I am developing in this chapter, will have done its job well if it helps some of those trapped in the deathly nightmare of poverty and oppression to acquire new metaphors to plait their stories or analyze their conditions and to dream of a sweet place and to envision a meaningful future of freedom, justice, and beloved community.

King's Philosophical Conceptualization of Home

Let us begin with one of King's mature articulations of his philosophical outlook as conveyed in a prophetic vision titled, "The World House," a chapter in his book *Where Do We Go from Here: Chaos or Community?* He wrote:

> However deeply American Negroes are caught in the struggle to be at last at home in our homeland of the United States, we cannot ignore the larger world house in which we are also dwellers. Equality with whites will not solve the problems of either whites or Negroes if it means equality in a world society stricken by poverty and in a universe doomed to extinction by war. All inhabitants of the globe are now neighbors.[9]

This passage captures two dimensions of King's thought that are of paramount importance for our limited purpose in this chapter. He succinctly sets forth his deep conviction about the connection between the domestic struggle and worldwide human rights, but he also clearly links the theme of an African American sense of homelessness and his notion of the world house. The theme of homelessness is more clearly spelled out in an address King gave to an Operation Breadbasket gathering in Chicago in 1967:

> On the Statue of Liberty we read that America is the mother of exiles, but it does not take us long to realize that America has been the mother of its white exiles from Europe. She has not evinced the same maternal care and concern for her black exiles who were brought to this country in chains from Africa, and it is no wonder that our slave-worn parents could think about it and they could start singing in a beautiful soul song, in a beautiful sorrow song—"Sometimes I feel like a motherless child." It was this sense of estrangement and rejection that caused our forebears to use such a metaphor.[10]

In prioritizing home—or what we may call *ontological homeness*—as the philosophical foundation for social-ethical analysis, King situated himself in an enduring everyday black philosophical-theological tradition.

One word to express the plight of African Americans is "homelessness," with its sense of uprootedness. America has never made African Americans, torn from their homeland, feel at home. Whites never wanted them to feel at home and did not consider them as sisters and brothers. Consequently, part of African Americans' struggle—from the era of chattel slavery to the civil rights movement and sadly even today—has been to make America home, to be integrated into a home they have built with whites, Native Americans, Asians, and other groups.

Malcolm X captured well this sense of homelessness of a whole race in the United States when he, in language not typical of King, told an audience in Cleveland in 1964: "No, I'm not an American. I'm one of the 22 million black people who are victims of Americanism. One of the . . . victims of democracy, nothing but disguised hypocrisy. So, I'm not standing here speaking to you as an American, or a patriot, or a flag-saluter, or a flag-waver—no, not I! I'm speaking as a victim of this American system. And I see America through the eyes of the victim. I don't see any American dream; I see an American nightmare!"[11]

The philosopher-mystic Howard Thurman, who greatly influenced King, has the theme of homelessness running through his major works. You encounter it in his relentless commentaries on the death of communities, the absence of a sense of belonging in one's own country because of segregation, and the socially imposed feeling that blacks do not count as human beings worthy of dignity.[12] Thurman writes: "Every man lives under the necessity for being at home in his own house, as it were. He must not seem to himself to be alien to himself. This is the thing that happened when other human beings relate to him as if he were not a human being or less than a human being."[13] White racism, he argues, treats blacks as people that do not count or do not belong in America. In *Jesus and the Disinherited*, he writes: "There are few things more devastating than to have it burned into you that you do not count and that no provisions are made for the literal protection of your person." When this ground of personal dignity is denied blacks they cannot feel that they belong to the United States or get the collective confirmation of their roots in it.[14] Instead of getting confirmation, African Americans have been looked at in contempt. Is the torture or trauma of "double consciousness" as depicted by W. E. B. Du Bois not somewhat connected to the tragic devastations of homelessness? In a voice filled with anguish and lament, Du Bois asks, in *The Souls of Black Folk* (1903): "Why did God make me an outcast and a stranger in mine own house?"[15]

Drawing from the "Negro spirituals," Peter Paris, the eminent African American social ethicist, also speaks of the black condition as a matter of loss of home, loneliness, forsakenness, and the like. In his 2005 essay, "When Feeling Like a Motherless Child," he argues that nothing can surpass this sense of homelessness or loneliness than the metaphor of the motherless child:

Few can imagine the pain and suffering of a people who were afflicted and abused in every conceivable way. Abducted from a continent where their dignity had been ascribed in accordance with their family's status and forcibly brought to a land where they were afforded no dignity whatsoever, their loneliness was dreadful. In fact, that dread was expressed nowhere more aptly than in the words, "Sometimes I Feel Like a Motherless Child, a Long Ways from Home." The familiar imagery of *mother* and *home* are altogether appropriate when speaking about the African experience because the family constituted then and now the paramount social reality. In fact, none would dispute that the family is a necessary condition for the development of personhood. Thus, to "feel like a motherless child" is virtually unimaginable to African peoples, because every woman is actually called "mother" by everyone, and similarly every older man is called "father." Thus, no place is safer and more secure for African children than the African village. For an African to "feel like a motherless child" symbolizes the experience of radical alienation that destroys both persons and the communities to which they belong.[16]

The sense of homelessness conveyed by the spirituals not only captured the dreadful plight of blacks and the tradition of protest and hope but also demonstrated something about the philosophical point of departure for the social and ethical analyses of their human condition in America. Many African American ethicists, theologians, and philosophers have been deeply affected by these salient dimensions of the spirituals. Take, for instance, the scholarship of Paris. His essays exude the rueful lamentation of a motherless child mingled with the hope of escape from the misery of alienation and degradation—escape to heaven.[17] Like the old spirituals, Paris's ethical analyses are conversations with America about blacks' experience of pain and suffering, struggle and striving, and the unity of protest and hope in their religious thought—all carried out in plaintive tones and sad rhythms.[18] With the simplicity of his prose, precision and clarity of thought, and the evocative power of his analytical descriptions, his essays have a mournful beauty to them.

James H. Cone, the brilliant father of black theology, reinforces this point in his book *The Spirituals and the Blues*, that the theme of homelessness is a red thread that runs through the stories of African Americans. The inner logic or pathos of the spirituals convey something about the tripartite framework I identified above as the dynamic and organizing principle of King's thought. Drawing from his analysis of the spirituals, Cone writes: "The actual physical brutalities of slavery were minor in comparison to the loss of the community. That was why most of the slave songs focused on 'going home.' Home was an affirmation of the need for community. It was the place where mother, father, sister, and brother had gone. . . . But most of all, they wanted to be reunited with their families which had been broken and scattered in the slave marts."[19]

Anytime I read about the brutal, macabre experience of enslaved Africans, my blood boils and I feel the sensation of a creepy, uncanny encounter with an unnameable evil force. Historian of religion Charles H. Long says that the land of America feels strange to him. In the early 1960s, the African American scholar met with the great theologian Karl Barth at the University of Chicago and asked him: "How do you like this strange place called the United States?" We do not have the exact response of Barth to Long's question. We only have Barth's acknowledgement of it in his American edition of *Evangelical Theology: An Introduction*: "This is what I was asked by a dusky theological colleague (not a Roman Catholic this time, but a literally black colleague) with a subtle smile." Long, in an essay published in 1969, made the following comment in response to Barth's published words, and it further attests to the feeling of homelessness that haunts and informs the scholarship of African American theologians and ethicists, including Martin Luther King Jr.: "In putting this question to [Barth] I was at the same time echoing for myself the constant enigma of my native land—the fact that my native land has always been for me a strange place. Barth's description of me as a 'dusky theological colleague . . . a literally black colleague' is an important locus of this strangeness."[20]

My colleague at Boston University, Walter Earl Fluker, the Martin Luther King Professor of Ethical Leadership and editor of the Howard Thurman Papers Project, has drawn heavily from the tropes of home and homelessness to inform his analysis of the black church in his 2016 book, *The Ground Has Shifted*. Fluker, an astute thinker, in an original contribution that draws from the work of Toni Morrison, combines the two tropes with those of diaspora and exile to reconceptualize home. He posits home not as a destination but as quest for a sense of wholeness. "Home [is] not escape or inscape, but a yearning for freedom, sense of identity, and a place to stand in the *center of the world*."[21] Such a home, he argues, is best imagined as an exilic space, an existential/aesthetic condition antithetical to vibrant human flourishing, yet not without hope.[22] In another place, he writes:

> Privileging Exile provides a more excellent way, a more powerful space in which to locate the contemporary struggle of African American existence because it is a more accurate depiction of where we are: exiled from one another, from ourselves and even from the land of our birth—exiled in a space of death, a national imaginary that is dysfunctional for the overwhelming majority of black people

who exist not as citizens, but as resident aliens or worse. Exile also captures the yearning for home, which is where we must go and become in order to enter a different social and political purpose.[23]

This kind of conceptualization of the human condition of blacks is very evident in King's thought. Home is a symbol deployed to capture his fundamental idea of the oneness of humanity, the ontological unity of all peoples, and a vision of global communion. This symbol is often expressed in the language of mutuality and single fabric of existence. For instance, King writes:

> We are caught up in an inescapable network of mutuality; tied in a single garment of destiny. Whatever affects one directly, affects all indirectly. As long as there is poverty in this world, no man can be totally rich even if he has a billion dollars. As long as diseases are rampant and millions of people cannot expect to live more than twenty or thirty years, no man can be totally healthy, even if he just got a clean bill of health from the finest clinic in America. Strangely enough, I can never be what I ought to be until you are what you ought to be. You can never be what you ought to be until I am what I ought to be.[24]

A meaning of home comes through in this short passage. You are at home when you are accepted by others who are living in the same place with you as one of their own, and they care enough for your own flourishing. You are at home when you are allowed to partake of all society has to offer. Malcolm X once compared blacks being at home to that of being at the dinner table. "I am not going to sit at your table and watch you eat with nothing on my plate, and call myself a diner," he said. "Sitting at the table doesn't make you a diner, unless you eat some of what's on that plate." [25]

This notion of home as participation, as sitting at a common table, sharing nourishment, and flourishing together—at the level of a country or the entire world—translates into love and justice, two ideas that underpinned King's praxis. He conceptualized love as the "supreme unifying principle of life," vital for the beloved community, and justice as the removal of all obstacles that thwart fellowship and as the rebuilding of broken homes (communities) and the end of alienation.[26] Justice was also conceptualized as the vital force of life—an ontological power, if you will. King believed that racial and economic justice would someday become a reality "because the arc of the universe is long but bends toward justice."[27] No wonder, Cone argues: "There was a close interrelationship between love and justice in King's thinking: Love and its political expression, integration—occupied the center of his thinking, while justice—and its political expression, desegregation—became the precondition or the means of achieving love. But looking at the problem from another angle, King also advocated that love, expressed in nonviolent protest, was the only means of achieving justice, which he equated with desegregation."[28]

Love and justice are integral to King's understanding of the world house as a universal, inclusive, and embracing site for livelihood and human flourishing for all God's children, irrespective of their faith. The absence of this peaceful world house in his days must have deeply wounded his heart. One senses profound pain in his plaintive appeal for economic justice, for a caring home for poor people of the world: "Two-thirds of the peoples of the world go to bed hungry at night. They are undernourished, ill-housed and shabbily clad. Many of them have no houses or beds to sleep in. Their only beds are the sidewalks of the cities and the dusty roads of the villages."[29] The levels of poverty and economic injustice that so staggered King have not abated. In the United States and around the world too many people still experience homelessness in the sense of being cut off from a caring home and suffering severe economic deprivations. King wonders (as do I): "Why should there be hunger and privation in any land, in any city, at any table when man has the resources and scientific know-how to provide all mankind with the basic necessities of life?[30] As King grappled with questions like this he increasingly rejected any notion of capitalism as functional in the world house. This questioning attitude was one of the factors that led him to expand his vision of the civil rights movement. As Kenneth L. Smith, one of his professors during his years at Crozer Theological Seminary, put it: "As King came to a deeper understanding of the relation between racial oppression, class exploitation, and militarism, he moved beyond civil rights for blacks to the need for basic structural changes within the capitalistic system: the nationalization of basic industries, massive federal expenditures to revive center cities and to provide jobs for ghetto residents, and a guaranteed annual income for every adult citizen of the U.S."[31]

Homelessness as Economic Dislocations

In her book *The New Jim Crow* (2010), Michelle Alexander documents the growing economic inequality between blacks and whites in the United States, a trend sustained and exacerbated by the mass incarceration of African Americans. The income and wealth inequality so evident today, according to Alexander, is partly explainable by the collapse of inner-city economies:

> During the late 1970s, jobs had suddenly disappeared from urban areas across America, and unemployment rates had skyrocketed. In 1954, black and white

youth unemployment rates in America were equal, with blacks actually having a slightly higher rate of employment in the age group sixteen to nineteen. By 1984, however, the black unemployment rate had nearly quadrupled, while the white rate had increased only marginally. This was not due to a major change in black values or black culture; this dramatic shift was the result of deindustrialization, globalization, and technological advancement. Urban factories shut down as our nation transitioned to a service economy. Suddenly African Americans were trapped in jobless ghettos, desperate for work.[32]

The collapse of the job opportunities came at a time when the country was also pushing to build more prisons as racial minorities were targeted by national drug policy, "tough on crime policies," and the reduction of funding for public housing. Decades after the death of King, blacks and other minorities are experiencing brutal levels of income inequality buttressed by mass incarceration. Millions of African Americans are not really *at home* in America; they are warehoused, segregated, or confined to a caste system, a veritable symbol of economic inequality. "The fact that some African Americans have experienced great success in recent years does not mean that something akin to a caste system no longer exists," Alexander writes. "No caste system in the United States has ever governed all black people; there have always been 'free blacks' and black success stories, even during slavery and Jim Crow."[33]

The current rising levels of income inequality offer us vivid pictures of economic homelessness, portraying millions of poor Americans who are not at home in their own country. This inequality mirrors the widening gap between the rich and the poor all over the world. This gap between the haves and the have-nots signifies multiple forms of uprootedness, varied types of existential disconnection. Owing to space constraints, I will limit the discussion to only three of them: (1) uprootedness of active, relational presence of human beings with one another (inequality); (2) uprootedness of blacks and other minorities from the core dynamics of human flourishing (displacement from enjoying the fruits of American democracy and prosperity); and (3) uprootedness from space (differentials in availability of opportunities in different neighborhoods).

The United States is deeply divided economically. There is a wide racial divide in this economic disparity, and a gender gap in pay hits women of color with a double whammy. One crucial effect of racism is that black lives are valued less than those of whites, creating what scholar Eddie Glaude calls the "value gap."[34] Finally, we have the differential spatiality of life opportunities. Poverty and income inequality are often linked to geographical spaces. Persons living in different zip codes have differing opportunities available to them to actualize their potential and flourish. Below I will focus on the uprootedness of blacks in America's economic home and explore the deep connections between poverty and race. This focus will allow me to shed ample light on the other two types of uprootedness. The U.S. economy is profoundly racialized, with socio-economic forces undergirding and causing income inequality and differentials in capability to flourish.

The Color Gap: Poverty and Racialization

The American economy is split. There is a sharp division between the 1 percent and the rest of society. The economy is split by racism. There is division between blacks and whites, and a division between whites and nonwhites as a whole. Nobel Prize–winning economist Joseph Stiglitz declares: "We do have a divided society . . . America has been growing apart, at an increasingly rapid rate." Stiglitz laments that the impact of an increasingly divided society reaches beyond what the stark data portray. It shows up "in health, education, and crime—indeed in every metric of performance. While inequalities in parental income and education translate directly into inequalities of educational opportunity, inequalities of opportunity begin even before school—in the conditions that poor people face immediately before and after birth, differences in nutrition and the exposure to environmental pollutants that can have lifelong effects. So difficult is it for those born into poverty to escape that economists refer to the situation as a 'poverty trap.'"[35]

The American poverty trap has a color line. Minorities of color in general live below the standard of well-being of the white majority. Poverty is defined or marked by racism as much as anything else. Indeed, the attention of many scholars is increasingly drawn to the theme of "poverty and racialization of the economy" in their examination of economic inequality.

What is racialization? My hope is that we are not too quick to reduce or constrict the meaning of the term. How does it cause poverty in the United States? I will suggest five ways. First, "racialization of the economy" refers to the structural inequalities that exist in the United States and are keyed to, marked by, and driven by race or skin-color discrimination. Second, the term "racialization of the economy" points to the increasing vulnerability of citizens of color to early death and shorter than average life expectancy. Third, racialization of the economy is the near monopoly of benefits, positions, and economic opportunities in the United States by whites. Fourth, racialization of the economy is exclusion of minorities from the necessary economic, social, and public resources—to a degree that diminishes and destroys their capacity to actualize their God-given potential. Finally, racialization of the economy is a form of *police logic* of the American Empire, policing that renders certain racial groups permanently *part of no part* (in the conception of French philosopher Jacques Rancière): part of the demographic, economy, and polity that does not count.

The combined result of the logics and dynamics of these five forms of racialization is the absolute and relative poverty of minority groups. This twinning of poverty and racialization is not accidental. Poverty and racism define the United States as much as wealth and military power do. Picture the racialization of the U.S. economy as the five-pointed stars on the U.S. flag, with each point oozing poverty into the social fabric of black America. The whole assemblage of stars and stripes is set in order and driven by what perspicacious theologian Emilie Townes calls "fantastic hegemonic imagination."[36] There is an invidious imagination that holds the systemic, structural evil of racialized poverty firmly in place. It politicizes economic statistics to secure subordination, economic impoverishment, and immiseration of minority groups. In short, poverty as a product of racism is a cultural production. There is still a fantastic manipulative imagination aided by trickster Jacob's poplar rod of stripes in the land of the Puritans' New Israel of stars and stripes that make one partner rich at the expense of the other.

What are the five points of each star that drip poison, poverty, and human degradation and strangle hope? What are these points that kill dreams and forestall human flourishing? First, there is the spatial production of poverty—there is a geographical dynamic to poverty in the United States. Minorities and people of color often live in places where there are few opportunities for economic improvement. These zones are inimical to the accumulation of wealth because of policies such as redlining in the past. As sociologists Mel Oliver and Tom Shapiro stated in their book, *Black Wealth/White Wealth*: "Locked out of the greatest mass-opportunity for wealth accumulation in American history, African-Americans who desired and were able to afford home ownership found themselves consigned to central-city communities where their investments were affected by the 'self-fulfilling prophecies' of the FHA appraisers: cut off from sources of new investments . . . their homes and communities deteriorated and lost value in comparison to those homes and communities that the FHA appraisers deemed desirable."[37]

We often put more emphasis on income inequality when addressing economic injustice. It is time to put the accent on spatial inequality. Economists often consider spaces as "'containers for data' rather than a context for inequality and exploitation to play out," as British geographer Gareth Jones writes. There is pervasive inattentiveness to space when theologians or philosophers discuss economic inequality. As Jones argues, even eminent economists pay little or no attention to spatial political economy, neglecting geographical mobility or geographies of capital and its impact on nations and spaces: "The economic geography of global capitalism for the past forty years shows that capital will seek out a spatial fix to the crises of under/over accumulation. Fundamental to the power of capital, therefore, is its geographical mobility, to shape-shift from being something fixed to being a flow. The apotheosis of this transformation is finance capital."[38] Black neighborhoods in urban centers and cities have seen devastating declines, and the economic well-being of their residents has been reduced as unfettered capital and technological innovations, in their quasi-random, wind-like movements, abandoned them as spaces of surplus populations not immediately relevant to profit making. According to Martha Biondi, author of *To Stand and Fight: The Struggle for Civil Rights in Postwar New York City*, many black labor leaders of the 1960s and 1970s "called plant relocation and the deindustrialization of the urban core an attack on the gains of Black migrant workers" made by black workers after World War II.[39]

American cities are not designed to disperse economic activities that generate income and provide residents, especially those in poor neighborhoods, the wherewithal to enjoy flourishing lives. Rising inequality in the United States and economic disparities between racial groups cannot be divorced from the form and intensity of the ongoing major social cleavages in the fabric of cities. These cleavages too are related to spatial demographics. Widening economic disparity between rich and poor neighborhoods means decreasing integrity of the city and weakened mutuality of its parts; rich neighborhoods are not present and accountable to the poor ones as they are in a rightly ordered fellowship.[40]

Likewise, of course, capitalism is not designed to equally disperse the means for human flourishing. King understood this very well, and he began shifting the focus of the civil rights movement to his Poor People's Campaign to demand economic reforms in the interest of poor and working-class people of all colors. King considered the persistence of economic inequality an affront to human rights, and he demanded a radical reconstruction of the economy for the benefit of the have-nots. During his visit to Sweden in December 1964, en route to receive the Nobel Peace Prize, he stated: "We feel that we have much to learn from Sweden's democratic socialist traditions and especially from the manner in which you have overcome so many of the problems of poverty, housing, unemployment, and medical care for your people—problems that still plague far more affluent and powerful nations."[41] More will be said later in this chapter about the international implications of King's democratic socialist ideas and how they might be better understood in a global context today.

The second point of the star of empire relates to economic inequality. Thomas Piketty and Joseph Stiglitz in recent books have shown alarming growth rates of income inequality in the United States.[42] For black folks and other people of color, the condition is actually worse than is portrayed in their studies. The household income of blacks is far lower on the average than that of whites. The unemployment rates among minorities are higher than that of whites.

Piketty says that income inequality will worsen in the future because the rate of return of capital of the richest 1 percent of the American society is growing faster than the economy. He describes this as $r > g$ [where r is the rate of return on capital, and g is the growth rate of the economy], which points to a process (force) of divergence in the U.S. economy of the twenty-first century.

> When the rate of return on capital significantly exceeds the growth rate of the economy (as it did through much of history until the nineteenth century and as is likely to be the case again in the twenty-first century), then it logically follows that inherited wealth grows faster than output and income. People with inherited wealth need save only a portion of their income from capital to see that capital grow more quickly than the economy as a whole. Under such conditions, it is inevitable that inherited wealth will dominate wealth amassed from a lifetime's labor by a wide margin, and the concentration of capital will attain extremely high levels—levels potentially incompatible with meritocratic values and principles of social justice fundamental to modern democratic societies.[43]

According to Piketty, we are back in the days of "patrimonial capitalism," in which wealth is concentrated at the top and kept there by inheritance.[44] Minorities have less inherited capital than whites and generally do not own the capital whose rate of growth exceeds the rate of growth of the economy. Let me relate this to the spatial demographics and racism that I highlighted above. Sociologist Elizabeth Jacobs, in her criticism of Piketty's neglect of politics and racism in his book, makes the connection clear. She writes: "Because whites are more able to give inheritances or family assistance for down payments, due to historical wealth accumulation, white families buy homes and start accumulating capital on average eight years earlier than similarly situated black families. And because whites are more able to give financial assistance, larger up-front payments typically lower interest rates and lending costs for white families as compared with blacks. Much of this inequality in capital accumulation can be traced back to an early policy decision, which shaped access to capital in important ways."[45] Given this historical burden and continuing racial discrimination, blacks are not watching the gyrations of Piketty's now famous formula $r > g$; instead $r > g$ is watching them, mocking their absence from the orgies of accumulation and exploitation. This reminds me of what Malcolm X said about Plymouth Rock, upon which the first pilgrims landed when they arrived in America: "Our forefathers weren't the pilgrims. We didn't land on Plymouth Rock; the rock was landed on us."[46] Whites are today landing and dancing on Piketty's rock of wealth; tomorrow Piketty's rock will land on blacks. And the day after tomorrow, rocks from the hands of poor whites, blacks, Asians, and Hispanics, striking for equality and social justice, will fly on the streets of America. Piketty states over and over again that the increasing divergence between the rate of return on capital and the rate of growth of the economy is threatening to the values of social justice in democratic societies: "The inequality $r > g$ implies that wealth accumulated in the past grows more rapidly than output and wages. . . . Once constituted, capital reproduces itself faster than output increases. The past devours the future. The consequences for long-term dynamics of wealth distribution are potentially terrifying, especially when one adds that the return on capital varies directly with the size of the initial stake and that the divergence in the wealth distribution is occurring on a global scale."[47]

The third point of the star that drips its poison into black lives is a failing school system. Blacks, other minorities, and poor children in the United States are not given the kind of education that will prepare them for the economy of tomorrow. Add to this the digital divide between minorities and whites, and between the rich and the poor, and you catch a glimpse of the children of the barely breathing members of the permanent underclass being suffocated. All this means that the cruel income and wealth gap between whites and blacks—a veritable indicator of the racialization of the economy—will only widen in the future.

The fourth poisonous point of the five-pointed star is the prison-industrial complex. We have a criminal (law-and-order) system that seems to target minorities: to kill them on the street, judicially execute them, and imprison them en masse as a way of "keeping the streets safe"—safe, that is, for the rich class and the richest of the rich, capitalists.[48]

Finally, attention should be directed to the differential in the human development index of the various racial groups in this country. The HDI measures critical indicators of human welfare such as life expectancy and human capital. There is a huge discrepancy in these between whites and blacks and between the rich and the poor. The average 2015 HDI value (scaled from 0–10) for the United States was 5.03. For racial groups: Whites: 5.43; Latinos: 4.05; African Americans: 3.81; Asians: 7.21.[49] The United Nations *Human Development Report* for 2016 states:

African Americans' life expectancy is shorter than that of other ethnic and racial groups in the United States. African Americans also trail Whites and Asian
Americans in education and wages: Whites earn 27 percent more on average. In
some metropolitan areas the disparity is particularly striking. The life expectancy
of African Americans in Baltimore, Chicago, Detroit, Pittsburgh, St. Petersburg
and Tampa is now close to the national average in the late 1970s. The reasons are
complex but linked to a long history of legal and social discrimination.

Policies that improve educational achievement can expand opportunities for
African Americans and other racial and ethnic minorities in work and other areas. Equalizing educational achievement could reduce disparities in employment between African Americans and Whites by 53 percent, incarceration by 79
percent and health outcomes by 88 percent.

Differences in wages between African Americans and Whites are also related to discrimination in the job market. Discrimination accounts for an estimated one-third of wage disparities, all else (including education) being equal.
This indicates that policies are needed to ensure that skills and education are rewarded equally. Social pressures within the African American community can
limit choices and later life chances among adolescents. Being labelled as "acting White"—whereby high-achieving African American students are shunned in
some contexts by their peers for doing well academically—can discourage good
performance in school. Reducing the stigmatization of academic achievement
among African American youth could be a step towards reducing inequalities in
human development outcomes.[50]

The preceding analyses go to the heart of the politics of inclusiveness and exclusion and the distribution of citizens to assigned places. African Americans have
been treated as a surplus, not as a plus, in the U.S. economy, polity, and society
as a whole. For African Americans, the United States is really not the site of the
logic of emancipatory democracy and the radical, universal equality of all citizens. Following French philosopher Jacques Rancière, we can easily surmise
that African Americans are in the part of no part in American society, the part
that belongs to the whole but does not count.[51] Rancière believes that every society is split between those who count and those who do not, the part of no part.
A fundamental antagonism exists between the parts of the community. The part
that does not count wants to undermine the order of distribution, while the part
that dominates aspires to maintain the way things are, to continue the consen-
sual oppressive practices that reject the political logic of egalitarianism. The
part that dominates insists on holding on to the logic of the police state. Is being
part of a society and not being counted not analogous to King's view of home-

lessness or domestic exile? Are not civil rights struggles and African Americans' demands for equality quintessential examples of King's ideal of egalitarianism?

King's vision of equality led him to embrace democratic socialism as the political system necessary for the flourishing of all Americans. For King, democratic socialism was the means most likely to lead to prosperity for all in the world house. He combined his call for "a Bill of Rights for the Disadvantaged," which would insure a livable income for all, with advocacy for a sort of Marshall Plan for the benefit of poor people around the world. The uplift, empowerment, and well-being of all who suffered under the yoke of capitalism were critical in his quest for universal human rights. The economic program for the world house, King argued, was to be built not only on economic opportunity and justice but also on a moral foundation for all of God's children. The program, which assumed that poverty, racism, and militarism were interconnected and equally problematic, required what King called "a revolution of values."[52] His democratic socialist vision extended beyond capitalism and communism. King declared: "Each represents a partial truth. Capitalism fails to see the truth in collectivism. Communism fails to see the truth in individualism. Capitalism fails to realize that life is social. Communism fails to realize that life is personal. The good and just society is neither the thesis of capitalism nor the antithesis of communism, but a socially conscious democracy which reconciles the truths of individualism and collectivism."[53]

The realization of King's vision would require a fundamental restructuring of the logic and dynamics of the economies of the entire Western world, especially the United States. As historian Gerald McKnight observes: "King was proposing nothing less than a radical transformation of the Civil Rights Movement into a populist crusade calling for redistribution of economic and political power. America's civil rights leader was now focusing on class issues and was planning to descend on Washington with an army of the poor to shake the foundations of the power structure and force the government to respond to the needs of the ignored underclass."[54] The current levels of inequality in the United States and the rest of the world demonstrate that King's call for a populist crusade for economic equity is still relevant. In fact, it is more relevant today than in his time. What is holding things back?

What are urgently needed are the forms of political organization and alliances that can support the struggle for economic equality. King was very clear on the connection between political power and economic reforms. He theorized a connection between economic reforms, an increase in political power, political participation by those targeted as beneficiaries of the reforms, and the formation of effective political alliances.[55] Today there is a massive failure in political praxis, and this partly accounts for the nonrealization of King's economic-political dreams. This is the same conclusion that Frank L. Morris reached in the 1980s when he examined the implementation of King's economic ideas in the United States. He stated: "The political record since 1968 is mixed. There have been no major breakthroughs in the way of developing independent black political organizations or the forging of more effective political alliances with poor whites, organized labor or other ethnic minorities and oppressed people."[56]

Indeed, Martin Luther King Jr.'s political philosophy and radical political praxis offer us a powerful lens with which to theorize the failure of political struggles for economic justice, as well as the conditions of inequality, injustice, racism, poverty, and militarism, and they also allow us to critique homelessness and governance by the *axiom of inequality* and to deconstruct the logic of the police state in America. I need to add that, unlike today's philosophers of deconstruction, King always endeavored to offer hope or constructive proposals for rebuilding, or for building the world house. He was the dreamer par excellence.

Wherever King rendered searing analyses of homelessness, broken communities, or the workings of hate and injustice in America, he also offered an invigorating hope, a powerful dream of a home that engendered love and justice. On August 28, 1963, at the March on Washington, he powerfully expressed this dream in these memorable words:

> I have a dream that one day this nation will rise up and live out the true meaning of its creed, "We hold these truths to be self-evident, that all men are created equal." I have a dream that one day . . . sons of former slaves and the sons of former slave owners will be able to sit down together at the table of brotherhood. . . . This is our hope. . . . With this faith we will be able to work together, to stand up for freedom together, knowing that we will be free one day. . . . This will be the day when all God's children will be able to sing with a new meaning, "My country 'tis of thee, sweet land of liberty, of thee I sing.[57]

The coming of the day of God's children is not conceptually bound to Americans alone. That concept embraces King's magnificent vision of a world house, the love ethic, and the transformation of values informing neoliberal economics. As he once noted: "A genuine revolution of values means in the final analysis that our loyalties must become ecumenical rather than sectional. Every nation must now develop an overriding loyalty to mankind as a whole in order to preserve the best in their individual societies. This call for world fellowship that lifts neighborly concern beyond one's tribe, race, class, and nation is in reality a call for an all-embracing and unconditional love for all men [and women]."[58]

Now, how might King's world house vision help countries create fairer economic policies that undergird peaceful communities?

World House and the Global Economy

Amid the drift of civilizations from home to homelessness, how should human beings learn to live together? King envisioned the world house as a possible ethical solution to the devastations caused by racism, poverty, and militarism. Drawing from Jesus's parable of the prodigal son, who left his loving father and wasted his inheritance, King compared the effect of the absence of a *homelike* global economy to the misadventures of the son. The son eventually "came into himself" when he returned to his father's house. Like the prodigal son, human beings can only come to themselves and build a just, peaceful, and prosperous community for all God's children when they make up their minds to return to their father's house, the home of siblinghood where everyone has dignity and worth. The world—especially the United States—has gone too far afield and needs to return home. "America has strayed to the far country of racism and militarism," King wrote. "This unnatural excursion has brought only confusion and bewilderment. . . . It is time for all people of conscience to call upon America to return to her true home of brotherhood and peaceful pursuits."[59]

The movement toward a world house is therefore a drive toward reunion, a return to the site of livelihood, security, equality, and justice for all inhabitants of a shared, common earth. King thought of the world house as a pluralistic, global commons with some modicum of a world government. "As we grow and come to see the oneness of mankind and the geographical oneness of the world, made possible by man's scientific and technological ingenuity," he wrote, "more and more we are going to have to try to see our oneness in terms of brotherhood."[60]

Though the focus of the notion of world house is global, it is also ultimately directed at individual self-realization. King is clear, however, that every effort should be undertaken to make sure that individual fulfillment occurs in the context of community, as an expression of the substance of justice, peacebuilding, and the actualization of human potentiality in ways consistent with human dignity and with the unity of the community. The world house is a continuous process of individual self-realization and movement toward increasing, uniting communion. The separation that arises by each individual dynamic actualization is overcome or limited by its realization within the whole society and by virtue of mutual participation in each other's lives.[61]

World house is a vision of economic justice and human flourishing founded in a real world characterized by wrongdoings and conflicts. Economic injustice deprives individuals of the creative freedom to actualize themselves within the communities in which they belong. A just order enables an individual to actualize one's potential—to be what one essentially is, and its absence is tantamount to the denial of human dignity and the destruction of one's humanity. The fact that one person can deprive another of the capabilities and conditions needed to actualize potential is not immutable. Such power differentials ought to be—and can be—rebalanced. Such restructuring is also necessary—and possible—globally.

One of the central problems of the international economic system, as I showed in my 2008 book, *God and Money: A Theology of Money in a Globalizing World*, is the imbalance of power between a few powerful nations and the rest of the world, especially those in Africa, Latin America, and South Asia.[62] Instead of enhancing relationality and conditions in which all might flourish, the international economic system gives poor nations short shrift. One might say, borrowing from Hobbes, that the life of poor nations is nasty, brutish, and short. This might even be an understatement. Instead of aiding life in developing nations, the international economic system often deals death to them. The system is not organized for them to flourish. The present sets of relations in the international economic system are not organized in such a way that will allow developing economies to act in the international public realm equally and thus to join others in the common pursuit of development and greatness. It appears that they are forever condemned to mere survival and subsistence. The system needs to be reshaped into a more democratic structure, one that is more supportive of life. The global monetary system should be used to create, enhance, and sustain relationships between persons and nations in the global community, rather than allowing it to steal, and to kill, and to destroy, as said of the thief in John 10:10. *God and Money*, highlighting the importance of healthy relations and sociality in economic interactions, points to an alternative to the current predatory global economic system that would take global human community seriously. A reimagined alternative (the "Earth-Dollar System") aims to enable individuals and nations to participate fully in the preservation and progress of life, and for local and global communities to operate through their own agencies and in cooperation with others.

The generative energy that will keep the world house functioning, whether at the level of the global financial system or the local level in each community, is the *eros* of participation. Participation is the glue that holds together the kind of relationships necessary for peacebuilding, nonviolence, networks of care, and justice. Participation is the antidote to alienation, disconnection, and apathy. In our efforts to promote the world house, we should emphasize the idea of people acting together, having the right and the duty to share in the common good, and being able to play active roles in their communities. This also makes a claim on society and decision makers to consult persons on policies, projects, and decisions that affect them and their communities. The source of this right for an individual to be an active agent and to be in solidarity with others in the process of seeking and ordering the common good is simply membership in the community.

Here I resort to Catholic social teachings as a source to clarify my understanding of the theology of participation.[63] Participation is an inviolable and inalienable right of every member of the community, which means that such a right cannot be taken or surrendered. It flows from the understanding that the human being is a *social* being and that participation is essential for one's self-realization and flourishing. A person self-realizes, or self actualizes, through acting together with others. Participation enables the individual to participate in the life of God, to join in God's creative and sanctifying activity over the earth and its inhabitants, and to aid in ordering the universe and the common good.

Insofar as human beings are essentially social, beings-in-communion, human dignity and participation are best addressed in social relationships in community. Everyone is required to participate in the production of social goods and the creation of the common good. And society ought to enable each and every person to acquire the capabilities (such as the skills and competencies persons need to become the agents of their own development) that will allow one to so participate. This means that caring for poor people and victims of violence in the world house is not just about meeting their needs but also giving them enough power to meet their own needs. In summary, at the societal level it involves two things: capabilities and power (ensuring a dynamic balance of power between classes).

Participation in the economy of one's community or country is the principle means of participation in all modern societies. Participation in the economy is also an excellent moral lens to examine and assess economic and social justice. According to the National Council of Catholic Bishops in 1986: "The ultimate injustice is for a person or group of persons to be treated or abandoned passively as if they were nonmembers of the human race. To treat people this way is effectively to say that they simply do not count as human beings."[64] The persons are both wronged and harmed by their exclusion from participation.

Participation and economic justice are not about equality of economic outcomes among all citizens. Economic justice is about arranging the basic structures of society to protect the poor, weak, and marginalized, and Martin Luther
King Jr. knew this. This commitment to restructuring entails three principles or
policy guidelines in the context of the capitalist economy. First, to safeguard human dignity and provide for the necessary minimum level of participation in
the life of community, we must establish a floor, a basis for human flourishing,
and regard it as an obligation society must honor. Second, in order to encourage risk taking and entrepreneurship necessary for economic development, we
have to create incentives to spur additional efforts and allow people to maxi-
mize their own outcomes. Finally, in maximizing one's outcome (or income),
the conditions of others should not be worsened by one's actions. There is a
prohibition against doing harm to others.

Building the World House: The Enduring Challenge

This chapter has treated Martin Luther King Jr.'s vision of the world house against
the background of economic injustice and the rising significance of income inequality and class. I have presented the world house as a set of goods that members of society have a right to enjoy. The absence of the drive toward the world
house and equality anywhere means that persons are having their moral status
and well-being diminished. Seeing and working toward the world house—and
thus to economic justice, participation, nonviolence, dignity, equality, and freedom—are an excellent way to move toward improving and restoring that degraded status and well-being. Proponents of the world house as a philosophical construct and a political strategy aspire to build an environment for all God's
children to be treated with respect and to create the conditions for possible actualization of human potential.

It is vitally important to add that the building of the world house is not only
about setting up structures and stabilizing situations that give life meaning and
purpose and allow it to flourish. It is also about disrupting, dislocating, and tear-
ing down structures of society that negate or thwart life. It is about persons—
including poor and rich, colored and whites—"discerning the body" in which
they are incorporated. "Discerning the body," as Saint Paul informs us in First
Corinthians, is about being sensitive to things that cause alienation, division,
and fractures in the social body; being alert to the sufferings of its weak, marginalized, and disinherited members; and being not simply compassionate but
also wise enough to care for the well-being of the whole body under the impact
of God's spirit.

This chapter's focus on King's metaphor of the world house and related metaphors of family, home, dinner table, and so on clearly demonstrates his abiding concern for the economy, the necessary resources for maintaining and enhancing a meaningful life. Such a metaphor has enabled us to connect his thought with that of many of his contemporaries as well as that of several economists and theological ethicists from our time, more than fifty years later.

I have also suggested some ways of increasing the participation of the poor in the economies of the countries in which they live. Yet I am troubled, as you too may be, by the nagging question of how we might effect a cure for the problem of economic inequality. How do we gain economic justice in the United States, a country that is so greatly divided over the role of government in creating jobs with a viable wage and providing good health care, education, and housing? In the virtually two-party U.S. political system, it seems members of one party believe that the government has such a role, while members of the other believe it does not. With similar numbers on either side, we have a stalemate. So how do the ethics of the matter just discussed get translated into effective action? We all need to engage in social activism and politics in our communities to address this. And we ought to keep in mind not the least of King's lessons: his words were always spoken or written in the context of action aimed at remedying problems he and other human beings faced.[65]

NOTES

The epigraphs are from Martin Luther King Jr., "Nobel Lecture," University of Oslo, Oslo, Norway, December 11, 1964, King Papers, Library and Archives of the Martin Luther King Jr. Center for Nonviolent Social Change, Atlanta; Joseph E. Stiglitz, *Globalization and Its Discontents* (New York: W. W. Norton, 2002), 5.

1. Martin Luther King, "The Social Organization of Nonviolence," in *A Testament of Hope: The Essential Writings and Speeches of Martin Luther King, Jr.* (New York: HarperCollins, 1986), 623–26.

2. Martin Luther King, "The Current Crisis in Race Relations," in *Testament of Hope*, 89.

3. M. Douglas Meeks, *God the Economist: The Doctrine of God and Political Economy* (Minneapolis: Fortress, 1989), 3.

4. Martin Luther King, "I Have a Dream," in *Testament of Hope*, 217.

5. Martin Luther King Jr., "The Negro Is Your Brother" (aka "Letter from Birmingham Jail"), *Atlantic Monthly*, August 1963, https://www.theatlantic.com/magazine/archive/2018/02/letter-from-birmingham-jail/552461.

6. Meeks writes: "In the broadest sense I will mean by *oikos* access to livelihood. The household living relationships of the *oikos* are the institutional relationships aimed at the survival of human beings in society. *Oikos* is the way the persons dwell in the world toward viability in relation to family, state, market, nature, and God. *Oikos* is the heart of both ecclesiology and political economy." Meeks, *God the Economist*, 33.

7. Ibid., 36.

8. Thomas F. Jackson, *From Civil Rights to Human Rights: Martin Luther King, Jr. and the Struggle for Economic Justice* (Philadelphia: University of Pennsylvania Press, 2007), 326.

9. Martin Luther King Jr., *Where Do We Go From Here: Chaos or Community?* (Boston: Beacon Press, 1967; rpt. 1968, 2010), 177.

10. Variations of this quote can be found in Martin Luther King Jr., "The Crisis of Civil Rights," unpublished address, Operation Breadbasket meeting, Chicago, October 10–12, 1967, King Papers, Library and Archives of the Martin Luther King Jr. Center for Nonviolent Social Change, Atlanta; Martin Luther King Jr., "Transforming the Neighborhood," speech, NATRA (National Association of TV and Radio Announcers) Convention, Atlanta, August 11, 1967, King Papers; Lewis V. Baldwin, *The Voice of Conscience: The Church in the Mind of Martin Luther King, Jr.* (New York: Oxford, 2010), 106, 301n17; and Lewis V. Baldwin, *There Is a Balm in Gilead: The Cultural Roots of Martin Luther King, Jr.* (Minneapolis: Fortress, 1991), 42.

11. Quoted in James H. Cone, *Martin and Malcolm and America: A Dream or a Nightmare* (Maryknoll, N.Y.: Orbis, 1991), 1.

12. Howard Thurman, *The Luminous Darkness: A Personal Interpretation of the Anatomy of Segregation and the Ground of Hope* (Richmond, Ind.: Friends United Press, 1971); Howard Thurman, *Deep River and Negro Spirituals Speaks of Life and Death* (Richmond, Ind.: Friends United Press, 1975); Howard Thurman, *The Search for Common Ground* (Richmond, Ind.: Friends United Press, 1971); and Howard Thurman, *Jesus and the Disinherited* (Boston: Beacon Press, 1976).

13. Thurman, *Luminous Darkness*, 101.

14. Thurman, *Jesus and the Disinherited*, 39.

15. W. E. B. Du Bois, *The Souls of Black Folk* (New York: Penguin Books, 1989), 5.

16. Peter Paris, "When Feeling like a Motherless Child," in Sally A. Brown and Patrick Miller, eds., *Lament: Reclaiming Practices in Pulpit, Pew, and Public Square* (Louisville: Westminster John Knox, 2005), 112–13.

17. For his understanding of the notion of heaven in the spirituals as a principle of social criticism, see Peter J. Paris, "When Feeling Like a Motherless Child"; Peter J. Paris, "The Linguistic Inculturation of the Gospel: The Word of God in the Words of the People," in Brian K. Blount and Leonora Tubbs Tisdale, eds., *Making Room at the Table: An Invitation to Multicultural Worship* (Louisville, Ky.: Westminster John Knox Press, 2001), 80–81, 89–90; Peter J. Paris, "The Problem of Evil in Black Christian Perspective," in Douglas A. Knight and Peter Paris, eds., *Justice and the Holy: Essays in Honor of Walter Harrelson* (Atlanta: Scholars Press, 1989), 304.

18. I have adapted Paris's words from "When Feeling like a Motherless Child," 115–16, for my purposes here.

19. James H. Cone, *The Spirituals and the Blues: An Interpretation* (Maryknoll, N.Y.: Orbis, 2008), 59, 65.

20. Charles H. Long, *Significations: Signs, Symbols, and Images in the Interpretation of Religion* (Aurora, Colo.: Davis Group, 1999), 145.

21. Walter Earl Fluker, *The Ground Has Shifted: The Future of the Black Church in Post-Racial America* (New York: New York University Press, 2016), 100. Italics in original.

22. Ibid., 75, 81, 84–85, 96–102, 108–11, 114, 118, 132, 137, 155.

23. Ibid., 108–9.

24. Martin Luther King, "The American Dream," in *Testament of Hope*, 210.

25. Cone, *Martin and Malcolm and America*, 198.

26. King, *Where Do We Go From Here?*, 201.

27. Martin Luther King, "If the Negro Wins, Labor Wins," 201–7, in *Testament of Hope*, 207.

28. Cone, *Martin and Malcolm and America*, 64.

29. King, *Where Do We Go From Here?*, 187.

30. Ibid.

31. Kenneth L. Smith, "Equality and Justice: A Dream or Vision of Reality," *Report from the Capital*, 39, no. 1 (January 1984): 5.

32. Michelle Alexander, *The New Jim Crow: Mass Incarceration in an Age of Colorblindness* (New York: the End Press, 2010), 206.

33. Alexander, *The New Jim Crow*, 21, 50–51, 57, 144–45, 196.

34. Eddie S. Glaude Jr., *Democracy in Black: How Race Still Enslaves the American Soul* (New York: Broadway Books, 2016), 6, 9, 29–50.

35. Joseph E. Stiglitz, *The Price of Inequality: How Today's Divided Society Endangers Our Future* (New York: W. W. Norton, 2013), xxi, 3, 24–25.

36. Emilie M. Townes, *Womanist Ethics and the Cultural Production of Evil* (New York: Palgrave Macmillan, 2006), 11–12, 18–22, 104–5.

37. Mel Oliver and Thomas Shapiro, *Black Wealth/White Wealth: A New Perspective on Racial Inequality* (New York: Routledge, 1995), 18, quoted in Elizabeth Jacobs, "Everywhere and Nowhere: Politics in Capital in the Twenty-First Century," in Heather Boushey, Bradford Delong, and Marshall Steinbaum, eds., *After Piketty: The Agenda for Economics and Inequality* (Cambridge, Mass.: Harvard University Press, 2017), 533.

38. Gareth Jones, "The Geographies of Capital in the Twenty-First Century: Inequality, Political Economy, and Space," in Boushey, Delong, and Steinbaum, *After Piketty*, 280, 283.

39. Martha Biondi, *To Stand and Fight: The Struggle for Civil Rights in Postwar New York City* (Cambridge, Mass.: Harvard University Press, 2003), 286.

40. Nimi Wariboko, *The Charismatic City and the Resurgence of Religion: A Pentecostal Social Ethics of Cosmopolitan Urban Life* (New York: Palgrave Macmillan, 2014), 137–53.

41. Martin Luther King Jr., "Press Statement at Stockholm Airport Arrival," Stockholm, Sweden, December 12, 1964, King Papers.

42. Thomas Piketty, *Capital in the Twenty-First Century*, translated by Arthur Goldhammer (Cambridge, Mass.: Harvard University Press, 2014); and Stiglitz, *Price of Inequality*.

43. Piketty, *Capital*, 34–35.

44. Piketty, *Capital*, 168, 191–94, 308–12, 367–74, 477–593, 597, 618–19, 703–4, 746–48.

45. Jacobs, "Everywhere and Nowhere," 533–34.

46. Malcolm X, "Malcom X Warns, 'It Shall Be the Ballot or the Bullet,' Washington Heights, New York, March 29, 1964," AMDOCS, http://www.vlib.us/amdocs/texts/malcolmx0364.html.

47. Piketty, *Capital*, 746–47.

48. Mark L. Taylor, *The Executed God: The Way of the Cross in Lockdown America* (Minneapolis: Fortress, 2015); and Alexander, *The New Jim Crow*.

49. *Human Development Report 2016* (New York: United Nations Development Program, 2016), 60.

50. Ibid., 60–61.

51. Jacques Rancière, *Disagreement: Politics and Philosophy*, translated by Julie Rose (Minneapolis: University of Minnesota Press, 1998), 13.

52. King, *Where Do We Go from Here?*, 186, 196–97; and Martin Luther King Jr., *Why We Can't Wait* (New York: New American Library, 1963) 136–41.

53. King, *Where Do We Go from Here?*, 197.

54. Gerald McKnight, *The Last Crusade: Martin Luther King, Jr., The FBI, and the Poor Peoples' Campaign* (New York: Westview Press, 1998), 21–22. Also quoted in Alexander, *New Jim Crow*, 39.

55. King, *Where Do We Go from Here?*, 146–47, 154–66.

56. Frank L. Morris, "A Dream Unfulfilled: The Economic and Political Policies of Martin Luther King, Jr.," in David J. Garrow, ed., *Martin Luther King, Jr. and the Civil Rights Movement*, vol. 3 (Brooklyn, N.Y.: Carlson Publishing, 1989), 676.

57. King, "I Have a Dream," 219.

58. King, *Where Do We Go from Here?*, 201.

59. Martin Luther King Jr., "The Casualties of War in Vietnam, " in *"In a Single Garment of Destiny": A Global Vision of Justice*, edited by Lewis V. Baldwin (Boston: Beacon Press, 2012), 161.

60. Martin Luther King, "The Greatest Hope for World Peace," in *"In a Single Garment of Destiny,"* 149.

61. Paul Tillich, *Theology of Peace*, edited by Ronald Stone (Louisville: Westminster John Knox Press, 1990), 94.

62. Nimi Wariboko, *God and Money: A Theology of Money in a Globalizing World* (Lanham, Md.: Lexington Books, 2008).

63. Mark J. Allman, "A Thick Theory of Global Justice: Participation as a Constitutive Dimension of Global Justice," PhD diss., Loyola University of Chicago, 2003, 183–202.

64. National Council of Catholic Bishops, *Economic Justice for All* (Washington, D.C.: U.S. Catholic Conference, 1986), para. 77.

65. I wish to thank Peter J. Paris and Walter E. Fluker for their valuable comments on the first draft of this chapter. Thanks to Austin Washington, one of my doctoral students at Boston University, for proofreading the first draft.

CHAPTER 8
MARTIN LUTHER KING JR. AND THE NONVIOLENT TRANSFORMATION OF GLOBAL CONFLICT
BROADENING KNOWLEDGE OF NONVIOLENT ACTION IN THE GREAT WORLD HOUSE

MARY E. KING

I left India more convinced than ever before that nonviolent resistance is the most potent weapon available to oppressed people in their struggle for freedom.
MARTIN LUTHER KING JR., "My Trip to the Land of Gandhi"

Our ability to dismantle injustice and achieve a better world cannot be achieved by using the methods and tools of those who are pledged to a philosophy of violence, which usually leads to more violence. We cannot accept the culture of our foes, use the language of our adversaries, apply the weapons of our enemy, or behave like those who are traitors to their own humanity—and yet still be able to create societies that are compassionate, ethical, and just.
JAMES M. LAWSON JR.

The writings and orations of Martin Luther King Jr. conceivably comprise the largest collection of papers in the literature on nonviolent resistance. With King's stimulus and consequentiality a counterpart to that of Mohandas K. Gandhi, the American civil rights leader would become one of the most potent influences of the twentieth century, as groups and societies across the world adopted nonviolent struggle as a means of producing tangible alterations in the political order. The influence of both titans continues to inform and shape the world today. King's continuing impact on global nonviolent struggles correlates more closely than Gandhi's to recent research showing that in the twenty-first century, civil resistance has become the preferred choice for groups and societies seeking justice and rights, an end to oppression, or the collapse of dictatorships. Indeed, unarmed civilians challenging their adversaries through boycotts, massive processions, nonviolent occupations, strikes, vigils, and other nonviolent methods have become the most common form of struggle in today's world, and King is a central actor in the story of how this has happened.

The concept and doctrine of nonviolence has coursed through widely varying cultural, philosophical, political, religious, and spiritual traditions. Originating during ages past, the practice of nonviolent action can be documented in every culture in which it has been researched. The terms "nonviolence" and "nonviolent action" have precise meanings in scholarly studies, but in common parlance they refer to identifiable "nonviolent methods," applied within a conflict, which deliberately reject the harming of human life.[1] Adoption of civil resistance is generally either because remaining nonviolent will have the most persuasive effect and can enlist a varied range of resisters, or because resorting to armed violence is recognized as perilous against a heavily armed opponent.

Nonviolent methods with their infinite variety have identifiable features that unite them and are core characteristics of the technique or process of nonviolent action. Nonviolent in the sense that they do not harm the bodily welfare of the opposing human beings or inflict physical injury, the methods can be contentious, disruptive, boisterous, disorderly, cause economic pain, or raise emotionally charged issues from a state of being hidden or concealed into full view. Methods employ communications, psychology, specific properties of social power, and symbolism. They may act by withdrawing expected cooperation and compliance, or by doing something unanticipated. They can interrupt or disturb the usual operations of an institution, bureaucracy, or system. They often significantly raise the costs of maintaining the status quo and can dissolve the legitimacy of a tyrant. The outcomes from using such *active* methods cannot be predicted with precision, although considerable knowledge of sequencing and how the methods exert political pressure is often involved in determining how and when they are used.[2] Conscious methods are essential for engaging in nonviolent direct action, which is action applied directly to the perceived cause of an injustice or grievance and not working through representatives or agencies. Although a group of parliamentarians or government officials may resort to nonviolent methods, direct action is normally reserved for situations in which the institutions of politics have failed.

Nonviolent struggles have often behaved as predictors of democracy. This outcome is not ideological; nonviolent movements *tend* to lead to democratic results and the leaders that emerge are predisposed in favor of democracy. This is partly related to the demanding processes involved for groups and campaigns to decide their strategy, and to the rigors associated with individuals making the personal decision to undertake the risks and endure the penalties that may accompany nonviolent struggle—something that cannot be coerced.

The civil rights movement of the mid-twentieth century resulted in the most effective legislation ever passed in U.S. history for the ongoing effort to make the country inclusive of all its peoples and to expand their ability to exercise the fundamental rights guaranteed under the Constitution, among them access to public accommodations and the ballot. Yet King's pungently elaborated concerns in "The World House," the final chapter of his book *Where Do We Go from Here: Chaos or Community?*, raises the momentous question of how the human family of "black and white, Easterner and Westerner, Gentile and Jew, Catholic and Protestant, Muslim and Hindu" will learn "to live with each other in peace." His words ring with authenticity and power as he judges that "racism is still that hound of hell which dogs the tracks of our civilization."[3] If one believes his statement to be true to this day, then one must consider what impact King has had on nonviolent struggles in the great world house since his death.

The twenty-first century has seen a continuation of the significant role played by nonviolent campaigns of civil resistance in the construction, broadening, and defense of democracies. Correspondingly, once democratic forms of government have been established or restored, nonviolent methods from a large repertoire—such as processions, civil disobedience, draft or tax resistance, human chains, mass rallies, site occupations, strikes, and vigils—have retained their relevance in opposing injustice and unjust wars. It is not an exaggeration to say that Gandhi and King tutored humanity internationally in a potent, nonlethal process for correcting egregious abuses, grievances, suffering, and wrongs. They also represent the wave of the future insofar as non-Western, nonwhite intercontinental leadership must inevitably bend to demographics, because the greater part of the world community is not descended from European forebears. In this situation, accompanied by the failures, limitations, and corruption of the standard existing institutions of politics, there exists a grave need for continuing to authenticate and sustain the ability of nonviolent social movements to address critical issues of justice.

This chapter considers indicative global nonviolent struggles in exploring King's influence in the half-century since his death on the growing effectiveness of nonviolent action. It is also the case that overestimation of the efficacy of violent struggle and war is a problem in much of the world, including in the United States, in which King was rooted. Historical analysis for many nonviolent social movements has been imbalanced by an embedded conviction in the usefulness of violent means for national adhesion and awakening. Thus, the chapter opens with a suggestive review of the determinative role that civil resistance has had for U.S. history, part of the background for King's entry into worldwide leadership. Rarely do chronicles of nonviolent resistance become part of a nation's discourse or central to the popular view a country holds of its journey to liberation or self-determination.

King and Antecedents of Nonviolent Struggles

Nonviolent social movements have affected human history for millennia, from five secessions (comparable in effect to general strikes) by Roman plebeians between 494 and 287 BCE, such that by 471 they had won from the patricians the right to a tribune where they could assemble and elect representatives, to innumerable struggles to eradicate inhumane working conditions in nineteenth-century Britain and the United States.[4] U.S. social history provides abundant examples of mass nonviolent action carried out by average individuals such that it might be assumed that this panoply explains how Martin Luther King Jr. came to embrace nonviolent action, yet little evidence can be found that he was conscious prior to the 1955–56 Montgomery bus boycott of the forceful antecedents and array of significant nonviolent struggles in the nation's past.

King in his early and formative years would in all likelihood not have been taught chronicles in U.S. history from which he could have drawn lessons and models for the leadership that he would as an adult bring first to the civil rights movement and then to the world. The United States had ample grist for the mill for ardent historical analysis of its own nonviolent struggles, yet these episodes were more often ignored or effaced than acknowledged by the historians, educators, and commentators who have shaped the popular view of the nation's past. At other times, they were not recognized as being undertakings of nonviolent resistance. Labor unions had been major actors in improving conditions through collective bargaining, as they joined together seeking to raise wages and improve safety standards, over time developing capabilities to organize for workers' benefits and rights. Yet trade unions were customarily indifferent or antagonistic toward black membership, especially in the South, with the region's disdain for the right to organize and bargain collectively. Another salient example of an abundance of nonviolent struggles is the decade from 1765 to 1775, prior to the War of Independence, in which émigrés to the original thirteen colonies relied on boycotts, nonimportation and nonexportation strategies, protest demonstrations, methods of noncooperation, and committees of correspondence that coordinated resistance to British rule.

The resistance demonstrated in the Boston Tea Party and Stamp Act conspicuously manifested the settlers' political defiance of the Crown. The Stamp Act raised revenues by taxing coffee, sugar, textiles, and wine, in part to service London's debt from supporting the ten thousand British troops garrisoned in the United States. "Stamps," separately embossed vellum sheets or parchment purchased from official distributors, were necessary for clearing documents for ships, licenses, or deeds.[5] The act requiring them would be repealed in 1766, due to organized opposition by an elaborate network of artisans and merchants. When on December 16, 1773, colonists masquerading as Mohawks boarded three British ships and opened their cargo of 342 tea chests and dumped the contents into Boston harbor, they did so to oppose the imposition of a tea tax by the British Parliament, seated in London, where the colonies had no representation.[6]

A youthful Martin Luther King Jr. was likely taught about the colonists' exploits in an American history class, but almost certainly it would not have been explained as nonviolent struggle, civil disobedience, tax resistance, or part of a social movement. News outlets were the first to refuse to buy stamps, a form of noncooperation, well before there was a First Amendment guaranteeing freedom of speech.[7] The widespread use of nonviolent sanctions by colonists of all ages—including men, women, and children—was enforced by immeasurable but well-organized local extralegal committees.

Not only was the interconnected nonviolent action in the colonies ignored in chronicling the origins of the United States, but British and U.S. scholars working with original archival documents on both sides of the Atlantic have shown that nine or ten of the thirteen original colonies had actually won de facto independence from Britain and self-governance through civil resistance campaigns by 1775—a full year prior to the outbreak of the War of Independence.[8] Even today, schoolchildren are not exposed to this compelling chapter in U.S. history.

Thousands of social movements, protest drives, and nonviolent campaigns during the nineteenth and early twentieth centuries made claims and demands for the abolition of slavery, eradicating child labor, an eight-hour work day, prison reform, legal and political support for labor rights, tenant rights, professional benefits, and the ability to develop cooperatives (enterprises jointly owned by those who use its services) and to organize electric power.[9] In 1903, labor and community organizer Mother Jones organized hundreds of children to march from Philadelphia to the summer home of President Theodore Roosevelt in Oyster Bay, New York, to demand enforcement of child labor laws in Pennsylvania mines and silk mills. Although the president refused to meet with the child marchers, many of them missing fingers or bearing other infirmities from mining accidents, the March of the Mill Children drew attention to child labor. Precocious though King was, one cannot assume that he knew of the wide-ranging social correctives being fought for by diverse swaths of citizens with slender resources in ways deliberately chosen because they did not use violence or seek to harm the well-being of their adversaries.

Across the Atlantic, Quakers and Methodists led Britain's antislavery struggles, and in 1833, following multiple mobilizations, Parliament passed an emancipation act applicable throughout its empire, banning the slave trade. Yet the very same colonists who had organized a decade of civil resistance campaigns against British rule were extremely divided on the issue in the new nation they had established and would ultimately fight a gruesome civil war over the trade in human cargo. The Civil War would result in more military deaths than all other U.S. wars put together; six hundred thousand were killed at a time when the country had a population of thirty million.[10]

White Southern Baptists in the United States acceded to the institution of slavery, defended it, and for economic reasons compromised their denomination's fundamental commitment to individual freedoms. Georgia's constitution, adopted in 1733, prohibited slavery, but after approval by the powerful white Baptist leadership, many of whom owned slaves, its prohibitory clause was removed. The other major white Protestant denomination in the South, the Methodists, organized in 1784, initially condemned slavery in strong language, but by 1844, with a number of them now slave owners, had split from their northern counterparts because of their support for human bondage. Notwithstanding debate over whether to engage in antislavery work in their own entities or through interracial agencies, African Americans had by 1830 structured their own antislavery national convention in Philadelphia, which convened intermittently during the three decades of the abolitionist period and into the Civil War. By the 1830s, abolition had become the core of a massive nonviolent U.S. mobilization. The decades of antislavery campaigning prior to the Civil War directly signify one of the most concerted efforts in U.S. history to develop nonviolent means of struggle.[11]

Never was there an absence of resistance to slavery. African American forms of grassroots resistance had involved refusal to cooperate with systems of slavery from the earliest arrival of enchained Africans in the Americas, in the late fifteenth century. From 1492 to 1870, some eleven million enslaved Africans arrived in the Western Hemisphere. Disembarking Africans introduced resistance methods used on slave ships that derived from indigenous ancient and traditional forms of defiance. In what would become the United States, beside the comparatively rare organized violent revolts and uprisings, for three centuries slaves experimented with forms of noncooperation, including actions that are comparable to nonviolent direct action.[12] While abolitionists considered public speaking and publishing to be *indirect* action methods, those who were enslaved might use such oblique means to protect themselves as lying, careless use of tools, playing sick, and implementing work slowdowns. Nonviolent *direct*

action included boycotts, civil disobedience of "illegitimate" laws, and other actions aimed directly at the source of the wrong. Refusing to cooperate or obey,
slaves also escaped into swamps or forests and to the North, sang spirituals that
conveyed hidden meanings and urged resistance, signed petitions, and rejected
names given them by their owners.

The protracted campaigns against the New World's accommodation of slavery and the subsequent fights for its abolition were sometimes led by fugitive
or former slaves. In 1857, one such leader, Frederick Douglass, potently justified
the legitimacy of waging struggle:

> The whole history of the progress of human liberty shows that all concessions
> yet made to her august claims have been born of earnest struggle. . . . If there is
> no struggle there is no progress. Those who profess to favor freedom and yet de-
> preciate agitation, are men who want crops without plowing up the ground, they
> want rain without thunder and lightning. . . .
>
>   This struggle may be a moral one, or it may be a physical one, and it may be
> both moral and physical, but it must be a struggle. Power concedes nothing with-
> out a demand. It never did and it never will. Find out just what any people will
> quietly submit to and you have found out the exact measure of injustice and
> wrong which will be imposed upon them, and these will continue till they are
> resisted with either words or blows, or with both. The limits of tyrants are pre-
> scribed by the endurance of those whom they oppress.[13]

Pervaded with forms of nonviolent action, whether named as such or not, the
United States abounded with forms of noncooperation, understood and used
by those who suffered injustice, infringements, and tribulations.

Popular social movements are not easily held back or contained and often
have a transformational effect by opening political space for other claimants.
Civil resistance has a recognized tendency to make way for constituencies with
different grounds for using direct action. A salient example is pointed to by historian Carleton Mabee, who asserts that the first advocacy for sit-ins and protest rides in the United States may have been in 1838, when a policy of support
for such measures was adopted by the Antislavery Convention of American
Women.[14] Campaigners for the women's vote in New Zealand worked for decades before the country became the first to grant the franchise to women in
1893. By the end of the nineteenth century, a movement transcending national
boundaries was seeking to enfranchise women in nations across the globe. It is
now considered possibly the most effective *transnational* nonviolent movement
of the modern era.[15]

King Learns from Gandhi

In 1944, at age fifteen, Martin Luther King Jr. entered Morehouse College in Atlanta, where he encountered Benjamin E. Mays, a forceful presence as the college's president. Mays held campus-wide Tuesday-morning lectures in the chapel, where he repeatedly talked about the Indian independence struggles. These regular student assemblies led Martin to see the ministry as offering an intellectually engaging and potent means to confront white supremacy and its appalling manifestations. It was probably through Mays that Martin was introduced to the thinking of Mohandas Karamchand Gandhi, whom Mays had met in India in 1936. In his chapel remarks, Mays would often discuss his trip, the meeting, and Gandhi's outlook and philosophy of social action.[16]

Also at Morehouse, King was assigned to read Henry David Thoreau's essay "Resistance to Civil Government," which has sometimes been published as *On the Duty of Civil Disobedience*. Recalling his first encounter with Thoreau, King said he was "fascinated by the idea of refusing to cooperate with an evil system"—so moved that he reread the essay several times. It was what King described as his "first intellectual contact with the theory of nonviolent resistance."[17] "Unjust laws exist," said Thoreau, "shall we transgress them at once?"[18] Thoreau's defiance was a way of remaining true to his beliefs, a personal testimony of conscience, and his refusal to cooperate expressed his denial of support for a government that he deemed illegitimate because it condoned slavery and hoped to expand slave territory through the Mexican War. Thoreau was arrested for refusing to pay six years of delinquent poll taxes. Bailed out of jail by a relative, he transformed his brief incarceration into material for what became his famous lecture on noncooperation with government, delivered before the Concord Lyceum in February 1848. So far as anyone knows, Thoreau did not use the term "civil disobedience" in the lecture, and it does not appear in his essay.

In Thoreau's era, civil disobedience was mostly chosen by people or groups who had modest or no hopes of engendering broad political transformation. Six decades later, through Gandhi's refining of civil disobedience and gaining possession of all-India leadership, it had become a tool of mass action specifically pointed at political change.[19] Gandhi too had read Thoreau, although he regarded his exposure to the New England transcendentalist as confirming what he had already been formulating. The combined twentieth-century projections from both Gandhi and King were required to bring civil disobedience forcefully onto the world stage as a potent method of noncooperation capable of altering societies and politics under certain circumstances.

The inchoate U.S. freedom movement cannot be comprehended without appreciating the four decades of interaction and exchanges of knowledge between African Americans traveling abroad and the Gandhian independence struggles on the Indian subcontinent. Notwithstanding extended ocean voyages and propeller-driven airplanes, Gandhi's thinking was being transmitted some twelve thousand miles, ultimately reaching black leaders and intelligentsia in the United States. As historian Sudarshan Kapur has shown, between 1919 and 1955, Edward G. Carroll, James L. Farmer, Benjamin Mays, Channing Tobias, and Howard Thurman were among the African American students of Gandhian theories and methods who journeyed to India prior to King's emergence as a leader.[20] Also, for more than twenty years, Mordecai Wyatt Johnson, the president of Howard University, afforded an essential link between African Americans and the Gandhian campaigns, with ensuing travel to India by individuals such as James M. Lawson Jr. and Bayard Rustin. These travelers gained insights into Gandhian theories that held promise for application in the United States, and they brought selected awareness back to institutions with African American leadership and to other organizations. By the mid-1920s, pockets of the black community were also becoming aware through eager coverage in black-owned newspapers that Gandhi was developing strategies of resistance to European colonialism and oppression that might be appropriate for their use in the United States.

While a student at Crozer Theological Seminary in Chester (Delaware County), Pennsylvania, King heard a sermon by Mordecai Wyatt Johnson about the life and thinking of Gandhi. King later recorded that the message was "so profound and electrifying that I left the meeting and went out and bought half a dozen books on Gandhi's life and works."[21] Having thus embarked on a life-long encounter with Gandhi's understandings of the use of social power, King's comprehension would be furthered after meeting James M. Lawson Jr. at Oberlin College in 1957, where King was speaking at a time when Lawson, having returned from three years of teaching in India, was preparing for graduate work. Lawson explained to King that he had determined while in college that he would become a Methodist minister and go south to commit himself to dismantling segregation and racism. Absorbed by Lawson's experience in India, King noted that they were both the same age, twenty-eight. He implored Lawson: "Don't wait! Come now! You're badly needed. We don't have anyone like you!"[22]

By January 1958, Lawson was based in Nashville as southern field secretary of the Fellowship of Reconciliation (FOR), affiliated with the International Fellowship of Reconciliation, a peace organization formed in response to the revulsions of World War I and that resulted from an ecumenical conference in Constance, Switzerland, in 1914.[23] FOR, based in Nyack, New York, came into being in 1915. On arrival in Nashville, Lawson found that Glenn E. Smiley, a white, Texas-born Methodist minister, had become national field director of FOR. Smiley had been incarcerated as a conscientious objector during World War II, and along with Bayard Rustin he had been a field secretary with FOR during the late 1940s. Smiley had put together for Lawson a crowded schedule of workshops, including one at the first annual meeting of the Southern Christian Leadership Conference (SCLC) in Columbia, South Carolina, which would recur at every SCLC meeting as long as King lived. Lawson had begun teaching at Nagpur, in Maharashtra, at the crossroads of India, barely four years after Gandhi's assassination in 1948, and he was singularly knowledgeable from meeting volunteers who had worked with Gandhi and visiting their sites of struggle. In a role also apportioned with Rustin and Smiley, Lawson would become the critical agent in interpreting the basics of Gandhian nonviolent action for King, SCLC, and by 1960 the Student Nonviolent Coordinating Committee (SNCC).

Commencing with the 1955–56 Montgomery bus boycott, King would become the individual principally responsible for interpreting Gandhian reasoning and skill in the United States. It was he who persuaded elements of the black community that carefully chosen ideas and techniques from Gandhi could be effective in attacking white supremacy, a conclusion that was not foreordained. The movement of tens of thousands that coursed through the U.S. South between the Montgomery action and passage of the national Voting Rights Act in 1965 possessed a direct, if select, connection to the civil resistance experimented with and propounded by Gandhi.

During the Montgomery events, while the fundamental approach might have been described as nonviolent resistance and noncooperation, King's personal grounding, he wrote, was in Jesus's Sermon on the Mount, which he considered the foundation for the "dignified social action" of the bus boycott.[24] Yet as days passed, he would write in his 1958 book about Montgomery, *Stride toward Freedom*, that Gandhi's inspiration exerted its influence. This was partly because once the boycott began, seasoned professional students of the historic technique of nonviolent struggle descended on Montgomery, believing that King's leadership presented an extraordinary moment for confronting the persistence of injustice. They would eventually comprise an esteemed group of practitioners and theoreticians of nonviolent resistance, among them Lawson, Rustin, and Smiley. Working with them, often in the nightly tutorials they gave, King's comprehension grew. Persuaded that being true to one's conscience and faith left "no alternative but to refuse to coöperate with an evil system," King said that he had come to conceive of the movement "as an act of massive non-coöperation," such that he was seldom using the term "boycott."[25]

What King regarded as significant use of noncooperation had been articulated by Gandhi in 1905. Despite only being in his thirties then, Gandhi had formulated a compelling insight: "Even the most powerful cannot rule without the co-operation of the ruled."[26] King was in full possession of this knowledge in Montgomery, and it still reverberates today. The understanding that no system can stand if the population withholds its obedience and cooperation is rudimentary in nonviolent struggles. Although never meeting in person, Gandhi and King cumulatively would amplify and refine the use of the social power manifested in noncooperation, civil disobedience, silent vigils, and other forms of collective group action.

King's prescience reveals itself in what he said upon receiving the 1964 Nobel Peace Prize in Oslo, Norway. His remarks connected the nonviolent struggles of the U.S. freedom movement to the entire planet's need for disarmament. Remarking that the most exceptional characteristic of the movement was the direct participation of masses of people in it, and accentuating Gandhi's introduction of the "[nonviolent] weapons of truth, soul force, non-injury and courage," King also proffered his strongest proposal to date for waging nonviolent resistance on issues other than racial injustice. International nonviolent action, he said, could let global leaders know that, beyond racial and economic justice, human beings worldwide were concerned about world peace: "I venture to suggest . . . that the philosophy and strategy of nonviolence become immediately a subject for study and for serious experimentation in every field of human conflict, by no means excluding relations between nations . . . which [ultimately] make war."[27]

Telling journalists that he would donate the prize money to the civil rights movement, King returned home to engross himself in plans for the fifty-four-mile march from Selma to the Alabama capital of Montgomery, which would be the last large-scale and most consequential direct action for the movement. Even before this march, and remarkably so in the Mississippi programs of 1963 and 1964, the movement had begun turning toward political and economic organizing, including mock ballots and development of alternative, or parallel, political parties and social institutions. The latter are among the most advanced methods of nonviolent struggle, formulated by Gandhi in 1941 as part of a "constructive program," in which a new social reality could be built in the midst of the old order, including the construction of alternative, or parallel, institutions.[28]

Broadening the Knowledge of Nonviolent
Action in the Great World House

In the fifty years after the death of Martin Luther King Jr., more than fifty countries have experienced the disintegration of dictatorships and tyrannies, col-
lapses brought about by popular nonviolent mobilizations. King's thought is interwoven with the increasing comprehension of how nonviolent struggle works
and its accelerated transmission of ideas, both of which help account for this
process and technique spreading across the world. This chapter maintains that
the inheritance from King's legacy, his still potent ability to communicate, and
the ongoing resonance from his ideas and way with words have been decisive
in the transcultural spread of knowledge, which also reverberates in King's concept of the world house.[29]

A demonstrable turn to civil resistance in the decades since King's assassination has widened political reforms, hastened codification of human rights,
sped democratic transitions, offered frameworks for average citizens to pursue
social change, and in some cases lifted military occupations. Peoples, groups,
and societies have in the past half century achieved tangible political and social change in widely varying cultures and divergent political systems, remarkably often with laudable results. Civil resistance is not without limits, however,
and some failures have occurred, as in Burma (1988) and China (1989), both of
which led to substantial repression in these countries. The historic method of
nonviolent action for seeking change has subsequently grown, with its use as a
strategic force recognized by social scientists, policy makers, political analysts,
strategic-studies specialists, peacemakers, and international scholars of diverse
disciplines.

Completing a "Process of Democratization"

History had prodded King's generation to accept an "indescribably important
destiny," as he put it, "to complete a process of democratization which our nation too long developed too slowly, but which is our most powerful weapon
for world respect and emulation."[30] In the years immediately after King's 1968
death, by the early 1970s, Glenn Smiley, one of the professional tutors on nonviolent resistance who had been advising King and the SCLC, embarked on dis-
tributing King's writings in South America, often in the course of working with
a number of organizations on the continent seeking to build peace and equity with which he became involved. King's 1963 "Letter from a Birmingham

Jail" had inspired Adolfo Pérez Esquivel, an Argentine sculptor and professor of architecture, and others to create in 1974 a nongovernmental organization known as Servicio Paz y Justicia (SERPAJ), or Service to Peace and Justice Foundation. During the 1970s and 1980s, SERPAJ defended political prisoners in numerous military regimes in Latin America. Pérez Esquivel was jailed in 1976 in Ecuador, in the company of Roman Catholic bishops from North America and Latin America, and then expelled from the country. In 1977, he was incarcerated in Buenos Aires by Argentina's federal police. Held without trial for fourteen months and tortured, he was in prison when he learned that he would win the 1980 Nobel Peace Prize, in recognition of his work to defend human rights.

SERPAJ would eventually encompass some twenty Latin American countries in its work, including documentation of the catastrophic deaths faced by *desaparecidos*—citizens who tragically "disappeared" in late-twentieth-century "dirty wars," fomented in part by the United States and its backing of a political repression campaign called Operation Condor. According to Chilean sociologist Manuel Antonio Garretón, "The Southern Cone military regimes, more than other dictatorships, were institutionalized systems that deliberately produced and spread fear."[31] SERPAJ disseminated King's writings throughout the continent during the decades following King's observation that "decisions affecting the lives of South Americans are ostensibly made by their government, but there are almost no legitimate democracies alive in the whole continent."[32]

The military junta ruling Argentina (1976–83) sought to subdue all forms of opposition by methodically kidnapping people who spoke out against the regime. Between thirteen thousand and thirty thousand alleged subversives, supposed guerrillas, and their suspected sympathizers disappeared or were tortured and killed based on the weakest of evidence. They were buried in mass graves or their remains secretly interred in unidentified places.[33] Levels of fear were such that no one openly posed questions until a group of women—who met accidentally while walking the halls of governmental bureaucracies—stepped forward to hold the regime accountable for the disappearance of their children. They sought information concerning the whereabouts of their offspring even if that meant substantiation of their deaths.

On April 30, 1977, fourteen women came together on the central square of Buenos Aires, La Plaza de Mayo, in front of the Casa Rosada, the presidential palace, bearing photographs of their disappeared children. Calling themselves Las Madres de la Plaza de Mayo, the Mothers of the Plaza de Mayo, their request was an answer to one question: what happened to our children? From that date onward, every Thursday at 3:30 p.m. mothers and grandmothers of the disappeared came to the plaza, their numbers growing, wearing headscarves bearing pictures of their children, walking slowly in a dignified silent vigil to confront the authorities of a brutal regime. The conspicuous minimalism of their query echoed King's modest reasoning in Montgomery, when he explained the simple message of the boycott to the city's white community: "We can no longer lend our coöperation to an evil system."[34] Pérez Esquivel openly supported the mothers, notwithstanding continual harassment from the regime. On Mother's Day, October 5, 1977, 237 mothers included their names and identity card numbers on a half-page advertisement in the national newspaper *La Prensa*, calling for the truth regarding the disappearance of their children.

With King's writings spreading into Latin America, hundreds of thousands of people across much of the political spectrum in Chile's civil society became involved, including political parties, labor unions, grassroots organizations, and nongovernmental groups. They launched a nationwide "days of protest" campaign in 1983 against General Augusto Pinochet's dictatorship, which marked the beginning of sustained resistance by the opposition. It would yield results in October 1988, when Pinochet called a plebiscite to ratify his remaining in office another eight years. In response, the pro-democracy movement organized a "No" campaign, with intensive voter registration, public opinion surveys, television advertising, and canvassing of voters. In the run-up to the plebiscite, anti-Pinochet forces took advantage of the window for mobilizing and coordinated massive demonstrations and "go-slows" in which people at designated times slowed all public behavior and action. For instance, street sweepers would deliberately move their brooms slowly, and pedestrians would slacken their brisk walks to no more than an amble. Pinochet maneuvered to try to remain in office, but other officials of the military junta withdrew their support. In deciding to remain within the parameters of Pinochet's own 1980 constitution, the military and security forces accepted the eventual 54.7 percent majority vote of no, clearly demonstrating popular opposition. The presidency and democracy were restored through a series of transitional constitutional laws passed between 1981 and 1990.

The nonviolent ouster of military rule in Chile was echoed in Bolivia. After a general strike brought the country to an economic standstill in September 1982, the military stepped down, and the 1980 Congress was reconvened, with Hernán Siles Zuazo assuming the presidency in October. The sharing of King's writings and public addresses in Latin America contributed to an era in which movements of nonviolent resistance became generative in the creation, extension, and defense of democracy.

The Berlin Wall and Eastern Europe

From the 1960s forward, stimulated by the example of the U.S. civil rights movement and with awareness of Martin Luther King Jr.'s example spreading, followed by the antinuclear movement, the movement against the war in Vietnam, the women's liberation movement, and mobilizations against environmental degradation, nonviolent campaigns of civil resistance would address a range of wrongs and grievances. They were sometimes local but also involved tens of thousands, while still others were national mobilizations.

Until the French and American upheavals of the eighteenth century, the word "revolution" had referred to a sudden alteration in political direction with the goal of restoring an earlier order. Afterward, violence and bloodshed came to be equated with revolution. During the twentieth century, it sometimes seemed that violence and carnage had become the stock-in-trade of revolutionary movements. Some groups, among them Weatherman in the United States and the Red Brigades in Italy, argued that sabotage and violence, including bombings, comprised the only viable tool to address exploitation. About this mentality, King spoke logically: "This is no time for romantic illusions about freedom and empty philosophical debate. This is a time for action. What is needed is a strategy for change, a tactical program. . . . So far, this has only been offered by the nonviolent movement."[35] By the 1970s, a discernible shift had begun, away from the idealization of revolutionary violence, and some abused and subjugated peoples were asserting confidence in nonviolent struggle as the way that they could best rectify their situation.

During 1989–91, the citizens of Eastern Europe effectively disproved the presumption of violence as the strongest force. From Soviet-backed, communist-controlled regimes, fledgling democracies emerged, with civil resistance playing a primary role in how these new nation-states materialized. Regimes backed by the Soviet Union were disintegrated without resort to physical force or weaponry, except for Romania, where security forces turned violent. To Polish sociologist Janusz Ziolkowski, the dismantling of communist party states across Eastern Europe showed that "the popular image of revolution [was] itself undergoing a revolution." Ziolkowski writes: "A different revolutionary tradition has replaced that of 1848. It shows a respect for nonviolence and the rule of law and even a degree of forgiveness for those who have abused power. It is the tradition of Gandhi, Martin Luther King, Lech Walesa and Vaclav Havel."[36]

Democracies emerged without slaughter, accomplishing significant successes. These national nonviolent "revolutions" showed that armed insurrection is not the sole course of action available for aggrieved groups and societies, and, although not the only factor, they would play a role in the ultimate collapse of the Soviet Union.

The logic behind the selection of nonviolent resistance in the post–World War II Eastern bloc was coldly pragmatic on the part of the academicians, artists, authors, journalists, pastors, playwrights, political reformers, priests, scholar practitioners, and theater performers who used nonviolent action to change circumstances. Moscow had been able to maintain pervasive fear of Soviet military intrusion in the Eastern bloc by suppressing leaps toward freedom in 1953 (when the Soviet military put down East German workers' strikes and marches), in 1956 (crushing a Hungarian uprising), and in 1968 (leading the Warsaw Pact invasion to end the Prague Spring in Czechoslovakia). Even so, ordinary citizens in the Eastern bloc nation-states under communist rule after World War II, some within the Soviet Union, others occupied by the Soviet army at the close of the war, began the turn to nonviolent means in the 1970s. The Soviet signature on the 1975 Helsinki Accords, which became synonymous with human rights, ignited popular defiance, as Helsinki watch committees materialized across Eastern Europe to monitor adherence to the agreements. Essentially undetected, defiant committees began forming elsewhere throughout the Eastern bloc without official permission.

The social power arising from nonviolent action by citizens is not identical to that issuing from the state, although both types may assert themselves in the same sphere. The ostensibly weaker side can sometimes collapse the presumably stronger one. Arguments for fighting without violence were made not on grounds of pacifism but on a basis of both ethical and practical justifications, echoing Gandhi and King, as revealed in the immense outpourings of forbidden *samizdat* (Russian for "self-published") writings.

Government-suppressed literature was printed and covertly circulated, reaching prolific levels in Poland, Czechoslovakia, and Lithuania. Opposition movements such as Poland's Solidarity union (Solidarność), Czechoslovakia's Charter 77, the East German Pastors' Movement, and the Baltic states' popular fronts judged civil resistance the only realistic option, wanting no pretext for Soviet incursion. The activist intellectuals, many reading Gandhi and King and whose clandestine writings drove the spread of nonviolent resistance throughout the Eastern bloc, made practical arguments for choosing nonviolent struggle.[37] They wanted to stand in contrast to the ruthlessness and duplicity of the systems under which they had suffered.

Elements of King's influence or outright attribution of his exact words can be found in almost any civil resistance movement that one plumbs worldwide.

Yet Poland is particularly illuminating. As Soviet troops occupied Poland after World War II, wisdom on how to fight without bloodshed was being quietly, covertly shared. By the mid-1980s, two thousand samizdat titles were circulating regularly, some numbering tens of thousands of copies. These were often laboriously typed on onionskin paper with carbon copies, ten keyed at a time.

Prior to Poland's 1980 formation of Solidarność gaining world attention, committees of academicians were working together there during the 1970s with Roman Catholic laity and theologians. Starting in 1976, they came together with lawyers to assist the families of workers jailed, exiled, or fired due to suspected connections to two violent episodes associated with protests at one hundred factories over increases in food prices. Forming the Committee for the Workers' Defense (Komitet Obrony Robotników, or KOR), they hoped to unify Polish society. In 1977, refusing to function clandestinely, KOR became the first group to organize independently in the Soviet bloc without sanction from a communist regime. Historians Jacek Kuroń and Adam Michnik were members of this pioneering group.

Kuroń, who spent nine years in prison, partly for organizing student strikes and penning an open letter to the communist party, asserted, "By building independent organizations, society can erode totalitarianism from within."[38] As knowledge of methods of resistance spread, the Roman Catholic monthly *Wiez* (Bond) published translations of Gandhi and King.[39] A group that embarked on hunger strikes in 1977 to protest the arrest of nine members of KOR made specific references to Gandhi and King.[40]

The activist intellectuals advising KOR sought to fight for freedoms with ethical standards consistent with the goals they espoused, with a connection between means and ends, about which King himself had written extensively. KOR wanted a strong civil society, an independent political space not under government control. Janusz Ziolkowski stated plainly: "They wanted to be citizens, individual men and women with dignity and responsibility, with rights but also with duties, freely associating in civil society."[41] For those reimagining their lives without Soviet occupation, civil society was both a tactic and a "prefiguring of 'society-to-be.'"[42]

Solidarność was established in June 1980, after an explosion in the Lenin Shipyard in Gdańsk caused the deaths of eight workers. Instead of walking out as in a typical strike, the laborers began a sit-down strike, an extended work stoppage that nonviolently occupied the workplace. Kuroń spoke for the strike committee until the regime severed telephone lines and incarcerated him and Michnik. In short order, however, the party and state would recognize Solidarność as the union described itself: the first "independent, self-governing union" in an Eastern bloc communist country, possessing the right to strike. By late September 1980, Solidarność's membership exceeded ten million and enlisted 80 percent of the Polish workforce. With the backing of numerous Polish historians, like Kuroń and Michnik, Solidarność's leaders were not simply taking a principled stance on nonviolence. They wanted to end the sentimentalized spilling of Polish blood, the likes of which had accompanied Polish rebellions in the nineteenth century as the nation tried to remain whole from German and Russian predations.

In 1981, Poland's communist party-state instituted martial law, which would last for seven years, but the union persevered. Michnik, later editor of Poland's second-largest daily newspaper, *Gazeta Wyborcza* (Election Gazette), in 1985 wrote in *Letters from Prison and Other Essays* that the ethics of Solidarność and its rejection of armed force "has a lot in common with the idea of nonviolence as espoused by Gandhi and Martin Luther King Jr." In prison he penned: "The ethics of Solidarity is based on the . . . premise: that there are causes worth dying for. Gandhi and King died for the same cause as the miners in Wujek [striking workers who met their deaths three days after the Polish government's imposition of martial law], who rejected the belief that it is better to remain a willing slave than be a victim of murder."[43]

From February 6 to April 5, 1989, twenty-six Solidarity delegates along with ecclesiastical observers would meet with twenty-nine communist party representatives around a large round oak table to discuss Poland's future. Thirteen working groups conducted ninety-four sessions, often functioning until dawn. The talks between the formerly jailed and their jailers would result in an agreement that restructured Poland into a democracy. Women were involved, in large proportion, in all events and actions. The November 1989 opening of the Berlin Wall is often cited as the moment when the unraveling of the Soviet Union began. February 6, however, may more appropriately commemorate the date the Eastern bloc began its self-liberation. Not for the first time in history, a national nonviolent revolution was required to achieve the negotiations that reconstructed Polish governance.

The roundtable talks mark the commencement of other Eastern bloc upheavals and the eventual collapse of the Soviet Union. The East German party-state would on November 9, 1989, announce that all East German citizens could travel out of the country at will, without official permission. In December 1990, Solidarność cofounder Lech Wałęsa was elected president of Poland—becoming the first noncommunist leader in Eastern Europe in almost forty years.

The academicians, activists, intellectuals, artists, clergy, and others dwelling in the shadow of the Soviet Union comprehended a profound irony. As Czech playwright Václav Havel, who would later become president of his country, wrote: "The 'dissident' movements [of the Soviet Bloc] do not shy away from the idea of violent political overthrow because the idea seems too radical, but on the contrary, because it does not seem radical enough."[44] Rather, they wanted truly revolutionary change and to transform their societies. Solidarność had consciously set out not to topple the state or take power but to reform the existing system, create a free trade union to improve conditions for workers, win wider rights and freedoms, and achieve the recognition of a civil society. Some theoreticians see civil disobedience as a critical component of modern civil societies, by its keeping alive the visualization of a just and democratic society. Civil disobedience, Jean L. Cohen and Andrew Arato assert in their book *Civil Society and Political Theory*, may essentially constitute civil society.[45]

The increasingly transnational character of nonviolent movements abetted by King's influence can also be seen in how knowledge spread from the Balkans to the Caucasus early in the twenty-first century. Two decades after Solidarity launched the largest mass strikes in European history, national nonviolent mobilizations emerged in Serbia in the Balkans, Georgia on the Black Sea, and Ukraine in the Caucasus. These three struggles pressing for democracy and freedoms were related in the sense that youth groups were the harbingers for democratic formation and worked to transmit knowledge about civil resistance.

Gearing up to bring one million demonstrators to Belgrade to confront Serbia's Slobodan Milošević dictatorship, the youthful Otpor! (Resistance!) became the catalyst. Its eighteen thousand members activated a "get out the vote" campaign in February 2000, as thirty Serbian nongovernmental organizations joined the effort. On October 5, 2000, half a million people were in Belgrade from across the nation. When Milošević gave the order to shoot at the crowds, the special police forces and military disobeyed.[46] As general strikes and civil disobedience spread across the country, Milošević's rule ended that month. Police and security forces withdrew from view as hundreds of thousands more people arrived in Belgrade, some by the busload and some atop bulldozers and tractors festooned with banners proclaiming "Bulldozer Revolution." Political scientist Ivan Vejvoda says that "civil resistance in Serbia was an emphatically home-grown movement that underwent a long but eventually deep learning process," and he calls the experience of Otpor! members "a school for protest and leadership."[47]

Farther east, Otpor! emboldened student groups seeking to make similar democratic transitions in Georgia and Ukraine. A galvanizing group in Georgia, Kmara! (Enough!), was aided by Otpor! in planning nonviolent action and became instrumental in deposing the country's president, Eduard Shevardnadze in 2003, in Georgia's Rose Revolution. Pora! (It's Time!) became an animating force behind Ukrainian civil resistance, aided by Otpor! and Kmara! Dubbed the Orange Revolution, Ukraine's mobilization eventually produced a peaceful handover of power to the campaign's presidential candidate in 2004–5. Altering popular perception of what young catalysts can accomplish, the three youth organizations aided independent groups to bend taught theories into national mobilizations.[48] In their audacity, innovativeness, and energy, they were like SNCC in King's era.

Fifteen republics had comprised the Soviet Union; in 1991 the largest of them, Russia, became independent. Boris Yeltsin became the first popularly elected president of the Russian Federation in the wake of nonviolent resistance against an attempted military coup directed at Soviet leader Mikhail Gorbachev.

"A Freedom Explosion"

Bearing in mind that any worldwide esteem for the United States is linked to perfecting the country's democratic character, Martin Luther King Jr. understood that efforts "to win freedom from all forms of oppression" come "from the same deep longing that motivates oppressed people all over the world." In his view, the standing of the United States corresponded with the depth of its democratic participation, and he comprehended, "In a real sense the racial crisis in America is part of the larger world crisis." This duality of perception was an asset for aspiring peoples around the globe. King had not even reached his thirties when he discerned a truth that resounds for the United States today: "Without persistent effort, time itself becomes an ally of the insurgent and primitive forces of irrational emotionalism and social destruction."[49]

The Philippine nonviolent revolution of 1986 was brought about by a progression of massive nonviolent demonstrations that would bestow the name "people power" on nonviolent campaigns in which politically significant numbers take action, notably when seeking democratic transitions. Starting in 1983, a remarkably sustained campaign of civil resistance against the violence and electoral fraud of the Ferdinand Marcos regime led to its 1986 disintegration and restoration of the nation's democracy.

The Philippines had emerged from U.S. rule in 1946 with a constitution modeled on that of the United States, and President Marcos, after his reelection in 1969, had instated martial law in 1971. During the 1970s Marcos refashioned the constitution. The corrupt and repressive regime faced armed struggle from a secessionist Islamic insurrection on the island of Mindanao, and, during the 1980s, communist guerrilla units increasingly threatened its rule. In September

1983 the assassination of senator and opposition leader Benigno Aquino, upon his return to the country from exile, shifted passive acceptance of Marcos into active opposition. The country's middle class, its business sector, and Filipino Roman Catholics began to back the "people power" mobilization.

From 1983 to early 1986, the movement swelled as innumerable demonstrations and marches were organized, along with what were known as people's strikes to close businesses, factories, and offices, and in addition, labor strikes, boycotts, and sit-ins were prevalent. Nonviolent general strikes brought to a halt all economic activity, and these included public barricades to halt private motor vehicles.[50] Human rights groups, peasant organizations, student unions, teacher's associations, labor unions, and women's groups held "people's freedom marches" and major demonstrations, called "parliaments of the streets."[51]

Transmitting in 1986 from a Catholic-run radio station, Radio Veritas, the Roman Catholic Church urged Filipinos to come to Manila's Epifano de los Santos Avenue to demonstrate. As crowds surged in the hundreds of thousands, singing opposition anthems, and with nuns and priests leading prayer vigils, Radio Veritas broadcast around the clock readings from Gandhi's and King's collected works. Some later erroneously claimed that only seventy-two hours had been needed to collapse the Marcos regime. Yet lecturers Hildegard and Jean Goss-Mayr and Richard Deats of FOR, with which King was linked and worked laterally, had been teaching social ethics in the Philippines for twenty years in preparation for such a national mobilization.[52] Defections from the Philippine military, hidden support from the United States, and the cumulative effects of years of struggling against Marcos were also involved in his downfall. Corazon Aquino, Benigno Aquino's widow, became president on February 25, 1986.

South Africa's anti-apartheid struggle lasted for most of a century, and during the latter part of the twentieth century King's writings inspired and were cited by South African leader Albert Lutuli, who had been elected president-general of the African National Congress in 1952 and would remain in this role until his death in 1967. On the cutting edge of the anti-apartheid struggle, and at a time when the ANC was about to establish an armed wing, Lutuli's adamant stance on the necessity for nonviolent action was recognized when he became the 1960 Nobel Peace laureate.

South Africa's protracted efforts against apartheid would involve a coalescence of internal and external campaigns, domestic and international boycotts, third-party sanctions, violent and nonviolent tactics, and protections afforded by intercontinental and worldwide support, including backing from pro-democracy institutions, churches, unions, and human rights groups.

In 1961, the ANC established the Spear of the Nation as an armed front based outside South Africa, while sponsoring sabotage inside the country. Yet the ANC's armed wing could not bring majority rule to South Africa, and its incursions never reached its optimistic prediction of "people's war." On the contrary, the 1980s saw an upsurge of nonviolent resistance that involved some seven hundred affiliates of an extensive internal mobilization called the United Democratic Front (UDF). Notwithstanding the masculine iconography of violence expressed by an armed wing whose guerrilla warfare was at best "martial theatre," as political scientist Tom Lodge phrases it, the years of varying strategies in South Africa's anti-apartheid movement had by the mid-1980s shifted toward those of the wide-ranging UDF affiliates. The vitality of these affiliates arose from the townships, and each generally included a local civic organization, a women's group, and a youth congress, like a stool with three legs. Despite the apartheid regime's banning of political organizing, it was youth groups, students, women's groups, and inhabitants of townships who carried out campaigns by the hundreds (particularly rent and consumer boycotts, student boycotts, and countless strikes), the creation of alternative or parallel institutions, and other forms of defiance, together rendering it impossible for the system of apartheid to be maintained. Some young organizers introduced brutal violence, including "necklacing" with burning tires of alleged informers and collaborators.

The UDF galvanized significant rebellion against local councils in the townships, and this turned it into a popular insurgency. Gaining tangible international support through contributions and third-party economic sanctions, nonviolent civil resistance ultimately undermined the bases of power for the apartheid regime with stay-away strikes involving millions of participants and UDF noncooperation campaigns by the hundreds—particularly rent and consumer boycotts and student boycotts. The scale of the UDF rebellion is said to have been "unprecedented" with the enormity of its effective noncooperation.[53] This predominantly nonviolent African mass mobilization engrossed global audiences, which crested as they watched South Africa end apartheid in 1994 and elect Nelson Mandela as its first black president.

Elsewhere in Africa, dictatorships were ended in Madagascar and Benin. In Asia, East Timor won independence from Indonesia in 1999, after twenty-five years of occupation. In 2006, an eleven-year civil war in Nepal ended after nineteen days of mass demonstrations united the Nepalese people against their king, who surrendered absolute control and restored the parliament in major constitutional concessions. A campaign by Pakistani barristers in the "lawyers' movement" of 2009 returned the country's fired chief justice to the high court's bench. Also in Asia, a communist monopoly was ended in Mongolia.

The Gathering Experience with Nonviolent Struggle

The two most extensive endeavors of democratic reconstruction in the twentieth century, in two generations worldwide, resulted from nonviolent action combined with other elements and forces. The first unfolded with the national nonviolent revolutions of the former Eastern bloc in the 1980s and 1990s, leading to the dissolution of the Soviet Union and producing a diverse group of rough-hewn democracies. The second was the 2010–12 Arab Spring, present in several countries although interrupted and thwarted.

Arab nonviolent campaigns initially helped to disintegrate authoritarian governments in Tunisia, Egypt, Libya, and Yemen, yet these collapsed autocracies also resulted in catastrophes. Violence beset Libya; nearly thirty years of Hosni Mubarak's regime in Egypt was ended but followed by regression to authoritarian rule; multiple wars broke out in Syria; and counterrevolution in Bahrain was aided by Saudi intervention. An expressly nonviolent campaign in Yemen faced fierce government repression, creating a petri dish for war that began in 2015, resulting in some twenty-two million persons, nearly 75 percent of the population, reportedly in dire need of humanitarian assistance by 2019.[54] Other upheavals experienced mixed results in Iraq, Oman, Sudan, Algeria, and Morocco.

The first of the Arab nonviolent revolutions, Tunisia's in December 2010, caused the greatest sociopolitical change and entailed the least bloodshed. As social media reports from Tunisia sped through the Arab world, however, they could not in their brevity reveal the comparative preparedness of Tunisian institutions for this change, maturity that was not shared across the region. Imitator movements materialized in the contagion of Arab rebellion without apprehension that the Tunisian trajectory toward democracy had been extant for decades. However imperfectly, this had allowed civil associations, labor unions, and multiparty politics to develop, and for women's and human rights to grow. After the departure of dictatorial President Zine El Abidine Ben Ali, the Islamist political party An-Nahda exemplified the democratic prerequisite that political parties accept electoral results. Defeated in 2014 legislative elections, it conceded.

Protagonists of the Arab Awakening faced two major impediments: harsh reprisals by the targeted regimes and deficiencies in the conditions and institutional capacity of their societies for making peaceful transitions to pluralistic constitutional governance. Both stand as reminders that civil resistance can be used as a corrective for failing political systems, but it cannot be a replacement for democracy governed by a constitution. Only Tunisia had civil organizations resilient enough to ensure that its beleaguered new democracy would survive repeated challenges, as was recognized when the 2015 Nobel Peace Prize was awarded to a quartet of four such groups.

Along with fragile civil societies, the rest of the region also had limited planning for achievable goals, lack of groups designated to plan strategy, and a dearth of preparation for overhauling preexisting governing bodies. As most of the Arab campaigns eventually ran up against reassertions of autocracies, failures in preparation and planning for the new order revealed themselves. The fact that the new democracies had trivial transnational support was also consequential. The tragic outcomes of Arab Awakening reopened a long-standing debate on competence versus conditions, in which theoreticians of civil resistance often reemphasized the significance of skill with nonviolent techniques. Especially given the enormity of the larger ongoing Arab democratic quest, it seems prudent to argue that robust debate needs to continue, along with serious research as bade by Martin Luther King Jr.

Transformation of Conflict

Given momentum inspired by the media's publicizing of King's leadership internationally during his lifetime and subsequent worldwide commemoration of the meaning of his work and mission, the expanding record of nonviolent action as the preferable means for securing justice is increasingly seen to have transformative potential for groups and societies involved in acute conflict. Nonviolent struggle is time and again the only possible option for tangible change, its fusion of ethics and practicality often adopted when all other approaches have failed or because anything else will worsen the situation. Nothing is ignoble about choosing civil resistance for utilitarian reasons. Intrinsic to revolutionary nonviolence are popular participation, high regard for human rights, reverence for life, the pursuit of tangible correctives to injustice, and possibilities for "transformation of conflict," a term coined by Gandhi. While the term lacks precision, it implies change for the better and a desire to address social problems at their roots, consistent with King's perspective and ongoing influence. In examining King's influence, a preference is clearly evident for processes that are not simplistically reducible to victory or failure. As worded by clinical psychologist Brandon Hamber, "Transformation is a continuous aspirational progression."[55] Gandhi was asked in his advancing years whether nonviolent action was a program for the seizure of power, to which he replied: "A non-violent revolution is not a programme of 'seizure of power'. It is a programme of transformation of relationships ending in a peaceful transfer of power."[56] As early as 1957, King had presciently warned against triumphalism, saying that he wanted to "avoid the temptation of being victimized with a psychology of victors."[57] His emphasis on relational aspects of confronting the opponent led him to oppose a "win or lose" mentality. When striving to alter the behavior of an adversary, elicit definite responses, and achieve accommodation, nonviolent struggle is essentially interactive and seeks to modify the relationships involved in an underlying disagreement.

Civil resistance is not the same as management or resolution of conflict, even though both can result from nonviolent campaigns, and it can also lead to negotiations, although this is not guaranteed—hence the importance of planning and strategy. The contemporary concept of conflict transformation generally stresses deeply transforming the underlying relationships, structures, and systems that have brought injustice and violence into being. Though the study and experimentation that King urged in his 1964 address as Nobel laureate has yet to fully materialize, the field of peace and conflict studies is now the fastest growing of the social sciences. It offers an academic roost compatible with the technique of nonviolent resistance, although in both theory and practice nonviolent action is older than peace and conflict studies, having contributed many of its core insights, such as the need to separate the antagonist from the antagonism.

Moreover, nonviolent struggle can itself be viewed as a form of conflict transformation. Actual *resolution* of conflicts may be rare, and is often transient, with most acute conflicts being diminished, downgraded, or contained but seldom ended. Civil resistance is inherently transformational, as it seeks a transactional alteration in the power relationship between contending parties and to address the underlying causes of strain and injustice. Its presumptions of power focus on the relationships between the challengers and involve communicative action of two contenders reciprocally affecting or influencing each other. Depending on the goals of the protagonists, civil resistance can be aimed at a broad range of objectives, including a quest for dignity; replacing animosity, fear, hatred, stereotypes, and suspicion; reconciliation or forgiveness; or comprehension, consciousness, and even compassion and empathy.

The nonviolent method of fighting for social justice does not presume that all conflicts can be resolved by mediation or arbitration. Far from utopian in thought, theoreticians of nonviolent action assume that political conflict cannot be eradicated. They also respect the congruence of the means and ends—hence the prominence of maintaining nonviolent discipline. Some strife is grounded in such profound feelings of grievance that it cannot be solved until the underlying causes of conflict are fully addressed. Seeking compromise is reasonable in settling disputes that do not involve deep-seated questions of principle or egregious issues of social injustice, but others demand to be fully threshed before broaching the topic of resolution.

As King noted in *Stride toward Freedom*, during the Montgomery bus boycott he perceived nonviolent struggle to consist of five elements. "Nonviolent resistance is not a method for cowards; it does resist," he wrote. "This is ultimately the way of the strong . . . not a method of stagnant passivity." Second, "it does not seek the humiliation or defeat of the opponent" but rather seeks understanding and "to awaken a sense of moral shame in the opponent." Third, "the attack is directed against forces of evil rather than against persons" committing the wrong. Fourth, "the nonviolent resister is willing to accept violence if necessary, but never to inflict it." Fifth, the civil resister refuses to use "external physical violence but also internal violence of spirit." In this regard, King said he was thinking about *agape*, which in New Testament Greek meant disinterested understanding and "redemptive good will . . . seeking to preserve and create community."[58] This analysis of nonviolent action has since decidedly deepened. Yet even as nonviolent movements in our time have been able to collapse or disintegrate some fifty tyrannies and dictatorships, in part thanks to theory and praxis contributed by Gandhi and King, the rudiments that King disclosed in analyzing the Montgomery boycott reveal his bedrock relational sensibilities.

When contesting parties possess severely asymmetrical power, the smaller or weaker side may find it hard even to obtain a hearing apart from staging a nonviolent struggle, which can bring parity between the sides of an otherwise unbalanced relationship. This is an important property of nonviolent struggle. It may be the only way under lopsided circumstances to reach negotiations, transform a dispute, or resolve a conflict. King understood that civil resistance could work under asymmetrical circumstances, and he stated this clearly: "Nonviolent resistance is the most potent weapon available to oppressed people in their struggle for freedom."[59]

According to Peter Wallensteen, authority in peace studies at Sweden's Uppsala University, "The projects that exist within the peace research community all aim at understanding why conflicts occur or how they can be terminated."[60] Perceiving conflict to be part of the human condition, neither Gandhi nor King believed that political disputes *can* be "terminated" or eradicated. Far from being utopian, both Gandhi and King, and today's nonviolent theoreticians, tend to presume that political conflict cannot be eradicated. Gandhi understood solutions to last until they unraveled again. In this appraisal, some disputes must be fought, and certain struggles waged, albeit with nonviolent means.

Nonviolent Action and the World House

In 1962, a medical student at Atlanta's Emory University was given free housing at St. Joseph's Infirmary for the last two years of his medical education in exchange for being on call as an "extern." One of his tasks was to write a medical history on all new admissions to the Roman Catholic hospital in the commercial capital of Georgia, on nights when he was on duty. One evening he went into a private room at the end of the top floor in the facility, where the nursing nuns said that he did not need to take a history on a particular patient, explaining that the patient was Martin Luther King Jr., who was under the care of a private physician. This was the extern's first and only experience of a black patient being admitted to a white hospital in Atlanta, and almost no one knew of it, because King was given confidential status. When the senior medical student looked at King's chart, almost nothing was written there except "hypertension and exhaustion." He concluded that the diagnosis was a combination of depression and exhaustion, yet the private doctor had phrased it more benignly. Subsequently, the extern would learn that King had been hospitalized more than once for "exhaustion," which he considered most likely to have been coupled with depression.[61]

King would again be hospitalized in St. Joseph's Infirmary in October 1963 for exhaustion and a severe viral infection, when it was reported that he would receive the 1964 Nobel Peace Prize.[62] That was the same month that J. Edgar Hoover, director of the Federal Bureau of Investigation, sent a memorandum to Attorney General Robert F. Kennedy, asking permission for intelligence surveillance to wiretap King, which Kennedy would grant.[63] Disclosures half a century after King's death suggest that he paid a high personal price for taking on his mission. He had not sought leadership; it had been thrust upon him. After the Montgomery bus boycott, he grew to his full moral stature. He possessed a deeper, stronger sense of ethics than any other U.S. leader of the twentieth century. Around the world, people who lack familiarity with details about the U.S. civil rights movement know about King. The closest that the United States comes to commemorating nonviolent action as a recurring component in its history is the national federal holiday on King's birthday. Yet King was far from the desiccated civil hero depicted annually. Rather, he endures as an exemplar for how human beings can confront our long, drawn-out failure to tackle endemic racism and interethnic strife, the persistence of poverty, militarism, terrorism and all forms of violence, and the intensifying environmental crises.

It is difficult to assess precisely the degree of King's influence on the innumerable nonviolent struggles that have ameliorated or corrected worldwide injustices, including those discussed above that took place in Latin America, the Eastern bloc, South Africa, the Philippines, and the Arab world. King's body of work is often cited in papers from civil resistance campaigns and in histories of such struggles. In the twenty-first century, Gandhi's experiments and King's leadership continue to be analyzed, shared, and absorbed as nonviolent campaigns persevere and develop proficiency worldwide. Global awareness of the comparative strength and successes of civil resistance keeps growing, and King continues to represent and provide potent ways for aggrieved groups to make conscious, studied turns from violent to nonviolent means of fighting for freedom, democracy, and rights. The international exchange of practical lessons from nonviolent resistance is part of King's story. Far-flung individuals and groups continue to draw on his experience, ideas, philosophy, and wisdom.

An example of such interchange is the way that youth and student groups in the Balkans and Caucasus used their learning not to promote a model but to embark on a continuing process. For some years, Serbia's Otpor! leaders were part of a network of experienced planners that included veteran organizers from struggles in Georgia on the Black Sea, Lebanon, the Philippines, South Africa, and Ukraine who coached these groups. Political scientists visited Cairo in 2009 to share their work with forward-looking Egyptian academicians and reform-minded civil-society actors, sharing the basics involved in historic struggles. Televised spectacles of dictatorships disintegrating from the 1980s into the twenty-first century made it easier for people to see for themselves how large numbers can under certain circumstances, withholding cooperation and refusing to obey tyrants, collapse authoritarian regimes. Scholars increasingly hold exchanges through seminars and webinars, and academic research and curricula reach additional people worldwide more quickly and freely than ever before. Although communication still takes place one-on-one or in small groups, blogging and social media have enabled the immediate sharing of insights and allowed people in nonviolent campaigns worldwide to compare notes. Among the bloggers writing about Egypt's Tahrir Square occupation was Dalia Ziada, who, when asked whether the flow of knowledge in historical accounts, readings, or training had played any role in ending Hosni Mubarak's rule, explained:

> People mistakenly assume that Egypt's revolution was spontaneous. But we had been studying and learning for ten to fifteen years through study groups and nonviolent workshops, especially in 2007–2008. These workshops exposed us to cases of nonviolent action and they inspired us. I learned about the U.S. civil rights movement and translated a comic book on Martin Luther King into Arabic and distributed it through my blog and also in print. It was passed around widely.

> At first people didn't understand what nonviolent resistance was or why it was important, but gradually the knowledge empowered people and helped all of us believe that we could do this.[64]

New developments in quantitative research show that nonviolent civil resistance has become worldwide the most widespread and common form of engagement to bring about social change. This understanding is related to withdrawals from the fund of wisdom underwritten by Gandhi and King. Investigations by political scientists Erica Chenoweth and Maria J. Stephan have found that nonviolent campaigns succeed more than twice as often as armed struggles when seeking to remove national leaders from office or to achieve territorial independence, even in repressive nondemocracies. In studying 323 nonviolent, violent, and mixed movements between 1900 and 2006, they found that nonviolent campaigns succeeded 53 percent of the time versus 26 percent for armed insurrections. They conclude that a significant explanation for this relative success is that "moral, physical, informational and commitment barriers to participation are much lower for nonviolent resistance than for violent insurgency." This may be mainly attributable to nonviolent movements' abilities to recruit significantly larger numbers of participants than armed insurgencies, with groups engaged in nonviolent campaigns on average four times larger than those engaged in violent struggles or guerrilla warfare. The sheer numbers can be instrumental in modifying power relations. Although Chenoweth and Stephan found that state repression and structural factors may reduce a civil resistance campaign's prospects for success by nearly 35 percent, they discerned no structural conditions that determine movement outcomes. They show that countries experiencing popular nonviolent struggles are more likely to emerge from acute conflicts as democratic and as sustaining human rights and democracy, once established, compared to those experiencing violent insurgencies. "On the whole," they write, "nonviolent resistance campaigns are more effective in getting results and, once they have succeeded, more likely to establish democratic regimes with a lower probability of relapse into civil war."[65] Even more telling is Chenoweth's assertion that none of the nonviolent movements she studied had failed once they had achieved 3.5 percent participation by the population.[66] In other words, when the level of mass involvement reached 3.5 percent of the citizenry in a campaign studied by Chenoweth, the struggle reached its goals.

"What we are seeing now is a freedom explosion," King wrote in 1967, alluding to "the realization of 'an idea whose time has come,' to use Victor Hugo's phrase." His term "freedom explosion" is a remarkably apt idiom for conveying the horizon of this chapter. King's body of works has contributed materially to the growing effectiveness of nonviolent mobilization worldwide in the twenty-first century and will continue to inform those who populate its campaigns. He spoke of "the deep rumbling of discontent . . . the thunder of disinherited masses, rising from dungeons of oppression to the bright hills of freedom." Having noted that during five decades after King's death dictatorships and tyrannies were disintegrated in more than fifty countries by civil resistance, it is worth recalling too that nonviolent struggles have been identified going back to ancient times. Right through human history, groups of people have pursued justice, equality, and freedom using nonviolent methods, exerting cultural, economic, political, psychological, and social forms of power against oppressive groups or rulers. The growing capabilities of average people in the twenty-first century to fight for truth and justice with nonviolent strategies and methods match King's own declaration about an eruption of freedom, which he saw as "the widest liberation movement in history," in which "great masses of people are determined to end the exploitation of their races and lands."[67]

King's vision for the world house invokes a view that "all reality hinges on moral foundations," in which reciprocity between wealthy nations and poor nations can lead to enrichment for all.[68] His recognition of interdependence is closely allied to an inherent linkage between means and ends, a powerful tributary of thought abounding in nonviolent struggles. Proponents of civil resistance generally contend that means tend to determine the result achieved—thus the importance of maintaining nonviolent discipline. They reject notions of "all means of struggle" and the conceit of mixing nonviolent action with violent measures, as contended by ideologists for armed struggle, in that violent insurrection and nonviolent struggle rest on different understandings of power and its sources.

In his "World House" chapter of *Where Do We Go from Here?*, King explicitly repeats his 1964 challenge that "the philosophy and strategy of nonviolence become immediately a subject for study and for serious experimentation in every field of human conflict, by no means excluding the relations between nations. It is, after all, nation-states which make war, which have produced the weapons that threaten the survival of mankind and which are both genocidal and suicidal in character." "True nonviolence is more than the absence of violence," he goes on. He further states: "It is the persistent and determined application of peaceable power to offenses against the community—in this case the world community. As the United Nations moves ahead with the giant tasks confronting it, I would hope that it would earnestly examine the uses of nonviolent direct action."[69] King threw down an extraordinary gauntlet before the world and the UN, in that direct action confronts the wrong or grievance directly.

Unfortunately, in the five decades since King's prudent proposition for "study and serious experimentation," nonviolent civil resistance has never been allocated the support and backing for research that was allotted for fields such as international development, the environment, human rights, national security, and the building of democracies. Untold nonviolent indigenous struggles for justice remain unrecorded and may no longer be accessible for analysis. Even so, it is not too late to take King's advice.

Related to the acuity of his vision for the world house, King saw civil resistance as a progressive substitution for violence in specific situations, stating, "In the presence of the weapons we have ourselves created, it is as possible and as urgent to put an end to war and violence between nations as it is to put an end to poverty and racial injustice."[70] Explicitly believing that poverty, racism, and militarism could be altered through the intelligent use of nonviolent strategies, King recognized the human agency of nonviolent action, while understanding the necessity for policing and defense in human societies. Adam Roberts, international relations expert and former head of the British Academy, attaches importance to the tradition where nonviolent resistance, by becoming technologically advanced in both skills and strategy, could serve in functions previously allocated to armed force. The pivotal idea is that civil resistance can gradually be substituted for dependence on armed force, for instance in police and defense systems, yet this concept is contingent on a viable substitute. Gene Sharp, whose discernments from six decades of research place him as the foremost scholar of what he called nonviolent strategic action, raised the possibility that nonviolent struggle might with time substantially be substituted for deadly conflict if organized for explicit purposes and practiced after study, preparation, and strategic analysis. Regarding Sharp's advancement of a theory of "progressive substitution," Roberts judges Sharp as having done the most to develop this precedent of political thought into coherent and intelligible theory, "giving it a high degree of credibility, because he combined it with an analysis of political power, including that of dictatorial and totalitarian regimes."[71] Sharp explained how nonviolent sanctions might be incrementally exchanged for armed force:

> The concept of replacing violent sanctions with nonviolent sanctions in a series of specific substitutions is not utopian. To a degree not generally recognized, this already occurs in various conflict situations, even on scales which affect our domestic society and international relations. Far from being utopian, nonviolent sanctions build upon crucial parts of our past and present reality. Past cases, however, are only the crude beginnings of alternative nonviolent sanc-

tions. These could be refined and developed to increase their power potential, and adapted to meet society's genuine need for sanctions. . . .

The nonviolent technique is thus an underdeveloped political technique, probably at the stage comparable to violent conflict several thousand years ago. Hence, nonviolent struggle as waged to date may only have revealed a small fraction of its potential fighting power and effectiveness."[72]

King asserted, "All inhabitants of the globe are now neighbors."[73] Today this can be seen to be true. With billions of people worldwide, half the planet's population, possessing access to the Internet and the numbers steadily growing, the potential for sharing knowledge and ideas quickly across cultures means that some contemporary nonviolent mobilizations exhibit transnational qualities. Viral mobilizations allowed by the Internet, mobile phones, GPS technology, and virtual social networks are altering some aspects of nonviolent struggles. Groups coalesce and operate across borders, often because their grievances extend beyond rigid political boundaries. Targeted entities or adversaries may include a multilateral organization, such as the World Bank, International Monetary Fund, or World Trade Organization. Transnational forces inherently shape some issues (concerning climate change, for example) and policies of multinational corporations. The goal of a transnational mobilization might be to support a threatened human right, press for codification of an entitlement won through massive popular mobilization, compel recognition of women's rights and gender equity, fight Anthropocene global warming, or resist a war. Appearing just before Tunisia's 2010–11 nonviolent uprising, Evgeny Morozov's *The Net Delusion: The Dark Side of Internet Freedom* warned, however, that the democratizing effects of the Internet can correspondingly increase the effectiveness of repression, entrench dictators, menace bloggers, and make it riskier to promote democracy.[74]

Building Knowledge of Nonviolent Struggle

A virtually unlimited need exists for building knowledge of nonviolent struggle for addressing persistent conflict. Evidence for this is disclosed whenever present-day journalists label a complex campaign of nonviolent action for social change "protest," call a demonstration a "riot," or use the phrase "passive resistance," which Gandhi and Martin Luther King Jr. rejected as misleading, as nonviolent action is anything but passive.

Nonviolent action is not solely moral or ethical. To King, it was practical and the "only road to freedom."[75] After the end of the Montgomery bus boycott, he said, "the choice is no longer between violence and nonviolence. It is either nonviolence or nonexistence."[76] King was making the same point, in nearly identical language, in his final address, on April 3, 1968, in Memphis the night before he was killed.

Scholars have shown that transitions to democracy entailing violent action are less likely to result in sustainable democracy than those characterized by nonviolent civil resistance. In other words, the consolidation of democratic norms and values may be a consequence of the choice of methods rather than the other way around.[77] Those working on the relatively new field of peacebuilding know that countries experiencing popular nonviolent struggle are more likely to sustain human rights and democracy, once established, than when violent struggle was used.

Both Gandhi and King honed the practice of nonviolent action as it developed during the twentieth century into a means of projecting immense and effective political power. Often indebted to Gandhi and King, oppressed peoples today are learning alternative ways to fight without violence faster than the tyrants and oppressors are coming up with new ways to repress them.

Notwithstanding the fact that nonviolent action has grown in volume and significance on every continent since King's death, civil resistance has remained underdeveloped as a political technique. In the United States and internationally, fortitude has been lacking from major institutions in backing its validity and efficacy. These include religious denominations, the academy, labor unions (historically perhaps the largest users of nonviolent direct action in times gone by), and philanthropic institutions. More efforts are needed to educate at all levels about nonviolent action and its successes. We equally need empirical research and investment supporting the development and refinement of nonviolent action. Such support is currently minimal compared to the vast assets allocated to military and security studies.

Superior strength continues to be equated with violence. This assumption is a direct inheritance from the tradition of war as the ultimate arbiter of conflict. It is connected to the perception of war making (or violence) as a rite and manifestation of manhood, inspired by scriptures or the idea that magnitude of force exhibits depth of conviction. Violence has also been labeled a cleansing process. Yet nonviolent movements exhibit indomitability and great persistence. With their effectuality increasing, nonviolent struggles have proved effective despite the aggression of postcolonial administrations. They have continued and frequently succeed in the face of military occupations, dictators, tyrants, institutionalized racism, entrenched gender cruelty and discrimination, and shoot-first-and-ask-questions-later policing.

If anything, the use of nonviolent action will intensify. In pursuing research, as King advocated, those studying the contingencies of war and others undertaking peace studies should link together closely. Historian Christopher Clark, in considering the future of war, echoes King's concept of the world house: "The quest for peace, like the struggle to arrest climate change, requires that we think of ourselves not just as states, tribes, or nations, but as the human inhabitants of a shared space. It demands feats of imagination as concerted and impressive as the sci-fi creativeness and wizardry we invest in future wars. It means connecting the intellectual work done in centers of war studies with research conducted in peace institutes, and applying to the task of avoiding war the long-term pragmatic reasoning we associate with 'strategy.'"[78] Fifty years after his death, Martin Luther King Jr. continues to lead, showing that coherent alternatives to violence are not just possible but also necessary.

NOTES

The epigraphs are from Martin Luther King Jr., "My Trip to the Land of Gandhi," in *A Testament of Hope: The Essential Writings of Martin Luther King, Jr.*, edited by James M. Washington (San Francisco: HarperSanFrancisco, 1986), 25; James M. Lawson Jr., verbal communication with Mary E. King, reported in email to Lewis V. Baldwin, June 7, 2018.

1. This chapter could not have been written without Gandhi's originating a new, living language for the English-speaking world, including contemporary campaigns and movements. He coined or appropriated terms of lasting currency like "civil disobedience," "civil resistance," "noncooperation," "nonviolence," "nonviolent conflict," "nonviolent methods," "nonviolent revolution," "nonviolent sanctions," "techniques of struggle," and "transformation of conflict."

2. For definitions of nonviolent methods and historical examples, see Gene Sharp, *The Politics of Nonviolent Action*, pt. 2, *The Methods of Nonviolent Action* (Boston: Porter Sargent, 1973), 109–902.

3. Martin Luther King Jr., *Where Do We Go from Here: Chaos or Community?* (Boston: Beacon Press, 1967; rpt., 1968, 2010), 167, 173.

4. Max Cary and H. H. Scullard, *A History of Rome: Down to the Reign of Constantine*, 3rd ed. (New York: Palgrave, 1980), 65–66.

5. Walter H. Conser Jr., "The Stamp Act of Resistance," in Walter H. Conser Jr., Ronald M. McCarthy, David J. Toscano, and Gene Sharp, eds., *Resistance, Politics, and the American Struggle for Independence, 1765-1775* (Boulder, Colo.: Lynne Rienner, 1986), 22, 28.

6. During this action, no harm was done or threatened to individuals. See Ronald M. McCarthy, "Resistance Politics and the Growth of Parallel Governments in America, 1765-1775," in Conser, McCarthy, Toscano, and Sharp, *Resistance, Politics, and the American Struggle*, 482.

7. Ibid., 482–92.

8. See ibid., esp. 3–21. A concise chapter summarizing and reviewing this voluminous research is Walter H. Conser Jr., "The United States: Reconsidering the Struggle for Independence, 1765-1775," in Maciej Bartkowski, ed., *Recovering Nonviolent History: Civil Resistance in Liberation Struggles* (Boulder, Colo.: Lynne Rienner, 2013), 299–317.

9. William Gamson examined fifty-three "challenging groups" in U.S. society chosen from an original sample of historical references concerning forty-five hundred organizations that had mobilized an uninvolved constituency and made claims against a targeted group (1816 to 1934, primarily nineteenth century). William A. Gamson, *The Strategy of Social Protests*, 2nd ed. (Belmont, Calif.: Wadsworth, 1990) 19–22, 48–49.

10. Military historian Margaret Macmillan, broadcasting from Beirut, July 10, 2018, BBC Radio 4 Reith Lecture.

11. Ronald M. McCarthy and Gene Sharp, eds., *Nonviolent Action: A Research Guide* (New York: Garland, 1997), 118.

12. Carleton Mabee, *Black Freedom: The Nonviolent Abolitionists from 1830 through the Civil War* (New York: Macmillan, 1970), 52–53.

13. Frederick Douglass, "The Significance of Emancipation in the West Indies," speech, Canandaigua, New York, August 3, 1857, in *The Frederick Douglass Papers*, vol. 3, series 1, *Speeches, Debates, and Interviews, 1855-1863*, edited by John W. Blassingame (New Haven: Yale University Press, 1986), 204.

14. Mabee, *Black Freedom*, 115.

15. Fred Halliday, "Hidden from International Relations: Women and the International Arena," in Rebecca Grant and Kathleen Newland, eds., *Gender and International Relations* (Buckingham, UK: Open University Press, 1991), 162.

16. See Mary King, *Mahatma Gandhi and Martin Luther King, Jr.: The Power of Nonviolent Action*, 2nd ed. (New Delhi: Indian Council for Cultural Relations and Mehta Publishers, 2002), 92–97. http://unesdoc.unesco.org/images/0011/001147/114773e.pdf.

17. Martin Luther King Jr., *Stride toward Freedom: The Montgomery Story* (New York: Harper & Row, 1958), 91.

18. Henry David Thoreau, "Resistance to Civil Government," in Elizabeth P. Peabody, ed., *Aesthetic Papers* (1849; repr., New York: Cosimo Classics, 2005), vol. 7, 543.

19. Gene Sharp, introduction to Henry David Thoreau, *On the Duty of Civil Disobedience*, Peace News Pamphlet (London: Housmans, 1963), n.p.

20. See Sudarshan Kapur, *Raising up a Prophet: The African-American Encounter with Gandhi* (Boston: Beacon Press, 1992). Kapur conducted archival research on the Gandhian freedom movement in India in twelve black-owned U.S. newspapers, journals, and outlets such as the *Crisis*, organ of the National Association for the Advancement of Colored People, when W. E. B. Du Bois was its editor (1910–34). Kapur notes Du Bois's writings as "an important source" (4n7).

21. Martin Luther King Jr., *Stride toward Freedom*, 96.

22. Mary King, *Mahatma Gandhi and Martin Luther King, Jr.*, 132.

23. Richard L. Deats, "The International Fellowship of Reconciliation," in Roger S. Powers, William B. Vogele, Douglas Bond, and Christopher Kruegler, eds., *Protest, Power, and Change: Encyclopedia of Nonviolent Action from ACT-UP to Women's Suffrage* (New York: Garland, 1997), 178.

24. Martin Luther King Jr., *Stride toward Freedom*, 84.

25. Ibid., 51–52.

26. Mohandas K. Gandhi, "Russia and India," *Indian Opinion*, November 11, 1905, in K. Swaminathan, ed., *Collected Works of Mahatma Gandhi* (New Delhi, India: Publications Division, Ministry of Information and Broadcasting, Government of India, 1960–78), 5:8.

27. Martin Luther King Jr., "The Quest for Peace and Justice," in Frederick Haberman, ed., *Nobel Lectures, Peace*, vol. 3, *1951-1970* (Amsterdam: Elsevier, 1972), 338–43 (address of December 11,1964, upon receiving the 1964 Nobel Peace Prize).

28. Mohandas K. Gandhi, *Constructive Programme: Its Meaning and Place* (repr., Ahmedabad, India: Navajivan, 1948), 21–22.

29. See, for example, Erica Chenoweth and Maria J. Stephan, "How the World Is Proving Martin Luther King Right about Nonviolence," *Washington Post*, January 18, 2016.

30. Martin Luther King Jr., *Stride toward Freedom*, 196–97.

31. Manuel Antonio Garretón, "Fear in Military Regimes: An Overview," in Juan E. Corradi, Patricia Weiss Fagan, and Manuel Antonio Garretón, eds., *Fear at the Edge: State Terror and Resistance in Latin America* (Berkeley: University of California Press, 1992), 23.

32. King, *Where Do We Go from Here?*, 175.

33. Adam Bernstein, "Jorge Rafael Videla, Ruthless Argentine Junta Leader, Dies at 87," *Washington Post*, May 18, 2013.

34. Martin Luther King Jr., *Stride toward Freedom*, 51.

35. Martin Luther King Jr., "Nonviolence: The Only Road to Freedom [October 1966]," in *Testament of Hope*, 56.

36. Janusz Ziolkowski, "The Roots, Branches and Blossoms of Solidarnosc," in Gwyn Prins, ed., *Spring in Winter: The 1989 Revolutions* (Manchester, UK: Manchester University Press, 1990), 46.

37. For details on eight national nonviolent revolutions of the Eastern bloc, see Mary [Elizabeth] King, *The New York Times on Emerging Democracies in Eastern Europe*, TimesReference from CQ Press (Washington, D.C.: CQ Press, 2009).

38. Jacek Kuroń, "Overcoming Totalitarianism," in Vladimir Tismaneanu, ed., *The Revolutions of 1989* (London: Routledge, 1999), 200.

39. Adam Michnik, *Letters from Prison and Other Essays*, translated by Maya Latynski (Berkeley: University of California Press, 1985), 88–89.

40. Jan Zielonka, "Strengths and Weaknesses of Nonviolent Action: The Polish Case," *Orbis* (1986): 93; and Jan Zielonka, *Political Ideas in Contemporary Poland* (Aldershot, UK: Gower, 1989), 95.

41. Ziolkowski, "Roots, Branches and Blossoms of Solidarnosc," in Prins, *Spring in Winter*, 59.

42. John Feffer, "Uncivil Society," *In These Times*, November 15, 1993, 28.

43. Michnik, *Letters from Prison and Other Essays*, 89.

44. Václav Havel, "The Power of the Powerless," translated by Paul Wilson, in *Living in Truth*, edited by Jan Vladislav (London, UK: Faber and Faber, 1987), 93.

45. Jean L. Cohen and Andrew Arato, *Civil Society and Political Theory: Studies in Contemporary German Social Thought* (Cambridge, Mass.: MIT Press, 1994), 566–67. Cohen and Arato end their 771-page study with the chapter "Civil Disobedience and Civil Society."

46. Ivan Vejvoda, "Civil Society versus Slobodan Milošević: Serbia, 1991–2000," in Adam Roberts and Timothy Garton Ash, *Civil Resistance and Power Politics: The Experience of Nonviolent Action from Gandhi to the Present* (New York: Oxford University Press, 2009), 306, 312.

47. Ibid., 307, 314.

48. For details, see King, *New York Times on Emerging Democracies in Eastern Europe*.

49. Martin Luther King Jr., *Stride toward Freedom*, 191, 197.

50. Kurt Schock, *Unarmed Insurrections: People Power Movements in Nondemocracies* (Minneapolis: University of Minnesota Press, 2005), 75–76.

51. David G. Timberman, *A Changeless Land: Continuity and Change in Philippine Politics* (New York: M. E. Sharpe, 1991), 131–32.

52. See Hildegard Goss-Mayr, "When Prayer and Revolution Became People Power," *Fellowship*, March 1987, 8–11.

53. Tom Lodge, "The Interplay of Non-violent and Violent Action in the Movement against Apartheid in South Africa, 1983–94," in Roberts and Ash, *Civil Resistance and Power Politics*, 217–18, 228.

54. David Ignatius, "The Lesson We Should Learn from the Killing Fields of Afghanistan and Yemen," opinion, *Washington Post*, January 29, 2019.

55. Brandon Hamber, "Transformation and Reconciliation," in John Darby and Roger MacGinty, eds., *Contemporary Peacemaking: Conflict, Violence and Peace Processes* (Basingstoke, UK: Palgrave Macmillan, 2003), 228.

56. Mohandas K. Gandhi, "Non-violent Technique and Parallel Government," in *Non-violence in Peace and War*, vol. 2, edited by Bharatan Kumarappa (Ahmedabad, India: Navajivan, 1949), 8.

57. Martin Luther King Jr., "Give Us the Ballot—We Will Transform the South" (May 17, 1957), in *Testament of Hope*, 200.

58. Martin Luther King Jr., *Stride toward Freedom*, 102–5.

59. Martin Luther King Jr., "My Trip to the Land of Gandhi," in *Testament of Hope*, 25.

60. Peter Wallensteen, *Understanding Conflict Resolution: War, Peace, and the Global System* (Thousand Oaks, Calif.: Sage Publications, 2002), 17.

61. Peter G. Bourne, personal communication with the author, April 27, 2018, Fredericksburg, Virginia.

62. Gary M. Pomerantz, *Where Peachtree Meets Sweet Auburn: The Saga of Two Families and the Making of Atlanta* (New York: Scribner, 1996), 334–35.

63. See Ellen Nakashima, "National Security: FBI Director Urges Police and Civilians to 'See Each Other' More Clearly," *Washington Post*, May 26, 2016, for the reflection of former FBI director James Comey on how he kept Hoover's memorandum on his desk as a reminder of "why it is vital that power always be checked, overseen and constrained."

64. The author thanks Vanessa Ortiz, then an official with the U.S. Agency for International Development, for her account of Ziada's response. Vanessa Ortiz, personal communication with the author, March 16, 2011, Washington, D.C. For the comic book, see Dalia Ziada, "Can a Comic Book Change the Middle East?," http://daliaziada.blogspot .com/2009/05/can-comic-book-about-mlk-change-middle.html.

65. Erica Chenoweth and Maria J. Stephan, *Why Civil Resistance Works: The Strategic Logic of Nonviolent Conflict* (New York: Columbia University Press, 2011), 10, 68.

66. Erica Chenoweth, "The Success of Nonviolent Resistance: Erica Chenoweth at TEDxBoulder," November 4, 2013, YouTube, https://www.youtube.com/watch?v= YJSehRlU34w&vl=en.

67. Martin Luther King Jr., *Where Do We Go from Here?*, 169.

68. Clayborne Carson and Peter Holloran, eds., *A Knock at Midnight: Inspiration from the Great Sermons of Reverend Martin Luther King, Jr.* (New York: Warner Books, 1998), 10.

69. Martin Luther King Jr., *Where Do We Go from Here?*, 184.

70. Ibid.

71. Adam Roberts, introduction to Roberts and Ash, *Civil Resistance and Power Politics*, 9.

72. Gene Sharp, *Social Power and Political Freedom* (Boston: Porter Sargent, 1980), xi, 279.

73. Martin Luther King Jr., *Where Do We Go from Here?*, 167.

74. Evgeny Morozov, *The Net Delusion: The Dark Side of Internet Freedom* (New York: Public Affairs, 2011). In Britain the book is subtitled *How Not to Liberate the World*.

75. Martin Luther King Jr., "Nonviolence: The Only Road to Freedom," in *Testament of Hope*, 55.

76. Martin Luther King Jr., *Stride toward Freedom*, 224.

77. See Adrian Karatnycky and Peter Ackerman, *How Freedom Is Won: From Civic Resistance to Durable Democracy* (New York: Freedom House, 2005).

78. Christopher Clark, "This Is a Reality, Not a Threat," *New York Review of Books*, November 22, 2018, 54.

CHAPTER 9

EMBRACING DIFFERENCE
MARTIN LUTHER KING JR.'S WORLD HOUSE VISION AS A TEACHING RESOURCE FOR WOMEN AND QUEER LIBERATION

AMY E. STEELE, VICKI L. CRAWFORD, AND LEWIS V. BALDWIN

I still hear people say that I should not be talking about the rights of lesbian and gay people. . . . But I hasten to remind them that Martin Luther King, Jr. said, "Injustice anywhere is a threat to justice everywhere." I appeal to everyone who believes in Martin Luther King, Jr.'s dream, to make room at the table of brotherhood and sisterhood for lesbian and gay people.
CORETTA SCOTT KING

Paying attention to issues of gender, sexuality, and sexism in the legacy of King's civil rights movement leadership prompts us to disobey the very rules of subjugation that all movement participants sought to change. It adds incentive for *joining* their tradition of refusing to be quiet, be patient, and accept the God-given hierarchy of human worth reflected in traditional social practices.
TRACI C. WEST, "Gendered Legacies of Martin Luther King, Jr.'s Leadership"

There are competing claims today about the significance of Martin Luther King Jr.'s legacy in the struggle for women's and queer liberation. Some hold that King's life, thought, and social praxis are relevant to the emergence and shaping of a world free of patriarchy, sexism, and homophobia, while others either take a sharply opposing viewpoint or contend that no one is sufficiently authoritative to speak for King in these times.[1] The fact is that King himself never called for the eradication of discrimination based on gender identity and sexual orientation, even as he became increasingly radical toward the end of his life. In his last two books, and in numerous sermons and speeches, he insightfully targeted white supremacy, poverty and economic injustice, and war as barriers to creative living in the world house, but he totally ignored sexism and homophobia.[2] This neglect on King's part should not be casually dismissed, especially since he knew about the abuse and subjugation of women and gay people, had a great capacity for analyzing world problems, was known for his extraordinarily progressive global outlook, and advocated for the kind of "revolution of values" that placed "ecumenical" above "sectional" loyalties.[3] It is equally true that King did not live to witness the second wave of the women's movement (feminism) and the blossoming of the gay rights movement, both of which occurred in the decade after his death in April 1968.[4] In any case, King-led civil and human rights campaigns positively impacted the character, momentum, and direction of both movements, and activists in the feminist, womanist, and LGBTQ communities continue to view King as a resource and inspiration.[5]

This chapter explores the meaning of King's complex and important legacy for women and queer people in the world house. King's scope of analysis of the human condition is expanded to include the worldwide systems of gender discrimination and the sequestering of the human rights of lesbian, gay, bisexual, and transgender humans. The chapter begins with a discussion of King's thoughts on the meaning of conformity, transformed nonconformity, and the maladjusted personality and how these squared with his absence of attention to the gender hierarchy and the queer rights issue in the 1950s and 1960s. What is said here about King and women builds on what was provided earlier in chapter 5. Next, attention is devoted to the competing claims about how King would feel today about women and queer people and their plight in the world house. The discussion here takes seriously Traci C. West's thoughts on "the question of contextualization," which suggest King's ideas and actions around gender and sexuality are best understood when contextualized in his own time and not beyond.[6] From that point, King's significance as a teaching resource for women and queer activists is critically assessed. The theoretical framework for this discussion is largely based on a reading of bell hooks's groundbreaking analysis, which considers the interrelationship between gender, race, class, and sex. Also, the discussion considers Paulo Freire's theory of critical pedagogy, which encourages a philosophical and practical approach to education that is simultaneously innovative, nontraditional, and critical of reality and the human condition while also anticolonial, liberating, humanizing, and geared toward much-needed social change and global transformation.[7] Implied here are teaching strategies for pedagogues who aim to employ King's ideas in facilitating the discovery of liberative paths for women and queer folk. Finally, the chapter concludes with commentary on steps that might be taken in the future to rid the world house of the oppressive structures of patriarchy, sexism, and homophobia.

On the Gender Hierarchy and the Gay Issue

In versions of his sermon "Transformed Nonconformist," Martin Luther King Jr. brooded over the fact that he lived "in a generation when crowd pressures have unconsciously conditioned our minds and feet to move to the rhythmic drumbeat of the status quo." King went on to declare, "In spite of this prevailing tendency to conform, we as Christians have a mandate to be nonconformists."[8] He turned to the discipline of psychology to make essentially the same point:

> Modern psychology has a word that is probably used more than any other word. It is the word "maladjusted." Now we all should seek to live a well-adjusted life in order to avoid neurotic and schizophrenic personalities. But there are some things within our social order to which I am proud to be maladjusted and to which I call upon you to be maladjusted. I never intend to adjust myself to segregation and discrimination. . . . I never intend to adjust myself to the tragic effects of the methods of physical violence and to tragic militarism. I call upon you to be maladjusted to such things. . . . God grant that we will be so maladjusted that we will be able to go out and change our world and our civilization. And then we will be able to move from the bleak and desolate midnight of man's inhumanity to man to the bright and glittering daybreak of freedom and justice.[9]

But when it came to the abuse, marginalization, and subjugation of women and queer people in the world house, King was anything but a "nonconformist" or "maladjusted" personality. To the contrary, he was at best an ambivalent soul—one who claimed an unwavering opposition to bigotry, injustice, and intolerance in all forms while also remaining silent and noncommittal in the face of oppression based on gender and sexuality. Here his world house vision fell short in terms of both a person-oriented analysis and moral reach. With this and more in mind, James H. Cone, the father of black liberation theology, and for many years professor at New York's Union Theological Seminary, has written: "I find it ironic that the public King we witnessed on a national stage talked vociferously about social justice and civil rights for all people yet his personal life did not reflect the same ethos concerning women and gays." Cone opined that "the public King" was never apt to advocate justice for women and LGBTQ people because this would have further damaged his "already-waning popularity" with black Americans and President Lyndon B. Johnson.[10]

When it came to the status of women in the United States and worldwide, King was seemingly torn between the pressure to conform or adjust to the traditions of patriarchy and a determination to affirm the essential dignity, worth, and sacredness of all human beings, devoid of any considerations of gender, race, religion, and nationality.[11] King evidently sounded the note of a nonconformist when he convinced his wife Coretta that "he believed that women are just as intelligent and capable as men and that they should hold positions of authority and influence" and when he declared, in a sermon on family life in 1955, that women should no longer be submissive "to the dictates of a despotic husband."[12] King's frequent references to Galatians 3:28 should also be recalled here: "There is neither Jew nor Greek, there is neither slave nor free, there is neither male nor female; for you are all one in Christ Jesus."[13] King's thinking in this regard obviously reflected his tendencies toward nonconformism, pragmatism, biblical liberalism, and personal idealism. But he failed to consistently proclaim how the abuse, marginalization, and subordination of women violated both scripture and the principles of human dignity and worth. Moreover, his own family structure was and remained patriarchal, and he never surrendered the claim to his role as head of the family, even as his frequent absences left Coretta to handle most of the decision-making and daily activities relative to their home and children.

Although King was not as committed as some men in his time to preserving the well-established male-female gender hierarchy, which many felt was rooted in scripture and tradition, the images of "homemaker," "supportive wife," "motherhood," and "caretaker" always dominated his consciousness when it came to women and their chief functions in society and the world. Thus, he never took seriously Ella Baker's "group-centered leadership model" and Fannie Lou Hamer's idea of "an equal partnership between men and women" when considering the question of exactly who should lead in the struggle for civil and human rights.[14] King opted instead for the "male-dominated charismatic leadership model," which had been passed down to him largely through the traditions of the black church and the larger American culture.[15] This explains his failure to embrace a strong egalitarian ethic regarding gender relations in the many civil and human rights organizations with which he was associated over time, including the Montgomery Improvement Association, the Southern Christian Leadership Conference (SCLC), the Student Nonviolent Coordinating Committee, the American Committee on Africa, and the American Negro Leadership Conference on Africa.[16] King benefited enormously from the masses of women who organized southern cities for civic engagement and movement building but devalued and often overlooked their leadership capacities and organizing expertise. He refused to properly acknowledge the quality of leadership provided by Baker, Septima Clark, and Dorothy F. Cotton in the SCLC, Dorothy I. Height of the National Council of Negro Women, and Nannie Helen Burroughs of the black women's club movement, and he offered little moral and physical support for the political strategies of grassroots activists such as Hamer, Victoria Gray, and Annie Devine of the Mississippi Freedom Democratic Party, civil rights activist Gloria Richardson in Cambridge, Maryland, and Johnnie Tillmon of the National Welfare Rights Organization.[17] Moreover, King never brought a sense of gender equality to his analyses of freedom movements in Africa, Asia, and Latin America. Such glaring omissions in King's world house vision were never seriously addressed by the women around him, though Baker, Clark, Height, and Molly Martindale, who worked with King in the Chicago Freedom Movement in the late 1960s, to name a few, did raise the issue of his attitude toward women from time to time.[18]

King's unwavering commitment to nonviolence is legendary, but there is no record of him consistently addressing women as victims of domestic violence. This too must be considered in any discussion of his thoughts on the status and treatment of women in the world house. King himself was never known to be verbally, physically, and sexually abusive to women, but he largely ignored these problems and was not as vocal as he should have been about the male tendency to reduce women to sex objects and about the degree to which women suffered due to rape and other sexual violence.[19] Although King understood that women faced an unequal distribution of the physical, sexual, spiritual, and psychological violence in places like South Africa, India, and throughout the Muslim world, his writings and speeches on the world house make no mention of the problem. Even in his address to the Women's International League for Peace and Freedom in October 1965, King made no specific references to the maltreatment of women, even as he alluded to the pressing need to overcome war and racial and religious conflict in the world house.[20]

There will always be questions as to how King could be a conformist when faced with patriarchy and sexism and a nonconformist when it came to racism, poverty, religious bigotry and intolerance, and war. His views on the role of women in the world house not only exposed glaring inconsistencies in his personalism but also raised serious questions about the nature of his commitment to love as "the supreme unifying principle of life."[21] He wrote: "As Christians we must never surrender our supreme loyalty to any time-bound custom or earth-bound idea, for at the heart of our universe is a higher reality—God and his kingdom of love—to which we must be conformed."[22] King's difficulty was in applying this principle to daily life, especially when it came to the condition of the world's women. He was simply ill equipped to identify with the plight of women and, despite his otherwise amazing capacity for empathy, failed to treat patriarchy and sexism as glaring social evils in the world house. The time and

context in which King lived were saturated with the thought that the mistreatment of women was not as serious as the many other social ills that afflicted
humankind. Thus, he could speak of racism and economic injustice as perennial allies in a global context, as he did in *Where Do We Go from Here?*, while completely leaving gender inequality and oppression of women out of the equa-
tion.[23]

Much the same can be said regarding King's attitude toward homophobia,
which was not wholly unrelated to sexism and racism. While King never publicly attacked gay people, he nonetheless felt that male homosexuality was inconsistent with a healthy maleness or manhood. In the winter of 1958, after
leading the successful Montgomery bus boycott and forming the SCLC, King, in
a monthly column he wrote for *Ebony Magazine*, felt compelled to respond to a
youngster who expressed his sexual feelings in these terms: "My problem is different from the ones most people have. I am a boy, but I feel about boys the way
I ought to feel about girls. I don't want my parents to know about me. What can I
do? Is there any place where I can go for help?" King responded candidly:

> Your problem is not at all an uncommon one. However, it does require careful
> attention. The type of feeling that you have toward boys is probably not an in-
> nate tendency, but something that has been culturally acquired. Your reasons for
> adopting this habit have now been consciously suppressed or unconsciously re-
> pressed. Therefore, it is necessary to deal with this problem by getting back to
> some of the experiences and circumstances that lead to the habit. In order to do
> this I would suggest that you see a good psychiatrist who can assist you in bring-
> ing to the forefront of conscience all of those experiences and circumstances that
> lead to the habit. You are already on the right road toward a solution, since you
> honestly recognize the problem and have a desire to solve it.[24]

Both the boy's and King's references to homosexuality as a problem was telling
enough but quite understandable in a time when homosexuality was deemed
acquired and not natural, when Christians and adherents of other religions
considered it sinful, immoral, and even inhuman, when sodomy laws in many
states criminalized homosexual acts, when President Dwight D. Eisenhower
and Executive Order 10450 denounced homosexuality as perverse or deviant
behavior, and when the American Psychiatric Association considered homosexuals to be victimized by "a form of mental disorder."[25] In "that homophobic
era," as author Michael G. Long calls it, King obviously chose to conform to the
demands of religious orthodoxy, traditional sexual mores, and the status quo.[26]
Here again he failed to choose the path of "the maladjusted" or "the transformed nonconformist."

Any careful study of King's attitude toward queer people and homosexuality should focus, first and foremost, on his relationships with James Baldwin and Bayard Rustin, gay black men with whom he closely associated. King met both in the late 1950s and was drawn to them because of a shared interest in the South and in civil and human rights, especially for the oppressed worldwide. Baldwin and Rustin are treated separately here because the relationship of each to King reveals something quite interesting and unique about traditional notions of what constituted masculinity in those times and about how queer people related to the civil rights movement and its leadership. Baldwin, who had become an accomplished and highly regarded writer, was asked by *Harper's Magazine* to do a profile of King in early 1960, and from that point the two grew closer as friends and fellow activists.[27] At that time, Baldwin stated in a letter to King: "I am one of the millions to be found all over the world but more especially here, in this sorely troubled country, who thank God for you."[28] In his essay on King, Baldwin noted that King was unlike "any preacher I have ever met before." He added: "For one thing, to state it baldly, I liked him. It is rare that one *likes* a world-famous man—by the time they become world-famous they rarely like themselves, which may account for this antipathy."[29] Baldwin would later become more specific in offering his impression of King: "Martin's a very rare, a very great man. Martin's rare for two reasons; probably just because he is and because he's a real Christian. He really believes in nonviolence. He has arrived at something in himself which allows him to do it, and he still has great moral authority in the South. . . . Poor Martin has gone through God knows what kind of hell to awaken the American conscience."[30]

Baldwin experienced both deep joy and inner peace through his association with King, and although King most certainly knew about his homosexuality, the subject apparently never surfaced in their conversations, nor did it interfere in any fashion with their relationship, their collaborative efforts at fund-raising for the civil rights cause, and their demonstrating in the streets for justice. "We all worked together and kept the faith together," Baldwin asserted, and when King was assassinated in 1968, Baldwin moved permanently to France because, as he put it, "I couldn't stay in America. I had to leave."[31]

King's admiration and respect for Baldwin never wavered. When working with Baldwin, he saw not a homosexual but another human being committed to the transformation or amelioration of the human condition. He knew that aside from Baldwin's moral, physical, and financial support for the freedom cause, he was doing as much and perhaps more than any other writer to explain the struggle for a greater flowering of democracy and a higher human ideal. After reading Baldwin's celebrated work, *Nobody Knows My Name* (1961), which high-

lighted themes ranging from the role of blacks in the United States and Europe
to sexual identity, King, writing in a very personal way to Baldwin, commented:

> Please excuse me for taking the prerogative of addressing you by your first name,
> but I feel just that close to you. I have just finished reading *Nobody Knows My
> Name*, and I simply want to thank you for it. This collection of essays and lectures
> will certainly go down as a classic on the meaning of the social revolution that
> is taking place in the United States in the area of race relations. . . . Your analy-
> sis of the problem is always creative and penetrating. Your honesty and courage
> in telling the truth to white Americans, even if it hurts, is most impressive. I have
> been tremendously helped by reading the book, and I know that it will serve to
> broaden my understanding on the whole meaning of our struggle. . . .I hope you
> many more successful days as a writer. You are not only a great Negro writer; you
> are a great writer. In a most creative way you rose up from all the crippling restric-
> tions that a Negro born in Harlem faces, or anywhere in the United States for that
> matter, and plunged against a cloud-filled night of oppression new and blazing
> stars of inspiration. You make all of us proud to be Negroes.[32]

King said much of the same and more about Bayard Rustin, whose contributions in the civil and human rights fields were different in some ways from Baldwin's and similar in others. Unlike Baldwin, who perceptively interpreted the
lives and struggles of blacks and gay and bisexual men on paper, Rustin made
his mark through his involvement with pacifist organizations such as the Fellowship of Reconciliation and the War Resisters' League, as an activist who pi-
oneered in the theoretical and practical application of Gandhian methods
to address U.S. race relations, and as a leading strategist and organizer in the
civil rights movement. Rustin did share Baldwin's deep interest in the plight of
blacks, gays, and other oppressed people. Apparently Rustin's passion for social justice, equality of opportunity, and peace in the more general sense accounted for the kind of relationship that would develop over time between him
and King.

Rustin became a "Gandhian counselor" to King in early 1956, worked with
the Montgomery Improvement Association during the bus boycott, and figured
prominently in the formation and development of the SCLC.[33] He also became a
close friend of both King and his wife, Coretta, and in March 1960 organized and
headed the Committee to Defend Martin Luther King when King was falsely
accused of "evading Alabama state income taxes," charges that were dropped
after King's surprising acquittal by an all-white Alabama jury.[34] Soon after the
acquittal, Rustin, King, and A. Philip Randolph announced plans to march on
the national Democratic and Republican conventions, a move that, strangely

enough, first injected homosexuality into the relationship between Rustin and King. Democratic congressman Adam Clayton Powell Jr., envious of King's rapid rise to prominence and furious that he had not been consulted, opposed the idea of a march on the Democratic convention and, at the urging of southern Democrats whose support he needed to become chairman of the House Labor and Education Committee, threatened to allege a nonexistent sexual liaison between Rustin and King. Powell's apparent attempt at blackmail, according to Rustin, added to King's "anxiety about additional discussions of sex" for King knew how "potentially damaging" this could be. To avoid "an embarrassing public squabble," Rustin "quietly resigned" from his position in SCLC, a decision that brought considerable relief to King and to many of his ministerial associates who considered homosexuality deviant, sinful behavior and felt that Rustin's presence hurt the civil rights cause.[35] A decade prior to "the Powell debacle" involving Rustin and King, Congressman Powell, also senior pastor of Harlem's Abyssinian Baptist church, had variously described homosexuality as "abnormal," "unnatural," "sexual degeneracy," and "sex perversion" in a feature article in *Ebony* magazine. Powell strongly denounced what he termed "a trend of parading homosexuals" in the nation's churches, claiming that the "boys with the swish and the girls with the swagger are getting daily more numerous and more bold." He felt the problem demanded a "well-rounded and understanding sex instruction program" in churches.[36] Most ministers in King's SCLC shared Powell's views around these issues, and so did most in the black community and the larger American society. Rustin recalled that "a number of the ministers" close to King wanted him dismissed from the SCLC staff "because of my homosexuality."[37]

King was well aware of Rustin's homosexuality and its potential damaging effects on him and the movement, and the two talked "at length" about this and more. But King was still willing to work with Rustin because he saw in him, as in Baldwin, a figure of great talent and ability, and also one with a commitment to a higher purpose, a purpose larger than himself. In King's estimation, both men had demonstrated this beyond question, and Baldwin himself reminded King of this shared commitment when he declared, in the *Harper's* article on King, that King had "lost much moral credit" in the thinking "of the young" when he "allowed Adam Clayton Powell to force the resignation of his extremely able organizer and lieutenant, Bayard Rustin."[38] But Rustin felt that he meant a lot to King, was sensitive to the dilemma King faced in that situation with Powell, and had serious problems with Baldwin raising an issue he felt should attract as little publicity as possible. "I was distressed with his comment on me and my relation to you," said Rustin about Baldwin in a letter to King.[39] Perhaps with "the

Powell debacle" in mind, Rustin, seemingly downplaying the role his sexuality played in his relationship with King, said the following more than two decades later: "It is difficult to know what Dr. King felt about gayness except to say that I'm sure he would have been sympathetic and would not have had the prejudicial view. Otherwise he would not have hired me. He was under such extraordinary pressure about his own sex life. J. Edgar Hoover was spreading stories, and there were very real efforts to entrap him. I think at a given point he had to reach a decision. My being gay was not a problem for Dr. King but a problem for the movement."[40] On another occasion, Rustin appeared to offer a more nuanced explanation:

> Dr. King came from a very protected background. I don't think he'd ever known a gay person in his life. I think he had no real sympathy or understanding. I think he wanted very much to. But I think he was largely guided by two facts. One was that already people were whispering about him. And I think his attitude was, look, I've got enough of my own problems. I really don't want to be burdened with additional ones. Secondly, he was surrounded by people who, for their own reasons, wanted to get rid of me—Andy Young in particular, and Jesse Jackson.[41]

Although King was always concerned about how Rustin's communist sympathies might be used to confuse or distort the fundamental issues confronting the oppressed, this was never as much of a problem for him as Rustin's sexuality. King was actually "too embarrassed" to raise the issue at times, Rustin biographer Daniel Levine says, and Michael G. Long has documented many instances in which King's actions "were in direct response to Rustin's homosexuality."[42] Speaking to his personal lawyer Clarence B. Jones via telephone about Rustin, King said, "When he drinks, he would approach these students . . . and there was something of a reflection on me." King had concluded that Rustin "controls himself pretty well until he gets to drinking."[43] Even so, King found ways to employ Rustin's services in an advisory and organizational capacity, even after he had been forced out of the SCLC. King collaborated with A. Philip Randolph and others in choosing Rustin to "organize the March on Washington, of which he was one of the leaders," in August 1963.[44] In the fall of 1963, and in early 1964, King and Rustin actually "toyed with the idea" of Rustin becoming executive secretary of the SCLC, succeeding Wyatt Tee Walker. The feeling was that Rustin would bring "some order to office procedures and fund-raising." But both King and Rustin ultimately decided that such a choice would terrify "some of SCLC's leadership," and Andrew Young filled the position vacated by Walker.[45]

Rustin influenced King in profound, positive, and decisive ways. As an adviser to King, beginning with the Montgomery bus boycott in 1955-56, Rustin played a pivotal role in launching the modern phase of the black freedom movement.[46] There was no one more important to King when it came to the theoretical and practical application of Gandhi's views and techniques, and Rustin's contributions as a movement strategist and organizer contributed substantially to King's effectiveness and image as a freedom crusader at home and abroad. When King was struggling with whether or not to defy a federal court order during the Selma to Montgomery march in 1965, he turned for advice to Rustin, who insisted that King could not "allow the federal injunction to stop him from moving."[47] There were occasional disagreements between the two men in the late sixties, relative to concerns such as the Chicago Freedom Movement, Vietnam, and the Poor People's Campaign, but there was always mutual respect and admiration as well as a productive working relationship.[48]

King's attitude toward women and queer people reveal how amazingly difficult it can be for even highly moral and rational figures to break from the chains of conformity. This was especially the case in the 1950s and 1960s. During that era, women and gay people, along with black Americans and other people of color, constituted "the subordinate others" in the United States, and the crusades to free people from oppression based on gender and sexuality had not gained full force in this country, let alone in other parts of the world. Most women worldwide were engaged in unwaged domestic work and bearing and taking care of children and the home, or otherwise limited to positions as teachers, secretaries, nurses, and other lower-wage jobs. Misogyny and the sexual abuse and exploitation of women occurred on high levels, with little or no chance for the prosecution and conviction of assailants. Queer people and their communities kept low profiles to avoid persecution in the United States and elsewhere in the West, and in some countries around the world they faced torture, imprisonment, and even death. This was the world house in which King lived and struggled. Small wonder that he had essentially nothing to say about the debilitating and devastating effects of the global structures of patriarchy, sexism, and homophobia.

On Women's and Queer Rights: Decontextualizing King

Much debate has occurred since the death of Martin Luther King Jr. in 1968 about whether it is possible to distinguish between King as crusader for freedom and justice in his own historical context and King as understood by subsequent generations, for whom he is an authority, resource, and inspiration. King is evidently a figure from the past and cannot answer appeals to justify his positions on patriarchy, sexism, and homophobia, but these appeals give his quest

for a more just and inclusive world house a surplus of new meaning. King's biography functions primarily as the narrative of an individual life and not so
much as a reliable model for how the oppression of women and queer people
might be addressed in the world house today and tomorrow. These reflections
square with Traci C. West's thoughts on "the question of contextualization" as
it relates to King and the meaning of his legacy of ideas and activism for those
struggling in the post-King age against patriarchy, sexism, and homophobia.[49]

When confronting the issues of women and gay people, West, professor of
ethics and African American studies at Drew Theological Seminary in New
Jersey and an ordained elder in the United Methodist Church, suggests that it
makes more sense to read and treat King in context rather than *beyond* context.
The point is that the only evidence of what King might do and say today about
these issues is what he said and did in his own time. West compels us to wonder how it is even possible in these times for King, who died more than a half
century ago, to authoritatively speak to oppression based on gender and sexuality. Mindful of "the contemporary misuse of King" as "a teaching resource,"
West also challenges us regarding the risks involved in viewing King "as a soli-
tary font of truth" and in representing his views on women and gays as the same
as our own. She warns against our pervasive tendency to exploit King in making our moral claims, insisting that this actually amounts to a meaningless effort to create "a definitive, albeit fictional voice of King," to rely on "an overly in-
flated image" of him, or to treat him as "a man-god who confers moral authority
and political currency in order to increase the marginal status of people who are
already vulnerable to social identity based on discrimination and violence."[50]
West's challenge regarding "the question of contextualization" is relevant to the
discussion that follows.

The question of contextualization" (and "decontextualization") inevitably
surfaces in any serious debate about the position King would take on issues re-
lating to human oppression over the last half century. His widow, Coretta King,
was among the first to assert that he would wholeheartedly support dismantling patriarchal structures and the liberation and empowerment of women
cross-culturally. In her estimation, these are the only positions that her husband could possibly take in view of his oft-repeated assertion that "injustice
anywhere is a threat to justice everywhere" and his firm declarations regarding
"the interrelated structure of all reality." Convinced that her husband's thinking and actions concerning the subordination and marginalization of women
would correspond with her own, Coretta became a strong advocate for wom-
en's rights worldwide, especially in the United States and Africa, and for the
increased involvement of women in foreign policy.[51] In the 1970s, 1980s, and

1990s, King's legacy always figured prominently in Coretta's consciousness as she gave speeches on women's issues, supported women's causes and organizations, and welcomed leaders and activists from the United States and abroad to the Martin Luther King Jr. Center for Nonviolent Social Change in Atlanta to discuss matters pertinent to women.[52]

Martin Luther King III and Bernice A. King, Coretta and King Jr.'s son and daughter, have echoed their mother's belief that their father would be a proponent of women's liberation. Both feel that their father would view the women's rights cause as yet another human quest "for justice and equality" and therefore "worthy of his support."[53] They also share their mother's view that their father's vision of a common, unified humanity, as reflected in his stress on "the interrelated structure of all life and reality," suggests that such would be the case. Although Bernice rarely comments specifically on what she thinks her father's stand on women's issues would be today, in her reflections titled, "A World House Built on a Foundation of Cultural Development," she does mention the suppression of women in "every nation" and implies that "leadership development" in the interest of women is consistent with her father's world vision.[54] Like her mother, Bernice has alluded frequently to the women's struggle in her many speeches and interviews concerning her father's legacy, while denouncing what she calls the "patriarchal order in our nation and world."[55]

The theological ethicist Rufus Burrow Jr. agrees that King would be supportive of women's liberation today, while offering a different and more academic explanation. He writes: "While I concede that the most one can do is speculate as to whether King would have eventually renounced sexism, it seems reasonable to me that one do so, both in light of his personalistic method and his clearcut, overwhelming capacity to grow and change in the face of evidence and events that warrant it."[56] Burrow, a personalist himself, seems to be making two points here. First, he reminds us that personalism, which King conceded was "my basic philosophical position," affirms in principle and practice the intrinsic value of all human personality, "the fundamental communal nature of persons," "a passion for social justice," and "the possibilities of human beings when they allow themselves to become co-workers with God" and is therefore inconsistent with sexism.[57] Since King embraced personalism on metaphysical, philosophical, and theological grounds, Burrow believes he would have eventually reached a point where he could no longer live with the conflict between his personalist values and his sexist behavior. Second, King was enough of a pragmatist or realist that he would see at some point that harmonious and creative living in the world house could not happen as long as patriarchy, sexism, or any other form of injustice existed.[58]

Traci West identifies with the school of thought holding that, because King lived, thought, and functioned in a different age and context from ours, we have no way of knowing what stand he would take regarding sexism and women's rights today. West even questions whether the "lens of gender" is useful at all "for examining the legacy" of King's "iconic religious and political leadership." What is at issue here is not only what West terms "the gender dynamics of King's work with women leaders" but also, perhaps more importantly in our case, how this is interpreted in the twenty-first century world house.[59] Any thoughts about what King would do and say about women's rights in our context are seemingly pointless. Thus, those who argue about this cannot speak for King and are simply using his voice to lend credence or legitimacy to their own views.

The debate surrounding what might be King's position on queer rights has received considerably more attention in the last decade or so, nationally and worldwide. Much of the intensity and explosiveness regarding this issue can be associated with President Barack H. Obama's decision to come out in favor of same-sex marriage in 2012 and with the Supreme Court's affirmation of marriage equality on constitutional grounds in 2015. But the "dueling claims" about King and gay rights had begun years earlier, as more and more voices in the queer community started to publicly "position themselves within that tradition that produced Dr. King" and the civil rights movement.[60] This led to sharp and continuing divisions in King's family. Coretta Scott King gave numerous speeches in the 1990s and the early 2000s making the link between her husband, the civil rights movement, and the struggle for gay and lesbian dignity and rights.[61] She held that racism, sexism, anti-Semitism, and homophobia were essentially one and the same, and that bigotry and intolerance against any people "[set] the stage for further repression and violence that spread all too easily to victimize the next minority group."[62] In 2004, Coretta made headlines nationally and internationally when she publicly gave her support to same-sex marriage, calling it "a civil rights issue."[63] Martin Luther King III fully agreed with his mother, while other members of the King family disagreed.[64] Bernice King, a Baptist minister and lawyer, asserted, at a church gathering in New Zealand, "I know in my sanctified soul that my father did not take a bullet for same-sex marriage." In December 2004, she and Pastor Eddie Long of the New Birth Missionary Baptist Church in Lithonia, Georgia, led some ten thousand demonstrators to King's gravesite in Atlanta and called for a constitutional amendment banning same-gender marriage.[65] Alveda King, Bernice's first cousin, was also a participant in the march. Back in 1998, Alveda headed a group known as King for America and "barnstormed the country speaking at rallies against gay rights legislation." In 2005, she declared that her famous uncle was "a champion of the word of God" and not "a champion of gay rights." Aligned with conservative voices in the religious right, Alveda, to a much greater extent than Bernice King, continues to lend "her family name and voice against LGBTQ rights," constantly urging gays and lesbians to "repent and save yourself."[66]

The battle over King and gay rights has not escaped the ranks of civil rights leaders, some of whom knew and worked closely with King. "Some civil rights leaders find the comparison [between black civil rights and gay rights] apt," wrote Allen G. Breed in 2004, "but other blacks call it downright disgraceful."[67] C. T. Vivian, Joseph E. Lowery, Clarence B. Jones, Fred Shuttlesworth, Dorothy Cotton, Marian Wright Edelman, and Jesse Jackson, all of whom were involved with King's SCLC, have lined up in favor of gay rights, and so have Benjamin Chavis, Julian Bond, and John Lewis, who also knew and associated with King. The male civil rights leaders of this earlier generation tend to be more vocal about what might be King's position on these issues. Vivian argues that King would champion queer rights today because he "was a theologian" who began "with the fact that God loves everybody, and all men and all women are created by God." "He based his whole philosophy on God's love for all people," Vivian continues.[68] Lowery concedes that "blacks should clearly sympathize with the gay community's fight for rights," but points out, on the other hand, that "the sheer weight of U.S. history precludes too close a comparison." "Homosexuals as people have never been enslaved because of their sexual orientation," Lowery adds. "They may have been scorned; they may have been discriminated against. But they've never been enslaved and declared less than human." Jesse Jackson agrees, acknowledging that LGBTQ people are entitled to "equal protection under the law" but saying "gays were never called three-fifths human in the Constitution."[69] Jones, Chavis, Bond, and Lewis all agree that gay rights is "a civil rights issue," and all believe that King would understand as much and more while standing with the oppressed. The same holds true for Al Sharpton, William Barbour, Patrisse Cullors, Alicia Garza, and others who represent the more recent generation of social justice leadership.[70] In contrast, Fred Shuttlesworth, who collaborated with King in the Birmingham crusade, is said to have denied that King would be a proponent of LGBTQ rights. "Dr. King and I were not crusading for homosexuality," he allegedly remarked. "I've heard Dr. King speak out against homosexuality on many occasions. It is wrong to equate homosexuality with civil rights."[71]

Because King was a Baptist clergyman and an intellectual deeply interested in politics, it is equally important to consider ways in which the debate regarding King and gay rights has unfolded in ecclesial, academic, and political circles, especially among African Americans. Aside from C. T. Vivian, Joseph Lowery, Jesse Jackson, John Lewis, Benjamin Chavis, and other clergymen activists from the King era, few African American ministers have been willing to risk their reputations and livelihood by publicly invoking King's name in defense of queer rights. However, there are exceptions. The lesbian Yvette A. Flunder, pastor of the City of Refuge United Church of Christ in Oakland, California, and presiding bishop of the Fellowship of Affirming Ministries, has mentioned King's name and activities at times when affirming queer rights. In a letter to the *Washington Post* in 2009, Christine and Dennis Wiley, copastors at the Covenant Baptist United Church of Christ in Washington, D.C., invoked King's name and memory "in support of their pro-marriage equality position."[72] Clearly, most ministers wholeheartedly reject the mere mention of King's name in conversations about gay rights, particularly regarding same-gender marriage. In 2002, Nathaniel Wilcox, a Miami minister, insisted that King "would be outraged" because he was a minister who "believed in the word of God." "And if Dr. Martin Luther King was the man of God I think he was," Wilcox added, "then he preached against all sorts of immorality—including lying, stealing and homosexuality."[73] At a Des Moines, Iowa, rally in 2011, the Reverend Keith Ratliff Sr. insisted that there is absolutely nothing in King's sermons, speeches, and writings that indicate that he would favor "gay and lesbian marriages."[74] Many black clergy expressed such views with the clear backing of white ecclesial bodies such as the Southern Baptist Convention, which, ironically enough, has always shown an inability and even unwillingness to understand and apply King's views on freedom and equality.[75] As Coretta Scott King's stance in favor of gay marriage rights became more widely known in the first decade of the twenty-first century, individual male clergy like Jesse Lee Peterson, the radio host who led a black conservative religious group Brotherhood Organization of a New Destiny (BOND), either attacked her or questioned her motives.[76] Groups of black pastors met in Atlanta, Boston, and other cities and issued strongly worded declarations supporting traditional marriage and denouncing efforts to link the legacy of King and the civil rights movement to same-gender marriage.[77] The Atlanta megachurch pastor Eddie Long accompanied Bernice King to New Zealand, where the two voiced support for the conservative, anti-gay platform of Destiny of New Zealand, "a political party that began as an offshoot of Destiny Church in Auckland."[78] This gaudy display of anti-gay sentiment by Long and King's daughter overseas, perhaps more than any other step taken by ministers, was an assault on the very idea that King's vision of a world house includes queer communities and their liberation and empowerment.

Black and white intellectuals, some of whom have lectured or written on the relationship of the King legacy to gay rights, have been apt to use logic rather than the Bible and religion in asserting their views. When asked what position he thought King would take today on queer rights, Peter J. Gomes, the gay theologian, Plummer Professor of Christian Morals at Harvard Divinity School, and ordained Baptist minister, explained: "I don't like claiming dead prophets. One can speculate what he would say. But I don't want to say what he'd say."[79] While refusing to take a firm and unequivocal position on the question, Ravi Perry, professor of political science at Clark University in Massachusetts, declares: "There is no public or private record of King condemning gay people. Even the FBI's surveillance of King's private phone conversations didn't turn up any moment where King disparaged gay people. If Dr. King were anti-gay, there would likely be a sermon, a speech, a recording of some kind indicating such. And knowing how closely his phones were tapped, surely there would be a record of such statements."[80] Michael G. Long, professor of religious studies and peace and conflict studies at Pennsylvania's Elizabethtown College, who has written the only book on King, homosexuality, and gay rights, maintains that while King's position on gay rights is unclear, he would nonetheless be "a champion of gay rights today because of his view of Christianity." Taking seriously "the question of contextualization," Long notes that "Dr. King never publicly welcomed gays at the front gate of his beloved community," but "he did leave behind a key for them— his belief that each person is sacred, free and equal to all others." In this sense, Long asserts, "King's vision transcended his personal limitations."[81] Earl Ofari Hutchinson, the author of numerous books on politics and race in America, a frequent contributor to the *Huffington Post* and other publications, and an occasional guest commentator on CNN, MSNBC, and other news outlets, concludes that King likely would be a supporter of LGBTQ rights and that he, unlike his daughter Bernice, "would not have marched against gay marriage." Hutchinson reminds us that many of the "ultra-conservatives" who "have corralled a few black churchmen, some with stellar civil rights credentials," into endorsing "a constitutional amendment outlawing gay marriage" are the very same people who staunchly oppose affirmative action.[82] Traci West and James H. Cone, previously mentioned in this chapter, are among those intellectuals and academics who frame their thoughts on the King legacy and queer rights in light of the question of contextualization, suggesting that King was the product of a certain society and culture and that any credible discussion of what he felt about gay people and their condition should focus on the period in which he actually lived, spoke, and acted.[83] Anything else amounts to a "decontextualization" of King.

The motives of politicians who weigh in on the question of links between the King legacy and queer rights are always easy to detect, especially in a society and

world house in which attitudes toward gays and lesbians range from outright rejection to toleration to open acceptance. Former president Barack Obama is still
one of the very few high-ranking politicians willing to publicly support rights
for LGBTQ people, and in taking his stand in 2012 he saw himself acting very
much in the tradition of King and the civil rights movement. Other politicians
have emerged to claim that King would support the gay cause today. When a
group of black ministers put forth "a strongly worded statement" in Boston in
2004 condemning same-gender marriage and "denouncing" comparisons between the civil rights movement and the queer rights struggle, Byron Rushing,
a black state legislator in Massachusetts, lamented: "Martin Luther King is rolling over in his grave at a statement like this."[84] During that same period, Mayor
Jason West of New Paltz, New York, a white member of the Green Party, also
suggested that King would be against anti-gay bigotry, noting, "The people who
would forbid gays from marrying in this country are those who would have Rosa
Parks sit in the back of the bus."[85]

White political and religious conservatives, who would otherwise ignore
King's moral challenge around civil and human rights, have appealed to him
and his legacy to justify their opposition to same-sex marriage. In expressing total rebuke of the Supreme Court for legitimizing same-sex marriage, the conservative politician and former Republican presidential hopeful Gary Bauer
declared: "I think what we've seen is the concept of civil rights being hijacked
by all kinds of people who, I believe, if Martin Luther King were alive today, he
would be mortified by." Bauer argued: "I think Dr. King, being a pastor, would've
certainly understood the biblical definition of marriage, and I think he would've
been a powerful voice . . . for strengthening the family, for the need for children
to be raised with mothers and fathers."[86] Equally unhappy with the Supreme
Court's ruling on this issue, the National Organization of Marriage, a leading
group against marriage equality in the United States, "invoked Martin Luther
King Jr. and Supreme Court cases involving slavery and abortion—all in a call
for lawmakers and the public to overturn the Supreme Court's decision." The
group reasoned, strangely, that King's idea of "an unjust law"—"a human law
that is not rooted in eternal law or natural law"—actually applied in all of these
cases, including same-gender marriage.[87] But, on close examination, it is evident that the distinction King made between "just" and "unjust laws," in his celebrated "Letter from Birmingham Jail" (1963), actually benefits proponents of
gay marriage and not its opponents.[88]

Undoubtedly, questions about where King might stand on women's and
queer rights in the world house today will continue to cause conflict, and people on both sides of these issues will not cease to use King as a convenient po-

litical ploy to buttress their own opinions. But all who do so remain guilty of de-contextualizing the historical King for self-serving purposes or turning King into a useful symbol to promote their own moral visions and political agendas. But the reality is that what King would say and do about the oppression of women and LGBTQ people will remain unclear and questionable. We will never fully understand why he consistently suggested in principle that all forms of oppression are equally problematic while at the same time remaining silent and non-committal in the face of patriarchy, sexism, and homophobia. His failure to become a moral voice of provocation, advocacy, and affirmation for women and queer people will never make sense, especially in view of his deep commitment to a biblically rooted vision of humanity that transcends all artificial, sectarian, or tribal barriers. The best we can say is that King was a complex personality and indeed something of an enigma. He himself asserted on many occasions that "man is a duel personality"—"a bundle of contradictions, contraries, and conflicts."[89] The central question for today and tomorrow, then, is how to best use King's ideas in the continuing crusade to transform a world that seems increasingly antagonistic toward women's and queer realities.

Relevantizing King: Lessons for Women and Queer People

Despite Martin Luther King Jr.'s shortcomings as a voice of advocacy and liberator of the oppressed, his vision of the world house and the ways in which he articulated and pursued that vision provide opportunities for critical reflection around the type of social movement that might serve as a liberatory model that does not exclude women and LGBTQ people. In other words, King is indeed a teaching resource in that he continues to inform our understanding of what it means to pursue nonviolent and corrective action in cases where "the powers that be" refuse to act in the interest of justice and the common good. King's words still apply to the challenges inherent in the enduring struggle of all humans to live harmoniously, creatively, and productively in the world house. King believed that functioning in the world house at its best involves a lifelong intellectual and practical quest, particularly in terms of social criticism, moral thinking, sociopolitical praxis, and the living out of the highest communitarian ideal. Thus, when exploring King's world house vision as a teaching resource for women and the LGBTQ community in the twenty-first century, the works of Paulo Freire, the Brazilian educator and philosopher, and of bell hooks, the African American feminist writer and social activist, come to mind. Freire equips us with a "theory of critical pedagogy" and an important framework for engaging difference, and bell hooks helps us to understand the concept of "intersectionality" and how overlapping and interdependent systems of discrimination and oppression are perennially relevant to this discussion.[90]

King continues to inform our understanding of what it means to be truly human in a world that dehumanizes the "other." He pointed toward an understanding of revolution and redemption inclusive of the whole of human experience, or what Freire calls "humanization." "Humanization," writes Freire, "is affirmed by the yearning of the oppressed for freedom and justice, and by their struggle to recover their lost humanity."[91] Both Freire and King understood that critical-analytical thinking, or the development of a critical consciousness, is a first step in the humanization and liberation of the oppressed and the oppressor cross-culturally, not only intellectually, but also physically, spiritually, socially, politically, economically, and otherwise. This is why each stressed the importance of education and denounced the debilitating and devastating effects of miseducation. Freire insisted that education either functions as an instrument that facilitates conformity to the status quo or "it becomes the 'practice of freedom,'" or the process by which humans critically confront reality while seeking ways of transforming the world in the interest of a more healthy and inclusive human community.[92] This is much of what King had in mind when he observed that through "education we seek to change attitudes," to "change internal feelings," to "break down the spiritual barriers to integration" and community.[93] King referred to education as "a most vital and indispensable element," and he suggested that freedom of thought must be brought into educational systems and the processes of learning before those processes can translate into strategies and tactics for much-needed revolutionary change in the social, political, and economic spheres of any society.[94] But perhaps the more important point is that neither King nor Freire seems to parse a foundational understanding of humanization that addresses sexism and homophobia. While both present contradictions, they also propose helpful resources for teaching, especially since humanization—with its egalitarian entitlements of opportunities, pleasures, and responsibilities—is at the center of their thought and liberation models.

Freire and King are essentially one in highlighting the value of education in the definition and practice of freedom. Their ideas are a reminder to women and gay people that freedom is about more than merely struggling against the status quo or the structures of patriarchy, sexism, and homophobia. It is also about the right to define themselves and their world against that wall of assumptions that people outside of their communities hold about them. It is about liberating the mind and not simply the body. It involves an internal reckoning, or a process of self-analysis, that rejects the images the oppressive society and world have imposed upon them, while replacing those images with autonomy, self-definition, and responsibility. Freire sees this as "the struggle for humanization" or "human completion," and King as the freedom of the mind and the actual living out of the principle of the intrinsic "dignity and worth of human personality."[95] Both perspectives have pedagogical value for women and LGBTQ people who struggle daily against stereotypes, rejection, physical and psychological violence, and the lack of self-esteem. In other words, the struggle in these cases entails both internal and external forces.

Freedom for Freire and King is also about the practice of community in a global context. Freire's utopianism and King's world house are about humans moving toward ever new and greater possibilities of freer, richer, and more complete lives, individually and collectively. This necessarily includes working for the freedom and humanization of the oppressed as well as the oppressors, because the oppressors have to be liberated from their oppressive routines. For Freire, this is what "a liberating pedagogy" demands, and for King it merely speaks to "the interrelated structure of all reality."[96] There are clearly lessons here for those women, gays, and lesbians who define their struggle over and against, and not with, those who are responsible for their oppression. Movements and strategies for those oppressed on the basis of gender and sexuality cannot succeed without a deep sense of the kind of symbiotic relationship that exist between the oppressed and oppressors. Put another way, the oppressed-oppressor dichotomy employed by many women's and queer groups only undermines the potential for the humanization and liberation of all. This does not mean that the oppressed will always find common ground, much less solidarity, with the oppressor. It simply means that the goal for both should always be the greatest communitarian ideal possible.[97] Anything less, for Freire and King, is morally unjustifiable, socially irrelevant, and sociopolitically destructive.

The feminist author and social activist bell hooks also has much to offer in the further development of a liberation ethic for women and LGBTQ people in the world house. She shares Freire's and King's idea of education as the practice of freedom and community, but equally significant is her concept of intersectionality, which should stand as a challenge to women and queer people regarding the need to consider oppression based on gender, sex, race, and class as equally problematic and deserving of complete elimination. This more inclusive feminist theory recognizes the uniqueness of women's situation and "the long-standing idea of sisterhood," as so often highlighted by both feminists and womanists, but it insists simultaneously that all oppressed groups must accept and work with each other. Also, hooks's theory affirms "the importance of male involvement" in the struggle against injustice and inequality, arguing, as does Paulo Freire, that much-needed and lasting change cannot occur if they fail to make their contribution. This implies the need for new forms of coalition-building. Further, hooks advocates "a restructuring of the cultural framework of power," so that it finds the oppression of any group anywhere in the world unnecessary.[98] Such an inclusive liberation ethic could be instructive and beneficial in practical ways for women and LGBTQ communities as they think in terms of steps they might take to strengthen their cause today and tomorrow. This ethic is most certainly in line with King's world house vision, which values loyalties that are "ecumenical" over those that are "sectional."[99]

Freire and hooks are used here to frame a discussion of King's world house that might be more persuasive and useful to women and LGBTQ people in their struggle, especially since King was, as previously noted, never really an advocate of women's and gay causes. There are other ideas, consistent with Freire and hooks's concept of education as the practice of both freedom and community, that are applicable in referencing King as a resource for women's and queer liberation. In envisioning the world house, King not only thought in terms of the necessity to maintain critical consciousness as foundational for all humans, but also of the importance of the resolve to "search for truth," "to adjust to new ideas," to "reestablish the moral ends of our lives," "to resist collective evil," and to come to a fuller realization of "the social nature of human existence." Each of these merit further comment if its relevance to the plight and struggles of women and LGBTQ people is to be properly and convincingly established.

King often said that ideologies and structures that breed injustice and human oppression are constructed and maintained on a foundation of "untruth" and that truth is essential in any legitimate crusade for the fullest of freedom. "He who lives with untruth lives in spiritual slavery," he maintained. And quoting Jesus, he went on to assert: "Freedom is still the bonus we receive for knowing the truth. 'Ye shall know the truth, and the truth shall set you free.'"[100] King knew that untruth is a propaganda tool weaponized by the powers that be, not only to distort reality and misinform but also to thwart the efforts of the oppressed, to divide their ranks, and to confuse their supporters. In contrast, those consciously and purposefully committed to freedom and justice, especially among the oppressed, must always use truth to inform, to unite, and to push an agenda that is liberative and empowering. This invariably entails a willingness to face basic and even brutal truths about their history, their condition, and who they are as a people. King concluded that both education and communal consciousness have a role in the search for truth—in rising above "the horizon of legions of half-truths, prejudices, and propaganda," and truth-telling was among the messaging strategies he used to validate a movement for both civil and human rights. "I have been strongly influenced by the prophets of old and those who place the search for truth above expediency," he declared. "I would like to hope that I am not a consensus leader, constantly determining what is right and wrong by taking a sort of Gallup poll of the majority opinion."[101] In what is today being called "the post-truth era"—or the era of "fake news," "alternative facts," and "bizarre conspiracy theories"—King's refusal to sugarcoat reality, to embrace a relativistic ethic when it comes to truth and untruth, and to divorce truth from the physical, spiritual, and communal search for human liberation and wholeness is highly instructive for women and LGBTQ communities as they seek their rightful and secure place in the world house.[102]

In his reflections on the world house, King insisted that "our very survival depends" in part on our ability to "adjust to new ideas."[103] He often called upon the oppressed to keep "an open and analytical mind," to be receptive to "the best lights of reason," and to always delight in learning from others across the globe who have struggled against injustice and oppression.[104] In his own quest for civil and human rights, he learned from sources as varied as Rosa Parks, Marian Wright Edelman, James Baldwin, Bayard Rustin, the Indian leader Mohandas K. Gandhi, South African freedom fighter Albert Lutuli, and the Buddhist monk Thich Nhat Hanh. An eclectic thinker par excellence, King took ideas from these and many other sources and combined them into an intelligible whole, thereby fashioning a liberation ethic that he thought was essential for harmonious, creative, and productive living in the world house. Women and queer people have already discovered that any serious study of King's legacy is an intellectual journey fraught with frustration and risk, especially in view of his time, context, and the limitations of his worldview around issues of human oppression, but they can nonetheless benefit, theoretically and practically, from King's openness to learning from struggles for freedom and independence everywhere in the world. Also, there is much to be gained from an honest and enduring assessment of how King's world house vision might take on new hues and pertinence for women and LGBTQ people in the world house of today and tomorrow.

Much the same might be said about King's emphasis on the need to "reestablish the moral ends of our lives," particularly as we develop a fresh and more inclusive sense of who we are as a people, of what we should be about as a human family, and of what we should fight for and against. "Our hope for creative living in this world house that we have inherited lies in our ability to reestablish the moral ends of our lives in personal character and social justice," King wrote. "Without this spiritual and moral awakening, we shall destroy ourselves in the misuse of our own instruments." Bearing in mind King's oft-repeated assertion that "means and ends must cohere, because the end is preexistent in the means," those who seek to rid the world house of injustice and oppression based on gender and sexuality must remember that this endeavor hinges largely on a new awakening toward each other and the plight in which all oppressed people find themselves.[105] In light of their reading of King, women and the LGBTQ communities might ask: How do our personal moral ends shape our collective moral and political ends? What common moral ends define our local, national, and international lives? What might we discover as we awaken more to the falseness of the inferiorities and supremacies we have inherited, consciously or unconsciously?

Yet another consideration in this continuing crusade for women's and queer rights is the moral imperative "to resist collective evil," which commonly appears in the forms of unjust governments, laws, and other social codes and customs. "Noncooperation with evil is as much a moral obligation as is cooperation with good," King wrote, as he intellectually defended and practically applied nonviolence as the most moral means of eliminating injustice and oppression.[106] Drawing upon Socrates, Heraclitus, Saint Augustine, Saint Thomas Aquinas, Georg W. F. Hegel, Henry David Thoreau, Mohandas K. Gandhi, Richard Gregg, Reinhold Niebuhr, and others, King challenged the most creative and prophetic people in any society to resist unjust and oppressive systems, laws, and social practices with the goal of improving them.[107] Clearly, this is the continuing challenge confronting women and LGBTQ people as they evaluate the most doable and potentially workable strategies and tactics for achieving their liberation and empowerment. The important thing is to remain grounded fundamentally in a moral and ethical core.

No less significant is King's challenge to oppressors and the oppressed to fully realize and embrace "the social nature of human existence." As King frequently said, this means that humans are a part of each other—that they are interconnected and interdependent and must be ever mindful of their essential oneness as God's creation. "I can never be what I ought to be until you are what you ought to be," King declared, "and you can never be what you ought to be until I am what I ought to be." "This," he added, "is the interrelated structure of reality."[108] This is still another layer of that ideal of community that King considered absolutely essential in the world house, and ethical and theological dialogue with King around this principle could be fruitful for women and queer people as they continue to define and redefine their future and as they discover new loyalties and forge stronger alliances of conscience in their march toward the fullness of freedom, justice, and human dignity.

The foregoing discussion is not meant to suggest that King speaks authoritatively to contemporary issues of women's and queer rights. It only suggests that

King put forth ideas and values that are timeless in terms of what it means to be fully human and that critical reflection around some of those ideas and values might be useful to women and LGBTQ people as they continue the struggle against structural forms of oppression under the overarching global system of heterosexual male domination.

Beyond Patriarchy, Sexism, and Homophobia: The Future World House

The struggles for women's and queer rights have gained worldwide attention in the twenty-first century. Patriarchy, sexism, and homophobia continue to fragment the cultural, social, and political landscape nationally and globally. Unquestionably, the liberation of women and LGBTQ people remains a crucial and neglected dimension of the world house, and our worldview must interact with Martin Luther King Jr.'s in the creation of a global human situation that is better and more inclusive for them and the many other oppressed segments of the human family. We might begin by taking seriously King's challenge to develop "a world perspective" or to come to a better sense of our "global citizenship." For King, arriving at such an important sense of self-understanding and self-identity necessarily entails addressing and struggling against social evil wherever it exists in the world house. King pointed to his own identity as "a citizen of the world" in establishing a rationale for speaking out against apartheid in South Africa, poverty in India, the treatment of Jews in Russia, and the war in Vietnam, and moral, rational, and freedom-loving persons today must feel compelled to do likewise in the crusade against patriarchy, sexism, and homophobia.[109]

The world has changed since King's death, but much remains unchanged. Women still face misogyny and are victimized by discrimination, sexual abuse, and other forms of violence in every corner of the globe. In this twenty-first century, women remain subordinate to men in virtually every sphere of private and public life. LGBTQ people still constitute the marginalized other, are often forced to remain anonymous in Muslim countries, and are consistently the victims of condemnation, physical attack, hate crimes, and even death at the hands of homophobes everywhere. Even so, the future is not totally bleak for queer communities. In the United States and much of the Western world, queer people have found increasing acceptance among the general populations and are enjoying more privileges, including marriage equality, but the dilemma confronting them remains frustratingly and painfully real. Associated press journalist David Crary describes the tragically ambivalent climate that confronts LGBTQ

communities: "In much of the world, the push for gay rights has advanced in-
exorably in recent years. Countries which now allow same-sex marriage range
from Portugal to South Africa to Argentina.... Throughout the Arab world,
however, homosexual conduct remains taboo—it is punishable by floggings,
long prison terms and in some cases execution in religiously conservative Saudi
Arabia, and by up to three years imprisonment in relatively secular Tunisia. Iraq
and Yemen each experienced a surge of killing of gays [in 2009]."[110] This is a historic moment in much of the world house, a time when queer rights, for the first
time, are widely viewed and described as basic human rights. Barack Obama,
the forty-fourth president of the United States, used his position and influence
in the mounting global efforts to end discrimination against LGBT people. It
was an unprecedented example of a powerful world leader forthrightly engaging a highly controversial issue, thus casting himself in the image of what King
called "a transformed nonconformist." The step taken by Obama assumes even
more significance in that he is one who directly benefited from the philosophy
and leadership of King and the gains of the civil rights movement of the 1950s
and 1960s. This explains his deep ties to human rights advocacy for queers. The
Obama administration issued a statement calling on the United Nations "to
combat discrimination against gays and lesbians around the world," because of
concerns about the murder, harassment, and arrest of people due to their sexual orientation and gender identity.[111] The very humanity of gays and lesbians,
Obama and others declared, is at stake. Unfortunately, this very worthy cause
has not been endorsed and taken on by Donald J. Trump, the forty-fifth U.S.
president, and the forces of Trumpism.

    Due to the Internet, social media, and continuing advancements in science
and technology, the future of the world house looks promising on some levels yet discouraging on others, especially when the problems and challenges
still confronting humanity around gender and sexuality are considered. Martin Luther King Jr. understood in his own time that ingenuity and revolutionary
strides in science, technology, and other fields do not necessarily translate into
moral and spiritual growth and maturity. In fact, the opposite is more likely to
take place. This is why so much of King's appeal for a more creative and inclusive world house was aimed at the heart and soul of human beings. He talked a
lot about getting "the heart right" and about "redeeming" or "saving the soul" of
the United States and of humanity as a whole.[112] King realized that the barriers
to community in the great world house were not merely external (e.g., racism,
poverty, and war) but also, perhaps more importantly, internal (e.g., hatred,
greed, ignorance, and fear).[113] In his judgment, this is what made religion and
education so important, ideally, particularly since religion at its best changes

hearts, and education at its best improves the minds and the thinking of those truly willing and able to benefit from it.[114] Although King never provided answers for many of the chasms that fragment and continue to divide humanity, the sheer power of his appeals to the hearts, souls, and minds of both the oppressors and the oppressed may prove to be his greatest gift to those who look to him for meaning and inspiration in the growing crusade to liberate women and queer people in the world house. What matters most in this age of polarization and tribalism is not what King did or failed to do about these issues when he was alive. Far more important is how freedom-loving people today might expand on and make his world house vision more inclusive now and in the future.

NOTES

The first epigraph is quoted in Brian Dunlap, "What Would Martin Luther King Jr. Say about the Gay Rights Movement?," *Quora*, November 23, 2011; https://www.quora.com /What-would-Martin-Luther-King-Jr-say-about-the-gay-rights-movement; the second epigraph is from Traci C. West, "Gendered Legacies of Martin Luther King Jr.'s Leadership, *Theology Today*, 65, no. 1 (April 2008), 56.

1. See Traci C. West, "Gay Rights and the Misuse of Martin," in Lewis V. Baldwin and Rufus Burrow Jr., eds., *The Domestication of Martin Luther King, Jr.: Clarence B. Jones, Right-Wing Conservatism, and the Manipulation of the King Legacy* (Eugene, Ore.: Cascade Books, 2013), 141–42; Katie G. Cannon, *Black Womanist Ethics* (Atlanta: Scholars Press, 1988), 163, 165–67, 169–73; Dunlap, "What Would Martin Luther King Jr. Say?"; Robert Shine, "Martin Luther King's Words Call LGBT Catholics and Allies to Action," *New Ways Ministry*, January 18, 2016, https://ww.newwaysministry.org/2016/01/18/martin-luther-kings-words -call-lgbt-catholics-and-allies-to-action; Brandon Ambrosino, "What the Gay Rights Movement Should Learn from Martin Luther King, Jr.," *Time*, January 20, 2014, http:// time.com/2332/what-the-gay-rights-movement-should-learn-from-martin-luther-king-jr; Opal Tometi, Alicia Garza, and Patrisse Cullors-Brignac, "Celebrating MLK Day: Reclaiming Our Movement Legacy," *Huffpost*, March 20, 2015, https://www.huffpost .com/entry/reclaiming-our-movement-l_b_6498400.html; and Lewis V. Baldwin and Amiri YaSin Al-Hadid, *Between Cross and Crescent: Christian and Muslim Perspectives on Malcolm and Martin* (Gainesville: University Press of Florida, 2002), 171–99. Those advocating for other views on King include West, "Gendered Legacies," 41–56; Cheryl J. Sanders, *Empowerment Ethics for a Liberated People: A Path to African American Social Transformation* (Minneapolis: Fortress Press, 1995), 97–102; David Zimmerman, "Would Martin Luther King Jr. Have Supported the Gay Rights Movement," *Boston Spirit*, January 20, 2013, http:// archive.boston.com/lifestyle/blogs/bostonspirit/2013/01/would_martin_luther_king _jr_ha.html; "Did Martin Luther King Jr.'s Dream Include LGBTQ People Too?," *LGBTQ Nation*, January 2017, https://www.lgbtqnation.com/2017/01/martin-luther-king-jr-s -dream-include-lgbtq-people; Carolyn M. Brown, "Bernice King Defends Herself against Anti-Gay Remarks," *Black Enterprise*, August 21, 2013, https://www.blackenterprise.com /bernice-king-anti-gay-remarks; Curtis M. Wong, "Martin Luther King, Jr. Would Be 'Mortified' by the Gay Marriage Movement, Gary Bauer Claims," *Huffpost*, January 25, 2015, updated February 2, 2016, https://www.huffpost.com/2015/01/25/gary-bauer

-martin-luther-king-jr-_n_6541820.html; and German Lopez, "Top Anti-Gay Group Cites Martin Luther King in Opposition to the Supreme Court's Decision," *Vox*, June 26, 2015, https://www.vox.com/2015/6/26/8853369/gay-marriage-supreme-court-nom.

2. Martin Luther King Jr., *Where Do We Go from Here: Chaos or Community?* (Boston: Beacon Press, 1967; rpt., 1968, 2010), 167–202; Martin Luther King Jr., *The Trumpet of Conscience* (San Francisco: Harper & Row, 1967), 3–78; Clayborne Carson and Peter Holloran, eds., *A Knock at Midnight: Inspiration from the Great Sermons of Reverend Martin Luther King, Jr.* (New York: Warner Books, 1998), 69–75; and Martin Luther King Jr., "Address at the 50th Anniversary of the Women's International League for Peace and Freedom," Philadelphia, Pennsylvania, October 15, 1965, King Papers, Library and Archives of the Martin Luther King Jr. Center for Nonviolent Social Change, Atlanta.

3. On King and women and gay people, see Martin Luther King Jr., *The Papers of Martin Luther King, Jr.*, vol. 6, *Advocate of the Social Gospel, September 1948–March 1963*, edited by Clayborne Carson, Susan Carson, Susan Englander, Troy Jackson, and Gerald L. Smith (Berkeley: University of California Press, 2007), 212; and Bayard Rustin, *Time on Two Crosses: The Collected Writings of Bayard Rustin*, edited by Devon W. Carbado and Donald Weise (San Francisco: Cleis Press, 2003), 285, 292–93. On King and the world house and King's progressive global outlook, see Martin Luther King Jr., *Where Do We Go from Here?*, 167–91; Martin Luther King Jr., *Trumpet of Conscience*, 3–78; and Martin Luther King Jr., "Nobel Lecture," December 11, 1964, University of Oslo, Norway, King Papers; Martin Luther King Jr., *A Testament of Hope: The Essential Writings and Speeches of Martin Luther King, Jr.*, edited by James M. Washington (San Francisco: HarperCollins, 1986), 135–44, 279–86, 313–28, 617–33; and Martin Luther King Jr., "Doubts and Certainties Link: An Interview," unpublished transcript, London, England, February 1968, King Papers.

4. According to some sources, the early gay rights movement extends as far back as 1924, when Henry Gerber, a German immigrant, founded the Society for Human Rights in Chicago. This is said to have been "the first documented gay rights organization in the United States." Although the movement gradually emerged from that time and "saw some early progress in the 1960s," it was not until the late 1960s and 1970s that it significantly increased in terms of vitality, activism, and visibility. See "Gay Rights," History .com, https://www.history.com/topics/gay-rights/history-of-gay-rights.

5. John J. Ansbro, *Martin Luther King, Jr.: The Making of a Mind* (Maryknoll, N.Y.: Orbis Books, 1982), xv; Shine, "Martin Luther King's Words Call LGBT Catholics and Allies to Action"; Ambrosino, "What the Gay Rights Movement Should Learn"; Tometi, Garza, and Cullors-Brignac, "Celebrating MLK Day"; Madison Feller, "9 Black Activists on How Martin Luther King, Jr.'s Legacy Inspires Their Work," *Elle*, April 4, 2018, https://www.elle .com/culture/career-politics/a19673268/black-activists-martin-luther-king-jr-legacy -anniversary-assassination; "Lessons from the Civil Rights Movement: An Interview with Damu Smith," *Reimagine! RP&E Journal* (Race, Poverty and the Environment), http://www .reimaginerpe.org/node/917; and Monica A. Coleman, "Lessons on Action, Love and Death: A Young Womanist Encounter with the Legacy of Martin Luther King, Jr.," unpublished paper, August 2014, 1–23. The word "feminist" is used here to describe women of different national, racial, religious, and cultural backgrounds who are committed to the complete elimination of patriarchy and the full liberation of women. "Womanist," a term taken from the works of Alice Walker, refers to black women, many of whom are clergy and trained theologians, who share essentially the same commitments.

6. See West, "Gay Rights and the Misuse of Martin," 141–56; and West, "Gendered Legacies of Martin Luther King, Jr.'s Leadership," 41–56.

7. "bell hooks," Wikipedia, https://en.wikipedia.org/wiki/Bell_hooks. Though hooks did not use the word "intersectionality" in her *Feminist Theory*, first published in 1984, the meaning of the word is essentially spelled out in the topic of that book's first chapter. bell hooks, *Feminist Theory: From Margin to Center*, 2nd ed. (Cambridge, Mass.: South End Press, 2000), 1–17. For Freire, see "Paulo Freire," Wikipedia, https://en.wikipedia.org/wiki/Paulo _Friere; Paulo Freire, *Pedagogy of the Oppressed*, translated by Myra Bergman Ramos (New York: Herder and Herder, 1970), 27–186; and Paulo Freire, *Education for Critical Consciousness* (New York: Seabury Press, 1973), 1–82.

8. Martin Luther King Jr., *Strength to Love* (1963; repr., Philadelphia: Fortress Press, 1981), 17.

9. Martin Luther King Jr., *Testament of Hope*, 14–15; and Martin Luther King Jr., *The Papers of Martin Luther King, Jr.*, vol. 4, *Symbol of the Movement, January 1957–December 1958*, edited by Clayborne Carson, Susan Carson, Adrienne Clay, Virginia Shadron, and Kieran Taylor (Berkeley: University of California Press, 2000), 276.

10. "Did Martin Luther King Jr.'s Dream Include LGBTQ People Too?"

11. King often said the likes of this: "And when we truly believe in the sacredness of human personality, we won't exploit people, we won't trample over people with the iron feet of oppression, we won't kill anybody." One can only imagine what such a statement means in light of the abuse and subordination of women. See Martin Luther King Jr., *Trumpet of Conscience*, 72.

12. Coretta Scott King, *My Life with Martin Luther King, Jr.*, rev. ed. (New York: Henry Holt, 1993), 57–58; King, *Papers of Martin Luther King, Jr.*, vol. 6, 212.

13. *Papers of Martin Luther King, Jr.*, vol. 4, 124; Martin Luther King Jr., *The Papers of Martin Luther King, Jr.*, vol. 3, *Birth of a New Age, December 1955–December 1956*, edited by Clayborne Carson, Stewart Burns, Susan Carson, Peter Holloran, and Dana L. H. Powell (Berkeley: University of California Press, 1997), 378–79, 417; and Martin Luther King Jr., *Trumpet of Conscience*, 72.

14. Vicki Crawford, Jacqueline A. Rouse, Barbara Woods, Broadus Butler, Marymal Dryden, and Melissa Walker, eds., *Women in the Civil Rights Movement: Trailblazers and Torchbearers, 1941–1965* (Brooklyn: Carlson Publishing, 1990), 60–65, 213; and Baldwin and Al-Hadid, *Between Cross and Crescent*, 182–93.

15. Baldwin and Al-Hadid, *Between Cross and Crescent*, 185.

16. Charles M. Payne, *I've Got the Light of Freedom: The Organizing Tradition and the Mississippi Freedom Struggle* (Berkeley: University of California Press, 1995), 195–96, 419; Lynne Olson, *Freedom's Daughters: The Unsung Heroines of the Civil Rights Movement from 1830 to 1970* (New York: Scribner, 2001), 133, 144–45, 188; Rosetta E. Ross, *Witnessing and Testifying: Black Women, Religion, and Civil Rights* (Minneapolis: Fortress Press, 2003), 191; and Lewis V. Baldwin, *Toward the Beloved Community: Martin Luther King, Jr. and South Africa* (Cleveland: Pilgrim Press, 1995), 14–21, 32–57.

17. Bettye Collier-Thomas and V. P. Franklin, eds., *Sisters in the Struggle: African American Women in the Civil Rights–Black Power Movement* (New York: New York University Press, 2001), 185; Baldwin and Al-Hadid, *Between Cross and Crescent*, 187; and Michael K. Honey, *Going Down Jericho Road: The Memphis Strike, Martin Luther King's Last Crusade* (New York: W. W. Norton, 2007), 183.

18. Baldwin and Al-Hadid, *Between Cross and Crescent*, 182–83. Molly Martindale, who helped organize the Chicago Freedom Movement, recently recalled how women activists in that movement had begun to question sexism and patriarchy. See Mary Lou Finley, Bernard LaFayette Jr., James R. Ralph Jr., and Pam Smith, eds., *The Chicago Freedom Movement: Martin Luther King Jr. and Civil Rights Activism in the North* (Lexington: University Press of Kentucky, 2016), 352–56.

19. Septima Clark, *Ready from Within: Septima Clark and the Civil Rights Movement*, edited by Cynthia Stokes Brown (Trenton, N.J.: Africa World Press, 1990), 79.

20. Martin Luther King Jr., "Address at the 50th Anniversary of the Women's International League for Peace and Freedom."

21. Martin Luther King Jr., *Where Do We Go from Here?*, 190. Rufus Burrow was the first King scholar to stress the point of inconsistencies in King's personalism (personal idealism). See Rufus Burrow Jr., *God and Human Dignity: The Personalism, Theology, and Ethics of Martin Luther King, Jr.* (Notre Dame, Ind.: University of Notre Dame Press, 2006), 7–15.

22. Martin Luther King Jr., *Strength to Love*, 18.

23. Martin Luther King Jr., *Where Do We Go from Here?*, 173.

24. King, *Papers of Martin Luther King, Jr.*, vol. 4, 348–49; Michael G. Long, *Martin Luther King, Jr., Homosexuality, and the Early Gay Rights Movement: Keeping the Dream Straight?* (New York: Palgrave Macmillan, 2012), 39, 42; and John Blake, "What Did MLK Think about Gay People?," *CNN Belief Blog*, January 16, 2012, http://religion.blogs.cnn.com/2012/01/16/what-did-mlk-think-about-gay-people.

25. Long, *Martin Luther King, Jr., Homosexuality, and the Early Gay Rights Movement*, 43–44; and "Gay Rights," History.com.

26. Long, *Martin Luther King, Jr., Homosexuality, and the Early Gay Rights Movement*, 3.

27. Baldwin's profile of King was published under the title, "The Dangerous Road Before Martin Luther King," and it appeared in *Harper's Magazine*, 222 (February 1961): 33–42.

28. James Campbell, *Talking at the Gates: A Life of James Baldwin* (New York: Viking Penguin, 1991), 143; and Martin Luther King, *The Papers of Martin Luther King, Jr.*, vol. 5, *Threshold of a New Decade, January 1959–December 1960*, edited by Clayborne Carson, Tenisha Armstrong, Susan Carson, Adrienne Clay, and Kieran Taylor (Berkeley: University of California Press, 2005), 460–61.

29. See King, *Papers of Martin Luther King, Jr.*, vol. 5, 461n2.

30. James Baldwin, *Conversations with James Baldwin*, edited by Fred L. Standley and Louis H. Pratt (Jackson: University Press of Mississippi), 44.

31. Ibid., 85. Strangely, Michael Long essentially ignores King's relationship with Baldwin in *Martin Luther King, Jr., Homosexuality, and the Early Gay Rights Movement*.

32. King highly recommended Baldwin's *Nobody Knows My Name* to family, friends, and fellow activists and noted, "While I could not endorse all of Mr. Baldwin's opinions, they do make very stimulating reading." See Martin Luther King Jr., *The Papers of Martin Luther King, Jr.*, vol. 7, *To Save the Soul of America, January 1961–August 1962* (Berkeley: University of California Press, 2014), 286–87, 316.

33. Jervis Anderson, *Bayard Rustin: Troubles I've See: A Biography* (New York: HarperCollins, 1997), 69, 186–87, 189; Daniel Levine, *Bayard Rustin and the Civil Rights Movement* (New Brunswick, N.J.: Rutgers University Press, 2000), 94, 121, 155; and Long, *Martin Luther King, Jr., Homosexuality, and the Early Gay Rights Movement*, 78–83.

34. Levine, *Bayard Rustin and the Civil Rights Movement*, 118, 120; and Long, *Martin Luther King, Jr., Homosexuality, and the Early Gay Rights Movement*, 78-80.

35. Levine, *Bayard Rustin and the Civil Rights Movement*, 120-21; Rustin, *Time on Two Crosses*, 285, 292-93; and Anderson, *Bayard Rustin*, 229-30.

36. Powell quoted in Long, *Martin Luther King, Jr., Homosexuality, and the Early Gay Rights Movement*, 43, 83, 87.

37. Long, *Martin Luther King, Jr., Homosexuality, and the Early Gay Rights Movement*, 43-46; and Rustin, *Time on Two Crosses*, 285, 292, 302.

38. Anderson, *Bayard Rustin*, 231; Levine, *Bayard Rustin and the Civil Rights Movement*, 121-22; Rustin, *Time on Two Crosses*, 292, 301-2; and King, *Papers of Martin Luther King, Jr.*, vol. 7, 152.

39. King, *Papers of Martin Luther King, Jr.*, vol. 7, 152. Rustin actually insisted that King not include his name in the acknowledgments and index of his first book, *Stride toward Freedom* (1958), knowing that both his homosexuality and communist ties might be used against both King and the movement. King accepted the advice, much to the disappointment of some of Rustin's friends and acquaintances. See Anderson, *Bayard Rustin*, 209-10.

40. Long, *Martin Luther King, Jr., Homosexuality, and the Early Gay Rights Movement*, 83; and Rustin, *Time on Two Crosses*, 292.

41. Rustin, *Time on Two Crosses*, 302.

42. Levine, *Bayard Rustin and the Civil Rights Movement*, 121, 155; and Long, *Martin Luther King, Jr., Homosexuality, and the Early Gay Rights Movement*, 3.

43. Quoted in Levine, *Bayard Rustin and the Civil Rights Movement*, 121, 155. Ellipses in original.

44. Rustin claimed that "Dr. King was never happy about my leaving" the SCLC. See Rustin, *Time on Two Crosses*, 285-86, 293-94, 300-301; and Long, *Martin Luther King, Jr., Homosexuality, and the Early Gay Rights Movement*, 3.

45. Levine, *Bayard Rustin and the Civil Rights Movement*, 155.

46. Anderson, *Bayard Rustin*, 4.

47. Levine, *Bayard Rustin and the Civil Rights Movement*, 182-83.

48. Ibid., 195, 198-99; Anderson, *Bayard Rustin*, 294; Rustin, *Time on Two Crosses*, 302.

49. See West, "Gendered Legacies of Martin Luther King, Jr.'s Leadership," 41-56; and West, "Gay Rights and the Misuse of Martin," 141-56.

50. West, "Gay Rights and the Misuse of Martin," 143-56; and West, "Gendered Legacies of Martin Luther King, Jr.'s Leadership," 41-56.

51. Coretta Scott King, "An Address at the National Conference on Civil Rights," unpublished notes, Fisk University, Nashville, Tennessee, April 5, 1986, files of Lewis V. Baldwin; Martin Luther King Jr. and Coretta Scott King, *Four Decades of Concern* (Atlanta: Martin Luther King Jr. Center for Nonviolent Social Change, 1986), 29, 31; Dunlap, "What Would Martin Luther King Jr. Say?"; and Coretta Scott King, "U.S. Needs More Willing Women Participation in Foreign Policy," *Tennessean*, March 1, 1988.

52. *International Tribute to Martin Luther King, Jr.* (New York: United Nations Centre against Apartheid, Department of Political and Security Council Affairs, 1979), 56; Coretta Scott King, "U.S. Needs More Willing Women Participation"; "About Mrs. Coretta Scott King," King Center (Martin Luther King Jr. Center for Nonviolent Social Change), http://www.thekingcenter.org/about-mrs-king; and "Statement from Dr. Bernice A.

King, CEO of the King Center, about Coretta Scott King—Reading of Her Mother's Letter by Senator Elizabeth Warren," King Center, https://web.archive.org/web/20170726160416 /http://www.thekingcenter.org/news/2017-02-statement-dr-bernice-king-ceo-king -center-about-coretta-scott-king-and-reading-her.

53. Quoted in Dunlap, "What Would Martin Luther King Jr. Say about the Gay Rights Movement?"

54. Bernice A. King, *Hard Questions, Heart Answers: Speeches and Sermons* (New York: Broadway Books, 1997), 124–27.

55. "Statement from Dr. Bernice A. King."

56. See Rufus Burrow Jr., "Some Reflections on King, Personalism, and Sexism," *Encounter* 65, no. 1 (Winter 2004): 9–38.

57. Ibid.; Martin Luther King Jr., *Stride toward Freedom: The Montgomery Story* (New York: Harper & Row, 1958), 100.

58. Burrow, *God and Human Dignity*, xiii, 70.

59. West, "Gendered Legacies of Martin Luther King, Jr.'s Leadership," 41–43, 56.

60. West, "Gay Rights and the Misuse of Martin," 142; and Ambrosino, "What the Gay Rights Movement Should Learn."

61. Brian Lewis, "Both Sides Should Be Gracious in Debate over Gay Rights: Commentary," *Tennessean*, January 24, 2004; "About Mrs. Coretta Scott King," 1; West, "Gay Rights and the Misuse of Martin,"141–42; "Did Martin Luther King, Jr.'s Dream Include LGBTQ People Too?"; and Dunlap, "What Would Martin Luther King Jr. Say about the Gay Rights Movement?"

62. Dunlap, "What Would Martin Luther King Jr. Say about the Gay Rights Movement?"

63. "Coretta Scott King Gives Her Support to Marriage Equality," *Mass Equality*, March 24, 2004, https://web.archive.org/web/20060621162543/http://www.massequality.org /supporters/allies_supp/2004_king.html; and Sherry Wolf, "Why Gay Marriage Is a Civil Rights Issue: What Do Socialists Say?," *Socialist Worker*, April 23, 2004, http://socialist worker.org/2004-1/496/496_07_GayMarriage.php.

64. Dunlap, "What Would Martin Luther King Jr. Say about the Gay Rights Movement?"; and Long, *Martin Luther King, Jr., Homosexuality, and the Early Gay Rights Movement*, 2, 29–30.

65. "Did Martin Luther King, Jr.'s Dream Include LGBTQ People Too?"; Zimmerman, "Would Martin Luther King Jr. Have Supported the Gay Rights Movement?"; Brown, "Bernice King Defends Herself against Anti-Gay Remarks"; Blake, "What Did MLK Think about Gay People?"; Earl Ofari Hutchinson, "King Would Not Have Marched against Gay Marriage," *San Francisco Chronicle*, December 14, 2004, https://www.sfgate.com/opinion /openforum/article/King-would-not-have-marched-against-gay-marriage-2663669 .php; and "Dr. King Being Used in Gay Marriage Debate: Letter to the Editor," *Tennessean*, January 21, 2005. There is irony in the fact that Bernice King would participate in such a march, considering that her father marched with James Baldwin and Bayard Rustin. See Lewis V. Baldwin, *The Voice of Conscience: The Church in the Mind of Martin Luther King, Jr.* (New York: Oxford University Press, 2010), 230–31.

66. "Did Martin Luther King, Jr.'s Dream include LGBTQ People Too?"; and Hutchinson, "King Would Not Have Marched against Gay Marriage."

67. Allen G. Breed, "Blacks Divided over Comparing Civil Rights Fight to Gay Marriage," *Tennessean*, March 7, 2004.

68. Blake, "What Did MLK Think about Gay People?"; Breed, "Blacks Divided over Comparing Civil Rights Fight to Gay Marriage"; Long, *Martin Luther King, Jr., Homosexuality, and the Early Gay Rights Movement*, 97; Kelly Brown Douglas, *Sexuality and the Black Church: A Womanist Perspective* (Maryknoll, N.Y.: Orbis Books, 1999), 88; and "Jesse Jackson: Gay Marriage Rights Are Not Civil Rights," *Gay.com*, February 17, 2004, http://www.free republic.com/focus/f-news/1080522/posts.

69. Breed, "Blacks Divided Over Comparing Civil Rights Fight to Gay Marriage."

70. Long, *Martin Luther King, Jr., Homosexuality, and the Early Gay Rights Movement*, 96–97; Breed, "Blacks Divided over Comparing Civil Rights Fight to Gay Marriage"; "Civil Rights Leader Comes out for Marriage Equality," *Nashville Pride*, February 6, 2004; Deb Price, "Blacks Who Haven't Forgotten Civil Rights for All," *Tennessean*, September 20, 2004; Earl Ofari Hutchinson, "Gay Marriage Is a Civil Rights Issue," *AlterNet*, December 9, 2003, http://archive.li/7fol4; Tometi, Garza, and Cullors-Brignac, "Celebrating MLK Day"; Feller, "9 Black Activists on How Martin Luther King, Jr.'s Legacy Inspires their Work"; and Dan White, "Black Lives Matter Cofounder Wows Capacity Crowd at MLK Convocation," UC Santa Cruz Newscenter, February 16, 2016, https://news.ucsc.edu/2016/02/mlk -convocation-featuring-alicia-garza.html.

71. Quoted in Long, *Martin Luther King, Jr., Homosexuality, and the Early Gay Rights Movement*, 22.

72. Quoted in West, "Gay Rights and the Misuse of Martin," 144.

73. Quoted in ibid., 142; and Hutchinson, "Gay Marriage Is a Civil Rights Issue."

74. Quoted in West, "Gay Rights and the Misuse of Martin," 144.

75. Michael G. Long, "Southern Baptists, Gay Rights and the Freedom Rhetoric of Martin Luther King, Jr.," *Huffington Post*, June 25, 2012, https://www.huffingtonpost.com /michael-g-long/southern-baptists-gay-rig_b_1624890.html; Hutchinson, "Gay Marriage Is a Civil Rights Issue"; and Breed, "Blacks Divided over Comparing Civil Rights Fight to Gay Marriage."

76. Lewis, "Both Sides Should Be Gracious in Debate over Gay Rights"; and Breed, "Blacks Divided over Comparing Civil Rights Fight to Gay Marriage."

77. West, "Gay Rights and the Misuse of Martin," 143; and "Coretta Scott King Gives Her Support to Marriage Equality."

78. Long, *Martin Luther King, Jr., Homosexuality, and the Early Gay Rights Movement*, 31.

79. Ibid., 72.

80. Quoted in Blake, "What Did MLK Think about Gay People?"

81. Ibid. We take a position similar to Long's, suggesting that what matters most is not so much what King said and did about gay rights in his time but rather how his principles of the dignity of personality and the full realization of the beloved community might be universalized to include all oppressed peoples today and tomorrow. See Baldwin, *Voice of Conscience*, 240–41.

82. Hutchinson, "Gay Marriage Is a Civil Rights Issue"; Hutchinson, "King Would Not Have Marched against Gay Marriage"; and Earl Ofari Hutchinson, *50 Years Later: Why the Murder of Dr. King Still Hurts* (Los Angeles: Middle Passage Press, 2018), 83–87.

83. West, "Gay Rights and the Misuse of Martin," 142–56; and "Did Martin Luther King, Jr.'s Dream Include LGBTQ People Too?"

84. Quoted in West, "Gay Rights and the Misuse of Martin," 143.

85. Quoted in Breed, "Blacks Divided over Comparing Civil Rights Fight to Gay Marriage."

86. Wong, "Martin Luther King, Jr. Would Be 'Mortified.'"

87. Lopez, "Top Anti-Gay Group Cites Martin Luther King." King raised this issue of "just" and "unjust laws" in his "Letter from Birmingham Jail" in 1963. See Martin Luther King Jr., *Why We Can't Wait* (New York: New American Library, 1963), 82–84.

88. Here the members of the National Organization for Marriage fail to understand and actually distort what King meant in distinguishing between "just" and "unjust laws." King's distinction actually swings in the favor of people without rights, not those determined to somehow curtail or deny rights. See King, *Why We Can't Wait*, 82–84.

89. King, *Papers of Martin Luther King, Jr.*, vol. 6, 95.

90. Freire, *Pedagogy of the Oppressed*, 27–56; Freire, *Education for Critical Consciousness*, 3–84; and hooks, *Feminist Theory*, 1–17. Kimberlé Crenshaw advanced "intersectionality theory" and expanded it a decade after hooks wrote about it without using the word "intersectional." See Kimberlé Williams Crenshaw, "Mapping the Margins: Intersectionality, Identity Politics and Violence against Women of Color," *Stanford Law Review*, 43, no. 6 (July 1991): 1241–99.

91. Freire, *Pedagogy of the Oppressed*, 28.

92. Freire, *Pedagogy of the Oppressed*, 15, 57–118; and Freire, *Education for Critical Consciousness*, 1–60.

93. Martin Luther King Jr., *Stride toward Freedom*, 33–34.

94. Martin Luther King Jr., "Field of Education a Battleground," speech, United Federation of Teachers, New York City, July 15, 1965, King Papers; Martin Luther King Jr., "Revolution in the Classroom," unpublished address, Georgia Teachers and Education Association, Atlanta, April 31, 1967, King Papers; and Baldwin, *Toward the Beloved Community*, 182.

95. Freire, *Pedagogy of the Oppressed*, 28–31; Martin Luther King Jr., *Strength to Love*, 98–99; King, *Papers of Martin Luther King, Jr.*, vol. 6: 86–88, 120, 333, 441; and Martin Luther King Jr., *Where Do We Go from Here?*, 43, 123, 155.

96. Freire, *Pedagogy of the Oppressed*, 33–40, 69; "Paulo Freire," Wikipedia; Martin Luther King Jr., *Where Do We Go from Here?*, 181; Martin Luther King Jr., *Trumpet of Conscience*, 69–70; and Martin Luther King Jr., *Testament of Hope*, 625–26.

97. Freire, *Pedagogy of the Oppressed*, 34–40; "Paulo Freire," Wikipedia; and Martin Luther King Jr., *Where Do We Go from Here?*, 167–91.

98. "bell hooks," Wikipedia; bell hooks, *Feminist Theory*, 1–17.

99. Martin Luther King Jr., *Where Do We Go from Here?*, 190.

100. Ibid., 67.

101. Martin Luther King Jr. to Mr. Sam Wyler, July 20, 1967, King Papers.

102. Ruth Marcus, "Welcome to the Post-Truth Presidency," *Washington Post*, December 2, 2016, https://www.washingtonpost.com/opinions/welcome-to-the-post-truth -presidency/2016/12/02/baaf630a-b8cd-11e6-b994-f45a208f7a73_story.html.

103. Martin Luther King Jr., *Testament of Hope*, 619–20.

104. Martin Luther King Jr., *Strength to Love*, 147.

105. Martin Luther King Jr., *Testament of Hope*, 621; and Martin Luther King Jr., *Trumpet of Conscience*, 71.

106. Ansbro, *Martin Luther King, Jr.*, 110–62; and Martin Luther King Jr., *Stride toward Freedom*, 212.

107. Ansbro, *Martin Luther King, Jr.*, 110–62.

108. King, *Strength to Love*, 70.

109. King, *Trumpet of Conscience*, 31, 63, 68.

110. David Crary, "Gays Are Concerned in Egypt, Tunisia: New Leadership May Be Harsher," *Tennessean*, May 22, 2011. Our brackets.

111. "U.S. Demands Gay Rights Support at UN Council," *Newsmax.com*, March 22, 2011.

112. Carson and Holloran, *Knock at Midnight*, 6–7, 196–97.

113. Walter E. Fluker, *They Looked for a City: A Comparative Analysis of the Ideal of Community in the Thought of Howard Thurman and Martin Luther King, Jr.* (Lanham, Md.: University Press of America, 1989), 129–35.

114. Martin Luther King Jr., *Stride toward Freedom*, 33–34, 36.

CHAPTER 10

ALL OVER THE WORLD LIKE A FEVER
MARTIN LUTHER KING JR.'S WORLD HOUSE AND THE MOVEMENT FOR BLACK LIVES IN THE UNITED STATES AND UNITED KINGDOM

MICHAEL B. MCCORMACK AND ALTHEA LEGAL-MILLER

In one sense the civil rights movement in the United States is a special American phenomenon which must be understood in the light of American history and dealt with in terms of the American situation. But on another and more important level, what is happening in the United States today is a significant part of a world development. . . . All over the world like a fever, freedom is spreading in the widest liberation movement in history.
MARTIN LUTHER KING JR., *Where Do We Go From Here?*

We are #BlackLivesMatterUK. In Solidarity with our black family all over the world fighting racist violence. Join us. Follow us.
BLACK LIVES MATTER UK

"Racism is no mere American phenomenon," proclaimed Martin Luther King Jr. in his final book published before his death, *Where Do We Go from Here: Chaos or Community?* (1967). Understanding that global capitalism rests partially upon a foundation of structural racism, King continued, "Its vicious grasp knows no geographical boundaries." As such, King necessarily positioned racism beyond the nation-state and within a genealogy of globalized capitalism. His awareness of the ever-increasing dissolution of borders, to enable the global flow of capital, inspired a resistance that would seek to dismantle racialized borders that kept global citizens estranged through processes of discrimination, perpetual war, ghettoization, and marginalization. For King, it would be ordinary citizens of a world house, not governments, who would take up the mantle of global justice, casting away notions that "the United States and Great Britain . . . [were] the moral bastions of our Western world."[1] The 2016 U.S. presidential election of Donald J. Trump and the UK's Brexit referendum to leave the European Union have rekindled performative anxieties about the diminished standing of the United States and UK as moral guardians of social democracy. In January 2018, Senate Minority Leader Charles Schumer (D-N.Y.), lamented that the "moral authority" that let America "bring a light to the world" was "declining under President Trump's leadership, and declining rapidly."[2] Likewise, Saira O'Mallie, the UK director of the antipoverty ONE campaign, cautioned that an insular post-Brexit Britain could undermine the perception of "millions of people . . . who see the UK as a moral leader."[3] The periodic drama of Western nations bewailing the loss of moral ground at once serves to reinforce the fiction that such a status ever existed. Indeed, as King explained more than fifty years ago, the United States and UK were deeply implicated in global manifestations of white supremacy.[4]

The global and complex machinery of key intersecting oppressions, which King prioritized as poverty, racism and war, has long been the focus of U.S. and UK transnational resistance, particularly within the black Atlantic. Theorized and deployed most prominently by Paul Gilroy, the concept of the black Atlantic draws attention to how the transatlantic trade in African enslavement generated an African diaspora that produced "intricate connections among the nations and empires clustered round the Atlantic Ocean, with profound consequences for all those places and all their inhabitants that have endured to the present day."[5] King's keen awareness of the ever-growing global interconnectedness of daily lives and struggles is, in part, exemplified through his political activism as a black Atlantic sojourner, in the tradition of Olaudah Equiano and Frederick Douglass, who travelled to the UK in an effort to realize his vision of the World House.

In 1964, King stopped off in London, en route to Oslo, Norway, where he would receive the Nobel Peace Prize, to share his oft-repeated message that "the problem of racial injustice is not limited to any one nation . . . [but] spreading all over the globe." His overarching framework of racism as a global phenomenon did not prevent King from offering a British-specific analysis. Undeterred by members of the UK white supremacist League of Empire Loyalists (shouting "Keep Britain white!"), King stated: "Right here in London and right here in England, you know so well that thousands and thousands of colored people are migrating here from many, many lands—from the West Indies, from Pakistan, from India, from Africa. And they have the just right to come to this great land, and they have the just right to expect justice and democracy in this land."[6] King's sixth and final journey to the UK took place in 1967, where he visited the North East of England to receive an honorary doctorate in civil law awarded by the University of Newcastle upon Tyne.[7] As he had done less than three years earlier in London, King again positioned racialized injustices as a global reality with local particularities, restating, perhaps more emphatically after years of international travel, "More and more I have come to realize that racism is a world problem."[8]

A half a century later, U.S. and UK activist families, with loved ones killed in racialized encounters, are crossing the Atlantic to engage in transnational critiques. In 2012, Sybrina Fulton and Tracy Martin, the parents of Trayvon Martin, traveled to the UK in an act of solidarity and advocacy for UK campaigns against institutional racism and violence. The Martin family met with Doreen Lawrence, the mother of black British teenager Stephen Lawrence, who was the victim of a racially motivated murder by white youths in 1993, which was compounded by failures of the criminal justice system to bring adequate redress. "As soon as I heard about Trayvon's death, I wanted to stretch a hand out over the water," Lawrence recalled, further articulating that she immediately "understood what they were going through."[9] Marcia Rigg, the sister of Sean Rigg, a black British man who died in police custody after prolonged restraint in 2008, traveled to California with a coalition of UK families that included Stephanie Lightfoot-Bennett, sister of Leon Patterson (who died in police custody in 1992), Shaun Hall (brother of Mark Duggan, who was fatally shot by the police, which prompted uprisings across Britain, in August 2011), and Kadisha Burrell-Brown (whose brother Kingsley Burrell died in police custody while detained under the Mental Health Act in 2011). Coordinating and connecting with U.S. families impacted by racialized state violence, including the uncle of Oscar Grant, was, as Rigg put it, a vital "journey across the Atlantic . . . to start a global conversation on deaths in custody and state violence, as well as to bridge our struggles."[10] As King predicted, global conversations would be increasingly enabled through "cybernation," which would contribute to the "architectural pattern of the large world house in which we are living."[11] Indeed, U.S. and UK black Atlantic crossings are also electronic, as exemplified by the powerful statement sent by Black Lives Matter in support of UK protests sparked by the death of black British teenager Mzee Mohammed, who died after being restrained by Merseyside Police in Liverpool, England, in 2016. Their litany of remembrance for stolen black lives in the UK read: "We send you solidarity, as we see Mzee Mohammed. We see Sarah Reed. We see Jermaine Baker, the 1,558 people killed by police in the UK and your struggle to gain justice for them. When you lose your family, know that we see that loss and we feel it too. We are all family."[12]

Rising from the global "dungeons of oppression," King envisioned the emergence of a global family, or a "worldwide brotherhood," as he termed it, that would insist upon situating and interpreting national struggles within a much broader international and global framework.[13] "Consciously or unconsciously,"

King wrote, the black American was increasingly "caught up by the spirit of the times, and with his black brothers of Africa and his brown and yellow brothers in Asia, South America and the Caribbean, the United States Negro is moving with a sense of urgency toward the promised land of racial justice."[14] To be sure, the spirit of *our* times demands an account of the frustrated, ongoing black freedom struggle in such a global and expansive frame. As such, this chapter explores the contemporary relevance of King's global vision of the world house for a younger generation of activists continuing the legacy of local and transnational struggles for freedom in the United States and the United Kingdom.

The chapter considers how activists in the United States and the UK make critical and creative use of King as an inspirational, if contested figure in and beyond their respective social and geopolitical locations. We pay special attention to particular ways that millennial U.S. and UK activists engaged in contemporary black liberation movements draw upon, contest, reimagine, and/or begin to embody and materialize King's vision of a world house, in a historical moment when resurgent ideologies of narrow, ethnocentric nationalisms threaten the possibility of multicultural democratic societies in which all people in general, and black people in particular, can survive and thrive together. In a more theoretical register, we place King's vision of the world house in critical conversation with contemporary social and cultural theorists such as Stuart Hall, Paul Gilroy, and Toni Morrison, each of whom describes fraught notions of "home" and "belonging" in the postcolonial or neocolonial era. Moreover, the chapter calls attention to the ways diasporic, feminist, and queer activists have deployed notions of intersectionality in order to imagine alternative, deepened, and/or expanded meanings of King's vision of creative living in the world house as they live into what King described, more than fifty years ago, as an ever-widening, global movement for the liberation of humanity.

Persistent Racism and the Globalization of Resistance

On July 10, 2016, following the police killings of Alton Sterling and Philando Castille, in the United States, thousands of young people took to the streets of London, initiating the first of many Black Lives Matter demonstrations in the United Kingdom. Although these were largely framed as demonstrations of solidarity for "our American brothers and sisters," Maryam Ali, a founder of the Black Lives Matter chapter in London, cautioned individuals not to "forget that racism is a worldwide thing . . . [and] very prevalent."[15] Professional and amateur photographers captured an array of scenes from a demonstration that began at the U.S. Embassy in London before thousands marched and shut down one of the world's longest shopping strips, Oxford Street, in central London. The intercultural demonstration saw predominately young and black protesters demarcate space for black life in the heart of an architectural landscape that unabashedly displays the gains of Britain's involvement in both transatlantic slavery and colonialism. Protesters held signs bearing witness to the worth of black lives against a cross-circulated sonic milieu of U.S.-inspired chants, including "Stop Killing Us", "How Many More," "Hands Up, Don't Shoot," "No Justice, No Peace," and "Black Lives Matter." Not unlike Ethiopian Israelis who used the refrain "Baltimore Is Here" during a 2015 protest against police abuse and racism in Israel, U.S. chants in London functioned as transnational vehicles that could be read in local context.[16] Others, however, evoked the language of Jamaican diasporic black British youth culture, as exemplified by a makeshift placard that read, in black spray-painted capital letters, encircled by dripping red paint appearing to signify blood, "Stop Killing the Mandem."[17]

Among the signifiers of black Atlantic youth protest, captured by photographer Janine Wiedel, is an image of a black female protester holding a painted canvas of Dr. King, thrown into relief by the arresting presence of iconic Britishness—the Clock Tower, popularly known as Big Ben. The head-and-shoulders portrait of a suit-wearing King with hands up and palms facing out is almost entirely painted in black and white, with the exception of a red tie and a single red capitalized word written on each of King's palms, together saying, "DON'T SHOOT."[18] The black-and-white portrait appears to emphasize the temporality and pastness of King, yet he is simultaneously refracted through a legible millennial lens and redeployed into a contemporary landscape via one of the signature chants of protests after the police shooting of Michael Brown in Ferguson, Missouri, "Hands up, don't shoot!"

Janine Wiedel's photograph, part of her exhibition titled Black Lives Matter UK, offers a useful entry point into a consideration of how U.S. and UK millennial activists refigure and recontextualize King as well as transnational struggles, materialities, and futures. The contemporary relevance of borders and fortification—perhaps the antithesis of "the world house"—is dramatically illustrated through xenophobic U.S. calls to "Build That Wall" and the UK anti–European Union slogan, "Take Back Control." Against these articulations of white nationalism, however, journalist Steven W. Thrasher asserts, Black Lives Matter has "kicked off a new, borderless kind of politics about the value of black life worldwide."[19] Demonstrating King's famed pronouncement that "injustice anywhere is a threat to justice everywhere," African American youth activists from Ferguson, Missouri, have traveled to the UK and Palestine (after young Palestinians visited Ferguson) in order to unite or reunite with other struggles.[20] "If Black

Lives Matter can connect black Missourians, Baltimoreans, Palestinians and Is-raelis," Thrasher suggests, "it can cross any border."[21]

Seen in this light, it is understandable why a young black woman in the UK would wield a seemingly anachronistic and monochromatic image of King, su-perimposed with bold red signifiers of contemporary and globalized antiracist struggle. Indeed, it could be argued that King's vision of the great world house anticipates the scenes of struggle and solidarity demonstrated in urban streets from Louisiana to London in the summer of 2016 and beyond. By the late 1960s, King had begun to articulate a more radical, though consistently nonviolent vi-sion of social transformation. Recognizing the growing militancy of liberation movements in the United States and around the world, King observed: "Once the aspirations and appetites of the world have been whetted by the marvels of Western technology and the self-image of a people awakened by religion, one cannot hope to keep people locked out of the earthly kingdom of wealth, health and happiness. Either they share in the blessings of the world or they organize to break down and overthrow those structures or governments which stand in the way of their goals."[22]

King's notion of a great world house may strike contemporary audiences as politically naïve or irredeemably utopian in its articulation of an idealistic global society governed by principles of religious morality and liberal univer-salism. Nevertheless, his prophetic vision offers a powerful critique of the per-sistence of the exclusionary and violent politics of white supremacy, capitalism, and militarism that continues to necessitate transnational movements for liber-ation in the twenty-first century. For instance, King's critiques of militarism take on urgent contemporary meaning in light of militarized police forces, which have provoked the chant "Hands up, don't shoot." Thus, the "DON'T SHOOT" on King's palms in the young British woman's placard is less anachronistic than it may seem at first. Moreover, King's vision clearly recognizes the inevitability of increasingly disruptive movements for justice and equality as long as the global masses of humanity—people of color, to be sure—continue to be denied access to the recognition and resources reserved for the privileged and powerful in the West.

Though steadfastly committed to his nonviolent convictions, King described the upsurge in resistance among people of color, striving toward thriving and not merely surviving, as "revolutionary times" that demanded fresh perspec-tives. According to King, to fail to develop new dispositions consistent with such times was nothing short of tragic. While every society has its guardians of the status quo, or those "fraternities of the indifferent" who are "notorious for sleeping through revolutions," King insisted that it is imperative to "remain awake through great periods of social change." And, in his estimation, people of color and conscience across the globe had been awakened, were on the move, and could be compared to a "great tidal wave" surging forward toward freedom. Nevertheless, King seemed concerned about the sustainability of such a movement over time. While the "awakening" of the masses was reason to be encouraged, more important was "remaining awake." Indeed, for King, the very survival of humanity was at stake in "our ability to stay awake, to adjust to new ideas, to remain vigilant and to face the challenge of change."[23]

Perhaps it is noteworthy, then, that among black millennials in the United States, the popular vernacular phrase "Stay woke," which quickly spread across social media and beyond the United States, has come to describe the imperative to remain vigilant concerning the ever-shifting systemic injustices and political machinations that impinge upon their everyday lives. For black millennial activists, remaining "woke," as a mode of social consciousness, involves no less than keeping track of the interlocking systems of global oppressions that render the lives of people of color, black people in particular, vulnerable and dispensable. While "staying woke" to antiblack racism and other modes of oppression emerged in the vernacular culture of black youth in the United States, it nevertheless resonates with experiences of many black Britons in the United Kingdom. For example, one black British university student asserted: "Black Lives Matter, political movements—social media have revolutionized the way we see race, crime, and social injustice. There is a re-awakening for everyone. Everyone is involved in something—some kind of politics."[24]

It is sometimes argued that given the smaller black population and relatively fewer police shootings, there is little rationale for a movement for black lives in the United Kingdom. Racism, it is argued, is an American problem. Indeed, there is a sense in which social movements such as the U.S. civil rights movement and Black Lives Matter are uniquely American phenomena responding to distinctively American modes of antiblack racism, and the manifestations of such movements in the United Kingdom tend to be more responsive to racial injustices in the United States than to local issues affecting black communities in the UK. However, this should not discount the significance of such international displays of solidarity and exchange in resistance to global and local manifestations of antiblack racism. As Patrisse Cullors, a cofounder of Black Lives Matter in the United States, has argued: "The focus on the U.S. is so intense and hyper-vigilant. It doesn't allow for Black Americans to see ourselves as part of a global movement. . . . I think we need a shift. We need to have a much more integrated theory but also practice around all Black lives globally."[25]

To be sure, as if in anticipation of such arguments, King insisted that the injustices that motivate such movements are not isolated to the United States and that black Americans are not alone in their antiracist yearnings for freedom from oppression. Cullors expresses urgent questions for black Americans: "Why are we so focused on only *our* Black lives? Why aren't we thinking of the Black lives across the globe? We know that our folks are suffering. I think that has to do with the US being so US-centered. We're going to have to work actively to push ourselves out of that narrative."[26] If Cullors stresses the need for black Americans to decenter their own experiences in order to become better global allies in a broader, more diasporic struggle for black lives, Natalie Jeffers, a cofounder of Black Lives Matter UK, articulates the inverse as a necessity in her context. Jeffers puts it this way: "We really are focused on sharing the British narrative. . . . It might have taken the shocking images from deaths in the U.S. to awaken young people, but they're aware of oppression at an individual household level; they see what happens within our communities."[27] Similarly, Marcia Rigg, black British activist and cochair of the United Families and Friends Campaign, a coalition of individuals impacted by deaths in police, prison, and psychiatric custody, notes that "when we have protested on the streets across our country we have shouted out the names of Michael Brown, Trayvon Martin, Oscar Grant, Sandra Bland, Freddie Gray and more in solidarity with the U.S. We want the world to be aware of the names of the deaths in the UK too and for them to be remembered during this struggle."[28] That sorrowful roll call of people of color in Britain who have died during or following police contact includes Cynthia Jarrett (1985), Leon Patterson (1992), Joy Gardner (1993), Shiji Lapite (1994), Wayne Douglas (1995), Brian Douglas (1995), Ibrahim Sey (1996), Christopher Alder (1998), Roger Sylvester (1999), Azelle Rodney (2005), Sean Rigg (2008), Habib "Paps" Ullah (2008), Jimmy Mubenga (2010), Kingsley Burrell (2011), Mark Duggan (2011), Merlin "Smiley Culture" Emmanuel (2011), Adrian McDonald (2014), Sheku Bayoh (2015), Jermaine Baker (2015), Sarah Reed (2016), Mzee Mohammed (2016), Dalian Atkinson (2016), Shane Bryant (2017), Edson Da Costa (2017), Darren Cumberbatch (2017), Rashan Charles (2017), and Kevin Clarke (2018).

More directly addressing the issue of state-sponsored violence against black bodies, Jeffers claims, "There might be fewer guns used in the UK, but there is a war going on against black people."[29] As black British writer Siana Bangura explains: "In the UK, a black person is less likely to be shot dead on the streets than their counterpart in America. But we are more likely to be detained with brute force and left to die at the hands of neglectful officers. The racism in Britain's justice system is insidious, but deadly nonetheless."[30] Although the UK organization Inquest reports that 178 black people have died in police custody or following police contact in England and Wales between 1990 and 2018, a UK police officer has not been successfully prosecuted for involvement in a black death since two officers were found guilty of assault against David Oluwale, a British Nigerian, who was killed in 1969. For UK black communities, the absence of any convictions for police brutality–related black deaths in fifty years "seems to have given police officers a sense that they can take life with impunity."[31]

The systemic devaluation of black lives is discernible through numerous inequalities that disproportionately affect the everyday lives of black communities in the UK. Joshua Virasami, a young British-born Mauritian activist in the UK, opines, "Black lives don't matter in the UK—if you are poor and black, the colour bar is a lived reality." Black disproportionality, he says, is evident "from big wage gaps to unemployment, low educational attainment to stop-and-search, incarceration to deaths in police custody and prisons."[32] Indeed, while black people make up about 3 percent of the UK population, they constitute 10 percent of all police deaths in custody and a colossal 30 percent of those shot dead by the police.[33] Michelle Alexander's critical analysis of the U.S. criminal system, in *The New Jim Crow: Mass Incarceration in the Age of Colorblindness*, has had a profound impact on U.S. mainstream and academic framing of criminal system issues.[34] It has also bolstered the organizing of U.S. campaigns to end mass incarceration, such as the Veterans of Hope Project, which has "developed an interfaith study guide for *The New Jim Crow* written in honor of Rev. Dr. Martin Luther King Jr."[35] Its transnational reach in the UK, though still undetermined, invites possibilities for new forms of solidarity and collective activism, particularly in light of the startling statistic that the proportion of black people incarcerated in the UK is almost seven times the share of the population, compared to the United States, which incarcerates black Americans at a rate of four times greater than the population share.[36]

In the wake of the Brexit vote in the United Kingdom and the election of Trump as the forty-fifth president of the United States, many have noted a rampant increase of public articulations and acts of racism and xenophobia. As Jeffers sees it: "After Brexit, people are seeing the direct change in language online, aware of being seen as another in your own country. People of colour even being told to 'go home'. There were vans bearing racist slogans being driven round British streets. We know there's a direct link between street racism and state racism."[37] Indeed, reported hate crimes involving racial and religious discrimination saw a 29 percent spike in 2016–17 (which according to the Home Office was partially a reflection of increased hostilities "around the time of the EU referendum").[38] Police officers have used routine arrests to collect and store DNA profiles from three-quarters of black British men between the ages of eighteen and thirty-five.[39] Such twenty-first-century challenges require not only "staying woke" but also mobilization and movements of resistance.

In *Al Jazeera*, Virasami articulated his sense of what is at stake for his generation of activists in the ongoing and international struggle of people of African-descent against interlocking systems of oppression: "I believe the movement has one fundamental objective—the self-determination and emancipation of black people from a global system of 'white-hetero-patriarchal' capital which subjugates us at the mercy of the profits of a corporatocracy, the same captains of industry who have run this violent operation for centuries."[40] Virasami, in ways that both echo and expand upon the critiques of Martin Luther King Jr., articulates a position that addresses the particular concerns of a generation of black millennials that has been awakened to an intersectional analysis of oppression necessary for any effective black liberation struggle. For instance, Virasami's use of "white-hetero-patriarchal" deploys additional categories of identification and struggle that are absent from King's thought but central to contemporary movements for justice. To be sure, any contemporary notion of a world house, a metaphor rooted in notions of family, domesticity, and intimate relationality, would be unthinkable without confronting the gender and sexual politics that all too often render the home a site of violence. It can certainly be argued, however, that this more expansive analysis is in keeping with King's insistence on remaining vigilant, facing the challenges of change, and struggling to give birth to new systems of justice and equality.

In addition to such concerns with an intersectional politics of identity and issues of class and capitalism, younger generations of activists have also given particular attention to environmental injustice. The Flint water crisis and the protests against the Dakota Access Pipeline are but two poignant examples that have garnered significant attention among activists in the United States. In the context of the United Kingdom, Black Lives Matter protests also took on environmental concerns, framed as a particular threat to people of African descent across the globe. Indeed, this issue became prevalent during a demonstration in the UK that involved a number of activists—all white—blocking a runway at London City Airport. As one explanation of the rationale for why the London City Airport was shut down, #BlackLivesMatterUK tweeted: "By 2050 there will be 200 million climate refugees. Black people are the first to die, not the first to fly, in this racist climate crisis." Other statements posted to various social media platforms and circulated in alternative channels of communication during and subsequent to the demonstration decried "the UK's environmental impact on black people."[41]

This framing was met with disdain or suspicion by both critics and supporters of the burgeoning Black Lives Matter movement in the United Kingdom. For critics, framing undeniably important environmental issues as a "racist climate crisis" was unnecessarily divisive and threatened to undermine much-needed efforts for environmental change.[42] Among supporters of the movement for black lives, the emphasis on the environment was read as yet another attempt by white activists to appropriate a black-led movement, shifting attention away from state-sponsored violence against black bodies and toward issues more palatable to white liberal audiences. However, black activists and organizers of the protest countered that the deployment of white bodies at London City Airport was strategically considered, much like that of white Freedom Riders during the U.S. civil rights movement in the 1960s, as a means of reducing the burden on black bodies already inordinately vulnerable and subject to state violence. In addition, activists argued that environmental injustice disproportionately affects poor, black people in the United Kingdom and across the globe—especially in underdeveloped regions of Europe's former colonies, more accurately regions underdeveloped by European colonialism.

Thus, Black Lives Matter UK's linkage of planes, privilege, poverty, pollution, and people of color calls to mind the following observation by social theorist Paul Gilroy: "This is not the globalized mindset of the fortunate, unrestricted traveler or some other unexpected fruit of heavily insulated postscarcity and indifferent overdevelopment. It is a critical orientation and an oppositional mood triggered by comprehension of the simple fact that environmental and medical crises do not stop at national boundaries and by a feeling that the sustainability of our species is itself in question."[43] Thus, though the London City Airport protest, with its concern for environmental racism, appears to be well beyond the horizon of King's vision, it points back to one of the central challenges that King saw threatening the viability of the world house. The London City Airport protest raised provocative questions concerning the relationship between environmental injustice and the restriction of black mobility. Furthermore, when Black Lives Matter UK activists "called for open borders to allow those being adversely affected by climate change to move to other parts of the world," they pressed hotly debated issues of immigration and the militarized policing of national borders.[44]

Migrants, Muslims, and Postcolonial Melancholia

At the time when Martin Luther King Jr. wrote "The World House," the last chapter of his last book, he was acutely aware of the challenges of a postcolonial world, in which the formerly colonized were migrating toward the "homelands" of their former colonizers, challenging the racial superiority and politics of socio-spatial relations established under colonial regimes. As King aptly noted: "For several centuries the direction of history flowed from the nations and societies of Western Europe out into the rest of the world in 'conquests' of various sorts. That period, the era of colonialism, is at an end. East is moving West. The earth is being redistributed." King's account of postcoloniality captures a set of dynamics that present significant possibilities and severe challenges for his vision of a world house inhabited by humanity in all of its regional, racial, and religious diversity. Indeed, despite the promise of such "revolutionary times," King recognized, "The postcolonial period is more difficult and precarious than the colonial struggle itself."[45] Gilroy describes the precariousness of the postcolonial period in terms of "the cultural disorientation that accompanies the collapse of imperial certainties into post-colonial nihilism."[46] Whether or not one sees Gilroy's use of "nihilism" as an accurate description here, there is little doubt that he has captured the sense of uncertainty that follows in the wake of imperial decline—uncertainty that creates intense anxieties and contestations around notions of place, space, identities, belonging, and home.

In her 2017 collection of essays, *The Origin of Others*, writer and literary theorist Toni Morrison wrestles with the fraughtness of such fragile concepts as they are impacted by this "journey of the colonized to the seat of the colonizers." In the closing essay, "The Foreigner's Home," Morrison writes, "The spectacle of mass movement draws attention inevitably to the borders, the porous places, the vulnerable points where the concept of home is seen as being menaced by foreigners."[47] Elsewhere in "Home," Morrison describes the aftermath of such mass movement of people across borders. As she puts it, "The contemporary world's work has become policing, halting, forming policy regarding, and trying to administer the movement of people." In such a moment, Morrison argues, the very notions of nation and citizenship are constantly being redefined in response to the purportedly threatening presence of "exiles, refugees, *Gastarbeiter*, immigrants, migrations, the displaced, the fleeing, and the besieged."[48] Morrison describes a situation in which coming to terms with "foreignness," in terms of the incoming "others" *and* dominant subjectivities within the host society, leads to a "rapidly disintegrating sense of belonging" among those in the host society.

In a similar vein, Gilroy uses the more theoretical language of "postcolonial melancholia" to describe, in part, "the morbid culture of a once-imperial nation that has not been able to accept its inevitable loss of prestige in a determinedly postcolonial world." As Gilroy develops his argument concerning the "pathological formation" of postcolonial melancholia, he describes the phenomenon, in turns, as "[the] guilt-ridden loathing and depression that have come to characterize Britain's xenophobic responses to the strangers who have intruded upon it more recently" and subsequently a "postimperial hungering for renewed greatness."[49] It should be obvious that "the appeal of being great again," which Gilroy described in 2005 with reference to the UK, matches perfectly the expressions of resurgent white nationalism evident in the 2016 presidential campaign slogan of Donald Trump, "Make America Great Again," and the "Let's put the Great back in Britain" refrain of Brexit supporters. Of course, such perceived greatness is always already bound to conceptualizations of cultural and social formations determined by the normativity of whiteness and the exclusion of blackness.

Morrison's description of perceived threats to such Eurocentric sociocultural formations of "greatness" reminds us of how our refusal to come to terms with the presence of, proximity to, and prominence of "others" leads us to "cling manically to our own cultures, languages, while dismissing others'; . . . makes us legislate, expel, conform, purge, and pledge allegiance to ghosts and fantasy."[50] In the United Kingdom and United States, viciously and often violently xenophobic policies and public performances of "patriotism"—a pledging allegiance to ghosts and fantasy to be sure—clearly position the anti-immigration ideologies of "Take Back Control" and the White House prioritization of "America First" over any notion of King's uncompromisingly global vision of the world house. In *The Fateful Triangle: Race, Ethnicity, Nation*, Stuart Hall argues that this is due, in part, to the ways that world migrations are shifting not only global relations of power but also "forever disturbing the delicate balance of subordination on which [the West's] supposed purity and originary genius were constructed." Furthermore, Hall contends: "The so-called culture wars, which in the United States have had a highly particular cutting edge along the racialized borders of these lines of cultural contestation, must nonetheless be now reconceptualized in terms of this wider, more historically differentiated, global political development."[51]

In the United Kingdom, similar ideologies take on particular resonance and occasion passionate resentment toward those Gilroy calls "postcolonial citizen-migrants" seeking to enter the borders of their former colonizers. Here Gilroy is worth quoting at length: "The immigrant is now here because Britain, Europe, was once out there; that basic fact of global history is not usually deniable. And yet its grudging recognition provides a stimulus for forms of hostility rooted in the associated realization that today's unwanted settlers carry all the ambivalence of empire with them. They project it into the unhappy consciousness of their fearful and anxious hosts and neighbors. Indeed, the incomers may be un-wanted and feared precisely because they are the unwitting bearers of the im-perial and colonial past." Gilroy's description of ambivalence, anxiety, fear, and hostility toward those whose black and brown bodies bear witness to the colo-nial past takes on particular meaning with reference to those continental Afri-can and Caribbean immigrant communities attempting to cultivate a sense of belonging and home in the UK. Despite such attempts at belonging, these Af-rican diasporic immigrants—many born in the United Kingdom or living there for decades—are, more often than not, erroneously imagined as "unwanted alien intruders without any substantive historical, political, or cultural connec-tions to the collective life of their fellow subjects." As a result, these migrants be-come subject to the "structure of feeling" that Gilroy describes in terms of not only guilt and fear but also "powerful feelings of aggression . . . articulated as racist politics."[52] Gilroy's work attempts to come to terms with the reasons why a wide-ranging set of anxieties and fears, among whites, have been mapped onto blacks and immigrants in ways that exacerbate racism and nationalism in re-sponse to perceived problems thought to be associated with such "strangers and aliens." In theoretical dialogue with Gilroy, Hall grapples with the histori-cally specific modes of racism wherein the calling into question of "cultural be-longing" comes to function "as coded language for race and color" in Britain. Such contestation over "cultural belonging" frustrates the realization of King's vision of the world house and the possibilities for its realization in the twenty-first century.

Clearly, Morrison, Gilroy, and Hall raise provocative theoretical and practi-cal questions that haunt King's world house. Indeed, how does King's notion of the world house take on contemporary meaning in contexts in which white Brits and Americans are becoming increasingly anxious about their sense of belonging in "their own homes"? More pressing perhaps, how does the world house address Morrison's description of the ways that African Americans and African diasporic people throughout the world are subject to a status of "not being at home in their homelands; of being exiled in the place where they be-long."[53] These theoretical postulations and inquiries take on greater concrete-ness and urgency in the testimony of Natasha Nkonde, an activist and "post-colonial citizen-migrant" hailing from Zambia, a former British colony. In an interview with South East London–based poet and journalist Bridget Min-amore, Nkonde recounts the relationship between Brexit and her own involve-ment in Black Lives Matter UK. For Nkonde, the increase in racism and xeno-phobia unleashed by Brexit was a catalyst for activism among a number of black Britons, young people in particular. Moreover, Nkonde recounts the sense of alienation among young blacks in the UK, especially black migrants from the African diaspora. "You grow up ticking all the boxes and doing all the things you should be doing as a good black person, a good black immigrant," she says. "But you find yourselves not able to access things in the same way your white peers can." Nkonde adds: "Some people have gone through the immigration system, jumped through all the hoops, done everything they need to do. But all the promises they were given about citizenship? . . . The things that we were promised we are not getting, and it's being exposed."[54]

No doubt Nkonde's frustrations with being denied "all the promises" associated with British citizenship echo King's acknowledgement of the impatience of those people who are perpetually "locked out of the earthly kingdom of wealth, health and happiness."[55] Giving voice to the particular frustrations of black migrants seeking to make a home in the British wing of the world house, Nkonde insists, "We've gone back to the 60s when it comes to access to housing; landlords aren't renting to people with foreign sounding names." With explicit language that might have offended King's moral sensibilities, yet with exasperated longing that would have surely evoked his empathy, Nkonde concludes, "My parents have worked this hard to get me citizenship, I'm a British citizen, and I can still not be able to get a home because of my fucking name."[56] Indeed, Nkonde's frustrations comport well with King's prior observation concerning the unfathomability of certain "luxuries" among those prior to his generation, whose children have come to demand access to the resources their parents or grandparents could hardly envision.[57] The importance of Nkonde's insistence on a social reversion to the 1960s should not be missed as it underscores the significance of our returning to King and the creative uses that young activists make of his persona, speeches, writings, and public demonstrations in the making of their contemporary demands.

Indeed, a striking photograph from the London Black Lives Matter demonstration in July 2016 captures a young black Muslim woman, dressed in all black and holding a sign high above her head that reads, "Injustice anywhere threatens justice everywhere."[58] Among other things, this image suggests the ways King remains a resource for a diverse group of activists striving toward the realization of a more democratic and just society. Of course, this black British Muslim woman, wielding the words of an American Christian minister, also speaks to the significance of the interplay between racial justice and religious tolerance—and indeed pluralism—implicit in King's vision of the world house. This is especially significant in light of the racialized Islamophobia and anti-Muslim violence that characterizes anti-immigration rhetoric and the policing of borders in the UK and the United States. Below her paraphrasing of King, the Muslim woman in the photograph, presumably living in the UK, added the particularly American phrase "United we stand." In the context of the London demonstration, this sign undoubtedly signifies black British solidarity with black American activists in the United States. However, as a black and "visibly Muslim" woman, her sign signifies additional identifications and solidarities in struggles against the intertwining of racial and religious discrimination that threatens her belonging in the world house, even as her black, partially veiled, Muslim body is itself perceived as a threatening signifier of terror.[59]

To be sure, intellectuals and activists in the United Kingdom and the United States are increasingly recognizing and emphasizing the connections between Islamophobia, anti-blackness, and anti-immigration. In his 2018 *American Islamophobia: Understanding the Roots and Rise of Fear*, Khaled A. Beydoun offers a nuanced approach to the intersections between anti-Islamic and anti-black racism in the United States.[60] According to Beydoun, "Reckoning with Islamophobia requires situating it within the American context that feeds and foments it, which perils a broad population of could be victims that manifest the multi-layered diversity of the country they strive to call home." Of course, this striving among Muslims to call the United States home is frustrated by state-sponsored efforts, such as Trump's proposed travel bans, to keep Muslims outside of the United States or at its margins. Yet Beydoun's analysis insists upon viewing the marginalization of Muslims in the United States not only in terms of a long-standing Orientalism that must be understood in its own right, but also in light of the nation's history of antiblack racism. Beydoun writes, "Islamophobia in the United States is, in great part, a racial project, spawned by a master discourse that drove European supremacy and today powered by popular views and state policy seeking to safeguard its domestic progeny, white supremacy."[61] Thus, for Beydoun, Islamophobia must be seen as a particular manifestation of white supremacy. In *Islamophobia and Racism in America*, Erik Love goes further, insisting: "There is a common ancestry in America's worst racial sins: the campaigns leading to genocide of Native Americans, the brutal reign of chattel slavery, the *de jure* system of Jim Crow segregation, Japanese American internment camps, mass incarceration, deportation, and Islamophobia. All of these stem from White supremacy."[62]

Beydoun also sees a range of oppressions, such as racist policing and the school-to-prison pipeline, intersecting with Islamophobia in the United States, and he argues for a framing of these issues in ways that demonstrate their convergence. As such, it becomes clearer why issues such as Islamophobia must be linked to antiblack racism and social movements such as Black Lives Matter.[63] In a thoroughgoing article for the Black Youth Project, "Solidarity Can't Work without Understanding that Blackness Has a Role in Every Struggle," New York–based writer and storyteller Hari Ziyad attempts to make plain these convergences in response to Donald Trump's proposed "Muslim ban." In the article, Ziyad stresses the importance of the Movement for Black Lives taking up "so many causes not immediately recognized as Black—like the rights of Palestinians and Indigenous water protectors," while also insisting that such causes not contribute to the erasure of blackness and the suffering black bodies that are often marginalized within other marginalized communities with whom they share familial, social, and/or cultural ties. For Ziyad, "It's also crucial to understand that there are people at the intersections of communities who exemplify the greatest challenges to each of the causes we view as distinct. This is especially important when it comes to understanding the globalizing nature of anti-Blackness."[64]

Isra Amin Ibrahim, a Sudanese American university student, underscores Ziyad's point in a piece entitled, "Why We Must Stop De-Centering Black Muslims in the Fight against Islamophobia." Arguing for greater solidarity among black and nonblack Muslims in light of the anti-Islamic rhetoric and policy proposals of the Trump administration, Ibrahim offers a heartfelt plea that attempts to highlight her multiple and overlapping communities of identification, solidarity, and accountability as a young, black, immigrant Muslim woman living in the United States. Ibrahim concludes her piece by declaring, "I write for you [nonblack Muslims in the United States] and my Black Sudanese and Somalian immigrant family who exist between the genocidal structures of anti-Black racism, Islamophobic violence, and xenophobic tactics."[65] When such convergences as Isra Ibrahim embodies are denied or downplayed within nonblack and black marginalized communities—due in part to an adoption of antiblack sentiments, as a means of avoiding further marginalization—Ziyad argues that this "[leaves] Black people vulnerable even in the spaces they call home."[66] It is this persistent vulnerability, experienced at the intersections of anti-blackness and other complex modes of oppression, in the spaces black people already call home, that creates contradictory experiences of resonance and dissonance with King's hopeful vision of the world house for many young black folks in the United States and UK.

Black Millennials' International and Intersectional Activism

Of course, Martin Luther King Jr. was acutely aware that his vision of the great world house might never be realized. He also believed that if the seeming permanence of racism should thwart this vision, it would inevitably mean the end of Western civilization and indeed humanity as we have known it. For King, following Arnold Toynbee, at the root of the decline and ultimate demise of civilizations was their "failure to respond creatively to the challenges impinging upon them." Following this line of thought to its logical conclusion, King insisted that "if Western civilization does not now respond constructively to the challenge to banish racism, some future historian will have to say that a great civilization died because it lacked the soul and commitment to make justice a reality for all." Thus, the eradication of racism globally was for King an urgent moral and indeed spiritual imperative. King described such antiracist work as "our hope for creative living in this world house that we have inherited."[67]

In *Postcolonial Melancholia*, Gilroy too argues for a kind of "creative and negative thinking" that he sees as necessary for the possibility of dwelling together in multicultural democracies free from racism and the very category of race itself—what he calls "convivial metropolitan cultures." Similar to King, Gilroy also makes use, albeit critically, of domestic metaphors to discuss the simultaneous desirability and difficulties of living together with difference. In part, the difficulties arise from the realization that those whose privileges have heretofore allowed them to feel most at home, whether in the UK or the United States, are being met with demands to not only equitably share space and resources with others but also to make cultural adjustments to accommodate "the challenging presence of racially different people." In Gilroy's account, such challenges are more often than not seen as "intrusions by immigrants, incompatible blacks, and fascinating, threatening strangers." It is this sense that these racial and religious others are threatening intruders rather than kindred inheritors of the world house that Gilroy suggests calls into question the "desirability of that unchosen multicultural destination."[68]

In the midst of widening socioeconomic fissures in Britain, Gilroy finds such "hope for creative living" in the "enduring quality of resistance" among the country's young people. While he readily acknowledges that these inequalities strain the possibilities of recognizing commonalities across difference, he nevertheless sees in the British context a critical shift in social formations among British youth "in which factors of identity and solidarity that derive from class, gender, sexuality, and region have made a strong sense of racial difference unthinkable to the point of absurdity."[69] While it is beyond the scope of this chapter to provide a nuanced account of Gilroy's use of the terms "identity," "solidarity," and "race," it is important to note that he treats each of these terms as freighted with ideological baggage, as prone to misconception and deeply contested. As such, Gilroy should not be understood to be making a claim about British youths that suggests that they are presently living in a postracial society, though it is clear from his other writings that such a society would be desirable for Gilroy.[70] Rather, his longstanding argument that race is a product of racism and not the other way around helps to clarify his view about the social formation and racial identifications of British youth. If we keep in mind his argument that identity has much to do with "the interplay between subjective experiences of the world and the cultural and historical settings in which those fragile, meaningful subjectivities are formed," then Gilroy's claim seems to be that multiple axes of difference have shaped the experiences and subject formation of a generation of British youth in profound ways. Gilroy asserts that while "identity is always bounded and particular" and irreducible to "sameness," the kinds of sharp racial distinctions that have heretofore marked the neocolonial or postcolonial eras no longer remain compelling for—and indeed are being actively resisted by—a critical mass of young people in the UK.[71]

Against such racialized modes of identification that perpetuate social divisions and inequalities, Gilroy envisions the possibilities—brought about by these young people—of "the building of a multicultural nationality that is no longer phobic about the prospect of exposure to either strangers or otherness." It is the building of such a society, for Gilroy, that requires "creative and negative thinking." Such thinking would render race little more than "a virtual reality given meaning only by the fact that racism endures."[72] Of course, in the meantime racism does indeed endure as does the significance and matter of race as a social construction and lived reality. And it is precisely because of its tenacious endurance that young people across the black Atlantic have had to redouble their efforts as of late to, as King put it, "root out the last vestiges of racism" so that they may realize the possibilities of being at home in the world house.[73]

A 2016 documentary film, *Generation Revolution*, captures this spirit of resistance among British youth and their struggles toward creative living, or being at home, in the house that empire built. The film, directed and produced by Usayd Younis and Cassie Quarles, follows the work of five young black activists, between eighteen and twenty-three years old, and their organizations (London Black Revolutionaries, R Movement, and the Black Dissidents) between 2014 and the summer of 2016. Each motivated by her or his own experiences with racism in Europe, the young activists in *Generation Revolution* engage in various forms of direct action on behalf of black and brown but also poor people, women, and other marginalized groups in the UK. While the oppression of black and brown bodies is at the center of these various modes of activism, it is clear that to various degrees these young activists embrace complex and intersectional identities that lead them to a range of resistance tactics intended to undermine multiple forms of injustice and oppression simultaneously. Indeed, Arnie, the twenty-four-year-old founder of London Black Revolutionaries (LBR or Black Revs), insists that while his group has not hesitated to organize demonstrations such as We Can't Breathe ("a solidarity 'die-in' for Eric Garner") and Black Brunch (a demonstration to call attention to the economic displacement of black communities in Brixton, London), it is not a single-issue organization. To the contrary: "We're not just about fighting racism, we'll fight everything."[74]

Arnie's comments came in response to questions raised following one of LBR's more prominent direct action initiatives—pouring concrete over anti-homeless spikes laid in front of a local grocery store, to protest the rise of "defensive architecture" designed to exclude "'unwanted' behaviors and people."[75] The documentary's footage of the direct action against the marginalization and criminalization of homeless people—intertwined as it is with issues of poverty, lack of affordable housing, gentrification, and the public policing of socially stigmatized bodies—especially black and brown bodies—dramatizes the complexity and creativity of activism among black youth in the UK. To cement (quite literally) in the public imagination the solidarity at the heart of this direct action, the Black Revs declared, via social media, "Do not let the media hide the fact that this was direct action by the dispossessed (in this case Black and Asian people) fighting for other dispossessed people."[76] Joshua Virasami, also involved in the Black Revs and committed to an intersectional approach to fighting interlocking forms of oppression, insists that his generation of activists is "going to build a beautiful, loving, family of resistance," a sentiment that deeply resonates not only with King's world house but also his vision of the beloved community.

Tay, the youngest of the activists featured in the film, is a soft-spoken eighteen-year-old for whom Martin Luther King Jr. is an inspiring figure, yet he is wary of identifying fully with the masculine and messianic persona and performance associated with King. He confesses, "I'm not the most charismatic, Malcolm X, Martin Luther King-esque speaker. I'm just a baby boy, living my life." Despite his self-effacement, Tay is portrayed as a skilled community organizer like King and an activist in an organization that resists hierarchical leadership in favor of a more egalitarian approach reminiscent of U.S. organizer Ella Baker. In a community forum, Tay describes his organization as follows, "We are R Movement, an intersectional revolutionary organization." R Movement's commitment to intersectional activism is on display from the outset as Tay works with other leaders to organize "Why I Need Feminism," a forum for young people and activists. During one scene, one of the members of R Movement, a young black man named Jeremiah who attends the workshop contends: "You can't achieve something that has such a moral base like freedom without empathy. Like, how can you fight for the freedom of someone that you don't feel for?" A few moments later, Jeremiah, who also works as a youth mentor, can be seen brainstorming ideas for his "I Need Feminism Because . . ." sign, before eventually settling on the message "Patriarchy Is Poison." Jeremiah's prose is more poetic but carries a sentiment similar to an LBR sign that reads, "State Violence Kills Women." As the above suggests, the film is particularly attentive to the ways gender politics is deeply infused into the self-identification and activism of these organizations. In a particularly poignant scene, however, the film captures an exchange between Tay and a young black woman who is part of a feminist organization and who interrogates his gender politics. While Tay insists that R Movement is about resisting every system of oppression, including "white supremacy, patriarchy, and capitalism," the young black feminist activist gives full voice to her skepticism in a manner that deserves to be quoted in full:

> I get scared of black male activists . . . because I've met a lot of misogynistic ones. So . . . I'm looking at you sideways. It's just really hard to, like, trust people. Whenever I say to a black man, 'I'm a black feminist' they always say, 'Why are you trying to, like, divide us? Oh, this is what the white man wants.' And it's, like, well, you're not really giving a fuck about me as a woman. You're coming at it from a male perspective. But you have to understand . . . black males, you have it hard, but as black women, it's like we don't even exist.

Tay can be seen listening intently before affirming the legitimacy of the young woman's concerns and citing concrete examples of R Movement's commitment to progressive gender politics, which seems to alleviate her apprehensions concerning the possibility of collaborating with Tay and his self-proclaimed "intersectional and revolutionary" organization. The film's portrayal of these interactions offers a glimpse into how young activists negotiate tensions around identity politics that often arise within contemporary activist movements and threaten to derail them. At the same time, it shows how these young black male and female activists are collaboratively and creatively challenging reified notions of black masculinity and messianic male leadership that have often undermined the full liberatory potential of previous movements for black liberation, including the King-led U.S. civil rights movement. Moreover, the film shows young black women, such as twenty-five-year-old Tej and twenty-four-year-old Alex, claiming prominent leadership roles in street-level activism from the Black Brunch to the "die-in" demonstrations protesting police violence and deaths related to "Europe's refugee crisis." Indeed, as the film progresses, both Tej and Alex pose critical and fundamental challenges to the leadership, strategies, and tactics of Arnie, London Black Revolutionaries' male founder, in ways that seemingly expose unexamined vestiges of hierarchical and patriarchal notions of activism and leadership that he claims to resist. At the film's end, searching for alternative and more creative ways of living into her intersectional identities as a black woman activist, Tej seeks the most effective way to intervene in the crisis of homelessness among those who have seemingly been evicted from the world house.[77]

Generation Revolution concludes with scenes from the summer of 2016, the year the Black Lives Matter movement erupted in the UK and five years after the state-sponsored killing of Mark Duggan. Alex and a host of other black women are portrayed at the forefront of those Black Lives Matter UK demonstrations. They are simultaneously committed to local injustices in London and in solidarity with Black Lives Matter activists in the United States. This returns us, full circle, to Janine Wiedel's photographic exhibition of the London protest in solidarity with Black Lives Matter in the United States. Inside the frame of one representative image, a diverse sea of protesters floods Oxford Street. Fists are raised, cell phones record, and makeshift signs display antiracist messages bearing witness to the value of black lives. The crowd is mostly young, black, and female, yet men, whites, and other people of color are clearly present in this protest. A person of apparent South Asian descent is huddled next to a person of African descent; perhaps the two are sharing their respective experiences of, perspectives on, or motivations for participating in the demonstration. A sign of solidarity occupies a prominent place in the center of the frame, its holder invisible behind an ethnically ambiguous woman wearing a loose-fitting hijab. The message, written in black magic marker that bleeds onto the cardboard: "Asians 4 Black Lives Matter."[78]

Beyond the World House as a Utopian Vision

In an ironic and undoubtedly incomplete way, the photograph described above captures something not only of Gilroy's hopes for British youth, but also of Martin Luther King Jr.'s vision of the great world house. Of course, the fact that the photograph captures a scene of protest arising from ongoing state-sponsored violence against black bodies in the twenty-first century is a clear indication that King's vision has not been realized, as some would argue it never will be. In her introduction to an aptly titled collection of essays, *The House that Race Built: Black Americans, U.S. Terrain*, literary and cultural theorist Wahneema Lubiano argues, "The United States is not just the domicile of a historically specific form of racial oppression, but it sustains itself as a structure through that oppression."[79] Taking Lubiano earnestly, one certainly wonders not only whether such a house, built upon and structured by the antidemocratic forces of white supremacy, could ever bear the weight of becoming the world house King envisioned. To be sure, King too saw racism as the "treacherous foundation" on which both the United States and United Kingdom were built and as the "corrosive evil" that had the potential to be the downfall of all of Western civilization. To his mind, a "failure to respond creatively" to the challenges of racism—including, especially, the forced labor, economic exploitation, and wars waged upon black and brown bodies—would certainly mean the demise of the West. In a prescriptive tone, King declared that the avoidance of this fate was predicated upon a "spiritual and moral reawakening," and he challenged humanity to forge bonds of global solidarity and "work all over the world with unshakable determination to wipe out the last vestiges of racism."[80]

Thus, King's world house is not merely a utopian vision of universality and "brotherhood." As the opening epigraph to this chapter suggests, the world house that King imagined would be the result of a global and ever-expanding liberation movement that involved a great mass of people "determined to end the exploitation of their races and lands." More than fifty years ago, King claimed that no one familiar with history should be surprised by the uprisings of the oppressed, especially the formerly colonized of the world, as "the oppressed cannot remain oppressed forever" and "the yearning for freedom eventually manifests itself."[81] Unfortunately, those familiar with history are not surprised that oppression remains deeply entrenched in our societies. Of course, they should be even less surprised that a new generation of young activists continues to manifest fierce yearnings for freedom.

While King was initially concerned with such "yearnings for freedom," or the sociopolitical, economic, and spiritual strivings among black Americans, he came to insist upon situating and interpreting those struggles within a much broader global framework. Young activists in the Black Lives Matter movement, such as Patrisse Cullors in the United States, echo the necessity of such international solidarity. For Cullors:

> Anti-Black racism has global consequences. It is completely and absolutely necessary that, as Black people in the United States, we do not center the struggle around a domestic fight for our "civil rights." Rather, this is a broader fight for the Black diaspora, both on the continent and across the globe. It's essential that we center this conversation and also our practice in an international frame. If we don't have those critical dialogues, if we don't have that praxis around internationalism, we won't have a movement that is about all Black lives.

From her perspective, as an artist and activist in the United States, Cullors describes the Black Lives Matter movement in terms of "some of the most vibrant, creative responses to state violence." Much of the vibrancy and creativity of the

movement has undoubtedly been the result of thoroughly intersectional commitments to LGBT and queer people who have been centered in the Black Lives
Matter movement. Moreover, the movement's cofounders argue, it is only when
such people are centered—those most vulnerable to being cast outside of various literal and metaphorical home spaces—that the possibility of "saving" all
black lives can be realized. For Patrisse Cullors, this means, "We aren't going to
give up parts of our community in an effort to save some of our community."[82]

In this sense, Cullors and other young activists in Black Lives Matter draw
upon but radicalize King's insistence that "all *men* are interdependent" (emphasis added).[83] When Cullors insists, "It's either all of us, or it's none of us," with reference to Black trans women who have been "iced out of our communities," she
simultaneously affirms, critiques, and reimagines King's masculinist and hetero-
normative, if otherwise inclusive vision of the world house, in which, "all of life
is interrelated." As King put it: "The agony of the poor impoverishes the rich; the
betterment of the poor enriches the rich. We are inevitably our brother's keeper
because we are our brother's brother. Whatever affects one directly affects all
indirectly."[84] While Cullors's internationalist and abolitionist vision of democracy is most often rightly compared to Angela Y. Davis's, one can no doubt also
hear the powerful and persistent influence of King's "hope for creative living in
the world house" in her articulation of a vision of a "society that has no borders,
literally. It's a society that's based on interdependence and the connection of all
living beings. It's a society that is determined to facilitate a life that is full of respect, a life that is full of honoring and praising those most impacted by oppression." For Cullors, such a society is profoundly moral, as King knew it must be if
the global human family is to survive and thrive together. Cullors also imagines
this society as "deeply spiritual," as King envisioned a society worthy of the ap-
pellation "the great world house," a truly liberated world for all of God's children
to call home.[85]

NOTES

The epigraphs are from Martin Luther King Jr., *Where Do We Go From Here: Chaos or Community?* (Boston: Beacon Press, 1967; rpt., 1968, 2010), 169; inaugural tweet from Black
Lives Matter UK, July 15, 2016, https://twitter.com/ukblm/status/754013084432338944.

1. Martin Luther King Jr., *Where Do We Go from Here?*, 173.

2. Jordain Carney, "Schumer: America's 'Moral Authority' Declining under Trump,"
The Hill, January 3, 2018, http://thehill.com/homenews/senate/367274-schumer
-americas-moral-authority-declining-under-trump.

3. Karen McVeigh, "Cutting Aid While Leaving EU Will Make Britain More Insular, May
Warned," *Guardian*, April 20, 2017, https://www.theguardian.com/global-development
/2017/apr/20/aid-eu-britain-insular-theresa-may-tory-manifesto.

4. In exposing the transnational nature of white supremacy, King uses the national policy of apartheid in South Africa as a "classic example of organized and institutionalized racism" that is bolstered and "virtually made possible by the economic policies of the United States and Great Britain." King, *Where Do We Go from Here?*, 173.

5. Brian Ward, *Martin Luther King in Newcastle upon Tyne: The African American Freedom Struggle and Race Relations in the North East of England* (Newcastle upon Tyne, UK: Tyne Bridge Publishing, 2017), 16.

6. Martin Luther King Jr., "Speech at City Temple Hall," London, December 7, 1964, quoted in Ward, *Martin Luther King in Newcastle upon Tyne*, 47.

7. Ibid., 51.

8. Thomas A. Mulhall, "On Racism and War as Global Phenomena: Martin Luther King, Jr. and the World Council of Churches," in Lewis V. Baldwin and Paul R. Dekar, eds., *"In an Inescapable Network of Mutuality": Martin Luther King, Jr. and the Globalization of an Ethical Ideal* (Eugene, Ore.: Cascade Books, 2013), 102.

9. Jerome Taylor, "Trayvon Martin's Parents Call for an End to Racial Profiling in Britain," *Independent*, May 11, 2012, https://www.independent.co.uk/news/uk/home-news/trayvon-martins-parents-call-for-an-end-to-racial-profiling-in-britain-7737747.html.

10. Marcia Rigg, "'We Must Unite Globally against Police Brutality': Marcia Rigg on Building an International Coalition," November 9, 2015, https://fergusonsolidaritytour.com/.

11. Martin Luther King Jr., *Where Do We Go from Here?*, 169.

12. Steven Hopkins, "Veteran British Racism Campaigner Has Message to Black Lives Matter ahead of London Riots Anniversary," *HuffPost*, UK ed., July 30, 2016, https://www.huffingtonpost.co.uk/entry/london-riots-anniversary-nothing-has-changed-since-mark-duggan-shooting-claims-race-advocate-still-fighting-for-justice_uk_578f5a54e4b011978b131e84.

13. Martin Luther King Jr., *Where Do We Go from Here?*, 169, 171. Linda T. Wynn notes that while King's ideas about a "world house" were inclusive in intent, they were nevertheless often conveyed through the use of male gender-specific language, which may partially be indicative of his sexism. See Linda T. Wynn, "Beyond Patriarchy: The Meaning of Martin Luther King, Jr. for the Women of the World," in Baldwin and Dekar, *"In an Inescapable Network of Mutuality,"* 59.

14. Martin Luther King Jr., *Where Do We Go from Here?*, 170.

15. Lindsey Bever, "Why Black Lives Matter Has Gained Momentum in a Country Where Police Shootings Are Rare," *Washington Post*, July 10, 2016, https://www.washingtonpost.com/news/worldviews/wp/2016/07/10/why-black-lives-matter-has-gained-momentum-in-a-country-where-police-shootings-are-rare?/.

16. Steven W. Thrasher, "Black Lives Matter Has Showed Us: The Oppression of Black People Is Borderless," *Guardian*, August 9, 2015, https://www.theguardian.com/commentisfree/2015/aug/09/black-lives-matter-movement-taught-black-oppression-borderless-michael-brown.

17. "Mandem" is diasporic Jamaican patois for "men," "boys," or "group of males." See Lindsey Bever, "Why Black Lives Matter Has Gained Momentum."

18. Janine Wiedel, *Black Lives Matter* UK, Photo, 2016, Social Documentary Network, https://www.socialdocumentary.net/exhibit/Janine_Wiedel/3728.

19. Thrasher, "Black Lives Matter Has Showed Us."

20. Martin Luther King Jr., *Why We Can't Wait* (New York: New American Library, 1964), 77.

21. Thrasher, "Black Lives Matter Has Showed Us."

22. King, *Where Do We Go from Here?*, 176. The latter words of this quote, concerning the "overthrow" of structures and governments, are rarely associated with King, whose philosophy of nonviolence has been conveniently interpreted in ways that have been used to chastise and discredit the tactics and morality of contemporary activists.

23. Ibid., 170–71.

24. Sadhyi Dar, "How Black Lives Matter Is Changing British Universities," *Nation*, September 12, 2017, https://www.thenation.com/article/how-black-lives-matter-is-changing-british-universities-.

25. Patrisse Cullors quoted in Christina Heatherton, "#BlackLivesMatter and Global Visions of Abolition: An Interview with Patrisse Cullors," in Jordan T. Camp and Christina Heatherton, eds., *Policing the Planet: Why the Policing Crisis Led to Black Lives Matter* (London: Verso, 2016), 38.

26. Ibid., 39.

27. Natalie Jeffers quoted in Tracy McVeigh, "Why Activists Brought the Black Lives Matter Movement to the UK," *Guardian*, August 6, 2016, https://www.theguardian.com/uk-news/2016/aug/06/black-lives-matter-uk-found-vital-social-justice.

28. Hopkins, "Veteran British Racism Campaigner Has Message."

29. McVeigh, "Why Activists Brought the Black Lives Matter Movement to the UK."

30. Siana Bangura, "We Need To Talk about Police Brutality in the U.K.," *Fader*, March 29, 2016, http://www.thefader.com/2016/03/29/police-brutality-uk-essay.

31. Eric Allison and Simon Hattenstone, "Now We Know the Shocking Facts of Deaths in Custody, Will Theresa May Act?," *Guardian*, November 2, 2017, https://www.theguardian.com/commentisfree/2017/nov/02/deaths-in-custody-government-report-theresa-may.

32. Joshua Virasami quoted in Alasdair Soussi, "Do Black Lives Matter in the UK?," *Al Jazeera*, December 30, 2016, https://www.aljazeera.com/indepth/features/2016/12/black-lives-matter-uk-161226031336218.html.

33. Kiri Kankhwende, "#BlackLivesMatter in Britain Too: Why Does Our Media Care Less?," *Open Democracy*, April 19, 2016, https://www.opendemocracy.net/ourbeeb/kiri-kankhwende/blacklivesmatter-in-britain-too-why-does-our-media-care-less.

34. Michelle Alexander, *The New Jim Crow: Mass Incarceration in the Age of Colorblindness* (New York: New Press, 2010).

35. "The New Jim Crow: A Case Study on the Role of Books in Leveraging Social Change," New Press, promotional material, November 2014, 3, https://mediaimpactfunders.org/wp-content/uploads/2014/12/The-New-Press-NJC-Case-Study-Nov20141.pdf.

36. Randeep Ramesh, "More Black People Jailed in England and Wales Proportionally Than in U.S.," *Guardian*, October 11, 2010, https://www.theguardian.com/society/2010/oct/11/black-prison-population-increase-england.

37. McVeigh, "Why Activists Brought the Black Lives Matter Movement to the UK."

38. The Home Office is the lead UK government department for immigration and passports, drugs policy, crime, fire, counterterrorism and police. See Aoife O'Neill, *Hate Crime, England and Wales, 2016/17*, Home Office Statistical Bulletin 17/17 (London, UK:

Home Office, 2017), https://assets.publishing.service.gov.uk/government/uploads
/system/uploads/attachment_data/file/652136/hate-crime-1617-hosb1717.pdf.

39. Bangura, "We Need to Talk about Police Brutality in the U.K."

40. Virasami quoted in Soussi, "Do Black Lives Matter in the UK?"

41. Krishnadev Calamur, "Black Lives Matter's U.K. Protest," *Atlantic*, September 6,
2016, https://www.theatlantic.com/news/archive/2016/09/black-lives-matter-in-the-uk
/498731/.

42. Calamur, "Black Lives Matter's U.K. Protest."

43. Paul Gilroy, *Postcolonial Melancholia* (New York: Columbia University Press, 2010),
75.

44. Calamur, "Black Lives Matter's U.K. Protest."

45. King, *Where Do we Go from Here?*, 170, 179.

46. Gilroy, *Postcolonial Melancholia*, 113.

47. Toni Morrison, *The Origin of Others* (Cambridge, Mass.: Harvard University Press,
2017), 94.

48. Toni Morrison, "Home," in Wahneema H. Lubiano, ed., *The House that Race Built:
Black Americans, U.S. Terrain* (New York: Pantheon Books, 1997), 10.

49. Gilroy, *Postcolonial Melancholia*, 107, 90, 95.

50. Morrison, *Origin of Others*, 109–10.

51. Stuart Hall, *The Fateful Triangle: Race, Ethnicity, Nation* (Cambridge, Mass.: Harvard
University Press, 2017), 150.

52. Gilroy, *Postcolonial Melancholia*, 90, 100–101.

53. Morrison, *Origin of Others*, 100.

54. Bridget Minamore, "2016: A Year of Black Lives Matter in Britain," *Grazia*, February
1, 2017, https://graziadaily.co.uk/life/real-life/2016-year-black-lives-matter-britain.

55. Martin Luther King Jr., *Where Do We Go from Here?*, 176.

56. Minamore, "2016: A Year of Black Lives Matter in Britain."

57. Martin Luther King Jr., *Where Do We Go from Here?*, 176.

58. Wiedel, "Black Lives Matter UK," Photo, 2016.

59. For a detailed discussion of the term "visibly Muslim," see Emily Tarlo, *Visibly Muslim: Fashion, Politics, Faith* (New York: Bloomsbury, 2014).

60. Khaled A. Beydoun, *American Islamophobia: Understanding the Roots and Rise of Fear*
(Oakland: University of California Press, 2018).

61. Khaled A. Beydoun, "Rethinking Islamophobia," *Al Jazeera*, March 12, 2018, https://
www.aljazeera.com/indepth/opinion/rethinking-islamophobia-180312085500278.html.

62. Erik Love, *Islamophobia and Racism in America* (New York: New York University
Press, 2017), 85.

63. Unfortunately, such issues are not often linked. Internal racial and ethnic divisions among U.S. Muslim communities continue to undermine recognition of ways
white supremacy frustrates the possibilities of African Americans and Muslims to truly
"belong" or be at home and ways it perpetually threatens "others."

64. Hari Ziyad, "Solidarity Can't Work without Understanding that Blackness Has a
Role in Every Struggle," *Black Youth Project*, April 18, 2017, http://blackyouthproject.com
/solidarity-cant-work-without-understanding-blackness-role-every-struggle/.

65. Isra A. Ibrahim, "Why We Must Stop De-Centering Black Muslims in the Fight
against Islamophobia," *RaceBaitR*, February 1, 2017, http://racebaitr.com/2017/02/01/we
-must-stop-de-centering-black-muslims/.

66. Ziyad, "Solidarity Can't Work without Understanding."

67. Martin Luther King Jr., *Where Do We Go from Here?*, 173, 176.

68. Gilroy, *Postcolonial Melancholia*, 119–20.

69. Ibid., 120.

70. See, for instance, Paul Gilroy, *Against Race: Imagining Political Culture Beyond the Color Line* (Cambridge, Mass.: Harvard University Press, 2000).

71. Ibid., 98.

72. Gilroy, *Postcolonial Melancholia*, 99, 119.

73. Martin Luther King Jr., *Where Do We Go from Here?*, 174.

74. Cassie Quarless and Usayd Younis, *Generation Revolution* (United Kingdom: Black and Brown Films, 2016).

75. Karl De Fine Licht, "Hostile Urban Architecture: A Critical Discussion of the Seemingly Offensive Art of Keeping People Away," *Etikk i praksis: Nordic Journal of Applied Ethics* 11, no. 2 (2017), 27–44.

76. Quarless and Younis, *Generation Revolution*.

77. Ibid.

78. Janine Wiedel, "Black Lives Matter UK."

79. Wahneema H. Lubiano, *The House That Race Built: Black Americans, U.S. Terrain* (New York: Pantheon Books, 1997), vii.

80. Martin Luther King Jr., *Where Do We Go From Here*, 169, 173–74, 176.

81. Ibid., 169, 170.

82. Heatherton, "#BlackLivesMatter and Global Visions of Abolition," 35, 38, 40.

83. Martin Luther King Jr., *Where Do We Go from Here?*, 181.

84. Ibid.

85. Heatherton, "#BlackLivesMatter and Global Visions of Abolition," 40. In her essay "Home," in *The House That Race Built*, Toni Morrison insists that she "applauds" and is "indebted to" those intellectuals who have attempted to do the work of "clearing intellectual and moral space where racial constructs are being forced to reveal their struts and bolts, their technology and their carapace, so that political action, legal and social thought and cultural production can be generated sans racist cant, explicit or in disguise." Morrison also references "Martin Luther King's hopeful language" in her genealogy of intellectuals who have attempted to imagine a world free of racial hierarchy. Unlike King, however, Morrison rejects the metaphor of "house," insisting upon a radical distinction between "house" and "home." In terms of the former, Morrison argues that all too often those who claim to be committed to antiracist work are unwittingly reinforcing the structures of the "race house" by their reification of boundaries and borders between "inside" and "outside" and other binary conceptualizations of our presence and proximity to one another. Against this tendency, Morrison is in search of a "new space," that is wide and open, a place that is no longer marked by the anxiety of belonging. This is not "the house that race built," but another world altogether. She insists, "I have never lived, nor has any of us, in a world in which race did not matter," but she envisions such a world, sans racism, that can be imagined as home. Morrison, "Home," 11.

PART III
ENVISIONING, PURSUING, AND SHAPING THE FUTURE WORLD HOUSE
WHERE DO WE GO FROM HERE?

CHAPTER 11
THE WORLD AS A "SINGLE NEIGHBORHOOD"
THE GLOBAL ETHICS OF MARTIN LUTHER KING JR.

HAK JOON LEE

The large house in which we live demands that we transform this worldwide neighborhood into a world-wide brotherhood. Together we must learn
to live as brothers or together we will be forced to perish as fools.
MARTIN LUTHER KING JR., *Where Do We Go From Here?*

He shall judge between many peoples,
and shall arbitrate between strong nations far away;
they shall beat their swords into plowshares,
and their spears into pruning hooks;
nation shall not lift up sword against nation,
neither shall they learn war any more;
but they shall all sit under their own vines and under their own fig trees,
and no one shall make them afraid;
for the mouth of the LORD of hosts has spoken.
MICAH 4:3–4 (NRSV)

In his last Sunday morning sermon, "Remaining Awake through a Great Revolution," delivered only a few days before his death, Martin Luther King Jr. illustrated the shocking nature of a transformation taking place in the world with the
example of Rip Van Winkle, a character in Washington Irving's short story, who
had slept for twenty years through the American Revolution. King warned that,
like Rip Van Winkle, many people were sleeping without realizing how radically
the world was changing through the triple revolutions of technology, weapons, and human rights. While achievements in these areas were fascinating, he
noted, they were frightening because they posed new challenges and risks. King
warned that humanity needed new vision, ethics, and attitude to cope with the
new reality because the underdevelopment or lack of "the new attitudes, the
new mental responses, that the new situation demands" had become "the great
liabilities" of social life.[1]

The massive transformation in the world that King described is now termed "globalization."[2] Today we are seeing the globalization that King described in his own time, but it is accelerated and intensified as if on steroids. The speed and impact of globalization have increased sharply over the last several decades, and, as King warned, tens of millions of Americans have slept through the transformation without recognizing its radical nature. They are now waking up in shock and anger and struggling to find their place in a globalizing world.

In fact, technocrats and neoliberal oligarchs have kept people complacent or ignorant for a long time while a neoliberal race to the bottom has been exploiting poor people and racial and ethnic minorities, destroying communities, displacing peoples, and devastating nature. These destructive trends have now come home to roost. Seeing the rosy capitalist promise of endless material success turn into a nightmare of joblessness, competition, and shrinking social welfare benefits, poor people feel fearful, betrayed, and angry. Brexit, the election of Donald John Trump as U.S. president, and the rise of illiberal democracy in the West are examples of such angry reactions to the impact of globalization. Xenophobic religious radicals and white supremacists exploit these emotions for their own extremist agendas of religious terrorism, nativism, and white nationalism.[3] While the emotions of these xenophobes are understandable, their responses are more reactionary than constructive. Disillusioned by the current political arrangement of neoliberal political economy, they mistakenly direct their emotional energy at immigrants and racial or religious minorities, who are themselves victims of global corporations and power elites.

The world seems to be in disarray. Despite the promise of economic prosperity and liberal cosmopolitanism, neoliberalism is incapable of guiding and organizing this rapidly shrinking world. As King presciently pointed out, the world needs a new moral vision and ethics that are commensurate with the new reality that globalization has brought and is bringing about.

The Relevance of King's Global Vision and Ideas

Although Martin Luther King Jr. died more than a half century ago, and although globalization has drastically accelerated since then, King's vision and ideas are still relevant. King was probably one of only a few people who genuinely understood in his day the promises and threats of globalization and worked to make it a positive force for humanity. King called for the revolutionary transformation of values for humanity, and his vision of the "great world house" describes the direction and contours of the moral transformation befitting a globalizing world.

King's public ministry was closely tied with the new political and social reality that globalization was creating. For example, King's time, in the aftermath of World War II, was an era in which a global civil society began to emerge more concretely through various independence movements, international organizations (such as the UN and its agencies), and moral discourses of democracy and human rights (exemplified by the UN Universal Declaration of Human Rights in 1948). King's movements used the various dynamics, mechanisms, and organizations of this nascent global civil society—mass media, NGOs, liberation movements worldwide, human rights laws, international bodies, and coalitions—for political and moral change. For example, King used the international media and power structures to galvanize international pressure on America. He also actively worked with the UN and its agencies and appealed to international human rights laws.

Critically engaging with current forms of global ethics, this chapter studies King's theology, ethics, and practices as resources for constructive global ethics in the twenty-first century. I claim that King makes unique contributions to current scholarly discussions and practices of global ethics through his carefully conceived global vision of "the great world house," his deep understanding of timeless political realities, and his actual grassroots political practices. In particular, King addresses the reality of systematic inequality and the necessity of common morality in a creative tension or balance between the communal and the political, and the global and the local, which current approaches of global ethics often miss.

The importance of King's contribution to the project of global ethics lies first and foremost in his actual involvements in global peace and justice throughout his adult life. His global ethics emerged from his political praxis rather than theoretical speculations. Recognized as a champion of global peace and justice during his life, he made an impact on these, especially with regard to racism, militarism, and classism. His movement leadership shows how a global vision and global ethics can be doubly effective, impacting change locally and worldwide.

The Emerging Discipline of Global Ethics

Global ethics is an emerging discipline focused on the growing challenges of globalization. While global ethics, like traditional ethics, is a human intellectual endeavor to critically reflect on human normative decisions and actions relying on certain standards of right and wrong, good and bad, and fitting and unfitting, it is different from traditional ethics as it takes "the globe as the proper scope of ethics" and seeks to enhance the common good of humanity and the entire planet instead of the interests of a particular group or nation.[4] Accordingly, global ethics, in its deliberations, attempts to take into account the perspectives, rights, and needs of all concerned parties—individuals, institutions, and nations—and to keep in mind the common good. The rise of global ethics is prompted by the recognition that humanity, despite its differences, shares a common destiny, and that, for its survival, it needs to address the challenges facing it with shared moral responsibilities and collaboration. Many pressing global issues (e.g., nuclear threats, terrorism, economic inequality, global warming, religious and racial conflicts, migration, epidemics, human trafficking, and organized crime) are interrelated in their scope and nature. These problems are not all new, but their nature and dynamics have drastically changed due to globalization, which has increased their urgency and called for massive global cooperation to solve. That is, as the nature and scope of these ethical challenges are global, solutions should be global as well, and global ethics intends to assist these solutions by providing clarity and guidance with moral analyses, deliberation, and action.

In developing a normative framework for all of humanity, current theories of global ethics are built on traditional ethical approaches, such as deontology (natural law, human rights, Kantian ethics), teleology (utilitarianism), and areteology (Aristotelian virtue ethics).[5] Global ethics, however, regardless of its methodologies, tends to be universalistic in its attempt to provide a transnational framework of collective identity (global citizenship) and moral adjudication. It is characterized by extensive efforts to establish a shared moral ground or method that is accessible and applicable to all of humanity. That is, it goes against cultural or moral relativists, and it claims that certain ideas of goods, norms, and virtues are shared by all humans regardless of their religious, cultural, and ethno-racial backgrounds, and that meaningful moral discourse on these goods, norms, and virtues is possible among different groups. For example, a deontological approach (using natural law theory and human rights theory) sees that certain norms, such as nonmaleficence, sanctity of life, human dignity, compassion, justice, the golden rule, truth telling, and equality, are universally found or can be established across different cultures and religions.[6] Once ratified, these norms have binding authority; it is the moral duty of every person to respect and abide by these norms. Similarly, virtue ethicists believe that some virtues developed in a community (e.g., generosity and truthfulness) are globally applicable. Likewise, a utilitarian theory asserts that all humans tend to pursue happiness (pleasure) and to avoid pain and suffering, and it sees the principle of utility (the greatest happiness for the greatest number of people) as the universal basis of ethics.

The premise of global ethics is that once a certain norm, ethical method, or virtue is found to be universally authoritative, then it is applicable to all similar places and times. However, because of this universalistic orientation, global ethics experiences a few theoretical and practical difficulties, as indicated by the following reflections on ethical minimalism and the question of implementation.

Ethical Minimalism

Global ethics, especially in its deontological form, is often guilty of ethical minimalism or abstractionism. In other words, as it attempts to secure only a minimum consensus among different religious and cultural groups, it tends to be abstract and general while often disregarding local traditions and interpretive histories. However, it is doubtful whether such an abstract ethic can have binding authority over local people to the extent that it can motivate and influence their actions. Martin Robra's following critique is correct: "The universalized 'ethical minimum' cannot replace what does not yet exist: a shared global ethos and ethic, one rooted in a socially and ecologically sensitive global cultural vision backed by 'moral communities' and 'moral formation' which provide its viable environment."[7]

With its emphasis on the universal, global ethics tends to underestimate the role of local religious or other cultural rituals and traditions in interpreting and applying norms, shaping virtue, and motivating people to ethical action. Despite increased interreligious interactions, morality is still legitimated by a local, social, and cultural ethos, no matter how ineffable or meager such an ethos may be. Furthermore, the processes of defining, interpreting, and adjudicating global norms, ideals, and virtues often reflect a dominant worldview (usually Western) and the political-economic interest of rich and powerful nations and their power elites who currently control major global institutions and resources. For these reasons, global ethics or ethical claims are often suspected of being driven by the agenda of Western imperialism and hegemony.

In sum, global ethics cannot be imposed from above as universal regulative moral codes but should be voluntarily accepted by local communities. Global ethics should be global in scope, not only in terms of ethical analysis but also by participation in ethical deliberation and decision-making. Namely, global ethics requires the global participation of people in the process of deliberation, as one can easily see.

Implementation: Disparity of Power

Global ethics faces a challenge in not only how we find common goals, norms, and procedures that are accepted by local communities but also in how to implement them. This question of implementation is not unique to global ethics. It applies to all forms of ethics because knowing what is right, good, or fitting and *doing* it do not necessarily coincide. However, the concern about implementation exponentially grows because of its global scope. In addition, the question of implementation is more acute for global ethics because it operates in a context without any established structure of justice as opposed to a well-functioning nation-state. One task of global ethics is to assist the establishment of such a structure at a global level.

A crucial question, then, is how to address the power disparities between nations, racial or ethnic groups, and cultural communities and rectify the inequitable distribution of valuable resources (water, food, etc.), which are the immediate sources of injustices today. Achieving minimum justice requires checks and balances to power and correction of its abuses and misuses. The powerful seldom voluntarily give up their power and control but rather use their privileged information, institutional positions, and governmental resources to protect and expand their self-interest. So ethical declarations alone cannot undo deeply embedded injustices. Ethicist Lisa Cahill is right in saying: "The central obstacle to global ethics, therefore, is not mainly intellectual ignorance of commonalities in human nature that make certain goods necessary to human well-being. It is unwillingness to distribute community resources equitably, and to extend participation in basic goods to all human individuals and groups."[8]

Grassroots political engagements are necessary to rectify injustices and build global democracy. As injustices take a global form, global coalition-building and global collective practices are no less important than finding global norms and values in remedying problems.

One sees that ethical decision-making and implementation of global ethics are intimately associated with the development of global civil society and genuine global democracy. This means that ethical decision-making should no longer be controlled by powerful nations and corporations but should be shared among people at the grassroots level, and implementation requires ongoing checks and balances of power through global institutions and structures, grassroots organizing, and efforts led by NGOs.[9]

However, current approaches of global ethics do not adequately address these crucial concerns. Rather, one sees the two interrelated gaps between the global and the local and between theory and practice. There is a loyalty or trust gap on the part of local people toward global visions, norms, and virtues, just as there are power gaps between rich and poor and between whites and people of color, which impede the recognition, acceptance, and implementation of global ethics. Therefore, a challenge for global ethics is finding a plausible methodology that bridges these gaps.

In the following discussion, I examine how Martin Luther King Jr.'s ethics helps to bridge these two gaps. While many projects of global ethics tend to prioritize the global over the local and theory over practice, King's ethics maintains a creative tension and balance between the global and the local and between theory and practice, thus bridging the loyalty or trust and power gaps. At the heart of King's ethics is the synthesis of a seemingly contradictory relationship of the communal and the political, the global and the local. These double syntheses are instrumental in addressing the challenges that current global ethics projects face. For example, while recognizing the importance of moral norms (e.g., freedom, equality, fairness, and solidarity) for global peace and justice, King did not commit the fallacy of ethical minimalism, as many current proponents of global ethics do. Instead, King smoothly integrated these norms into his vision of the great world house, virtue formation, and political practices of nonviolence in the framework of communal-political ethics.

King's Communal-Political Ethics

I identify Martin Luther King Jr.'s ethics as communal-political ethics.[10] Developed out of his actual struggles for social justice, which started with the Montgomery bus boycott in 1955–56, King never separated the struggle for justice (the political) from the building of the community (the communal). While communal ethics upholds the community as the goal of human existence, based on the interdependent nature of this existence, the political is concerned with human responsibility and exertion toward that goal, through the liberation of the oppressed in particular. That is, while the communal offers the goal for all human endeavors, the political indicates a method to achieve it. Politics is understood as a collective process of coordinating and adjudicating diverse, often conflicting values, claims, and interests in achieving the beloved community. The immediate objective of politics is justice, but its ultimate goal is the beloved community. While the first necessary step toward the beloved community is the removal of social injustices such as racism, classism, and militarism, it ultimately cannot be built by legal means alone. It requires the conversion of hearts and minds through the communal power of love expressed through nonviolent resistance.[11]

King's communal-political ethics is expressed in his various key concepts such as justice, love, resistance, reconciliation, desegregation, and integration, as well as in his priestly and prophetic ministry, all assisting his work of community organizing and coalition-building for civil rights and peace and against poverty. King's communal-political ethics consistently informed and guided his actions, with the two dimensions constantly complementing, checking, and balancing each other.

Elements of King's Communal-Political Ethics

Martin Luther King Jr.'s communal-political ethics can be elaborated in terms of vision, norms, virtues, and practices, which respectively refer to the teleological (goal-oriented), deontological (duty-bound), areteological (virtue-bound), and praxiological (transformation-oriented) dimensions of his ethics. Although King never systematically organized these four elements into a coherent global ethics, these elements are prominent and organically interrelated in his speeches, writings, and political activities. If the communal is closely associated with the teleological and areteological (vision and virtue), the political has to do with the deontological and praxiological (norms and practice) dimensions, though they are never separate.

VISION

As mentioned in the opening of this chapter, King was convinced that in order to meet the various challenges that globalization poses, a revolutionary transformation of values and a restructuring of social relationships are necessary. For King, such a transformation includes loyalty to an encompassing moral vision for all humanity, and he introduced "the great world house" or simply "world house" as such a vision.[12] The great world house is an ecumenical-moral vision that helps to guide and coordinate various human activities in a compressed world. The vision of the great world house appeals to people of diverse cultural and religious backgrounds so that they can work on the common task of global peace and justice, moving beyond any selfish pursuit of career, power, or group interests that undermine the common good of humanity. King wrote: "We have inherited a large house, a great 'world house' in which we have to live together—black and white, Easterner and Westerner, Gentile and Jew, Catholic and Protestant, Moslem and Hindu—a family unduly separated in ideas, culture and interest, who, because we can never again live apart, must learn somehow to live with each other in peace."[13] Without such a vision, globalization poses more risks and threats than opportunities.

"Great world house" implies an inclusive, harmonious, interracial, and intercultural society defined by freedom, justice, and love. In this society, all individuals enjoy full and equal citizenship through participation in decision-making and contributing to the common good, regardless of skin color, religion, nationality, and class. All people are included as brothers and sisters in the family of humankind. The foundation of this vision was King's belief that human beings are essentially social and interdependent and that a good community not only meets the human desire for belonging but also is indispensable for the actualization of human potential and happiness.

From a political perspective, King's vision of the world house is not a naïve fantasy. It is actually instrumental in infusing a world perspective in people, in dismantling structural injustices (colonialism, economic exploitation, and militarism—the impediments to the great world house), and in building mutual alliances and voluntary collaboration among all races, religions, and nationalities beyond narrow loyalties and partial interests.

The need for such a vision was based on King's political experiences struggling against social injustices. Through his upbringing in an African American community, he learned that social transformation of harsh and dehumanizing injustices required a hopeful vision.[14] People will seldom act unless motivated. A vision invokes the motivating energy of hopefulness, which directs people's commitment to a moral cause. A well-crafted, articulate vision not only enables people to see a different future, it also brings together the otherwise fragmented energies and talents of a people.[15] Consequently, a hope-filled moral vision undermines the claim by the oppressors that the current situation is for the best or is even the only one possible.

King's moral vision of the world house is unique and somewhat daring. While some advocates of global ethics intentionally avoid discussing a metaphysical end of history and humanity in their attempts to secure a common moral ground across diverse cultures and religions and also avoid the potential conflict of goods between diverse groups, King did not hesitate to speak of the world house as the common end for humanity.[16]

NORMS

Martin Luther King Jr., like many proponents of global ethics, recognized the indispensability of a common moral ground for a just and peaceable global society, and he affirmed core moral norms that other proponents upheld, namely human dignity, freedom, equality, justice, love, solidarity (unity), nonviolence, and tolerance. For King, these norms were the minimum requirements in building the great world house.

Human solidarity is the bedrock principle of King's communal vision of the world house. He declared: "The universe is so structured that things do not quite work out rightly if men are not diligent in their concern for others. The self cannot be self without other selves. I cannot reach fulfillment without thou. . . . All life is interrelated."[17] He also frequently preached: "He who works against community is working against the whole of creation."[18]

Created in the image of God, each human being, King held, has intrinsic worth and dignity. Neither derived from nor conferred by the state, but encompassing all human beings, respect for human dignity is universally binding and indivisible; it applies to every person and all aspects of human life. Justice is to recognize the *imago Dei* of each person, the intrinsic worth of each person, and so act on that basis. Grounded in his belief in human dignity, King firmly upheld the norms of freedom and equality of all humans and fully endorsed the idea of human rights, both civil-political rights and economic-social rights.[19] King's "Letter from Birmingham Jail" (1963) is a well-known defense and articulation of human dignity based on natural laws. He declared in the letter, "Any law that uplifts human personality is just. Any law that degrades human personality is unjust."[20]

King was also firm on justice. For him, justice was not a mere social construction but something engrained in the moral order of the universe. He declared, "There is something in the universe that unfolds for justice," and he noted multiple times the importance of the conviction that "the universe is on the side of justice."[21] This belief in the universal authority of justice had an empowering effect on King and his followers. In their struggles, they endured hardship and challenges, all the while believing in God's final guarantee of justice.

King's communal-political method organically and synthetically harmonizes these moral norms. In the framework of his communal-political ethics, these norms are interrelated and mutually balancing. For example, the sanctity and solidarity of humanity are inseparable as all human beings are made in the image of God, the *imago Dei*. All humans are spiritually united; each person is responsible for protecting and promoting the sanctity of others.[22] Similarly, without this balancing and corrective work, love becomes merely romantic and emotional, justice becomes impersonal and legalistic, and power turns abusive. The demand of love prevents us from instrumentalizing or using others for profits, as justice serves as the minimum requirement of love.

King's firm belief in human dignity, freedom, and justice guided his struggles against racism, classism, and militarism. For King, these moral norms served as the criteria for social critiques of injustices, a common moral ground around which people might rally, as well as guidelines for legislation and public policy.[23] These norms were useful not only for naming injustices but also for forming coalitions with other religious groups to achieve justice based on a shared moral ground.

Virtues

Like proponents of global ethics, especially virtue theorists such as Rosalind Hursthouse and Martha Nussbaum, Martin Luther King Jr. emphasized various virtues as integral to his communal-political ethics, including love, forgiveness, forbearance, fortitude, justice, practical wisdom, and hopefulness, and he himself strove to embody these virtues.[24]

In cultivating virtues, King relied on education and communal practices such as nonviolent resistance. Since virtues are first formed in the context of family life, King believed that education in global ethics should start at home, and he encouraged mothers to inculcate the world perspective into their children.[25] Churches are also important in fostering this perspective through their teachings and moral examples. In a similar vein, King, in his last years, called for the revolutionary transformation of values with a mind toward the entirety of humanity rather than a particular people or a nation-state. He stated: "A genuine revolution of values means in the final analysis that our loyalties must become ecumenical rather than sectional. Every nation must now develop an overriding loyalty to mankind as a whole in order to preserve the best in their individual societies."[26] Knowing that human actions and the moral nature of society are more powerfully shaped by the desires of a moral agent than by mere knowledge of moral norms alone, King sought to mold these inner desires into a durable morality through a global vision and concomitant sustained practices.

At the same time, King noticed that virtues are developed in actual struggles for justice when people work in collaboration with others sharing the same moral vision of the great world house. He used nonviolence to build virtuous and cosmopolitan citizens of the world house. That is, for King, nonviolent resistance indicated not only political action but also a collective moral practice necessary to the formation of virtues.[27] King believed nonviolent resistance engendered moral and spiritual changes in its practitioners (e.g., a new sense of self-respect, courage, and strength) by helping channel the discontent and anger of ordinary people toward a noble cause.[28] By refusing to harm others and committing to a high moral cause, nonviolent struggles form public virtues such as fortitude, forbearance, hopefulness, justice, and—first and foremost—respect for life. Nonviolent resistance requires a high degree of discipline and maturity in resisting the temptation to violently retaliate.

On the basis of this awareness, King, with the assistance of James Lawson, used training programs and workshops to teach the life and discipline of nonviolence.[29] Before demonstrations, admonition sessions on nonviolence were held, in which songs, prayers, and scripture readings evoked images of nonviolence. Participants were taught to love rather than hate opponents and to suffer violence if necessary rather than inflict it upon others.[30] In addition, King demanded that participants sign a commitment card that delineated the ten commandments of nonviolence.[31]

POLITICAL PRACTICE

In a Kingian framework, the task of global ethics is not only normative but also political. Martin Luther King Jr. recognized that persuasion and vision alone cannot subvert injustices since oppressors never voluntarily give up their power and privilege.[32] Instead, power must be checked by another countervailing power. With this in mind, King employed a strategy of nonviolent resistance to overcome social injustices and to construct the great world house.

According to King, nonviolent resistance achieves its political objective in several respects. First, by publicly denouncing and refusing to comply, nonviolent struggles challenge unjust social systems. By dramatizing social evils, they bring to the surface the hidden contradictions, injustices, and tensions of society so that its members may collectively reflect on their moral state and condition. Second, nonviolent resistance amasses political power by garnering goodwill and favorable opinions from the public. Third, nonviolence undermines an unjust social system by pricking the conscience of the oppressors, forcing them to feel shameful of their moral hypocrisy and complicity in an evil system.[33] When the oppressed stand up for their cause and exercise moral virtues such as fortitude, patience, and forgiveness in the face of vicious and brutal attacks, the presumed moral and psychological superiority of the oppressor is unsettled.

In King's way of thinking, nonviolent resistance refuses to separate moral ends from moral means and achieves a morally consistent and politically effective social transformation while simultaneously attending to the reality of power and community building.[34] Nonviolence also creates the condition for mutual understanding and negotiation by disarming the fear associated with violence.

Throughout his life, King was convinced of the normativity and effectiveness of nonviolent resistance. He gave eyewitness accounts of the positive fruits of nonviolence he had seen in many places. In the last years of his ministry, he applied his nonviolent method internationally. He proposed nonviolent action as a superior method in resolving social injustices in a global society. In a highly interdependent world, he believed that international pressures, such as sanctions, collective protest, UN declarations and appeals, and boycotts, were not only ethical but also more effective than war in overcoming the evils of racism, colonialism, classism, and militarism. For example, he was convinced that the problems of Latin America and Africa could be better solved by "a solid, united movement, nonviolently conceived and carried through," putting pressure on international power structures.[35]

Dialectically interrelated, the four components—vision, norms, virtues, and political practice—offer a coherent framework of the theory and practice of King's ethics. This dialectic relationship of the four elements shows how King's ethics integrates moral knowledge and desires, as well as theory and practice. These four components mutually inform and sustain each other, evoking noble human desires (vision), coherently guiding decisions (norms) and actions (political practice), and instilling virtues in its agents. While the world house serves as the ultimate goal of every moral endeavor and political struggle, political practice denotes a means in building the world house, while moral norms and virtues, in turn, mediate and integrate vision and practice as reliable moral reference points. While the vision of the world house pulls and holds people together locally, political practice offers the opportunity for people to collaborate with each other locally in accomplishing the demands of a global moral vision in their own contexts. Similarly, virtues arise when persons participate in various political practices that aim to actualize the vision. That is, the shared vision and norms are internalized into enduring dispositions and habits in the participants as they actually live them out through collective struggles against social injustices.

At the same time, the vision, norms, and virtues keep political practice from being expedient or incidental. Due to their organic interdependence, the lack of any one component inevitably affects the whole edifice of King's ethics. Thanks to the balanced and dialectical relationship of the four elements, King's ethics is militant but not violent, confrontational but not antagonistic, transformative but not destructive.

The Global-Local Dialectic:
Kingian Thought and Social Praxis

Along with the communal-political, the global-local dialectic (glocality) was central to King's ethical thinking and practices.[36] Glocality was quite natural to King because he lived in the enmeshed African American community, broader U.S. society, and global community. Living in a crucial transitional time of a globalizing world, he was conscious of his social location in the suffering African American community in the context of the emerging interdependent world.

Being aware of the interdependent nature of human existence and the increasingly compressed social reality in a globalizing world, King did not separate the local and the global in his political struggles. A local injustice is tied to global injustice, he saw, and vice versa. Accordingly, a local struggle for justice should be pursued in the context of global justice. For example, King did not separate democracy in the United States and other countries. He tied African American struggles to those of other people of color across the world. He viewed the civil rights movement in the United States in its global context, emphasizing that "the struggle for freedom forms one long front crossing oceans and mountains."[37] Such convictions led King to advocate for the human rights of the Vietnamese people and poor people throughout Africa, Asia, and Latin America, despite unrelenting suspicion and criticism from his opponents as well as supporters. For King, democracy and human rights as a universal moral ideal can never be confined to national boundaries.

King's appeal to global vision and norms was partly political by intent. He recognized that entrenched social evils could not be dismantled by the local struggles of African Americans alone. They needed the support of the federal government and world opinion. Hence, King used both local and global resources in dismantling injustices. His glocality is found in his creative interplay between the local, the national, and the global. For instance, the Montgomery boycott was successful by virtue of both the national and international publicity it garnered and by the intervention of the federal government.

Clearly, King's ardent advocacy of a cosmopolitan moral vision and values was rooted in deep local religious traditions—namely, African American Christianity. His movement generated its energy and a collective sense of mission from black religious and other cultural traditions. Religion was the inspirational and organizational backbone of black people's militancy against injustice. Moreover, King relied on local African American religious and civic organizations to organize and train nonviolent warriors to march and demonstrate. For example, the uncompromising resilience of fifty thousand participants in the yearlong Montgomery bus boycott demonstrates faith as an inspiring power for social transformation. Without deeply rooted spiritual and moral convictions and strong local support, King's movement would have been unable to dismantle the deeply entrenched system of segregation.

King's glocal approach was productive in building a broad political coalition of diverse racial, ethnic, religious, and civic groups and organizations. The logic of a coalition is to work for the common good while still maintaining the identity of one's own group. In other words, it can operate through a framework of the global-local nexus. King built a coalition by identifying a local struggle with the global cause of justice (anticolonialism, anti–economic exploitation, anti-militarism), drawing a diverse group of people in the process.[38]

Kingian Goals and Public Theology

How, then, did King creatively mediate, balance, and harmonize the global and the local without collapsing one into the other? He relied on public theology to achieve the objective. King was a competent cultural and theological translator who was capable of fluently communicating a local moral dialect into a global language (a lingua franca) and vice versa. Robert Franklin mentions King's glocal public theological ability:

> King possessed a remarkable capacity to communicate his dream, indeed, the nation's dream and destiny, to all rational people.... He worked the resources of his southern black Baptist heritage, especially its song, prayer, homiletic, and theatric traditions, in order to make its particular wisdom available to everyone. He was convinced that the black experience of suffering, coping, and transcending or overcoming the traumas of oppression could serve as a socially therapeutic model of the world's struggling people.[39]

Public theology is a genre of theological discourse that communicates the specific moral vision, claims, and views of a particular religious community to a wide audience in seeking mutual understanding and desired ethical changes. It articulates the theological and moral claims and views of a particular religious tradition to the public, appealing to the universal validity and warrants of their beliefs. Public theology is glocal in nature since it is theologically grounded in a particular religious community (the local) but publicly relevant (the global). Public theology is ethical in nature. It not only offers a critique of social injustices but also seeks a common moral ground to bring diverse groups together for collective actions. To a considerable degree, King's effectiveness as the leader of a movement came from his glocal and public theological ability to frame the African American struggle in universal moral terms, reaching out in goodwill to many people across the nation and the world without losing a deep anchor in a local spiritual and cultural tradition and its organizational resources.

For King, public theology was the instrument of both moral persuasion and political coalition-building. Unlike proponents of secular moral philosophies and religious fundamentalists, King and his followers saw no contradiction between Christianity and a public pursuit of democracy and human rights. Through his masterful use of public theology, King succeeded in embedding the movement in a universal vision and norms. In doing so, he energized many civic institutions, associations, and grassroots movements for democracy and justice, and he elevated the civil rights movement into a worldwide human rights and democracy crusade.

Plausibility and Relevance of King's Ethics in a Global Context

This chapter has examined how Martin Luther King Jr.'s communal-political ethics serve as resources for a constructive global ethics in the twenty-first century. King saw the rising global scope and nature of moral threats to humanity, advanced a new moral vision, and used expansive universal norms, values, and goods to guide human aspirations and actions in addressing the challenges. However, he did so by respecting local traditions and history, and he empowered people at the grassroots level to confront the global power disparity. In addition, collaborating with other people and with global institutions such as the UN, King worked hard to construct a minimal global structure of justice (international laws) and a vibrant global civil society.

King's ethics has theoretical plausibility and practical relevance in addressing the challenges globalization presents. By reconciling universality and particularity, theory and practice, it addresses two key methodological difficulties of global ethics—loyalty gaps and power gaps—difficulties in collective deliberation and social transformation. King's global-local dialectic reconciles universality and particularity, while his communal-political ethics connects normative vision and values to political practice.

As such, King's ethics overcomes the fallacy of the liberal enlightenment that chooses the abstract universal over the particular (thus excluding religious movements and traditions from the public square), and of cultural relativism (postmodern deconstructionism) or ethnocentrism that chooses the particular over the universal. Instead, it offers a third way between secular liberal democracy and nationalism/authoritarianism. In this sense, King's ethics offers a wonderful resource to criticize current institutional arrangements and various political ideologies and practices in contemporary global society, namely the kinds of neoliberal oligarchy, superpower hegemony, religious terrorism, and nationalism/authoritarianism that reject the solidarity of humanity, deny dignity, and instead prioritize self-preservation and expansion of political and material interests at the expense of others, at times violently, consequently endangering our common existence.

Can others adopt King's ethics? My answer is *yes*. King's example has already been making an impact on the lives of numerous people around the world. He proved that coalition-building among diverse religious and other cultural groups is possible through deliberation and solidarity, working for justice and the common good. King's vision and norms are translatable to other religious and cultural groups if people are willing to work for the common good of humanity and the planet and are also willing to accept others as members of the same family. King's ethics relies on a method of public theology and actual community organizing in mediating the global and the local, the communal and the political, and, by learning from him, each community may develop the perspective and competence to harmonize its particular history and culture with the common good, while collaborating with others in dismantling injustices.

Humanity is at a crossroads between the accelerating power of globalization (that calls for the reorganization of life around the globe) and its ensuing injustices and problems (resulting from the abuse of powers and exploitation of inactivity and inequality). As King asked in his last book, *Where Do We Go from Here: Chaos or Community?*, humanity as a whole is now facing two extreme options. Chaos leads to conflicts, even war. The only remaining option is to build a moral community, with just laws and institutions, on a global level and on the basis of a new revolutionary vision and norms. As King pleaded, instead of being imprisoned by fear, a will to power, and competition, we need to galvanize the best nature of humanity—creativity, imagination, and moral commitment—in coping with challenges. In our efforts, King can still be a guiding star shining in the dark night of our current civilizational crisis, and his ethics can guide us to build a new and more just global civilization.

NOTES

The first epigraph is from Martin Luther King Jr., *Where Do We Go From Here: Chaos or Community?* (Boston: Beacon Press, 1967; rpt., 1968, 2010), 171; the second is from the *New Revised Standard Version of the Bible*.

1. Martin Luther King Jr., "Remaining Awake through a Great Revolution," in *A Testament of Hope: The Essential Writings and Speeches of Martin Luther King, Jr.*, edited by James M. Washington (New York: HarperCollins, 1986), 268, 269.

2. Despite the widespread discussion of globalization as a major social phenomenon today, there is no consensus on its definition, nature, scope, and implications. Generally speaking, "globalization" refers to the growing interconnection of the world due to advances in science, technology, and the expansion of the economy. Technological advances, particularly in communication, transportation, and trade, have accelerated and expanded the flow of people, goods, culture, and symbols across borders, while pre-

senting drastic challenges to almost every aspect of our lives: politics, economy, popular culture, ecology, education, and so on. No one can pinpoint when this process exactly started; however, no one can deny that the current form of globalization has been influenced by Western colonialism, which in turn is motivated by territorial expansionism and economic accumulation that proceeded through the enslavement and exploitation of indigenous peoples.

3. See Pankaj Mishra, *Age of Anger: The History of the Present* (New York: Farrar, Straus and Giroux, 2017).

4. Heather Widdows, *Global Ethics: An Introduction* (Durham, UK: Acumen, 2011), 5.

5. Ibid., 30–67.

6. In particular, a Kantian approach to global ethics claims that this is possible through the use of rationality; it relies on the method of the categorical imperative or similar derivatives, such as John Rawls's idea of "an original position," or "a veil of ignorance."

7. Martin Robra, "Affirming the Role of Global Movements for Global Ethics," *Ecumenical Review* 52, no. 4 (2000): 473.

8. Lisa Sowle Cahill, "Toward Global Ethics," *Theological Studies*, 63, no. 2 (2002): 341.

9. Orion Kriegman describes the same concern: "[Despite] the upsurge of civil society activity, in the form of NGOs and social movements, over the past few decades . . . existing social movements have not found a way to effectively balance the creative tension between pluralism and coherence to provide a collective framework for theory and action. Without a shared framework, it is hard to imagine how the latent potential would coalesce into a global systemic movement. The development of a shared framework will depend on new forms of leadership to facilitate engaged dialogue inclusive of diverse voices." *The Dawn of the Cosmopolitan: The Hope of a Global Citizens Movement* (Boston: Tellus Institute, 2006), 16.

10. Hak Joon Lee, *We Will Get to the Promised Land: Martin Luther King, Jr.'s Communal-Political Spirituality* (Cleveland: Pilgrim, 2006), 85–108.

11. Martin Luther King Jr., "An Experiment in Love," in *Testament of Hope: The Essential Writings and Speeches of Martin Luther King, Jr.*, edited by James Melvin Washington (San Francisco: HarperCollins, 1991), 20.

12. It is an expansion and international application of his idea of the beloved community that he first introduced at the end of the Montgomery bus boycott.

13. Martin Luther King Jr., *Where Do We Go From Here?*, 167.

14. See Lewis V. Baldwin, "Martin Luther King, Jr., the Black Church, and the Black Messianic Vision," *Journal of the Interdenominational Theological Center* 12, nos. 1–2 (Fall 1984/Spring 1985): 103–7.

15. The efficacy and enduring impact of such a vision is attested to by the popularity of King's "I Have a Dream" speech, which helped people dream of a different future for the United States and the world.

16. Hans Küng and Karl-Josef Kuschel, eds., *A Global Ethic: The Declaration of the Parliament of the World's Religions* (New York: Continuum, 1993).

17. Martin Luther King Jr., "The Ethical Demands for Integration," in *Testament of Hope*, 122.

18. Martin Luther King Jr., *Stride toward Freedom: The Montgomery Story* (New York: Harper & Row, 1958), 106.

19. King often invoked freedom and equality, citing the Declaration of Independence

and the U.S. Constitution, to defend the African American struggle for civil rights. Martin Luther King Jr., "Pilgrimage to Nonviolence," in *Testament of Hope*, 35.

20. Martin Luther King Jr., "Letter from Birmingham City Jail," in *Testament of Hope*, 293.

21. Martin Luther King Jr., "The Power of Nonviolence," in *Testament of Hope*, 13–14.

22. King, "Ethical Demands for Integration," 122.

23. For example, King appealed to the norms of human sanctity, freedom, and equality to criticize segregation, while invoking the norms of love and solidarity to build unity and coalitions among different religious and civic groups.

24. Lee, *We Will Get to the Promised Land*, 196. For more specific discussions of King's virtues, see Peter J. Paris, *The Spirituality of African Peoples: The Search for a Common Moral Discourse* (Minneapolis: Fortress, 1995).

25. Martin Luther King Jr., "What a Mother Should Tell Her Child," sermon, Ebenezer Baptist Church, Atlanta, May 12, 1963, King Papers, Library and Archives of the Martin Luther King Jr. Center for Nonviolent Social Change.

26. Martin Luther King Jr., "A Time to Break Silence," in *A Testament of Hope*, 242; and King, *Where Do We Go from Here?*, 190.

27. Martin Luther King Jr., "Suffering and Faith," in *Testament of Hope*, 41; and Martin Luther King Jr., *Stride toward Freedom*, 89.

28. Martin Luther King Jr., "Pilgrimage to Nonviolence," 39.

29. Martin Luther King Jr., "Why We Can't Wait," in *Testament of Hope*, 536–37.

30. Martin Luther King Jr., "Stride toward Freedom," in *Testament of Hope*, 448–49.

31. The ten commandments: 1.) Meditate daily on the teachings and life of Jesus; 2.) remember always that the nonviolent movement in Birmingham seeks justice and reconciliation—not victory; 3.) walk and talk in the manner of love, for God is love; 4.) pray daily to be used by God in order that all men might be free; 5.) sacrifice personal wishes in order that all men might be free; 6.) observe with both friend and foe the ordinary rules of courtesy; 7.) seek to perform regular service for others and for the world; 8.) refrain from the violence of fist, tongue, or heart; 9.) strive to be in good spiritual and bodily health; 10) follow the directions of the movement and of the captain of a demonstration. Martin Luther King, Jr., "Why We Can't Wait," in *Testament of Hope*, 537.

32. King, "Letter from Birmingham City Jail," 292.

33. This had to do with what Richard Gregg calls "moral jiujitsu," which is related to King's understanding of the employment of nonviolence and how it impacts both the victims of injustice and the perpetrators of injustice. See John J. Ansbro, *Martin Luther King, Jr.: Nonviolent Strategies and Tactics for Social Change* (New York: Madison Books, 2000), 146–51.

34. Martin Luther King Jr., "Love, Law, and Civil Disobedience," in *Testament of Hope*, 45.

35. Martin Luther King Jr., *The Trumpet of Conscience* (San Francisco: Harper & Row, 1967), 62.

36. Rufus Burrow Jr. traces King's glocal orientation to personalism: "King knew that there can be no universal without particulars and that the universal and particular mutually inform each other. . . . Personalistic method forces one to think globally while working locally and being ever mindful of how local and global issues are interconnected." Rufus Burrow Jr., "King's Beloved Community Ideal: Making the Connections," *Journal of Religion* 77, no. 3 (July 1997): 444.

37. "Martin Luther King: Speech about South Africa," *Racism Review*, January 17, 2011, http://www.racismreview.com/blog/2011/01/17/mlk-speech-about-south-africa/.

38. King's commitment to coalition-building and the democratic process is revealed in the SCLC's emphasis on the "intergroup and interpersonal living." See Martin Luther King Jr., *Where Do We Go from Here?*, 62. This emphasis reflects dialectical thinking that attempts to embrace the diversity of groups and persons while seeking a new political and moral synthesis that serves as a common ground.

39. Robert M. Franklin, *Liberating Visions: Human Fulfillment and Social Justice in African American Thought* (Minneapolis: Fortress, 1990), 139.

CHAPTER 12

TOWARD A HIGHER GLOBAL IDEAL
MARTIN LUTHER KING JR., THE WORLD HOUSE, AND THE CHALLENGES OF TOMORROW

LEWIS V. BALDWIN

We have to be a blessing by being for peace and freedom for ourselves, for our
families, for our friends, for our neighbors, for our nation, for our world.
MARTIN LUTHER KING JR., "Address at the 50th Anniversary of the
Women's International League for Peace and Freedom"

When met with hardship, when confronting disappointment, Dr.
King refused to accept what he called the "isness" of today. He
kept pushing towards the "oughtness" of tomorrow.
BARACK H. OBAMA

Much has already been said in this volume about Martin Luther King Jr. as a
global citizen who thought and acted in his own historical context and who,
more than a half century after his death, remains an authority, resource, and
inspiration for people worldwide. This focus on King, both in context and beyond context, shows that there is a certain timelessness about the issues and
concerns he addressed relative to the global human condition. Undoubtedly,
the power of his ideas, the example of his leadership, and the quality of his efforts for a more just, peaceful, and inclusive world still offer lessons for humanity's ongoing quest for creative living in the great world house.[1]

This chapter, the last in this book, casts a new and revealing light upon
King and his meaning for the future of humankind and the world. It holds that
King's radical and progressive vision of the great world house is greatly needed
in the twenty-first century and that his ideological and practical quest to bring
that vision to vivid life will have enduring resonance for generations to come.
The growing number of memorials that attest to the enduring quality of King's
global citizenship and human rights advocacy are discussed at some length,
and so are the ways in which the contemporary forces of globalization are both
consistent and inconsistent with King's world house vision. Special attention is

devoted to those aspects of King's thought and social praxis that offer a workable model for continuing global transformation. Moving from the premise that King's call for "a revolution of values and priorities" is crucial in achieving the fullness of the great world house as an empirical reality, the discussion turns more specifically to how certain of his ideas, values, and activities constitute a resource for the continuing enrichment of our understanding of the stakes and possibilities of world community and peace.[2] Appropriating the image and significance of King in this manner is audacious, since it requires conjecture, but nothing less is acceptable if we are to grasp why millions from every corner of the earth still appeal to King to justify their positions on a range of cultural, social, intellectual, religious, economic, and political questions.

A Symbol of Global Citizenship and Human Rights Advocacy

Great leaders in world history have two lives—one that extends throughout their sojourn on earth and a second that begins at death and continues as long as their lives, ideas, and activities remain powerful and meaningful.[3] This is most certainly the case with Martin Luther King Jr., who, due to the rising number of memorials dedicated to him, has become a global icon of unmatched proportions. In the United States alone, more than nine hundred cities have a street named for King.[4] Countless churches, schools, college and university dormitories, libraries, museums, public housing developments, community centers, social service centers, hospitals, bridges, parks, sculptures, statues, and other public works bear his name and image.[5] Martin Luther King Jr. Day is a U.S. federal holiday celebrated annually on the third Monday in January.[6] A thirty-foot granite statue of King, the first memorial to an African American on or near the National Mall in Washington, D.C., attracts millions of visitors from around the globe.[7] In Atlanta, King's birthplace, the Martin Luther King Jr. Center for Nonviolent Social Change stands as perhaps the greatest monument to King's legacy, and Morehouse College's Martin Luther King Jr. International Chapel as the most prominent religious memorial dedicated in King's honor. Both are also visited each year by countless people from various countries. These and the many new memorials continually appearing across the United States symbolize that King represented "the brightest and best" in terms of American values, ideals, and traditions.[8] They also suggest that King's dream for America and for humanity as a whole is as much alive as the eternal flame that burns in front of his crypt at the King Center in Atlanta.[9]

Less well known are the many King memorials that exist in other parts of the world. King's birthday is either celebrated or recognized in more than one hun-

dred countries, and Ghana, India, Liberia, Mexico, Rwanda, and the Virgin Is-
lands are among the many countries having issued commemorative stamps in
his honor since his death.[10] In African and Caribbean countries, countless annual events—from worship services to special lectureships to scholarly sympo-
sia concerning King's life and work—have occurred over time, his picture hangs
on the walls of homes, his books line the shelves of libraries, and babies are
named after him.[11] As in the United States, streets and highways, schools, social
service agencies, and parks bear King's name worldwide. A number of churches
in Hungary are named for him. A list of other King memorials across the global
landscape includes the Martin Luther King Jr. Center in Cuba; the Martin Luther King Jr. Mural in Sydney, Australia; the Boulevard Martin Luther King in
Nantes, France; Martin Luther King Park in Paris; Martin Luther King Park in
Vienna; Martin Luther King Jr. Forest in Israel; a statue in London that honors
King's martyrdom; and Piazza Martin Luther King, a square in Borgo San Lo-
renzo, Italy.[12] No other American, including the nation's presidents, is receiving
such worldwide recognition, which is certainly ironic considering how African
American men are routinely stereotyped and debased.

King deserves to be memorialized and even sculpted in stone because his
name and image are and will always be associated with a globalized rights culture. The King memorials around the globe are in large measure monuments of
recognition: they recognize both King's global citizenship and his commitment
to freedom, human dignity, justice, peace, and opportunity for humans everywhere. They attest to his vital role in insuring the full realization of civil rights
and human rights for all. They celebrate his devotion to the highest human and
ethical ideal, which involved promoting nonviolent responses to world problems while also preparing humanity as a whole to live creatively and harmoniously in what he variously termed "the beloved community," "the new world order," "the Promised Land of freedom, justice, and integration," "the Kingdom of
God on Earth," "the New Jerusalem," and "the great world house."[13]

The countless memorials dedicated to King's honor also constitute different
methods of remembrance and are therefore monuments of *memory*. They speak
to the world's desire to remember the man and the noble causes for which he
gave his life, and in this sense they are about recalling and preserving history
while also offering historical lessons. Put another way, they say a lot about how
the living cross-culturally choose to remember King the historical figure and
about their sense of what needs to be sustained. They also guarantee that important episodes in history are not overlooked or forgotten.[14] Evidently, King
memorials tell a powerful story about a dark but rich and productive past, and
they help humanity to understand its present existential situation. They are de-

signed to make history come alive for those who lived during the King years and especially for those who did not, and they are one means by which King speaks to humanity today and by which he will continue to do so in the future.

Equally significant are the ways in which King memorials serve as monuments of *meaning*. Specifically, they express some of humanity's shared and most cherished values, priorities, and traditions as well as aspects of its deep-seated feelings and motivations. In other words, they in many ways represent who and what human beings are and hope to be, and this is especially true for those who see something of themselves in King's image. King constantly pointed out that each human being is "two selves," the "higher" or "good self" and the "lower" or "evil self," and "the great burden of life," he declared, "is to always try to keep that higher self in command."[15] King memorials or monuments, in some sense at least, represent the best within human beings everywhere, the best that any can aspire to become. They are, in short, symbols of the better selves of all humans.

King memorials are also monuments of *inspiration*. They are designed throughout the world to rekindle conversations around civil and human rights, to recharge calls for much-needed social change, and to inspire the well-meaning to ascend to greater heights in the ongoing struggle against bigotry, intolerance, and injustice.[16] For some, King memorials are not only for inspiration but also for instruction and understanding. For the millions who admire King, this is about enlarging the reach of the human endeavor, keeping his dream alive, and insuring that it becomes a sustaining vision for all freedom-loving people. As journalist Ted Rayburn puts it, this is about advancing "the unfinished agenda of King's 'holy crusade.'"[17]

There is, at the same time, inherent danger in making King's legacy all about memorials or monuments. Kenneth L. Smith, one of King's former professors at Crozer Theological Seminary in Chester, Pennsylvania, raised this issue in an article in May 1984, a few months after the U.S. Senate voted overwhelmingly in favor of the King national holiday. Responding to the oft-repeated claim that "the holiday would have 'symbolic importance,'" Smith retorted: "That is true, but symbolic of what?" Smith wondered if the holiday might "assume simply a symbolic significance transcending its actual effect, thus turning King into just another irrelevant plastic hero like Superman." Smith went on to question whether it would be "symbolic of history or ritualistic hoopla." Pushing further, he asked: "Will the holiday be another example of what Max Weber called 'the routinization of charisma?'"[18] Such questions might well apply to all monuments dedicated to King's memory.

Freedom-loving peoples across the globe could benefit from sustained con-

versations about the meaning and significance of the notable variety of memorials they have created and continue to create in King's honor. Memorials for
great leaders may or may not stand the test of time, but are holiday celebrations,
monuments, murals, and other forms of memorabilia the best ways to pay hom-
age to King and the cause for which he suffered martyrdom? Is this in keeping
with what King himself said about how he wanted to be remembered? Are there
better ways to pay tribute to King as a symbol of a globalized rights culture?[19]
These are questions that should not be ignored or casually dismissed, especially
as the world engages in dialogue and a fruitful rethinking of King's legacy and
how it can best be understood and advanced today and tomorrow.

What the world's creators and supporters of King memorials have not said
is perhaps more significant than what they *have* said about their motivations
and about the merits and disadvantages of their methods of honoring King. As
indicated previously, there is much value in the ways in which the world honors and memorializes King, but what about the potential disadvantages of such
practices? Sadly, monuments have become ways of super-humanizing King, of
making him "larger than life" and even deifying him.[20] Highlighting "the dangers of adulation," Lauren Jefferson, quoting historian Mark Metzler Sawin
in 2014, wrote: "King's posthumous transformation from man to superhero is
'dangerous,' Sawin said, because such moral leaders are not 'giants,' but regular people 'who stumbled and wandered and worried as they strove to make a
better world.'"[21] Dorothy F. Cotton, who worked closely with King in his Southern Christian Leadership Conference, serving as director of its Citizenship Education Program, offered a similar observation two years earlier: "Massive numbers of people nationwide and in other countries deify Martin Luther King Jr.
But I think now of what Andy [Young] said in a phone conversation with me
recently: 'Martin didn't need *us* to do that,' to deify him. 'He needed us to *help*
him.' And we did. He needed us to be friends. And we were."[22] Monuments to
King's memory are perhaps more genuinely meaningful when his admirers understand that there is a clear difference between remembering, honoring, and
celebrating him on the one hand, and deifying or showing reverence for him on
the other.

Critics are not wrong in suggesting that memorials or monuments have also
become part of larger efforts to domesticate King, to co-opt his legacy, or to
make his image more palatable and acceptable to the powers that be, especially
the religious and political establishments in the United States.[23] Memorializa-
tion in such cases is about celebrating not the radical King but a fictional King,
or the King who has been reduced by many to a curious, gentle, harmless southern black Baptist preacher who localized unearned suffering, redemptive love,

and nonviolence as the core of the Christian faith. Speaking to "the clarity with which" King connected the domestic fight for equality to international politics, in particular poverty and war," British scholar Joe Hoover asserts that stressing the "international aspects of King's thinking" is one way of countering efforts to co-opt or domesticate him:

> It challenges the interpretation of King as an insufficiently radical leader offered by some critics, and the co-option of King's legacy not only by "moderate" liberals but also by conservative political figures in the U.S. King has become a symbol in the public consciousness of a safe reformism and a favorite icon for the type of liberal who abhors radicalism above any other political sin. As Michael Eric Dyson says, "Thus King becomes a convenient icon shaped in our distorted political images. He is fashioned to deflect our fears and fulfill our fantasies. King has been made into a metaphor of our hunger for heroes who cheer us up more than they challenge or change us."[24]

The power of King's legacy is actually hijacked and abused in some ways when so many of the images of him are projected purely in response to the needs and aspirations of certain sectors of this society and world.[25] Many people in the United States and abroad do not want King memorialized at all, in any form whatsoever, but since they are powerless to prevent the construction of monuments to his memory, their last resort is to somehow distort the meaning and importance of both his person and legacy.[26] In such an atmosphere, King memorials can easily be used against King and the values he embraced and sought to promote globally.

Monuments in King's honor should be substantive, reminding humanity of his unfinished work in the areas of economic justice and international peace, while also impacting the ways the world moves forward in the quest for greater human rights and community.[27] So far they have done little to actually bring people together across the artificial barriers of nationality, culture, race, ethnicity, religion, and politics, and they remain to some degree a source of resentment and polarization within the human family. They cannot convey true meaning or relevance by simply elevating the historical King and attracting visitors from every corner of the globe. They only do so to the extent that they contribute to the breaking down of barriers between peoples while also inspiring prophetic social witness and activism in the interest of a freer, stronger, and better humanity.[28] Otherwise, King monuments are in danger of becoming, in a material sense, little more than works of art and sculpture that testify to the power of human creativity or to the architectural and artistic heritage of different world cultures.

King never wanted memorials or monuments of any kind created and dedicated in his honor, and he said as much and more in a sermon delivered weeks
before his death at Atlanta's Ebenezer Baptist Church, located next door to what
would become the Martin Luther King Jr. Center for Nonviolent Social Change.
King wanted to be remembered instead for his struggle to love, serve, liberate,
and empower humanity.[29] But since increasing numbers of memorials or monuments in his honor exist worldwide, the best humans can do cross-culturally
is to view them in a new light or find inspiration from them to make their own
unique contributions to creative and harmonious living in the world house.
In other words, honoring King in the years ahead should be about service, not
monuments and statues.

The Great World House as an Elusive Phenomenon

Martin Luther King Jr. had the sort of serenity that passionately confronted the
world of human need, and he was always striving for a richer vision of humanity's universality in an interconnected, interrelated, and interdependent world.
He envisioned a great world house or "a planetary order" in which all artificial barriers that separate humans, particularly in terms of nationality, race, religion, culture, and ideology, are transcended, and in which the fruits of "life,
liberty, and the pursuit of happiness" are available "for all."[30] The processes of
globalization, as currently managed by powerful international corporations
and business elites, are usually associated, at least on paper, with a similar vision. That is mainly because they encourage vanishing borders between different countries and the advancement of global justice, democratic freedoms, human rights, and international integration through the transnational sharing of
the kinds of ideas, values, material goods, and services that meet the economic,
intellectual, cultural, social, political, and religious needs of the entire human
family.[31] Even so, any discussion of King's global vision vis-à-vis contemporary
globalization theory and praxis is risky, mainly because King is a figure from the
past, whose thought and activities were tailored specifically to human interests
and needs in his own times.[32]

Globalization existed in some form during King's lifetime, and he actually
commented on some of its essential ingredients in the late 1960s, though he
never used the term.[33] He repeatedly referred to "modern scientific and technological revolutions" and how they had led to "a world of geographical oneness,"
and he favored more international integration and cooperation through trade,
access to technology and capital, and other means.[34] Thus, it is not oxymoronic
to speak of the global King and to consider how his world house ideal might

take on new hues and pertinence for those who hope and struggle for more legitimate and meaningful processes of globalization in today's vastly different
and rapidly changing world.[35] The contemporary phenomenon of globalization
is more complicated than King could have ever imagined, with advantages and
disadvantages for humans everywhere, and it does not always lend itself to what
King considered creative living in the great world house. However, proponents
and supporters of globalization—which involves "the removal of barriers to free
trade and the closer integration of national economies"—believe that it has the
potential to create better living conditions across the globe by solving some of
the deep-seated problems that still threaten the unity, welfare, and survival of
the human race.[36] While some of the ideas associated with globalization echo
those put forth by King, the problem lies in the practical application of those
ideas in the daily lives of ordinary people around the world.

Globalization increases international relationships between people and
strengthens cross-cultural contacts, which is consistent in some measure with
King's unifying vision for humanity. People of different nationalities, ethnic
and racial backgrounds, classes, and religious and political persuasions are being brought together not only through the usual processes of immigration, advanced means of travel, and international tourism, but certainly through media
and telecommunications. Today's global media, including the Internet, facilitate
the spreading and sharing of language, music, and other forms of popular culture at a staggering rate, benefiting especially once-isolated communities or societies. According to some globalization theorists, "Cultural exchange is the best
way to establish strong people-to-people links," but this has unfortunately led to
the dominance of Western cultures over others.[37] King himself recognized the
growing global trend toward people-to-people contacts and cross-cultural links
in his own time, viewing this as primarily a by-product of scientific and technological ingenuity, but he apparently had something qualitatively different in
mind when speaking of the necessity for human interconnectedness worldwide.
Convinced that "the self cannot be self without other selves," he spoke of humanity in terms of "geographical togetherness," "a single neighborhood," and
"geographical oneness," insisting that this increasing pattern was inevitable, and
he believed, for example, that all cultures had something worthy to bring to a
fruitful intermingling of spiritual values. "The new world is a world of geographical togetherness," King declared as early as 1956, and he insisted that the challenge of the future involved making the world "spiritually one."[38] Although religious movements were among the first cultural forces to globalize, the processes
of globalization in their current forms are not taking spirituality very seriously
if they consider it at all.[39] If at all interested, the movers and shakers of global-

ization could possibly find some significance in King's vision of a world house characterized not only by a thriving geographical, economic, and cultural interconnectedness but also by an abiding sense of life as rooted in the sacred realm.

As noted above, an integral component of globalization is the expanding transnational flow and circulation of ideas and information via media and telecommunications. This is widely viewed as one of globalization's greatest benefits, especially for what are perceived as the more undeveloped or underdeveloped areas of the world. To some degree, greater and faster access to media and mass communication, not simply information but knowledge through the Internet, actually do serve the interests and needs of people on every continent.[40] Having a strong background in academics, King himself appreciated and marveled at the explosion of ideas, information, and knowledge in the United States and other Western nations in the mid- and late twentieth century, and he imagined the tremendous possibilities this heralded for the further enlightenment of humankind. In his estimation, widespread ignorance, the distrust of and resistance to new ideas, and deficiencies in sharing information and knowledge transnationally and cross-culturally constituted other barriers to communication and association between brothers and sisters in the world house. But King also believed that this would change for the better over time, especially with the coming of new scientific and technological revolutions and ever-increasing global connectivity.[41] In this regard, King was prescient.

A different scenario is unfolding, however, with globalized economics. Globalization is routinely pitched as a strategy that benefits rich and poor countries by (1) pushing free trade, which supposedly promotes economic growth, creates jobs, makes corporations more competitive, and lowers prices for consumers; (2) eliminating tariffs, value-added taxes, subsidies, and other trade barriers that inhibit multinational expansion, economic gains, and geopolitical cooperation; (3) increasing access to markets and the exportation of cheap goods; and (4) assisting poor countries through infusions of foreign capital and technology, thereby stimulating economic development and spreading prosperity.[42] King saw evidence of such global economic trends even in his own lifetime, and he too supported the freedom of countries to exchange goods and services with each other, the removal of trade barriers, and more access to global markets and technology. He challenged all "wealthy nations" in his time—"America, Britain, Russia, Canada, Australia, and those of Western Europe"—to "see it as a moral obligation to provide capital and technical assistance to the underdeveloped areas."[43] While all of these global economic policies figured, at least to some degree, into King's world house vision and are viewed as advantages of globalization today, their "adverse side" should not be overlooked. The

"current trajectory of globalization" is not succeeding in bringing "the promised benefits" to developed or developing countries, a problem reinforced by
the narrow nationalist and antiglobalization tendencies in countries such as the
United States, Britain, and Greece.[44] There are still barriers to free trade, such
as value-added taxes, which are very high in Europe.[45] Moreover, economic exchange has become yet another means by which powerful nations exploit and
"assert their dominance" over weaker nations in the name of globalization, thus
reinforcing patterns of neocolonialism.[46] This is most evident with the United
States, and it explains why many throughout the world view globalization "as
reinforcing American wealth and dominance."[47] Today's managers of globalization can learn much from King, who frequently warned against what he labeled
"a new form of paternalism" and "neo-colonialism." King consistently critiqued
wealthy nations, especially the United States, for using foreign aid "as a surreptitious means to control the poor nations." "Ultimately," King wrote, "foreign aid
programs must be motivated by a compassionate and committed effort to wipe
out poverty, ignorance and disease from the face of the earth."[48]

The effects of globalization on workers represent another area in which King
is still meaningful. King consistently advocated and fought for gainful employment and better living conditions and wages for "the least of these," or "the have-
nots," in the world house.[49] The processes of globalization are working very well
for Wall Street and multinational corporations, especially for the latter's owners,
managers, executives, and investors. Multimillionaires and billionaires benefit
from the exportation of jobs from wealthy and powerful nations to poorer ones,
and they are becoming more and more rich and powerful by exploiting tax shel-
ters to avoid paying taxes, paying slave-labor wages, and maintaining poor and
unsafe working conditions.[50] Clearly, globalization is not particularly beneficial
for working-class peoples, especially in the case of blue-collar workers. In the
United States, for example, workers face pay cuts from employers who threaten
to transfer jobs overseas. The exportation of jobs abroad is, in turn, contributing
to the deindustrialization of America, which is also adversely affecting workers. Furthermore, free trade is not promoting the kind of economic growth that
leads to robust job creation and lower prices for consumers. Consequently,
the existing global economic order is not significantly reducing poverty, raising living standards, or ending high levels of unemployment. Global inequality continues and is evident even in the polluted environment and the many
health challenges that confront poor people.[51] King was fully convinced that the
United States and other superpowers possessed the technology and resources
to end poverty and economic injustice worldwide, but he questioned their will
to do so. Even so, he called for a renewed sense of global mission to employ the

unemployed, to feed the hungry, to shelter the ill housed, and to heal and provide for the sick, the unwanted, and marginalized. For globalization's advocates
and enthusiasts, King's words remain instructive: "The agony of the poor impoverishes the rich; the betterment of the poor enriches the rich. We are inevitably our brother's keeper because we are our brother's brother. Whatever affects one directly affects all indirectly."[52]

King's sense of bonds and obligations between all members of the human
family is equally relevant to the larger question of the relationship between globalization and advancements in democratic freedoms, global justice, and human rights. Some globalization theorists believe that increased economic development and prosperity in poor countries creates the conditions for the
spread of democracy and respect for global justice and human rights "with no
colonialist designs."[53] Others suggest that globalization has brought into being
"an active global civil society" that is making such developments more possible.[54] But these claims are open to debate, and they are most certainly not supported by the abundant evidence. Until recently, globalization "had a crucial
political dimension"—"the American-led worldwide promotion of free elections and democratization"—but it now seems to undermine democracy while
replacing "the old dictatorships of national elites" with "new dictatorships of
international finance."[55] Largely because of the ways in which globalization is
implemented, the concept of global justice is rendered essentially nonexistent,
as each country commits to a conception of justice appropriate to its history,
culture, traditions, geopolitical context, and stage of development.[56] Although
"human rights are increasingly recognized as global norms" and are being redefined as such in many instances, globalization's role in the continuing exploitation of poor and developing countries, the victimization of workers, and
the subordination of women speaks more to its dehumanizing aspects and potential.[57] To the contrary, King's world house vision was about promoting democratic freedoms at home and abroad, advancing the cause of universal justice, and finding a greater role in what he termed "the human rights revolution"
of his times.[58] Put another way, in both principle and practice he stood for a
healthy leveling of democracy in the direction of greater justice, rights, and privileges for all human beings, and this was central to his call for a fresh core of
globally shared values. Thus, King remains, to some extent, a rich resource for
alternative and new reflection around these and many other issues pertinent to
globalization and its potential role in the shaping of a higher human ideal.[59]

Of special significance in this regard is globalization's engagement with violence and human destruction. Opinions on this vary widely. For example, supporters of globalization insist that "more markets and more democracy" con-

stitute "the cure for group hatred and ethnic violence around the world," but others see that "the global spread of markets and democracy" turns friends into competitors and is therefore "a principal, aggravating cause of group hatred and ethnic violence throughout the non-Western world."[60] In some places ethnic and religious differences have masked the underlying economic causes of many wars in this age of globalization.[61] Sadly, the emergence of a more economically interconnected and interdependent world has not eliminated the prospects for war and the reality of war.[62] In fact, warfare and violence in all forms (domestic, structural, political, state sponsored, and terroristic) has actually increased in recent decades despite the processes of globalization, a trend fueled in large measure by the tremendous availability of assault weapons and the stockpiling of weapons of mass destruction, by the shifting circumstances that encourage biowar, and by all too many humans who view violence as a means of promoting legitimate ends.[63] King predicted as much and more toward the end of his life, as he reflected on the futility and senselessness of violence, on "the destructive power of modern weapons," on the threat of "nuclear co-annihilation," and on those "determiners of our destiny" who are "talking peace while preparing for war."[64] He was obviously a globalist himself, and it is difficult to explain why his nonviolent world vision is receiving so little attention from the managers of globalization and the growing number of scholars who are tracing the impact of this phenomenon on the entire landscape of humanity.

For those who cherish the King legacy, the critical issue today and tomorrow is not simply violence as a threat to human life or existence but also *ecological* violence, or systematic damage to the environment. Economist Joseph E. Stiglitz has concluded that "caring for the environment" is, among other considerations, "necessary if the potential benefits of globalization are to be achieved."[65] But this is not happening in today's world. To the contrary, multinational corporations, which drive the forces of globalization, are often accused of an absence of concern for the environment, of mismanaging natural resources, of ecological damage, and of tolerating "environmental degradation" in the interest of "a higher GDP."[66] One case in point is their abysmal failure to embrace and promote the highest standards necessary to prevent or limit air and water pollution and the emission of greenhouse gases by motor vehicles, all of which contribute to public health challenges worldwide.[67]

Also important is the significant reduction in rainforests. "At current rates of destruction," according to some statistics, "the world's rainforests—with all their plants and animals and planetwide weather-controlling canopies of trees—are expected to be 90 percent wiped out by the year 2030." The award-winning author, international relief worker, and psychotherapist Thom Hartmann has addressed, in more specific terms, the sheer magnitude of the threat of declining environmental conditions and of increasingly destructive natural disasters to the world's plant and animal species. He reports that marine animal populations, for example, "are crashing," with worldwide fish catches declining "by some 26.5 percent between 1988 and 2001" alone. These problems are compounded by "the huge population pressure" the world faces. It is estimated that the global population "will stabilize somewhere between 8.5 and 12 billion during the next century," and that "ninety-five percent of these newcomers will live in the world's poorest countries," a development that could spell deeper trouble in a world of rapidly declining resources.[68] Apparently, King, having a sense of the sacredness of the earth, highly valued the vitality of the environment and the resources of nature, and he saw in his day a human family increasingly confronted "with the problem of excess population in relation to resources." He asserted, "This problem will be greatly diminished by wiping out poverty." He added: "When people see more opportunities for better education and greater economic security, they begin to consider whether a smaller family might not be better for themselves and for their children. In other words, I doubt that there can be a stabilization of the population without a prior stabilization of economic resources."[69] Thus, King has something to add to conversations about how the processes of globalization might treat the environment, manage natural resources, stem the tide of ecological violence, and prevent the crashing of ecosystems.

In this current age of globalization, the world house remains an elusive phenomenon because it still has not been fully realized, especially as envisioned by King. It is not excessive to claim that King's ideas and values, especially his world house ideal, can be useful in redefining and reshaping globalization, in making it more ethical, equitable, humane, and productive, without enduring threats to the freedoms, cultural identities, and values of marginalized peoples. In this ideal, all peoples and countries might have an equal voice and an equal hand in crafting the policies that impact their daily lives. King's reflections on the world house offer challenging insights and creative ways to approach the rich variety and complexity of human experience, and they challenge the idea of globalization as an effort to impose the power and values of any one country or any one class of people over others. He was fully committed to the globalization of a higher human and ethical ideal, and by engaging with that ideal, the inhabitants of the world can become more sensitive to their interconnectedness, to their moral responsibilities toward each other, and to the stakes and possibilities of much-improved international relations. In short, King's world house provides a model for alternative and new reflections around the issues of globalization.[70]

Since King thought in terms of the globalization of an ethical ideal, he has something to say today about the role of ethics in the face of rapid globalization. This is not likely to be understood by those who assume that associating King with current streams in globalization is impossible or irrelevant. It is not merely a matter of considering global challenges today and conjecturing what King would say or do about them. It is also a matter of considering King's actual words and actions and seeing how their meaning endures in today's pluralistic and rapidly changing world. Clearly, King, with the foresight, instinct, and discernment of a prophet, had at least some sense of the challenges that globalization would ultimately pose for all humanity. Thus, it is not illogical to consider his ideas about the world house in the context of current discussions about globalization, especially at a time when some critics are charging that globalization is polarizing humanity and resulting in an even more unjust world. After all, the ultimate challenge still entails, as King so often said, affirming and investing in our shared humanity and saving our common world house.[71]

The World House as Unfolding Conundrum: The Path Forward

Martin Luther King Jr. was very clear about what would ideally constitute the great world house, and in this sense his thought was teleological. In his thinking, the world house was both *present* and *future*, and he spoke and wrote about this ideal in terms of *the now* and *the not yet*. He saw approximations of the world house in the 1960s, as he considered the many ways in which scientific and technological advances were bringing humans together physically and geographically, and he knew then that this ideal was continuously in a state of becoming. Uncomfortable with "the isness" of the present world order, he envisioned humanity as always "reaching up for the eternal oughtness" of tomorrow's world order.[72] The world house would be increasingly actualized in history, and most certainly in the future, King thought, but he also knew that it was unattainable as a perfect human and ethical ideal, mainly because of the glaring and enduring realities of sin and evil on a personal and social level.

Progress toward the full realization of the world house in the future could be enabled by finding meaning and inspiration in King's call, made in the last year of his life, for what he termed "a revolution of values." King was, in principle and practice, a globalist who felt that such a revolution was much needed to accompany the scientific, technological, and "freedom revolutions engulfing the earth."[73] Undoubtedly, a careful reading of his vast repertoire of sermons, speeches, interviews, and writings yields principles and values useful for the future advancement of a more meaningful globalized rights culture and a greater realization of the world house as an empirical reality. This is not about speaking for King, making political uses of him, representing his ideas as our own, or promoting him as an authoritative voice with answers to all of the most pressing global questions of today and tomorrow.[74] Rather, it is about reflecting on the enduring significance of King's radical and progressive vision of the great world house and about being open to absorbing any wisdom and insights he provides for the continuing improvement of the human condition in the twenty-first century.

The paths leading to the great world house in the years ahead confront every human being with demands and challenges, which include, first of all, developing *a heightened and more vital sense of global citizenship*. King labeled himself "a citizen of the world," and his insistence on a model of responsible and effective global citizenship—which demands "a world perspective," a sense of oneness with all other humans, and a willingness to consistently speak out on international affairs—is becoming more and more important in this rapidly shifting age of social media.[75] Global citizenship at its best means that members of the human family can no longer live and function merely as inhabitants of a town, city, state, or nation. Every single inhabitant of today's world is, knowingly or unknowingly, a global citizen, and the continuing challenge for future generations involves taking on the demands and responsibilities that such an identity and status entail. The very survival of the world house, as King so often conceded, will depend greatly on the ability of people everywhere to ultimately reject categorically the Manichean division of the world into *us* versus *them*.

In a larger sense, this is about the need for *a richer vision of humanity's universality in an interconnected, interrelated, and interdependent world*. This was uppermost in King's mind whenever he talked and wrote about the social nature of human existence or "the interrelated structure of all life and reality":

> All men are interdependent. Every nation is an heir of a vast treasury of ideas and labor to which both the living and the dead of all nations have contributed. Whether we realize it or not, each of us lives eternally "in the red." We are everlasting debtors to known and unknown men and women. When we rise in the morning, we go into the bathroom where we reach for a sponge which is provided for us by a Pacific Islander. We reach for soap that is created for us by a European. Then at the table we drink coffee which is provided for us by a South American, or tea by a Chinese or cocoa by a West African. Before we leave for our jobs we are already beholden to more than half of the world.[76]

King elaborated further, noting that "all humanity is caught in an inescapable network of mutuality, tied in a single garment of destiny, and whatever affects one directly, affects all indirectly." "I must be concerned about what happens to men and women in Asia, Africa, South America, and Europe," he proclaimed. And he went on to insist that "our loyalties must become ecumenical rather than sectional"; to declare that "other-preservation," not "self-preservation," is "the first law of life"; and to call for "a world-wide fellowship that lifts neighborly concern beyond one's tribe, race, class and nation" to "an all-embracing and unconditional love for all."[77] King was speaking here of a globally responsible ethic of community, coexistence, and cooperation, with love as "the supreme unifying principle of life."[78] These are timeless values, echoed in very recent times in the voices and actions of groups ranging from Occupy Wall Street to Black Lives Matter to the Me Too movement to the hundreds of thousands of youth worldwide who are leading the March for Our Lives against guns, all of which evoke King's memory and legacy. They cannot be casually ignored, nor should they be dismissed by future dwellers in the great world house. Despite the ways in which the ever-flowing streams of technological advancements continue to bring humanity together geographically, the world is perhaps more divided spiritually and morally than at any time in the past. This is not likely to change drastically with the next generation of world house occupants. King's eternal appeal is indeed a warning for future generations: "We must either learn to live together as brothers [and sisters], or we are all going to perish together as fools."[79]

King's reflections on *the indispensability of a "shift from a 'thing'-oriented" to a "'person-oriented' society" and world* also have lasting value for the world house of tomorrow.[80] King was never really comfortable or satisfied with a nation and world in which material things were valued far more than flesh-and-blood human beings, and this should be the case with every rational and moral person concerned about human civilization's continuous and seemingly inevitable drift toward moral and spiritual ruin. King was fully convinced of the intrinsic dignity and worth, and indeed the sacredness, of all human personality.[81] He maintained that "when machines and computers, profit motives and property rights are considered more important than people, the giant triplets of racism, materialism, and militarism are incapable of being conquered."[82] The validity of this point is painfully revealed around the world today, as materialism invades every vestige of human existence, and as white supremacy, sexism, anti-Semitism, xenophobia, Islamophobia, homophobia, hate crimes, outright warfare, and the destruction of human beings through "ethnic cleansing" continue unchecked and unabated. King located the sacredness of all human beings in the *imago Dei* principle, which means that each person is a reflection of the divine image, and, in the years ahead, human salvation in the context of the world house will undoubtedly hinge largely on the capacity of its inhabitants to live out the true meaning of this principle. There is a continuing need for a kinship model of King's *imago Dei* concept, one that embraces the full humanity of all people and the dignity and sanctity of all persons. In short, this is about sharing King's vision of a world in which each individual is considered of infinite worth or value, irrespective of nationality, race, politics, religion, culture, or any other artificial human barrier.

The other real challenge in this regard is to forge *a fresh core of globally shared values that cherish the sacredness of human life and the significance of all life-giving forms*. This too would be consistent with King's global ethics. The essential value of human life was a central tenet of his worldview and also the driving force behind his personal quest for a more complete expression of the world house. This also explains King's advocacy and practice of nonviolence as both a personal and social ethic.[83] He was clearly in favor of universalizing the kinds of values, institutions, and structures that legitimize and protect human life. Many self-professed "pro-life" activists in today's world, especially in the United States, oppose abortion and stem cell research while simultaneously endorsing and even sanctioning capital punishment, violence against immigrants, the torture of Islamic terrorists, and war. King, in stark contrast, extended his concern beyond the beginnings of life to embrace the complete continuum of human existence.[84] Thus, his moral consistency around the question of reverence for human life offers a more sensible, workable, and beneficial model for the future world house.

Some King admirers are making a similar claim regarding his enduring relevance for preserving the life-giving power and resources of the environment and nature. This is also viewed as part of King's consistent and inclusive ethic of life.[85] Bill McKibben, a founder of the Grassroots Climate Campaign, has been inspired by King's nonviolent civil disobedience campaigns and feels that they are relevant to his own environmental activism.[86] John Blake of the Cable News Network (CNN) describes King as "an environmental hero," noting that King planted "the seeds for what would become our nation's now-thriving environmental justice movement." "People don't think of King as an ecological activist," Blake concludes, because "he didn't live long enough to see the environmental movement take off. . . . But he still inspires environmental activists because they say he was so eloquent in articulating a core belief of their movement"—namely "the interconnected nature of life."[87] King appreciated the beauty of the environment and its rich, life-giving "natural resources," and he also knew that unhealthy environments produce unhealthy people and vice versa. He frequently quoted Psalm 24:1—"The earth is the Lord's and the fullness thereof, the world, and they that dwell therein"—and he apparently viewed humans as caretakers of God's earth and was quite mindful of the importance of astute environmental stewardship. Much of what King shared about the abuse of the earth, declining natural resources, the global population explosion, and the many resulting health problems together suggest that he would have been in favor of government policies encouraging strict pollution standards, lower energy consumption, clean energy technology, and other environment-friendly policies.[88] Although Larry L. Rasmussen, author of *Earth-Honoring Faith: Religious Ethics in a New Key* (2016), may have gone a bit too far in calling King "one of the great ecological thinkers of the 20th century," it is safe to say that King should not be excluded from any serious conversation regarding the ongoing life and health of the planet Earth, especially in view of the life-threatening effects of climate change, the growing extinction of certain species, and the gradual elimination of entire ecosystems.[89] After all, the goal is to protect God's earth and all of God's creations from catastrophic damage and possible extinction. In other words, this is about saving the full continuum of planetary life forms that, when considered in connection with the larger issue of global environmental needs, are so essential to what King envisioned as creative and productive living in the great world house.

The world house could not be more deeply transformed than by a determined effort to also create *a sustainable culture of peacemaking and peacekeeping*. King was successful in forging a global ethic of peaceful coexistence out of his encounter with the New Testament's Sermon on the Mount, the philosophy of Mohandas K. Gandhi, and a range of other sources, and he is therefore a rich resource for thinking through the potentialities of nonviolence not only on an interpersonal and intergroup level, but also in an international context. King's hope for the ultimate elimination of war was vested in what he long called "the peace-loving peoples of the world" and, to a greater extent, in the United Nations, which he regarded as "a gesture in the direction of nonviolence on a world scale."[90] During the final year of King's life, as his global vision expanded and matured, he urged the nations of the world to move beyond an "intellectual analysis" of nonviolence to an employment of nonviolence as "an imperative for action," mainly because of the threat of "nuclear co-annihilation."[91] Thus, in this age of mass shootings, organized torture and terrorism, religiously based violence, and the threat of nuclear conflict between the United States and countries like North Korea and Iran, King remains and will continue to be a powerful and refreshing voice in any debate around the ethics of war and peace.[92] There should be a new appreciation for King's timeless lessons about the evils of violence and human destruction and the virtues of nonviolent resolution of conflict. It was he who reminded us that this is humanity's "last chance to choose" between "nonviolent coexistence and violent coannihilation."[93] This is still perhaps King's greatest and most enduring challenge to tomorrow's world house.

For King, the world house was ultimately about "a revolution of love and creativity" that would lead at some point to what he envisioned as a new humanity and "a new world."[94] In the days and years ahead, amid a din of loud voices, unreasonable and reasonable alike, King's calm voice will still be heard. His message of love, reconciliation, community, and peace will continue to be broadcast and received. That he goes on living, still giving hope to a hostile, tribalized, insecure, and violent world, assures us that his promise of the great world house will never be lost.

NOTES

The epigraphs are from Martin Luther King Jr., "Address at the 50th Anniversary of the Women's International League for Peace and Freedom," Philadelphia, October 15, 1965, King Papers, Library and Archives of the Martin Luther King Jr. Center for Nonviolent Social Change, Atlanta; Obama quoted in Martin Luther King Jr., *"In a Single Garment of Destiny": A Global Vision of Justice,* edited by Lewis V. Baldwin (Boston: Beacon Press, 2012), back cover. See also Associated Press, "Obama's Inauguration Day Is a Day for MLK, Jr.: Comments," WBUR News, https://www.wbur.org/news/2013/01/20/obama-inauguration -mlk; and Clayborne Carson and Kris Shepard, eds., *A Call to Conscience: The Landmark Speeches of Dr. Martin Luther King, Jr.* (New York: Warner, 2001), 107.

1. King's use of the metaphor of the world house apparently stretches as far back as December 1964, when he received the Nobel Peace Prize. See Martin Luther King Jr., "Nobel Lecture," University of Oslo, Norway, December 11, 1964, King Papers. For other such references, see Martin Luther King Jr., "Address at the 50th Anniversary of the Women's International League for Peace and Freedom"; Martin Luther King Jr., "Address at the Recognition Dinner," Dinkler Plaza Hotel, Atlanta, January 27, 1965, King Papers; and Martin Luther King Jr., "The World House," in *Where Do We Go from Here: Chaos or Community?* (Boston: Beacon Press, 1967; rpt., 1968, 2010), 167–91.

2. Martin Luther King Jr., *Where Do We Go from Here?,* 186.

3. Here I am paraphrasing a comment Adolph Berle made in a eulogy for President Franklin D. Roosevelt in 1945. See Kenneth L. Smith, "Equality and Justice: A Dream or Vision of Reality," *Report from the Capital,* January 1984, 4.

4. Ted Rayburn, "King's Central Message Must Not Fade," *Tennessean,* January 15, 2012; and Joey Garrison, "Nashville Might Rename Downtown Charlotte Avenue after MLK," *Tennessean,* March 4, 2018.

5. "In Memory of Martin Luther King, Jr.: Since His Death, Hundreds of Memorials Have Been Dedicated in Honor of the Famed Leader," *Ebony,* January 1986, 64, 66, 68, 70,

72; "MLK, Jr. Scholarship Banquet," *Tennessee Tribune* (Nashville), January 15–21, 2015; Lewis V. Baldwin, *To Make the Wounded Whole: The Cultural Legacy of Martin Luther King, Jr.* (Minneapolis: Fortress, 1992), 286–301; John Metcalfe, "Meet the 'World's Worst Martin Luther King, Jr. Statue' (Hint: It's Not in D. C.)," January 17, 2012, https://www.citylab.com/design/2012/01/meet-worlds-worst-martin-luther-king-statue-hint-its-not-dc/977; Derek H. Alderman, "With King Street Naming, One Journey Ends, Another Begins," *Star Tribune* (Minneapolis), March 6, 2002; and Derek H. Alderman, "Building on MLK's Legacy: Naming Streets Is One Thing, Seeking Equality Is Another," *Anniston (Ala.) Star*, January 16, 2012.

6. Nicole Crawford-Tichawonna, "Years of Persistence Led to Holiday: National Recognition for King's Birthday a Labor of Love for Many," *Tennessean*, January 14, 2018.

7. Lei Yixin, a Chinese master sculptor, created the statue of King. The choice of a sculptor from abroad caused some controversy, but the idea was very much in keeping with King's concept of the great world house. See Melanie Eversley, "Memorial to King Brings Some First-Day Visitors to Tears," *USA Today*, August 23, 2011; "The Martin Luther King Memorial: What You Will See," *USA Today*, August 26, 2011; John McDonnell, "A Dream Come True for Black Americans as Martin Luther King Statue to Sit between Lincoln and Jefferson on National Mall Is Unveiled," *Daily Mail*, February 17, 2011; https://www.dailymail.co.uk/news/article-1357909/Martin-Luther-King-statue-sit-memorials-Lincoln-Jefferson-National-Mall.html; Patrik Jonsson, "MLK Memorial: From China, with Love?," *Christian Science Monitor*, October 16, 2011, https://www.csmonitor.com/USA/2011/1016/MLK-Memorial-From-China-with-love; and Mitchell Landsberg, "Pick of Chinese Artist for King Statue Derided," *Tennessean*, July 28, 2007.

8. See Smith, "Equality and Justice," 5.

9. "In Memory of Martin Luther King, Jr.," 64; and Errin Haines, "Atlanta Shares King's Glow: Celebration Moves to D.C. for Obama's Inauguration," *Tennessean*, January 17, 2009.

10. Bonna M. de la Cruz, "King Pulpit Looked over the World: More than 100 Countries to Honor Civil Rights Leader," Tennessean, January 18, 1998; "In Memory of Martin Luther King, Jr.," 64, 66, 68, 70; "The World Honors MLK through Stamps: Commemorative Stamps Attest to High Esteem in Which Rights Leader Is Held at Home and Abroad," *Ebony*, January 1986, 82–84; and Baldwin, *To Make the Wounded Whole*, 286–301.

11. De la Cruz, "King Pulpit Looked over the World."

12. "In Memory of Martin Luther King, Jr.," 64, 66; Natalia Cruz, "A Bridge between U.S. and Cuban People," *People's Daily World*, May 6, 1987; Mo Elinzano, "25 Martin Luther King, Jr. Memorials in the U.S. and around the World," *Deseret News*, January 19, 2015, https://www.deseretnews.com/top/3020/0/25-Martin-Luther-King-Jr-memorials-in-the-US-and-around-the-world.html; Rachelle Sabourin, "20 Martin Luther King, Jr. Monuments around the World You Didn't Know Existed," *Complex*, January 20, 2014, https://www.complex.com/style/2014/01/martin-luther-king-jr-monuments; "Remembering Martin Luther King, Jr. beyond the Borders of the United States," Overseas Vote Foundation, January 13, 2012, https://www.overseasvotefoundation.org/remembering-martin-luther-king-jr . . . , accessed February 6, 2015.

13. "In Memory of Martin Luther King, Jr.," 64; , Martin Luther King Jr., *"In an Inescapable Network of Mutuality": Martin Luther King, Jr. and the Globalization of an Ethical Ideal,* edited by Lewis V. Baldwin and Paul R. Dekar (Eugene, Ore.: Cascade Books, 2013), 4–24; Martin Luther King Jr., *Where Do We Go from Here?*, 167–91; Martin Luther King Jr., "A Statement," unpublished, St. Augustine, Florida, June 17, 1964, King Papers; Martin Luther King Jr.,

"The Church on the Frontier of Racial Tension," Gay Lectures, Southern Baptist Theological Seminary, Louisville, Kentucky, April 19, 1961, King Papers; Martin Luther King Jr., *The Measure of a Man* (Philadelphia: Fortress Press, 1988), 35, 56; Martin Luther King Jr., "Annual Address to the Montgomery Improvement Association," First Annual Institute on Nonviolence and Social Change, Holt Street Baptist Church, Montgomery, Alabama, December 3, 1956, King Papers; Martin Luther King Jr., "The Desirability of Being Maladjusted," sermon, Chicago, January 13, 1958, King Papers; and Martin Luther King Jr., "A Realistic Look at Race Relations," speech, Second Anniversary of the NAACP Legal Defense and Educational Fund, Waldorf Astoria Hotel, New York City, May 17, 1956, King Papers.

14. "In Memory of Martin Luther King, Jr.," 64. Derek Alderman has written extensively on streets and other memorials dedicated in King's honor, and my treatment of King memorials as "monuments of memory" is indebted to his scholarship. See Derek H. Alderman, "Creating a New Geography of Memory in the South: The (Re)Naming of Streets in Honor of Martin Luther King, Jr.," *Southeastern Geographer*, 36, no. 1 (May 1996): 51–69; and Derek H. Alderman, "Martin Luther King Jr. Streets in the South: A New Landscape of Memory," *Southern Cultures*, 14, no. 3 (Fall 2008): 88–105.

15. Martin Luther King Jr., "The Prodigal Son," sermon, Ebenezer Baptist Church, Atlanta, September 4, 1966, King Papers; Martin Luther King Jr., "We Would See Jesus," sermon, Ebenezer Baptist Church, Atlanta, May 7, 1967, King Papers; and Martin Luther King Jr., *The Papers of Martin Luther King, Jr.*, vol. 6, *Advocate of the Social Gospel, September 1948–March 1963*, edited by Clayborne Carson, Susan Carson, Susan Englander, Troy Jackson, and Gerald L. Smith (Berkeley: University of California Press, 2007), 95–97.

16. Rayburn, "King's Central Message Must Not Fade"; Errin Haines, "King Holiday Recharges Calls for Social Changes," *Tennessean*, January 16, 2007; and Baldwin, *To Make the Wounded Whole*, 292.

17. Baldwin, *To Make the Wounded Whole*, 292; Andrea Young, "Martin Luther King, Jr.: The Legacy Lives," *Christianity and Crisis* 45, no. 22 (January 13, 1986): 532; and Rayburn, "King's Central Message Must Not Fade."

18. See Smith, "Equality and Justice," 5.

19. Canadian writer and arts administrator Rachelle Sabourin apparently cherishes the world's methods of paying tribute to King, suggesting that there is no "better way to remember the great man than with monuments created in his honor." Such a perspective is clearly open to debate. See Sabourin, "20 Martin Luther King, Jr. Monuments Around the World."

20. Lewis V. Baldwin, *Behind the Public Veil: The Humanness of Martin Luther King, Jr.* (Minneapolis: Fortress, 2016), 321–24; and Monica A. Coleman, "Martin Luther King: An American Icon," homily notes, 2005, http://www.geii.org/2005WPCU/prayer_worship/homily_notes_drm. . . , accessed January 31, 2005.

21. See Lauren Jefferson, "Professors Warn against 'Domestication' of Martin Luther King, Jr., Urge Renewed Focus on All Forms of Inequality," *EMU News*, January 25, 2014, https://emu.edu/now/news/2014/01/professors-warn-against-domestication-of-martin-luther-king-jr-urging-renewed-focus-on-all-forms-of-inequality.

22. Dorothy F. Cotton, *If Your Back's Not Bent: The Role of the Citizenship Education Program in the Civil Rights Movement* (New York: Atria Books, 2012), 265; and Baldwin, *Behind the Public Veil*, 321.

23. See Joe Hoover, "Martin Luther King, Jr. as an International Thinker?," *Disorder of Things*, January 21, 2011, http://thedisorderofthings.com/2011/01/21/martin-luther-king -as-an-international-thinker?; Jefferson, "Professors Warn against 'Domestication' of Martin Luther King, Jr."; Stephen Manning, "MLK Sculpture's Design Criticized: Federal Arts Panel Calls Statue Model 'Confrontational,'" *Tennessean*, May 10, 2008; Christopher Smith, "Cornel West on Obama and the Domestication of MLK's Legacy: 2 Comments," January 21, 2013, http://www.patheos.com/blogs/slowchurch/2013/01/21/cornel-west -on-obama-and-the-domestication-of-mlks-legacy; and Lewis V. Baldwin and Rufus Burrow Jr., eds., *The Domestication of Martin Luther King, Jr.: Clarence B. Jones, Right-Wing Conservatism, and the Manipulation of the King Legacy* (Eugene, Ore.: Cascade Books, 2013), 18. See also Traci West's discussion of "the misuse of King's name and reputation" to the service of certain interests and goals in Traci C. West, "Gay Rights and the Misuse of Martin," in Baldwin and Burrow, *Domestication of Martin Luther King, Jr.*, 141–56.

24. See Hoover, "Martin Luther King, Jr. as an International Thinker?"; and Martin Luther King Jr., *The Radical King: Martin Luther King, Jr.*, edited by Cornel West (Boston: Beacon Press, 2015), ix–xvi.

25. The very existence of memorials in tribute to King raises questions about the uses and abuses of him and his legacy at home and abroad. See Manning, "MLK's Sculpture's Design Criticized."

26. It has been argued that "King's 'fall from grace' is the primary context for understanding why there was (more than a decade of) resistance to naming a federal holiday in his honor." I submit that racism (or white supremacy) is a far more important factor in the resistance to all monuments in King's memory. See Crawford-Tichawonna, "Years of Persistence Led to Holiday."

27. Kenneth L. Smith makes this point in reference to the King holiday, and I am indebted to him for this idea. See Smith, "Equality and Justice," 5.

28. Rayburn, "King's Central Message Must Not Fade"; Beverly Keel, "Time for U.S. to Grow Up, Emulate Great Leaders," *Tennessean*, January 18, 2015; and Lucas L. Johnson, "Martin Luther King, Jr. and Our Responsibility to Stay Awake," *Fellowship*, Winter 2014, http://forusa.org/fellowship/2014/winter/martin-luther-king-jr-our-responsibility-stay -awake.

29. Clayborne Carson and Peter Holloran, eds., *A Knock at Midnight: Inspiration from the Great Sermons of Reverend Martin Luther King, Jr.* (New York: Warner, 1998), 185–86.

30. Significantly, King used a common or widely known phrase from the Declaration of Independence to further explain and clarify his vision of the world house. He used the phrase "great world house" in 1965, as his global vision was becoming more enlightened and explicit, because of its reference to three "unalienable rights" which, according to the framers of the Declaration, are granted to all humans by God, "their creator." See Martin Luther King Jr., "Address at the 50th Anniversary of the Women's International League for Peace and Freedom"; and Martin Luther King Jr., *Where Do We Go from Here?*, 167.

31. Viplav Mehta, in "What Are the Advantages and Disadvantages of Globalization?," *Quora*, October 23, 2016, https://www.quora.com/What-are-the-advantages-and -disadvantages-of-Globalization; Mike Collins, "The Pros and Cons of Globalization," *Forbes*, May 6, 2015, https://www.forbes.com/sites/mikecollins/2015/05/06/the-pros -and-cons-of-globalization; Baldwin and Dekar, "*In an Inescapable Network of Mutuality*,"

5; and Joseph E. Stiglitz, *Globalization and Its Discontents* (New York: W. W. Norton, 2002), 9–10.

32. In an earlier work, I treated King as "both a precursor to and critic of much of what is defined as globalization theory and praxis today." See Lewis V. Baldwin, "Living in the 'World House': Martin Luther King, Jr. and Globalization as Theory and Praxis," in Baldwin and Dekar, "*In an Inescapable Network of Mutuality*," 2–24.

33. The term "globalization" is said to have first appeared in a 1930 publication, *Towards New Education*, and it denoted at that time "a holistic view of human experience in education." In the 1960s, economists and other social scientists began to use the term, and the press picked it up in the 1980s. Since its inception, globalization has been greeted with "competing definitions and interpretations," "with antecedents dating back to the great movements of trade and empire across Asia and the Indian Ocean from the 15th century onwards." See "Globalization (or Globalisation)," Wikipedia, http://en .wikipedia.org/wiki/Globalization. Until recently, globalization was an unexamined concept in King studies, but it is now being used to break new ground in the field. For works that relate the term to King's global outreach, including his world house vision, see Lewis V. Baldwin, *The Voice of Conscience: The Church in the Mind of Martin Luther King, Jr.* (New York: Oxford, 2010), 216; Baldwin and Dekar, "*In an Inescapable Network of Mutuality*," 3–7; Hak Joon Lee, *The Great World House: Martin Luther King, Jr. and Global Ethics* (Cleveland: Pilgrim, 2011), 1–2, 15, 44–45, 131, 196; and Thomas A. Mulhall, *A Lasting Prophetic Legacy: Martin Luther King, Jr., the World Council of Churches, and the Global Crusade against Racism and War* (Eugene, Ore.: Wipf & Stock, 2014), 38, 63.

34. Martin Luther King Jr., *Where Do We Go from Here?*, 168–69, 174–81; and Martin Luther King Jr., *A Testament of Hope: The Essential Writings and Speeches of Martin Luther King, Jr.*, edited by James M. Washington (San Francisco: HarperCollins, 1986), 209.

35. Baldwin and Dekar, "*In an Inescapable Network of Mutuality*," 4–5.

36. Stiglitz, *Globalization and Its Discontents*, ix; Collins, "Pros and Cons of Globalization."

37. See "Globalization (or Globalisation)"; and Mehta, in "What Are the Advantages and Disadvantages of Globalization?"

38. Martin Luther King Jr., *Testament of Hope*, 138–39, 209; Martin Luther King Jr., *Where Do We Go from Here?*, 180; and Martin Luther King Jr., *The Trumpet of Conscience* (New York: Harper & Row, 1967), 69–70.

39. See "Globalization (or Globalisation)"; and Kent E. Richter, Eva M. Rapple, John C. Modschiedler, and R. Dean Peterson, *Understanding Religion in a Global Society* (Belmont, Calif.: Wadsworth, 2005), 134–36, 216–21, 245–48.

40. See "Globalization (or Globalisation)"; Mehta, in "What Are the Advantages and Disadvantages of Globalization,?"; Collins, "Pros and Cons of Globalization"; and Robert A. Sirico, "The Phenomenon of Globalization," *Religion and Liberty* 12, no 5 (July 20, 2010), https://acton.org/pub/religion-liberty/volume-12-number-5/phenomenon -globalization.

41. Martin Luther King Jr., *Where Do We Go from Here?*, 168–69; King, *Papers of Martin Luther King, Jr.*, vol. 6, 221; and Martin Luther King Jr., *Testament of Hope*, 138, 209–10, 213.

42. Collins, "Pros and Cons of Globalization"; Mehta, in "What Are the Advantages and Disadvantages of Globalization"; and "Globalization (Globalisation)."

43. See Martin Luther King Jr., *Where Do We Go from Here?*, 174, 178; and Martin Luther King Jr., *Trumpet of Conscience*, 69–70.

44. Stiglitz, *Globalization and Its Discontents*, 5, 247; Thad Williamson, David Imbroscio, Gar Alperovitz, and Benjamin Barber, *Making a Place for Community: Local Democracy in a Global Era* (New York: Routledge, 2002), 27; Gregory Korte, "Obama Warns Greece against Nationalism: In Birthplace of Democracy, President Talks Global Politics," *Tennessean*, November 17, 2016; and David Jackson, "Trump Targets Globalization and Trade: Assails Clinton, China and 'Failed Policies' for Job Losses," *Tennessean*, June 29, 2016.

45. See Collins, "The Pros and Cons of Globalization."

46. Mehta, in "What Are the Advantages and Disadvantages of Globalization?"; Amy Chua, *World on Fire: How Exporting Free Market Democracy Breeds Ethnic Hatred and Global Instability* (New York: Doubleday, 2003), 7; "Drawbacks of Globalization, Technology Expansion among Topics Highlighted, at Second Committee, Economic and Social Council Joint Meeting," United Nations, October 6, 2016, press release, https://www.un.org/press/en/2016/gaef3451.doc.htm; Alassane D. Ouattara, "The Challenges of Globalization for Africa," address sponsored by the World Economic Forum, Harare, May 21, 1997, International Monetary Fund, https://www.imf.org/en/News/Articles/2015/09/28/04/53/sp052197; and Thomas Pogge, *World Poverty and Human Rights* (Malden, Mass.: Blackwell Publishers, 2002), 19–20.

47. Chua, *World on Fire*, 7; and Stiglitz, *Globalization and Its Discontents*, 5.

48. King said so much about the need for the United States and other powerful Western nations to develop a higher regard for the sovereignty of all nations. This is part of what King had in mind as he constantly called upon America to provide much-needed moral leadership in the world. See Martin Luther King Jr., *Where Do We Go from Here?*, 169–70, 175, 178–79; "Martin Luther King Jr. Interview on the Merv Griffin Show," New York City, transcript, July 6, 1967, King Papers; and Baldwin, "Living in the 'World House,'" 9.

49. Martin Luther King Jr., *Where Do We Go from Here?*, 176–81; Martin Luther King Jr., "*In a Single Garment of Destiny*," 114–32; and Martin Luther King Jr., *Testament of Hope*, 27, 232–33, 623–26.

50. Collins, "Pros and Cons of Globalization"; and Thom Hartmann, *Unequal Protection: The Rise of Corporate Dominance and the Theft of Human Rights* (New York: Rodale, 2002), 166–68, 173–82, 242–43.

51. Collins, "Pros and Cons of Globalization." Joseph E. Stiglitz claims, "Because of globalization many people of the world now live longer than before and their standard of living is far better." This holds true for many people, especially in so-called developed countries, but certainly not in the poorest of poor countries. Some accounts of health matters in this age of globalization are not as optimistic as Stiglitz's. See Stiglitz, *Globalization and Its Discontents*, 4, 214, 247–48; Richard Horton, *Health Wars: On the Global Front Lines of Modern Medicine* (New York: New York Review Books, 2003), 127, 179–80, 472; and Ouattara, "Challenges of Globalization for Africa."

52. Martin Luther King Jr., *Where Do We Go from Here?*, 176–81.

53. Collins, "Pros and Cons of Globalization."

54. Stiglitz, *Globalization and its Discontents*, 214

55. Chua, *World on Fire*, 123; and Stiglitz, *Globalization and Its Discontents*, 247.

56. Pogge, *World Poverty and Human Rights*, 33.

57. Horton, *Health Wars*, 472; Richter, Rapple, Modschiedler, and Peterson, *Understanding Religion in a Global Society*, 376; and "Drawbacks of Globalization." King himself declared that "the technological revolution" of his time was not "strengthening democracy" but eviscerating it. He wrote: "Gargantuan industry and government, woven into

an intricate computerized mechanism, leave the person outside. The sense of participation is lost, the feeling that ordinary individuals influence important decisions vanishes, and man becomes separated and diminished." See Martin Luther King Jr., *Trumpet of Conscience*, 43–44.

58. Martin Luther King Jr., *Where Do We Go from Here?*, 167–202; Martin Luther King Jr., *Trumpet of Conscience*, 49–50; and Martin Luther King Jr., *Testament of Hope*, 280.

59. Baldwin and Dekar, "*In an Inescapable Network of Mutuality*," 7–11.

60. The latter position is set forth as "the sobering thesis" in Chua, *World on Fire*, 9.

61. See Steven Staples, "Ten Ways Globalization Promotes Militarism," *Rense ATL News*, September 5, 2003, https://rense.com//general41/prono.htm; and Baldwin, "Living in the 'World House,'" 21.

62. Baldwin, "Living in the 'World House,'" 21.

63. For an important source that evokes King's and Gandhi's names and memory in the context of a discussion around interrelated issues of "globalization, religion, ethics, violence, and peace," see Richter, Rapple, Modschiedler, and Peterson, *Understanding Religion in a Global Society*, 272–74. Speaking of anthrax and the infections it causes "as part of the threat to global security," Richard Horton goes on to charge that "globalization has fostered the conditions that will permit acts of biowar to flourish." See Horton, *Health Wars*, 127.

64. Martin Luther King Jr., *Where Do We Go from Here?*, 183; Martin Luther King Jr., *Trumpet of Conscience*, 58, 64, 70–71; and Martin Luther King Jr., "Address at the 50th Anniversary of the Women's International League for Peace and Freedom."

65. See Stiglitz, *Globalization and Its Discontents*, 216.

66. Richter, Rapple, Modschiedler, and Peterson, *Understanding Religion in a Global Society*, 272; Collins, "Pros and Cons of Globalization"; and Stiglitz, *Globalization and Its Discontents*, 218–19. Thom Hartmann notes, "In today's business environment, when corporations are run in ways that benefit the environment or their workers as much as their stockholders, they're at risk." See Hartmann, *Unequal Protection*, 196.

67. Williamson, Imbroscio, Alperovitz, and Barber, *Making a Place for Community*, 81–83; Richter, Rapple, Modschiedler, and Peterson, *Understanding Religion in a Global Society*, 303–6; and Stiglitz, *Globalization and Its Discontents*, 223–24.

68. Hartmann, *Unequal Protection*, 13; and Horton, *Health Wars*, 77.

69. Martin Luther King Jr., *Where Do We Go from Here?*, 177–78.

70. Baldwin, "Living in the 'World House,'" 23; and Martin Luther King Jr., *Where Do We Go from Here?*, 167–91.

71. Baldwin, "Living in the 'World House,'" 23–24; Martin Luther King Jr., *Where Do We Go from Here?*, 167–91; and Martin Luther King Jr., *Trumpet of Conscience*, 67–79.

72. See Irwin Abrams, ed., *The Words of Peace: Selections from the Speeches of the Winners of the Nobel Peace Prize* (New York: Newmarket, 1990), 57–58.

73. Martin Luther King Jr., *Where Do We Go from Here?*, 186.

74. Traci C. West has warned against such tendencies in our reading of King. See West, "Gay Rights and the Misuse of Martin," 142–43, 156. It has been argued that King is a figure from the past "with messages and methods evolved to fit the current reality during his lifetime" and that we have to be very careful about making him relevant for the present and future world. If we take this kind of thinking to the extreme, then perhaps we should reconsider our use of the Bible, which contains the teachings of Jesus, a figure who walked the earth and spread his messages nearly two millennia ago. See

Larry Boyer, "Is Martin Luther King, Jr. Relevant Today?," *Pulse Linkedin*, January 18, 2016, https://www.linkedin.com/pulse/martin-luther-king-jr-relevant-today-larry-boyer.

75. Martin Luther King Jr., *Trumpet of Conscience*, 68; Martin Luther King Jr., "What a Mother Should Tell Her Children," sermon, Ebenezer Baptist Church, Atlanta, May 12, 1963, King Papers; and Martin Luther King Jr., *Where Do We Go from Here?*, 181.

76. Martin Luther King Jr., *Where Do We Go from Here?*, 181; and Martin Luther King Jr., "What a Mother Should Tell Her Children." For a considerably longer version of this statement, see Martin Luther King Jr., *Trumpet of Conscience*, 69–70. See also Martin Luther King Jr., *Why We Can't Wait* (New York: New American Library, 1963), 77; and Baldwin and Dekar, "*In an Inescapable Network of Mutuality*," 12–24.

77. Martin Luther King Jr., *Where Do We Go from Here?*, 180–81, 190; Martin Luther King Jr., *Trumpet of Conscience*, 68; and Martin Luther King Jr., "What a Mother Should Tell Her Children."

78. Martin Luther King Jr., *Where Do We Go from Here?*, 190.

79. Martin Luther King Jr., *Trumpet of Conscience*, 68.

80. Martin Luther King Jr., *Where Do We Go from Here?*, 186.

81. Ibid. King owed much to personalism or personal idealism for this perspective. See Rufus Burrow Jr., *God and Human Dignity: The Personalism, Theology, and Ethics of Martin Luther King, Jr.* (Notre Dame, Ind.: Notre Dame Press, 2006), 69–87.

82. Martin Luther King Jr., *Where Do We Go from Here?*, 186.

83. See Martin Luther King Jr., *Strength to Love* (1963; repr., Philadelphia: Fortress, 1981), 151–52; and Martin Luther King Jr., *Trumpet of Conscience*, 68.

84. Baldwin, *Voice of Conscience*, 237–38.

85. In an interview toward the end of his life, King alluded to "the environmental conditions" that "scar the soul." In his thinking, there was no life-giving power apart from the health and well-being of the soul. See Martin Luther King Jr., "Doubts and Certainties Link: An Interview," unpublished transcript, London, England, February 1968, King Papers.

86. See Bill McKibben, "Martin Luther King's Legacy and the Power of Nonviolent Civil Disobedience: In Opposing the Keystone XL Oil Pipeline, Demonstrators Are Getting a Sense of the Civil Rights Leader's Courage," *Guardian*, Comment Network, August 25, 2011.

87. See John Blake, "Three Ways MLK Speaks to Our Time," CNN, January 15, 2018, http://www.cnn.com/2018/01/12/us/mlk-relevance-today/index.html.

88. King occasionally referred to the U.S. South as having "the most beautiful land," "rich with natural resources," and it is clear from some of his comments that he had some sense of environmental justice. See Martin Luther King Jr., "Speech at a Mass Meeting," Clarksdale, Mississippi, March 19, 1968, King Papers; Martin Luther King Jr., "The Meaning of Hope," sermon, Dexter Avenue Baptist Church, Montgomery, Alabama, December 10, 1967, King Papers; and Baldwin and Burrow, *Domestication of Martin Luther King, Jr.*, 174.

89. See Blake, "Three Ways MLK Speaks to Our Time." For a study that gives some attention to King and the African American religious experience in relation to environmental justice issues, see Tyson-Lord J. Gray, "Mercy, Mercy Me (The Ecology): Black Culture, Aesthetics, and the Search for a 'Green' Community" (PhD diss., Vanderbilt University, 2014).

90. See Martin Luther King Jr., "Farewell Statement," Delhi, India, March 9, 1959, King Papers; and Martin Luther King Jr., *Where Do We Go from Here?*, 184.

91. Martin Luther King Jr., *Trumpet of Conscience*, 64; and Martin Luther King Jr., "*In a Single Garment of Destiny*," 133.

92. Baldwin and Dekar, "*In an Inescapable Network of Mutuality*," 21.

93. Martin Luther King Jr., *Where Do We Go from Here?*, 191.

94. Martin Luther King Jr., *Trumpet of Conscience*, 50. King used the term "a new kind of man" instead of "a new humanity." See King, "Doubts and Certainties Link," 5; and Baldwin, *To Make the Wounded Whole*, 286.

AFTERWORD

The chapters in *Reclaiming the Great World House: The Global Vision of Martin Luther King Jr.* take as their point of departure King's belief in the interrelatedness of all persons as the fundamental basis for his conception of a world house. In our day, when connection across state and national borders is increasingly under assault, the idea of a worldwide interconnection of people may be nearly unfathomable. Within the United States, tensions across ideologies, gender and sexual identities, race, class, national origin, ethnicity, and other characteristics of persons inhibit many from thinking about being related to or in community with individuals and groups who are nonfamilial or dissimilar. Still, King argued that "all life is interrelated," that all persons "are interdependent," and that every "nation is an heir of a vast treasury of ideas and labor to which both the living and the dead of all nations have contributed."[1] The basis of interconnection embedded in this element of King's thinking is that interdependency arises from a legacy of "ideas and labor" upon which *everyone* draws. Persons of the current generation are not merely heirs of familial legacies but also beneficiaries, with everyone, of what humanity learns and gains. This wide view of legacy allows *Reclaiming the Great World House* contributors to think beyond era-bound concerns that may have limited King's imagining the fuller implications of the meaning and thrust of a world house ethic that he wrote "uplifts human personality."[2]

Contemporary issues relevant to affirming and uplifting all persons as siblings and citizens of the world house abound and, in a Kingian sense, continue to unfold, all the while enlightening new forms of exclusion and new opportunities to fulfill the world house vision. Today, for example, thinking about complete inclusion comprises the minimalist virtue of tolerance embedded in a "don't ask, don't tell" policy to prohibit exclusion of gay and lesbian persons. Current thought also to some degree entails *affirmation* of all queer persons while recognizing the reality of bisexual, transgender, and other sexualities as part of humanity's move to overcome the exclusionary gender binary system. Another contemporary reality that foregrounds the advancement of inclusive social ideals is the Me Too movement, which pushes beyond mere awareness of the need to affirm women. Me Too calls for unfettered women's access to, and recognition of women's contributions in, all strata of social and political realms. Me Too breaks open the "consent to assault" demanded as a levy for access that is, in essence, a reiteration of the power privilege that often, though not always, emerges as hetero-patriarchy.

During the popularization of #MeToo, another contemporary issue of exclusion—the challenge of appropriation as a type of erasure, commodification, and subordination—was foregrounded and addressed when celebrity Alyssa Milano took up Me Too advocacy and doubled back to acknowledge Tarana Burke's creation of the #MeToo hashtag and the founding of the Me Too movement. In the United States, young people have led—as some did during the civil rights movement—a new movement that has become the March for Our Lives against gun violence. In calling for an end to gun violence, March for Our Lives joins other voices calling for participatory democracy, or government that comports with the people's best ideals. This, too, echoes the civil rights movement: the idea of people, not politicians, leading the way to moral advances. These and other contemporary movements carry forward the world house ethic insofar as they contribute to the "treasury of ideas and labor" for future generations to advance interrelatedness in human community based on compassionate and passionate care and equity.

The inextricably linked virtues of love and justice are foundational in King's vision of human interrelatedness. Premised on equality and identified by King as "a more excellent way" that sometimes included "nonviolent protest," love seeking justice was King's interpretation of his Christianity as a tradition that engages the world and the political arena.[3] Love, King argues, is the virtue that surmounts the lethargy of complacency, loss of self-respect, individual security, and "do-nothingism"; love also overcomes the odium of losing faith, rejecting the dignity of one's opponent, and engaging in violence.[4] The virtue of love, King writes, requires that one behave as an "extremist in love," by which he means pursuing the cause of love through coming "to see that injustice must be rooted out by strong, persistent, and determined action."[5] King's use of the term "extremist for love" transposed the negative labeling of the 1963 protests in Birmingham, Alabama, as "extreme" to positive action pursuing justice. His ideas about an extreme, activist love being deployed against injustices are best explicated in the "Letter from Birmingham Jail" (1963), wherein King identifies "humiliation," "poverty," "segregation," and "lack of full participation"[6] as practices of injustice. Defining injustice as degrading "human personality," King writes, "Any law that uplifts human personality is just. Any law that degrades human personality is unjust." Citing conditions in Birmingham as a particular example of injustice, King continued, "All segregation statutes are unjust because segregation distorts the soul and damages the personality."[7] Such an analysis also applies in any serious discussion of threats to the human soul and personality in the context of the world house.

In the introduction to her compelling book *When They Call You a Terrorist: A Black Lives Matter Memoir*, Black Lives Matter (BLM) cofounder Patrisse Khan-Cullors laments the political reality of the United States having "5 percent of the world's population, but 25 percent of its prison population." Complexifying the lament, she notes incredulously that while the United States has a lopsided percentage of prisoners worldwide, this is "a prison population that, with extraordinary deliberation, today excludes the man who shot and killed a 17-year-old boy who was carrying Skittles and iced tea."[8] These observations are among the challenges undergirding Khan-Cullors's discussion of BLM demonstrators being called terrorists. Also, this labeling parallels charges made against King and other activists who were identified as extremists in their time. Another similarity is seeing the existence of the huge U.S. prison population and the labeling of BLM demonstrators as terrorists as practices of injustice. By naming these practices unjust, Khan-Cullors questions "the *logic* of equality, justice, and human freedom in the United States and all over the world." This logic, Angela Davis observes, is a means of "justifying the structural racism of such practices with references to due process and other ostensible legal guarantees of equality."[9] Perhaps the greatest challenges for manifesting a world house are the logics that sustain gender binaries, "consent" to sexual assault, violence as a solution, white supremacy, antiblack racism, and other practices that embody discursive arguments against human interrelatedness. That it is nearly unfathomable to think about humanity being interrelated in a great world house depends on the continuation of such logics, which permit normalization of these and other practices of injustice. The world house image asserts that the response to injustice is love.

To those who ask whether King's concept of active love seeking justice in the context of the great world house has relevance for the twenty-first century, #MeToo, the LGBTQ rights movement, March for Our Lives, Black Lives Matter, and other movements respond with a resounding "Yes!" This is a "yes" that recognizes that as this book is going to press in 2019, nothing seems further from capturing people's imagination everywhere than a version of Martin Luther King Jr.'s world house. It is a "yes" that knows we live in a time of hearts so broken by the dearth of love that many can no longer imagine the great world house as a goal for which to strive.[10] However, the "yes!" of these movements that have set their sights on lessening and eliminating specific injustices also is a "yes" that recognizes and believes in the vibrant, powerful legacy of the world house image. It is a "yes" that encourages actions aimed at overcoming the logics of divisions, aggression, violence, and subjugation. Racism, poverty, and war are the three great challenges that, according to King, must be solved in order to live together in the world house. Solving these problems, King writes, "will involve a revolution of values to accompany the scientific and freedom revolutions engulfing the earth." King concludes, "We must rapidly begin the shift from a 'thing'-oriented society to a 'person'-oriented society." Such a society overcomes the idea that "the giant triplets of racism, materialism and militarism are incapable of being conquered."[11] These ideas must be expanded to include sexism, binary hetero-patriarchy, religious bigotry and intolerance, and more. Imagining a different world is King's important and central legacy, but it requires "a revolution of values" and *new* logics aimed at "creating a world in which [we and] all of our children can thrive."[12]

Rosetta E. Ross
Professor of Religious Studies, Spelman College
Organizer and Founding Chair,
Daughters of the African Atlantic Fund

NOTES

1. Martin Luther King Jr., *Where Do We Go from Here: Chaos or Community?* (Boston: Beacon Press, 1967; rpt., 1968, 2010), 191, 192.

2. Martin Luther King Jr., "The Negro Is Your Brother" (aka "Letter from Birmingham Jail"), *Atlantic Monthly*, August 1963, https://www.theatlantic.com/magazine/archive/2018/02/letter-from-birmingham-jail/552461.

3. Ibid.

4. What King calls "do-nothingism" (individual complacency) correlates to the perhaps too frequent individual posture of focusing on the well-being of one's self and one's family to the exclusion of wider matters and social change. See ibid.

5. Ibid. Although the connection between love and action and love and justice became real to King through his study of Gandhi, Rufus Burrow discusses King's com-

mitment to love and his insights about the connection of love to action as deeply embedded through a heritage from King's southern Protestant elders and ancestors. See Rufus Burrow Jr., *Extremist for Love: Martin Luther King, Jr., Man of Ideas and Nonviolent Social Action* (Minneapolis: Fortress Press, 2014).

6. In his "Letter from Birmingham Jail," King's identification of "humiliation," "poverty," "segregation," and "lack of full participation" as injustices is asserted in the following phrases and statements respectively: "brutal injustice and shameful humiliation"; "smothering in an airtight cage of poverty in the midst of an affluent society"; "all segregation statutes are unjust because segregation distorts the soul and damages the personality"; and "an unjust law is a code inflicted upon a minority which that minority had no part in enacting or creating because it did not have the unhampered right to vote." See Martin Luther King Jr., "Negro Is Your Brother."

7. Ibid.

8. Patrisse Khan-Cullors and Asha Bandele, *When They Call You a Terrorist: A Black Lives Matters Memoir* (New York: St. Martins, 2017), 5–7.

9. Angela Davis, "Foreword," in Khan-Cullors and Bandele, *When They Call You a Terrorist*, xiii, italics added.

10. See Rita Brock's *Journeys by Heart: A Christology of Erotic Power* (Eugene, Oregon: Wipf and Stock, 1988), especially xi.

11. King, *Where Do We Go from Here?*, 196–97.

12. Khan-Cullors and Asha Bandele, *When They Call You a Terrorist*, 167.

SELECTED BIBLIOGRAPHY

ARCHIVAL SOURCES

American Committee on Africa Collection, Amistad Research Center, Tulane University, New Orleans.

James Hudson Papers, Carrie Meek–James M. Eaton Sr. Southeastern Regional Black Archives Research Center and Museum (Meek-Eaton Black Archives), Florida A&M University, Tallahassee.

Library and Archives of the Martin Luther King, Jr. Center for Nonviolent Social Change, Inc., Atlanta.
Coretta Scott King Collection.

Martin Luther King Jr. Papers Project ("King Papers"), Stanford University, California.

Martin Luther King Jr. Collection, Morehouse College, Robert W. Woodruff Library, Atlanta University Center, Atlanta.

Martin Luther King Jr. Papers, Howard Gottlieb Archival Research Center, Mugar Memorial Library, Boston University, Boston.

BOOKS

Abernathy, Ralph D. *And the Walls Came Tumbling Down: An Autobiography*. New York: Harper & Row, 1989.

Abrams, Irwin, ed. *The Words of Peace: Selections from the Speeches of the Winners of the Nobel Peace Prize*. New York: Newmarket Press, 1990.

Alexander, Michelle. *The New Jim Crow: Mass Incarceration in an Age of Colorblindness*. New York: New Press, 2010.

Allen, John. *Rabble-Rouser for Peace: The Authorized Biography of Desmond Tutu*. New York: Free Press, 2006.

Anderson, Jervis. *Bayard Rustin: Troubles I've Seen—A Biography*. New York: HarperCollins, 1997.

Anderson, Victor. *Pragmatic Theology: Negotiating the Intersections of an American Philosophy of Religion and Public Theology*. Albany: State University of New York Press, 1998.

Ansbro, John J. *Martin Luther King, Jr.: Nonviolent Strategies and Tactics for Social Change*. New York: Madison Books, 2000.

———. *Martin Luther King, Jr.: The Making of a Mind*. Maryknoll, N.Y.: Orbis Books, 1982.

Appiah, Kwame A. *Cosmopolitanism: Ethics in a World of Strangers*. New York: W. W. Norton, 2007.

Aristotle. *The Art of Rhetoric*. Penguin Classics. New York: Penguin Books, 1991.

Atkinson, Rowland, and Gary Bridge. *Gentrification in a Global Context: The New Urban Colonialism*. London, UK: Routledge, 2005.

Azaransky, Sarah. *The Worldwide Struggle: Religion and the International Roots of the Civil Rights Movement*. New York: Oxford University Press, 2017.

Bagley, Edith Scott, and Joe Hilley. *Desert Rose: The Life and Legacy of Coretta Scott King*. Tuscaloosa: University of Alabama Press, 2012.

Baldwin, James. *Conversations with James Baldwin*. Edited by Fred L. Standley and Louis H. Pratt. Jackson: University Press of Mississippi, 1989.

Baldwin, Lewis V. *Behind the Public Veil: The Humanness of Martin Luther King, Jr.* Minneapolis: Fortress Press, 2016.

———. *Plenty Good Room: A Bible Study Based on African American Spirituals*. Nashville: Abingdon Press, 2002.

———. *There Is a Balm in Gilead: The Cultural Roots of Martin Luther King, Jr.* Minneapolis: Fortress Press, 1991.

———. *To Make the Wounded Whole: The Cultural Legacy of Martin Luther King, Jr.* Minneapolis: Fortress Press, 1992.

———. *Toward the Beloved Community: Martin Luther King Jr. and South Africa*. Cleveland: Pilgrim Press, 1995.

———. *The Voice of Conscience: The Church in the Mind of Martin Luther King, Jr.* New York: Oxford University Press, 2010.

Baldwin, Lewis V., and Amiri YaSin Al-Hadid. *Between Cross and Crescent: Christian and Muslim Perspectives on Malcolm and Martin*. Gainesville: University Press of Florida, 2002.

Baldwin, Lewis V., and Rufus Burrow Jr. *The Domestication of Martin Luther King, Jr.: Clarence B. Jones, Right-Wing Conservatism, and the Manipulation of the King Legacy*. Eugene, Ore.: Cascade Books, 2013.

Baldwin, Lewis V., Rufus Burrow Jr., Barbara A. Holmes, and Susan Holmes Winfield. *The Legacy of Martin Luther King, Jr.: The Boundaries of Law, Politics, and Religion*. Notre Dame, Ind.: University of Notre Dame Press, 2002.

Baldwin, Lewis V., and Paul R. Dekar, eds. *"In an Inescapable Network of Mutuality": Martin Luther King, Jr. and the Globalization of an Ethical Ideal*. Eugene, Ore.: Cascade Books, 2013.

Bartkowski, Maciej, ed. *Recovering Nonviolent History: Civil Resistance in Liberation Struggles*. Boulder, Colo.: Lynne Rienner, 2013.

Beck, Don E., and Christopher C. Cowan. *Spiral Dynamics: Mastering Values, Leadership, and Change*. Malden, Mass.: Wiley-Blackwell, 2006.

Bell, Derrick. *And We Are Not Saved: The Elusive Quest for Racial Justice*. New York: Basic Books, 1987.

Bennett, Lerone, Jr. *What Manner of Man: A Biography of Martin Luther King, Jr.* 8th rev. ed. Chicago: Johnson Publishing, 1992.

Bertalanffy, Ludwig von. *General System Theory: Foundations, Development, Applications.* Rev. ed. New York: George Braziller, 1976.

Bess, Michael. *Choices under Fire: Moral Dimensions of World War II.* New York: Vintage Books, 2008.

Beydoun, Khaled A. *American Islamophobia: Understanding the Roots and Rise of Fear.* Oakland: University of California Press, 2018.

Biondi, Martha. *To Stand and Fight: The Struggle for Civil Rights in Post-War New York.* Cambridge, Mass.: Harvard University Press, 2003.

Bloom, Peter. *The Ethics of Neoliberalism: The Business of Making Capitalism Moral.* London, UK: Routledge, 2017.

Blount, Brian K., and Leonora Tubbs Tisdale, eds. *Making Room at the Table: An Invitation to Multicultural Worship.* Louisville: Westminster John Knox Press, 2001.

Blum, Edward J., and Paul Harvey. *The Color of Christ: The Son of God and the Saga of Race in America.* Chapel Hill: University of North Carolina Press, 2012.

Boesak, Allan A. *Black and Reformed: Apartheid, Liberation and the Calvinist Tradition.* Maryknoll, N.Y.: Orbis Books, 1984.

Boushey, Heather, J. Bradford Delong, and Marshall Steinbaum, eds. *After Piketty: The Agenda for Economics and Inequality.* Cambridge, Mass.: Harvard University Press, 2017.

Bowne, Borden P. *The Principles of Ethics.* New York: Harper & Brothers, 1892.

——. *Theism.* New York: American Book Company, 1902. First published 1887.

Branch, Taylor. *Parting the Waters: America in the King Years, 1954–63.* New York: Simon & Schuster, 1988.

Brock, Rita. *Journeys by Heart: A Christology of Erotic Power.* Eugene, Ore.: Wipf and Stock, 1988.

Brown, Robert McAfee, Abraham Joshua Heschel, and Michael Novak. *Vietnam: Crisis of Conscience.* New York: Herder and Herder, 1967.

Brown, Sally A., and Patrick Miller, eds. *Lament: Reclaiming Practices in Pulpit, Pew, and Public Square.* Louisville: Westminster John Knox Press, 2005.

Burrow, Rufus, Jr. *Extremist for Love: Martin Luther King, Jr., Man of Ideas and Nonviolent Social Action.* Minneapolis: Fortress Press, 2014.

——. *God and Human Dignity: The Personalism, Theology, and Ethics of Martin Luther King, Jr.* Notre Dame, Ind.: University of Notre Dame Press, 2006.

——. *Martin Luther King, Jr., and the Theology of Resistance.* Jefferson, N.C.: McFarland, 2015.

——. *Martin Luther King Jr. for Armchair Theologians.* Louisville: Westminster John Knox Press, 2009.

——. *Personalism: An Introduction.* St. Louis: Chalice Press, 1999.

Butler, Judith. *Precarious Life: The Powers of Mourning and Violence.* New York: Verso, 2004.

Cain, Patricia A. *Rainbow Rights: The Role of Lawyers and Courts in the Lesbian and Gay Civil Rights Movement.* New York: Routledge, 2018.

Calloway-Thomas, Carolyn, and John L. Lucaites, eds. *Martin Luther King, Jr., and the Sermonic Power of Public Discourse.* Tuscaloosa: University of Alabama Press, 1993.

Camp, Jordan T., and Christina Heatherton, eds. *Policing the Planet: Why the Policing Crisis Led to Black Lives Matter.* London, UK: Verso, 2016.

Campbell, James. *Talking at the Gates: A Life of James Baldwin.* New York: Viking, 1991.

Cannon, Katie G. *Black Womanist Ethics.* Atlanta: Scholars Press, 1988.

Carson, Clayborne, ed. *The Martin Luther King, Jr., Encyclopedia.* Westport, Conn.: Greenwood Press, 2008.

————. *Martin's Dream: My Journey and the Legacy of Martin Luther King, Jr.—A Memoir*. New York: Palgrave Macmillan, 2013.

Carson, Clayborne, and Peter Holloran, eds. *A Knock at Midnight: Inspiration from the Great Sermons of Reverend Martin Luther King, Jr.* New York: Warner Books, 1998.

Carson, Rachel. *Silent Spring*. New York: Houghton Mifflin, 1962.

Chenoweth, Erica, and Maria J. Stephan. *Why Civil Resistance Works: The Strategic Logic of Nonviolent Conflict*. New York: Columbia University Press, 2011.

Christie, Nancy, and Michael Gauvreau. *The Sixties and Beyond: Dechristianization in North America and Western Europe, 1945–2000*. Toronto: University of Toronto Press, 2013.

Chua, Amy. *Political Tribes: Group Instinct and the Fate of Nations*. New York: Penguin Press, 2018.

————. *World on Fire: How Exporting Free Market Economy Breeds Ethnic Hatred and Global Instability*. New York: Doubleday, 2003.

Clark, Kenneth B. *Prejudice and Your Child*. Middleton, Conn.: Wesleyan University Press, 1988. First published 1963.

Clark, Septima. *Ready from Within: Septima Clark and the Civil Rights Movement*. Edited by Cynthia Stokes Brown. Trenton, N.J.: Africa World Press, 1990.

Cohen, Jean L., and Andrew Arato. *Civil Society and Political Theory: Studies in Contemporary German Social Thought*. Cambridge, Mass.: MIT Press, 1994.

Collier-Thomas, Bettye, and V. P. Franklin, eds. *Sisters in the Struggle: African American Women in the Civil Rights–Black Power Movements*. New York: New York University Press, 2001.

Cone, James H. *Martin and Malcolm and America: A Dream or a Nightmare*. Maryknoll, N.Y.: Orbis Books, 1991.

————. *The Spirituals and the Blues: An Interpretation*. Maryknoll, N.Y.: Orbis Books, 1972.

Conser, Walter H., Jr., Ronald M. McCarthy, David J. Toscano, and Gene Sharp, eds. *Resistance, Politics, and the American Struggle for Independence, 1765–1775*. Boulder, Colo.: Lynne Rienner, 1986.

Coppa, Frank J., ed. *Encyclopedia of Modern Dictators: From Napoleon to the Present*. New York: Peter Lang, 2006.

Corradi, Juan E., Patricia Weiss Fagan, and Manuel Antonio, eds. *Fear at the Edge: State Terror and Resistance in Latin America*. Berkeley: University of California Press, 1992.

Cotton, Dorothy. *If Your Back's Not Bent: The Role of the Citizenship Education Program in the Civil Rights Movement*. New York: Atria Books, 2012.

Coulter, David L., John R. Wiens, and Gary D. Fenstermacher, eds. *Why Do We Educate? Renewing the Conversation*. Oxford, UK: Blackwell Publishing, 2008.

Crawford, Matthew B. *The World beyond Your Head: On Becoming an Individual in an Age of Distraction*. New York: Farrar, Straus, and Giroux, 2010.

Crawford, Vicki L., Jacqueline A. Rouse, Barbara Woods, Broadus Butler, Marymal Dryden, and Melissa Walker, eds. *Women in the Civil Rights Movement: Trailblazers and Torchbearers, 1941–1965*. Brooklyn: Carlson Publishing, 1990.

Darby, John, and Roger MacGinty, eds. *Contemporary Peacemaking: Conflict, Violence, and Peace Processes*. Basingstoke, UK: Palgrave Macmillan, 2003.

Davis, Ossie. *Life Lit by Some Large Vision: Selected Speeches and Writings*. New York: Atria Books, 2006.

Day, Keri. *Religious Resistance to Neoliberalism: Womanist and Black Feminist Perspectives*. New York: Palgrave Macmillan, 2015.

De Tocqueville, Alexis. *Democracy in America*. 1835. Translated and edited by Harvey Mansfield and Delba Winthrop. Chicago: University of Chicago Press, 2000.

Dewey, John. *Democracy and Education*. New York: Dover Publications, 2004. First published 1916.

Dixie, Quinton, and Cornel West, eds. *The Courage to Hope: From Black Suffering to Human Redemption*. Boston: Beacon Press, 1999.

Dorrien, Gary. *The Making of American Liberal Theology: Idealism, Realism, and Modernity, 1900–1950*. Louisville: Westminster John Knox Press, 2003.

Douglass, Frederick. *The Frederick Douglass Papers*, vol. 3, series 1, *Speeches, Debates, and Interviews, 1855–1863*. Edited by John W. Blassingame. New Haven, Conn.: Yale University Press, 1986.

Downing, Frederick L. *To See the Promised Land: The Faith Pilgrimage of Martin Luther King, Jr.* Macon, Ga.: Mercer University Press, 1986.

DuBois, W. E. B. *The Souls of Black Folk*. New York: Penguin Books, 1989. First published 1903.

Edwards, David L. *Christianity: The First Two Thousand Years*. London, UK: Continuum, 1998.

Faderman, Lillian. *The Gay Revolution: The Story of the Struggle*. New York: Simon & Schuster, 2016.

Fairclough, Adam. *To Redeem the Soul of America: The Southern Christian Leadership Conference and Martin Luther King, Jr.* Athens: University of Georgia Press, 1987.

Farris, Christine King. *Through It All: My Life, My Family, and My Faith.* New York. Atria Books, 2009.

Finley, Mary Lou, Bernard LaFayette Jr., James R. Ralph Jr., and Pam Smith, eds. *The Chicago Freedom Movement: Martin Luther King Jr. and Civil Rights Activism in the North*. Lexington: University Press of Kentucky, 2016.

Fluker, Walter E. *Educating Leaders for the Twenty-First Century*. Eugene, Ore.: Cascade Books, 2013.

———. *Ethical Leadership: The Quest for Character, Civility, and Community*. Minneapolis: Fortress Press, 2009.

———. *The Ground Has Shifted: The Future of the Black Church in Post-Racial America*. New York: New York University Press, 2016.

———. *They Looked for a City: A Comparative Analysis of the Ideal of Community in the Thought of Howard Thurman and Martin Luther King, Jr.* Lanham, Md.: University Press of America, 1989.

Francisco, Mranca. *Systems Theory: Perspectives, Applications and Developments*. Hauppauge, N.Y.: Nova Publishers, 2014.

Franklin, Robert M. *Liberating Visions: Human Fulfillment and Social Justice in African American Thought*. Minneapolis: Fortress Press, 1990.

Freire, Paulo. *Education for Critical Consciousness*. New York: Seabury Press, 1974.

———. *Pedagogy of the Oppressed*. New York: Herder and Herder, 1970.

Gamson, William A. *The Strategy of Social Protests*. 2nd ed. Belmont, Calif.: Wadsworth, 1990.

Gandhi, Mohandas K. *An Autobiography, or, The Story of My Experiments with Truth*. Boston: Beacon Press, 1993. First published 1927.

———. *Collected Works of Mahatma Gandhi*. 5 vols. Edited by K. Swaminathan. New Delhi, India: Publications Division, Ministry of Information and Broadcasting, Government of India, 1960–1978.

———. *Non-violence in Peace and War*. Ahmedabad, India: Navajivan Press, 1942.

———. *Nonviolent Resistance (Satyagraha)*. New York: Schocken Books, 1951.

Garrow, David J. *Bearing the Cross: Martin Luther King, Jr., and the Southern Christian Leadership Conference*. New York: William Morrow, 1986.

Giddings, Paula. *When and Where I Enter: The Impact of Black Women on Race and Sex in America*. New York: William Morrow, 1984.

Gilroy, Paul. *Against Race: Imagining Political Culture Beyond the Color Line*. Cambridge, Mass.: Harvard University Press, 2000.

———. *Postcolonial Melancholy*. New York: Columbia University Press, 2010.

Glaude, Eddie S., Jr. *Democracy in Black: How Race Still Enslaves the American Soul*. New York: Broadway Books, 2016.

Goudsouzian, Aram. *Sidney Poitier: Man, Actor, Icon*. Chapel Hill: University of North Carolina Press, 2004.

Grant, Rebecca, and Kathleen Newland, eds. *Gender and International Relations*. Buckingham, UK: Open University Press, 1991.

Green, Julie. *The Canal Builders: Making America's Empire at the Panama Canal*. New York: Penguin Books, 2009.

Haberman, Frederick, ed. *Nobel Lectures, Peace, 1951–1970*. Amsterdam, Holland: Elsevier, 1972.

Hall, Stuart. *The Fateful Triangle: Race, Ethnicity, Nation*. Cambridge, Mass.: Harvard University Press, 2017.

Hanh, Thich Nhat. *Living Buddha, Living Christ*. New York: Riverhead Books, 1995.

———. *Love in Action: Writings on Nonviolent Social Change*. Berkeley: Parallax Press, 1993.

Harris, Melanie L. *Ecowomanism: African American Women and Earth-Honoring Faiths*. Maryknoll, N.Y.: Orbis Books, 2017.

Hartmann, Thom. *Unequal Protection: The Rise of Corporate Dominance and the Theft of Human Rights*. New York: Rodale, 2002.

Havel, Václav. *Living in Truth*. Edited by Jan Vladislav. London, UK: Faber and Faber, 1989.

Heidegger, Martin. *Being and Time*. Translated by John Macquarrie and Edward Robinson. New York: Harper Perennial, 1962.

Henderson, Hazel, and Daisaku Ikeda. *Planetary Citizenship: Your Values, Beliefs, and Actions Can Shape a Sustainable World*. Santa Monica, Calif.: Middleway Press, 2004.

Holmes, Robert L. *On War and Morality*. Princeton: Princeton University Press, 1989.

Honey, Michael K. *Going Down Jericho Road: The Memphis Strike, Martin Luther King, Jr.'s Last Crusade*. New York: W. W. Norton, 2007.

hooks, bell. *Feminist Theory: From Margin to Center*. 2nd ed. Cambridge, Mass.: South End Press, 2000.

———. *Teaching to Transgress: Education as the Practice of Freedom*. New York: Routledge, 1994.

Horton, Richard. *Health Wars: On the Global Front Lines of Modern Medicine*. New York: New York Review of Books, 2003.

Houser, George M. *No One Can Stop the Rain: Glimpses of Africa's Liberation Struggle*. New York: Pilgrim Press, 1989.

Human Development Report 2016. New York: United Nations Development Program, 2016.

Hunter, James D. *To Change the World: The Irony, Tragedy, and Possibility of Christianity in the Late Modern World*. New York: Oxford University Press, 2010.

Hutchinson, Earl Ofari. *Fifty Years Later: Why the Murder of Dr. King Still Hurts*. Los Angeles: Middle Passage Press, 2018.

International Tribute to Martin Luther King, Jr. New York: United Nations Centre against Apartheid, Department of Political and Security Council Affairs, 1979.

Jackson, Thomas F. *From Civil Rights to Human Rights: Martin Luther King, Jr., and the Struggle for Economic Justice*. Philadelphia: University of Pennsylvania Press, 2007.

Jelks, Randall M. *Benjamin E. Mays, Schoolmaster of the Movement: A Biography*. Chapel Hill: University of North Carolina Press, 2012.

Jennings, Willie J. *The Christian Imagination: Theology and the Origins of Race*. New Haven, Conn.: Yale University Press, 2010.

Johnson, James Weldon, ed. *The Book of American Negro Poetry*. New York: Harcourt, Brace, 1922.

Jones, Clarence B. *What Would Martin Say?* New York: HarperCollins, Publishers, 2008.

Joseph, Gloria I., and Jill Lewis. *Common Differences: Conflicts in Black and White Feminist Perspectives*. Boston: South End Press, 1981.

Kafka, Franz. *Letters to Friends, Family, and Editors*. New York: Schocken Books, 1977.

Kapur, Sudarshan. *Raising up a Prophet: The African-American Encounter with Gandhi*. Boston: Beacon Press, 1992.

Karatnycky, Adrian. *How Freedom Is Won: From Civic Resistance to Durable Democracy*. New York: Freedom House, 2005.

Keck, Margaret E., and Kathryn Sikkink. *Activists beyond Borders: Advocacy Networks in International Politics*. Ithaca, N.Y.: Cornell University Press, 1998.

Keller, Helen. *The Story of My Life*. New York: Grosset & Dunlap, 1905.

Kender, Ibram X. *Stamped from the Beginning: The Definitive History of Racist Ideas in America*. New York: Nation Books, 2016.

Khan-Cullors, Patrisse, and Asha Bandele. *When They Call You a Terrorist: A Black Lives Matter Memoir*. New York: St. Martin's, 2017.

King, Coretta Scott. *My Life with Martin Luther King, Jr.* Rev. ed. New York: Henry Holt, 1993. 1st ed. published in 1969.

King, Coretta Scott, with Barbara Reynolds. *My Life, My Love, My Legacy*. New York: Henry Holt, 2017.

King, Martin Luther, Jr. *The Autobiography of Martin Luther King, Jr.* Edited by Clayborne Carson. New York: Warner Books, 1998.

———. *A Call to Conscience: The Landmark Speeches of Dr. Martin Luther King, Jr.* Edited by Clayborne Carson and Kris Shepard. New York: Warner Books, 2001.

———. *"In a Single Garment of Destiny": A Global Vision of Justice—Martin Luther King, Jr.* Edited by Lewis V. Baldwin. Boston: Beacon Press, 2012.

———. *The Measure of a Man*. Philadelphia: Fortress Press, 1988. First published 1959.

———. *The Papers of Martin Luther King, Jr.*, vol. 1, *Called to Serve, January 1929–June 1951*. Edited by Clayborne Carson, Ralph E. Luker, Penny A. Russell, and Louis R. Harlan. Berkeley: University of California Press, 1992.

———. *The Papers of Martin Luther King, Jr.*, vol. 2, *Rediscovering Precious Values, July 1951–November 1955*. Edited by Clayborne Carson, Ralph E. Luker, Penny A. Russell, Peter Holloran, and Louis R. Harlan. Berkeley: University of California Press, 1994.

———. *The Papers of Martin Luther King, Jr.*, vol. 3, *Birth of a New Age, December 1955–December 1956*. Edited by Clayborne Carson, Stewart Burns, Susan Carson, Peter Holloran, and Dana L. H. Powell. Berkeley: University of California Press, 1997.

———. *The Papers of Martin Luther King, Jr.*, vol. 4, *Symbol of the Movement, January 1957–December 1958*. Edited by Clayborne Carson, Susan Carson, Adrienne Clay, Virginia Shadron, and Kieran Taylor. Berkeley: University of California Press, 2000.

———. *The Papers of Martin Luther King, Jr.*, vol. 5, *Threshold of a New Decade, January 1959–December 1960.* Edited by Clayborne Carson, Tenisha Armstrong, Susan Carson, Adrienne Clay, and Kieran Taylor. Berkeley: University of California Press, 2005.

———. *The Papers of Martin Luther King, Jr.*, vol. 6, *Advocate of the Social Gospel, September 1948–March 1963.* Edited by Clayborne Carson, Susan Carson, Susan Englander, Troy Jackson, and Gerald L. Smith. Berkeley: University of California Press, 2007.

———. *The Papers of Martin Luther King, Jr.*, vol. 7, *To Save the Soul of America, January 1961–August 1962.* Edited by Clayborne Carson and Tenisha Armstrong. Berkeley: University of California Press, 2014.

———. *The Radical King: Martin Luther King, Jr.* Edited by Cornel West. Boston: Beacon Press, 2015.

———. *Strength to Love.* Philadelphia: Fortress Press, 1981. First published 1963.

———. *Stride toward Freedom: The Montgomery Story.* New York: Harper & Row, 1958.

———. *A Testament of Hope: The Essential Writings and Speeches of Martin Luther King, Jr.* Edited by James Melvin Washington. San Francisco: HarperCollins, 1986.

———. *The Trumpet of Conscience.* New York: Harper & Row, 1967.

———. *Where Do We Go from Here: Chaos or Community?* Boston: Beacon Press, 1967. Rpt., 1968, 2010.

———. *Why We Can't Wait.* New York: New American Library, 1963.

———. *The Wisdom of Martin Luther King, Jr.: An A–Z Guide to the Ideas and Ideals of the Great Civil Rights Leader.* Edited by Alex Ayres. New York: Penguin Books USA, 1993.

———. *The Wisdom of Martin Luther King in His Own Words.* New York: Lancer Books, 1968.

King, Martin Luther, Jr., and Coretta Scott King. *Four Decades of Concern.* Atlanta: Martin Luther King Jr. Center for Nonviolent Social Change, 1986.

King, Martin Luther, Sr., with Clayton Riley. *Daddy King: An Autobiography.* New York: William Morrow, 1980. Rpt., 2017.

King, Mary. *Mahatma Gandhi and Martin Luther King, Jr.: The Power of Nonviolent Action.* 2nd ed. New Delhi, India: Indian Council for Cultural Relations and Mehta Publishers, 2002. 1st ed. published in 1999.

———. *The New York Times on Emerging Democracies in Eastern Europe.* Times Reference from CQ Press. Washington, D.C.: CQ Press, 2009.

Kirk-Duggan, Cheryl A. *Refiner's Fire: A Religious Engagement with Violence.* Minneapolis: Fortress Press, 2001.

Knight, Douglas A., and Peter J. Paris, eds. *Justice and the Holy: Essays in Honor of Walter Harrelson.* Atlanta: Scholars Press, 1989.

Kripalani, Krishna, ed. *All Men Are Brothers: Autobiographical Reflections.* New York: Columbia University Press, 1958.

Kumarappa, Bharatan, ed. *Nonviolence in Peace and War.* 2 vols. Ahmedabad, India: Navajivan Publishing House, 1949.

Kung, Hans, and Kuschel, Karl-Josef, eds. *A Global Ethic: The Declaration of the Parliament of the World's Religions.* New York: Continuum, 1993.

Kuypers, Jim A., ed. *The Art of Rhetorical Criticism.* Boston: Allyn & Bacon, 2004.

Le Blanc, Paul, and Michael Yates, *A Freedom Budget for All Americans: Recapturing the Promise of the Civil Rights Movement in the Struggle for Economic Justice Today.* New York: Monthly Review Press, 2013.

Lee, Hak Joon. *The Great World House: Martin Luther King, Jr., and Global Ethics*. Cleveland: Pilgrim Press, 2011.

———. *Toward the Promised Land: Martin Luther King, Jr.'s Communal-Political Spirituality*. Cleveland: Pilgrim Press, 2006.

Levine, Daniel. *Bayard Rustin and the Civil Rights Movement*. New Brunswick, N.J.: Rutgers University Press, 2000.

Levy, Jacques E. *Cesar Chavez: Autobiography of La Causa*. New York: W. W. Norton, 1975.

Lewis, David L. *King: A Critical Biography*. New York: Praeger Publishers, 1970.

Long, Charles H. *Significations: Signs, Symbols, and Images in the Interpretation of Religion*. Philadelphia: Fortress Press, 1986.

Long, Michael G. *Against Us, but for Us: Martin Luther King, Jr. and the State*. Macon, Ga.: Mercer University Press, 2002.

———. *Martin Luther King, Jr., Homosexuality, and the Early Gay Rights Movement: Keeping the Dream Straight?* New York: Palgrave Macmillan, 2012.

Lorde, Audre, *Sister Outsider: Essays and Speeches*. Berkeley: Crossing Press, 2007.

Love, Erik. *Islamophobia and Racism in America*. New York: New York University Press, 2017.

Lubiano, Wahneema, ed. *The House that Race Built: Black Americans, U.S. Terrain*. New York: Pantheon, 1997.

Lucas, Scott, ed. *Britain and Suez: The Lion's Last Roar*. Manchester, UK: Manchester University Press, 1996.

Mabee, Carleton. *Black Freedom: The Nonviolent Abolitionists from 1830 through the Civil War*. New York: Macmillan, 1970.

Mandela, Nelson, and Mandia Langa. *Dare Not Linger: The Presidential Years*. New York: Farrar, Straus and Giroux, 2017.

Marcus, Eric. *Making Gay History: The Half-Century Fight for Lesbian and Gay Equal Rights*. New York: Harper Perennial, 2002.

Mays, Benjamin E. *Dr. Benjamin E. Mays Speaks: Representative Speeches of a Great American Orator*. Edited by Freddie C. Colston. Lanham, Md.: University Press of America, 2002.

McKnight, Gerald D. *The Last Crusade: Martin Luther King, Jr., the FBI, and the Poor People's Campaign*. New York: Westview Press, 1998.

Medearis, Angela Self. *Dare to Dream: Coretta Scott King and the Civil Rights Movement*. New York: Puffin Books, 1994.

Meeks, M. Douglas. *God the Economist: The Doctrine of God and Political Economy*. Minneapolis: Fortress Press, 1989.

Michnik, Adam. *Letters from Prison and Other Essays*. Translated by Maya Latynski. Berkeley: University of California Press, 1985.

Miller, W. Jason. *Origins of the Dream: Hughes's Poetry and King's Rhetoric*. Gainesville: University Press of Florida, 2015.

Mills, Kay. *This Little Light of Mine: The Life of Fannie Lou Hamer*. New York: Penguin Books USA, 1994.

Miranda, Francisco. *Systems Theory: Perspectives, Applications and Developments*. New York: Nova Publishers, 2014.

Mishra, Pankaj. *Age of Anger: The History of the Present*. New York: Farrar, Straus, and Giroux, 2017.

Mitchell, Mozella G., ed. *The Human Search: Howard Thurman and the Quest for Freedom, Pro-*

ceedings of the Second Annual Thurman Convocation. Martin Luther King Jr. Memorial Studies in Religion, Culture and Social Development. New York: Peter Lang, 1992.

Morozov, Evgeny. *The Net Delusion: The Dark Side of Internet Freedom.* New York: Public Affairs, 2011.

Morrison, Toni. *The Origin of Others.* Cambridge, Mass.: Harvard University Press, 2017.

Mulhall, Thomas A. *A Lasting Prophetic Legacy: Martin Luther King, Jr., the World Council of Churches, and the Global Crusade against Racism and War.* Eugene, Ore.: Wipf and Stock, 2014.

National Council of Bishops. *Economic Justice for All.* Washington, D.C.: U. S. Catholic Conference, 1986.

Niebuhr, Reinhold. *Moral Man and Immoral Society: A Study in Ethics and Politics.* New York: Charles Scribner's Sons, 1932.

Nkrumah, Kwame. *Neocolonialism: The Last Stage of Imperialism.* New York: International Publishers, 1966.

Norrell, Robert J. *Alex Haley and the Books that Changed a Nation.* New York: St. Martin's Press, 2015.

Nussbaum, Martha C. *For Love of Country?* New ed. Edited by Joshua Cohen. Boston: Beacon Press, 2000.

Oliver, Mel, and Thomas Shapiro. *Black Wealth/White Wealth: A New Perspective on Racial Inequality.* New York: Routledge, 1995.

Olson, Lynne. *Freedom's Daughters: The Unsung Heroines of the Civil Rights Movement from 1830 to 1970.* New York: Scribner, 2001.

O'Sullivan, Noel, ed. *Political Theory in Transition.* London, UK: Routledge, 2000.

Paris, Peter J. *The Spirituality of African Peoples: The Search for a Common Moral Discourse.* Minneapolis: Fortress Press, 1995.

Payne, Charles M. *I've Got the Light of Freedom: The Organizing Tradition and the Mississippi Freedom Struggle.* Berkeley: University of California Press, 1995.

Peabody, Elizabeth P., ed. *Aesthetic Papers.* New York: Cosimo Classics, 2005. First published 1849.

Penz, Peter, Jay Drydyk, and Pablo S. Bose, *Displacement by Development: Ethics, Rights and Responsibilities.* New York: Cambridge University Press, 2011.

Piketty, Thomas. *Capital in the Twenty-First Century.* Translated by Arthur Goldhammer. Cambridge, Mass.: Harvard University Press, 2014.

Pillay, Gerald J., ed. *Voices of Liberation*, vol. 1, *Albert Luthuli.* Pretoria, South Africa: HSRC Publishers, 1993.

Pogge, Thomas. *World Poverty and Human Rights.* Malden, Mass.: Blackwell Publishers, 2002.

Pomerantz, Gary M. *Where Peachtree Meets Sweet Auburn: The Saga of Two Families and the Making of Atlanta.* New York: Scribner, 1996.

Powers, Georgia Davis. *I Shared the Dream: The Pride, Passion, and Politics of the First Black Woman Senator from Kentucky.* Far Hills, N.J.: New Horizon Press, 1995.

Powers, Roger S., William B. Vogele, Douglas Bond, and Christopher Kruegler, eds. *Protest, Power, and Change: Encyclopedia of Nonviolent Action from ACT-UP to Women's Suffrage.* New York: Garland, 1997.

Prashad, Vijay. *The Darker Nations: A People's History of the Third World.* New York: New Press, 2007.

Prins, Gwyn, ed. *Spring in Winter: The 1989 Revolutions*. Manchester, UK: Manchester University Press, 1990.

Putnam, Lara. *Radical Moves: Caribbean Migrants and the Politics of Race in the Jazz Age*. Chapel Hill: University of North Carolina Press, 2013.

Raboteau, Albert J. *Canaan Land: A Religious History of African Americans*. New York: Oxford University Press, 2001.

———. *A Fire in the Bones: Reflections on African American Religious History*. Boston: Beacon Press, 1995.

Rallis, Sharon F., and Gretchen B. Rossman. *The Research Journey: Introduction to Inquiry*. New York: Guilford Press, 2012.

Rancière, Jacques. *Disagreement: Politics and Philosophy*. Translated by Julie Rose. Minneapolis: University of Minnesota Press, 1998.

Ransby, Barbara. *Ella Baker and the Black Freedom Movement: A Radical Democratic Vision*. Chapel Hill: University of North Carolina Press, 2003.

Reddick, Lawrence D. *Crusader without Violence: A Biography of Martin Luther King, Jr.* New York: Harper & Brothers, 1959.

Richter, Kent E., Eva M. Rapple, John C. Modschiedler, and R. Dean Peterson. *Understanding Religion in a Global Society*. Belmont, Calif.: Wadsworth, 2005.

Rieder, Jonathan. *The Word of the Lord Is upon Me: The Righteous Performance of Martin Luther King, Jr.* Cambridge, Mass.: Belknap Press of Harvard University Press, 2008.

Riggs, Marcia Y. *Plenty Good Room: Women Versus Male Power in the Black Church*. Eugene, Ore.: Wipf and Stock, 2008.

Roberts, Adam, and Timothy G. Ash. *Civil Resistance and Power Politics: The Experience of Non-Violent Action from Gandhi to the Present*. New York: Oxford University Press, 2009.

Roberts, J. Deotis. *Bonhoeffer and King: Speaking Truth to Power*. Louisville: Westminster John Knox Press, 2005.

Robinson, Joann Gibson. *The Montgomery Bus Boycott and the Women Who Started It: The Memoir of Joann Gibson Robinson*. Edited by David J. Garrow. Knoxville: University of Tennessee Press, 1987.

Robnett, Belinda. *How Long? How Long? African American Women in the Struggle for Civil Rights*. New York: Oxford University Press, 1997.

Rosenberg, Emily. *Spreading the American Dream: American Economic and Cultural Expansion, 1890–1945*. New York: Hill and Wang, 1982.

Ross, Rosetta E. *Witnessing and Testifying: Black Women, Religion, and Civil Rights*. Minneapolis: Fortress Press, 2003.

Rustin, Bayard. *Time on Two Crosses: The Collected Writings of Bayard Rustin*. Edited by Devon W. Carbado and Donald Weise. San Francisco: Cleis Press, 2003.

Said, Edward. *The Edward Said Reader*. Edited by Mustafa Bayoumi and Andrew Rubin. New York: Vintage, 2000.

Sanders, Cheryl J. *Empowerment Ethics for a Liberated People: A Path to African American Social Transformation*. Minneapolis: Fortress Press, 1995.

Schmidli, William M. *The Fate of Freedom Elsewhere: Human Rights and U.S. Cold War Policy toward Argentina*. Ithaca, N.Y.: Cornell University Press, 2013.

Schock, Kurt. *Unarmed Insurrections: People Power Movements in Nondemocracies*. Minneapolis: University of Minnesota Press, 2005.

Sen, Amartya. *Identity and Violence: The Illusion of Destiny*. Issues of Our Time. New York: W. W. Norton, 2006.

Senge, Peter M. *The Fifth Discipline: The Art and Practice of the Learning Organization*. New York: Doubleday, 1990.

Sharp, Gene. *The Politics of Nonviolent Action*, pt. 2, *The Methods of Nonviolent Action*. Boston: Extending Horizons Books and Porter Sargent, 1973.

——. *Social Power and Political Freedom*. Boston: Porter Sargent, 1980.

Shelby, Tommie, and Brandon M. Terry, eds. *To Shape a New World: Essays on the Political Philosophy of Martin Luther King, Jr*. Cambridge, Mass.: Belknap Press of Harvard University, 2018.

Shelp, Earl E., and Ronald H. Sunderland, eds. *The Pastor as Prophet*. New York: Pilgrim Press, 1985.

Skidmore, Thomas E. *The Politics of Military Rule in Brazil, 1964–1985*. New York: Oxford University Press, 1988.

Smith, Bernard. *Modernism's History: A Study in Twentieth-Century Art and Ideas*. Sydney, Australia: University of South Wales Press, 1998.

Smith, Kenneth L., and Ira G. Zepp Jr. *Search for the Beloved Community: The Thinking of Martin Luther King, Jr*. Valley Forge, Pa.: Judson Press, 1974.

Solomon, Robert C. *Introducing the Existentialists: Imaginary Interviews with Sartre, Heidegger, and Camus*. Indianapolis: Backett Publishing, 1981.

Songs of Zion. Supplemental Worship Resources 12. Nashville: Abingdon Press, 1981.

Stiglitz, Joseph E. *Globalization and Its Discontents*. New York: W. W. Norton, 2002.

——. *The Price of Inequality: How Today's Divided Society Endangers Our Future*. New York: W. W. Norton, 2013.

Tarlo, Emily. *Visibly Muslim: Fashion, Politics, Faith*. New York: Bloomsbury, 2014.

Taylor, Mark L. *The Executed God: The Way of the Cross in Lockdown America*. Minneapolis: Fortress Press, 2015.

Theoharis, Jeanne. *The Rebellious Life of Mrs. Rosa Parks*. Boston: Beacon Press, 2013.

Thoreau, Henry David. *On the Duty of Civil Disobedience*. Peace News Pamphlet. London, UK: Housmans, 1963.

Thurman, Howard. *Deep River and the Negro Spiritual Speaks of Life and Death*. Richmond, Ind.: Friends United Press, 1971. First published 1944.

——. *Jesus and the Disinherited*. New York: Abingdon Press, 1949.

——. *The Luminous Darkness: A Personal Interpretation of the Anatomy of Segregation and the Ground of Hope*. Richmond, Ind.: Friends United Press, 1971. First published 1965.

——. *The Search for Common Ground*. Richmond, Ind.: Friends United Press, 1971.

——. *With Head and Heart: The Autobiography of Howard Thurman*. New York: Harcourt Brace Jovanovich, 1979.

Tillich, Paul. *Theology of Peace*. Edited by Ronald Stone. Louisville: Westminster John Knox Press, 1990.

Tilly, Charles. *Social Movements, 1768–2004*. Boulder, Colo.: Paradigm Publishers, 2004.

Timberman, David G. *A Changeless Land: Continuity and Change in Philippine Politics*. New York: M. E. Sharpe, 1991.

Tismaneanu, Vladimir, ed. *The Revolutions of 1989*. London, UK: Routledge, 1999.

Torres, Camilo. *Revolutionary Priest: The Complete Writings and Messages of Camilo Torres*. Edited by John Gerassi. New York: Vintage Books, 1971.

Townes, Emilie M. *Womanist Ethics and the Cultural Production of Evil*. New York: Palgrave Macmillan, 2006.

Tutu, Desmond. *Crying in the Wilderness: The Struggle for Justice in South Africa*. Edited by John Webster. Grand Rapids, Mich.: William B. Eerdmans, 1982.

———. *Hope and Suffering: Sermons and Speeches*. Grand Rapids, Mich.: William B. Eerdmans, 1984.

Vance, J. D. *Hillbilly Elegy: A Memoir of a Family and Culture in Crisis*. New York: Harper & Row, 2018.

Vivian, Octavia. *Coretta: The Story of Coretta Scott King*. Minneapolis: Fortress Press, 2006.

Wallensteen, Peter. *Understanding Conflict Resolution: War, Peace, and the Global System*. Thousand Oaks, Calif.: Sage Publications, 2002.

Ward, Brian. *Martin Luther King in Newcastle upon Tyne: The African American Freedom Struggle and Race Relations in the North East of England*. Newcastle upon Tyne, UK: Tyne Bridge Publishing, 2017.

Wariboko, Nimi. *The Charismatic City and the Resurgence of Religion: A Pentecostal Social Ethics of Cosmopolitan Urban Life*. New York: Palgrave Macmillan, 2014.

———. *God and Money: A Theology of Money in a Globalizing World*. Lanham, Md.: Lexington Books, 2008.

Watley, William D. *Roots of Resistance: The Nonviolent Ethic of Martin Luther King, Jr.* Valley Forge, Pa.: Judson Press, 1985.

Weis, Monica. *The Environmental Vision of Thomas Merton*. Culture of the Land. Lexington: University Press of Kentucky, 2011.

Wheatley, Margaret J. *Leadership and the New Science: Discovering Order in a Chaotic World*. Rev. ed. San Francisco: Berrett-Koehler, 2006.

Widdows, Heather. *Global Ethics: An Introduction*. Durham, UK: Acumen, 2011.

Williamson, Thad, David Imbroscio, Gar Alperovitz, and Benjamin Barber. *Making a Place for Community: Local Democracy in a Global Era*. New York: Routledge, 2002.

Wills, Richard Wayne, Sr. *Martin Luther King Jr. and the Image of God*. New York: Oxford University Press, 2009.

Wink, Walter. *The Powers That Be: Theology for a New Millennium*. New York: Doubleday, 1998.

X, Malcolm, with Alex Haley. *The Autobiography of Malcolm X*. New York: Grove Press, 1965.

Young, William H., and Nancy K. Young. *The 1950s: American Popular Culture through History*. Westport, Conn.: Greenwood Press, 2004.

Zielonka, Jan. *Political ideas in Contemporary Poland*. Aldershot UK: Gower, 1989.

JOURNAL AND MAGAZINE ARTICLES, THESES, DISSERTATIONS, ETCETERA

Alderman, Derek. "Creating a New Geography of Memory in the South: The (Re)Naming of Streets in Honor of Martin Luther King, Jr." *Southeastern Geographer* 36, no. 1 (May 1996): 51–69.

———. "Martin Luther King Jr. Streets in the South: A New Landscape of Memory." *Southern Cultures* 14, no. 3 (Fall 2008): 88–105.

Allman, Mark J. "A Thick Theory of Global Justice: Participation as a Constitutive Dimension of Global Justice." PhD diss., Loyola University of Chicago, 2003.

Ambrosino, Brandon. "What the Gay Rights Movement Should Learn from Martin Luther King, Jr.," *Time*, January 20, 2014, 1–5, http://time.com/2332/what-the-gay-rights-movement-should-learn-from-martin-luther-king-jr.

Appiah, Anthony. "Education for Global Citizenship." In David L. Coulter, John R. Wiens, and Gary D. Fenstermacher, eds., *Why Do We Educate? Renewing the Conversation*, 107th Yearbook of the National Society for the Study of Education, vol. 1 (Boston: Wiley-Blackwell, 2008), 83–99.

Baldwin, James. "The Dangerous Road before Martin Luther King." *Harper's*, February 1961, 33–42.

Baldwin, Lewis V. "Martin Luther King, Jr., the Black Church, and the Black Messianic Vision." *Journal of the Interdenominational Theological Center* 12, nos. 1–2 (Fall 1984–Spring 1985): 93–108.

Beam, Joseph. "The Elder of the Village: An Interview with Bayard Rustin." *B/Out* 1, nos. 3–4 (1987): 17–19.

Berner, Erhard. "Poverty Alleviation and the Eviction of the Poorest: Toward Urban Land Reform in the Philippines." *International Journal of Urban and Regional Research* 24, no. 3 (June 28, 2008): 536–53.

Buffetrille, Katia. "Self-Immolation in Tibet: Some Reflections on an Unfolding History." *Revue d'Etudes Tibetaines* 25 (December 2012): 1–17.

Burrow, Rufus, Jr. "King's Beloved Community Ideal: Making the Connections." *Journal of Religion* 77, no. 3 (July 1997): 442–48.

———. "King's Dream and Multiculturalism: A Review Essay." *Encounter* 67, no. 2 (2006): 207–16. Review of James Echols, ed., *I Have a Dream: Martin Luther King, Jr. and the Future of Multicultural America* (Minneapolis: Fortress Press, 2004).

———. "Martin Luther King, Jr. and the Objective Moral Order: Some Ethical Implications." *Encounter* 61, no. 2 (Spring 2000): 221–23.

Cahill, Lisa Sowie. "Toward Global Ethics." *Theological Studies* 63, no. 2 (2002): 324–44.

Coleman, Monica A. "Lessons on Action, Love and Death: A Young Womanist's Encounter with the Legacy of Martin Luther King, Jr." Unpublished article, August 2014.

"Conversation in Ghana." *Christian Century*, April 10, 1957, 446–48.

Crawford, Vicki L. "Coretta Scott King and the Struggle for Civil and Human Rights: An Enduring Legacy." *Journal of African-American History* 92 (2007): 106–17.

Davies, William. "Neoliberalism: A Bibliographic Review." *Theory, Culture and Society* 31, nos. 7–8 (2014): 309–17.

Davis-Cohen, Simon. "Meet the Legal Theorists behind the Financial Takeover of Puerto Rico." *Nation*, October 30, 2017. https://www.thenation.com/article/meet-the-legal-theorists-behind-the-financial-takeover-of-puerto-rico.

Dunlap, Brian. "What Would Martin Luther King Jr. Say about the Gay Rights Movement?" *Quora*, November 23, 2011. https://quora.com/What-would-Martin-Luther-King-Jr-say-about-the-gay-rights-movement.

Feffer, John. "Uncivil Society." *In These Times*, November 15, 1993, 28–29.

Franklin, John Hope. "The Land of Room Enough." *Daedalus* 110, no. 2 (Spring 1981): 1–12.

Goss-Mayr, Hildegard. "When Prayer and Revolution Became People Power." *Fellowship* (Fellowship of Reconciliation), March 1987, 8–11.

Gray, Tyson-Lord J. "Mercy, Mercy Me (The Ecology): Black Culture, Aesthetics, and the Search for a 'Green' Community." PhD diss., Vanderbilt University, 2014.

Hudson, James. "Brotherhood in Christ." *Young Adult Quarterly*, September 27, 1953.

"In Memory of Martin Luther King, Jr.: Since His Death, Hundreds of Memorials Have Been Dedicated in Honor of the Famed Leader." *Ebony*, January 1986, 64–70.

Inwood, Joshua F. J. "Searching for the Promised Land: Examining Dr. Martin Luther King, Jr.'s Concept of the Beloved Community." *Antipode* 41, no. 3 (June 2009): 487–508.

"'I Remember Martin': People Close to the Civil Rights Leader Recall a Down-to-Earth and Humorous Man." *Ebony*, April 1984, 34–40.

Jordan, June. "How Shall We Know His Name? The Legacy of Martin Luther King, Jr.—20 Years On." *Christianity and Crisis*, May 18, 1987, 191–94.

Khan, Shah Alam. "Democratic Space—What Is That?" Countercurrents.org, June 3, 2009. http://www.countercurrents.org/khan030609.htm.

King, Martin Luther Jr. "The Negro Is Your Brother" (aka "Letter from Birmingham Jail"), *Atlantic Monthly*, August 1963, https://www.theatlantic.com/magazine/archive/2018 /02/letter-from-birmingham-jail/552461.

Lal, Vinay. "Pietermaritzburg: The Beginning of Gandhi's Odyssey." https://web.archive .org/web/20160307131455/http://www.sscnet.ucla.edu/southasia/History/Gandhi /Pieter.html.

Lee, Hak Joon. "Toward the Great World House: Hans Küng and Martin Luther King Jr. on Global Ethics." *Journal of the Society of Christian Ethics* 29, no. 2 (Fall/Winter 2009): 97–119.

Marable, Manning. "Along the Color Line: 'Developing Black Leaders.'" *National Baptist Union-Review* 92, no. 15 (December 1988): 6.

Mays, Benjamin E. "Pagan Survivals in Christianity." MA thesis, University of Chicago Divinity School, 1925.

Mills, Zachary W. "Talking Drum: Chicago's WVON Radio and the Sonorous Image of Black Lives, 1963–1983." PhD diss., Northwestern University, 2017.

Parmesan, Camille, and Cary Yohe. "A Globally Coherent Fingerprint of Climate Change Impacts across Natural Systems." *Nature*, January 2, 2003, 37–42.

Pérez, Myrna, and Vishal Agraharkark. "If Section 5 Falls: New Voting Implications." Brennan Center for Justice, June 12, 2013. http://www.brennancenter.org/publication /if-section-5-falls-new-voting-implications.

"Religion: Baptists in Berlin." *Time*, August 13, 1934.

Rivers, Larry O. "'Militant Reconciling Love': Howard University's Rankin Network and Martin Luther King, Jr." *Journal of African-American History* 99, no. 3 (Summer 2014): 223–50.

———. "'A New Social Awakening': James Hudson, Florida A&M University's Religious Life Program, and the 1956 Tallahassee Bus Boycott." *Florida Historical Quarterly* 95 (Winter 2017): 325–55.

Robins, Shani, and Richard E. Mayer. "The Metaphor Framing Effect: Metaphorical Reasoning about Text-Based Dilemmas." *Discourse Processes* 30 (2000): 57–86.

Robra, Martin. "Affirming the Role of Global Movements for Global Ethics." *Ecumenical Review* 52, no. 4 (2000): 471–78.

Smith, Kenneth L. "Equality and Justice: A Dream or Vision of Reality." *Report from the Capital*, January 1984, 4–5, 7.

Vetere, Arlene. "Structural Family Therapy." *Child Psychology and Psychiatry Review* 6, no. 3 (2001): 133–39.

West, Traci C. "Gay Rights and the Misuse of Martin." In Lewis V. Baldwin and Rufus Burrow, Jr., eds., *The Domestication of Martin Luther King, Jr.: Clarence B. Jones, Right-Wing Conservatism, and the Manipulation of the King Legacy*, 141–56. Eugene, Ore.: Cascade Books, 2013.

———. "Gendered Legacies of Martin Luther King Jr.'s Leadership." *Theology Today* 65, no. 1 (April 2008): 41–56.

Willis, Andre C. "Why Martin Luther King Jr. Stands Alone." *Root*, January 18, 2010. https://www.theroot.com/why-martin-luther-king-jr-stands-alone-1790878338.

"The World Honors MLK through Stamps: Commemorative Stamps Attest to High
   Esteem in Which Rights Leader is Held at Home and Abroad." *Ebony*, January 1986,
   82–84.
Young, Andrea. "Martin Luther King, Jr.: The Legacy Lives." *Christianity and Crisis*, January
   13, 1986, 531–32.
Zielonka, Jan. "Strengths and Weaknesses of Nonviolent Action: The Polish Case." *Orbis*
   30, no. 1 (Spring 1986): 91–110.

SERMONS AND SPEECHES

King, Coretta Scott. "Address at the National Conference on Civil Rights," Nashville,
   April 5, 1986. Notes in the personal collection of Lewis V. Baldwin.
King, Martin Luther, Jr. "Address at the 50th Anniversary of the Women's International
   League for Peace and Freedom," October 15, 1965, Philadelphia. Martin Luther King Jr.
   Papers, Library and Archives of the Martin Luther King Jr. Center for Nonviolent Social
   Change, Atlanta (hereafter King Papers).
———. "Address at the Initial Mass Meeting of the Montgomery Improvement Associ-
   ation," December 5, 1955, Holt Street Baptist Church, Montgomery, Alabama. King
   Papers.
———. "Address at the Recognition Dinner," January 27, 1965, Dinkler Plaza Hotel,
   Atlanta. King Papers.
———. "Annual Address to the Montgomery Improvement Association," December 3,
   1956, First Annual Institute on Nonviolence and Social Change, Holt Street Baptist
   Church, Montgomery, Alabama. King Papers.
———. "Beyond Vietnam," April 4, 1967, Riverside Church, New York City. Martin Luther
   King, Jr. Research and Education Institute, Stanford University, https://kinginstitute
   .stanford.edu/king-papers/documents/beyond-vietnam.
———. "The Casualties of the War in Vietnam," February 25, 1967, Nation Institute, Los
   Angeles. http://www.aavw.org/special_features/speeches_speech_king02.html.
———. "The Church on the Frontier of Racial Tension," April 19, 1961, Gay Lectures,
   Southern Baptist Theological Seminary, Louisville, Kentucky. King Papers.
———. "The Crisis of Civil Rights," October 10–12, 1967, Operation Breadbasket Meeting,
   Chicago. King Papers.
———. "The Death of Evil upon the Seashore," July 21, 1955. Sermon box, folder 174,
   Coretta Scott King Collection, Library and Archives of the Martin Luther King Jr. Cen-
   ter for Nonviolent Social Change, Atlanta.
———. "The Desirability of Being Maladjusted," January 13, 1958, sermon, Chicago. King
   Papers.
———. "The Dignity of Family Life," October 29, 1965, Abbott House, Westchester
   County, New York. King Papers.
———. "East or West—God's Children," September 13, 1964, Berlin, Germany. King
   Papers.
———. "Facing the Challenge of a New Age," November 27, 1962, Booker T. Washington
   High School Gymnasium, Rocky Mount, North Carolina. King Papers.
———. "Facing the Challenge of a New Age," June 20, 1965, valedictory address, Univer-
   sity of the West Indies, Mona, Jamaica. King Papers.
———. "Field of Education a Battleground," July 15, 1965, speech, United Federation of
   Teachers, New York City, King Papers.

———. "The Meaning of Hope," December 10, 1967, Dexter Avenue Baptist Church, Montgomery, Alabama. King Papers.

———. "Mental and Spiritual Slavery." Sermon outline, (n.d.), series 2, Martin Luther King Writings, Martin Luther King Jr. Collection, Morehouse College, Atlanta.

———. "The Negro Family," January 27, 1966, University of Chicago, Chicago. King Papers.

———. "Nobel Lecture," December 11, 1964, University of Oslo, Oslo, Norway. King Papers.

———. "The Other America," March 10, 1968, Local 1199 Salute to Freedom, Hunter College, New York City. King Papers.

———. "Pharisee and Publican," October 9, 1966. King Papers.

———. "President's Address," December 5, 1957, Montgomery Improvement Association, Montgomery, Alabama. King Papers.

———. "The Prodigal Son," September 4, 1966, Ebenezer Baptist Church, Atlanta. King Papers.

———. "The Quest for Peace and Justice," December 11, 1964, Nobel lecture, Oslo, Norway. https://www.nobelprize.org/prizes/peace/laureates/1964/king-lecture.html.

———. "A Realistic Look at Race Relations," May 17, 1956, speech, NAACP Legal Defense and Educational Fund, Waldorf Astoria Hotel, New York City. King Papers.

———. "Remaining Awake through a Great Revolution," March 31, 1968, sermon, National Cathedral, Washington, D.C. Martin Luther King, Jr. Research and Education Institute, Stanford University, https://kinginstitute.stanford.edu/king-papers /publications/knock-midnight-inspiration-great-sermons-reverend-martin-luther -king-jr-10.

———. "Remember Who You Are!" December 6, 1956, series 2, Martin Luther King Writings, Martin Luther King Jr. Collection, Robert W. Woodruff Library, Morehouse College, Atlanta.

———. "Revolution in the Classroom," April 31, 1967, address, Georgia Teachers and Education Association, Atlanta, King Papers.

———. "Speech at a Mass Meeting," March 19, 1968, Clarksdale, Mississippi. King Papers.

———. "Speech at Southern Methodist University," March 17, 1966, Dallas. https://www .smu.edu/AboutSMU/MLK#transcript.

———. "The State of the Movement," November 28, 1967, Southern Christian Leadership Conference staff retreat, Frogmore, South Carolina. King Papers.

———. "The Three Evils of Society," August 31, 1967, speech, Chicago. Transcribed by the author from a recording available online, https://www.youtube.com/watch?v=j8d -IYSM-08.

———. "Training Your Child in Love," May 8, 1966, Ebenezer Baptist Church, Atlanta. King Papers.

———. "Transforming the Neighborhood," August 11, 1967, NATRA (National Association of TV and Radio Announcers) Convention, Atlanta. King Papers.

———. "We Would See Jesus," May 7, 1967, Ebenezer Baptist Church, Atlanta. King Papers.

———. "What a Mother Should Tell Her Child," May 12, 1963, Ebenezer Baptist Church, Atlanta. King Papers.

———. "Where Do We Go From Here?," August 16, 1967, report to the Southern Christian Leadership Convention, Atlanta. Martin Luther King, Jr. Research and Education Institute, Stanford University, https://kinginstitute.stanford.edu/king-papers/documents /where-do-we-go-here-address-delivered-eleventh-annual-sclc-convention.

————. "Why Jesus Called a Man a Fool," August 27, 1967, sermon, Mount Pisgah Mission-
ary Baptist Church, Chicago. Martin Luther King, Jr. Research and Education Institute,
Stanford University, https://kinginstitute.stanford.edu/king-papers/documents
/why-jesus-called-man-fool-sermon-delivered-mount-pisgah-missionary-baptist.
Williams, Delores S. "Between Hagar and Jezebel: A Womanist Assessment of Martin
Luther King, Jr.'s Beloved Community," videotaped lecture, January 13, 1997, All Faith
Chapel, Vanderbilt University Divinity School, Nashville. Jean and Alexander Heard
Library, Vanderbilt University.

FILMS

Bagwell, Orlando, and W. Noland Walker, directors. *Citizen King*. DVD. Alexandria, Va.:
PBS Home Video, 2004.
Martin Luther King, Jr.: A Personal Portrait. VHS. Goldsboro, N.C.: Michaelis Tapes, 1987.
Younis, Usaid, and Cassie Quarles, directors. *Generation Revolution*. United Kingdom:
Black and Brown Films, 2016.

CONTRIBUTORS

VICTOR ANDERSON is the Oberlin Theological School Professor of Ethics and Society at the Vanderbilt University Divinity School, and he also serves as a professor in the Program of African American and Diaspora Studies in the College of Arts and Sciences at Vanderbilt. He is the author of *Beyond Ontological Blackness: An Essay on African American Religious and Cultural Criticism* (1995), *Pragmatic Theology: Negotiating the Intersection of an American Philosophy of Religion and Public Theology* (1999), *Creative Exchange: A Constructive Theology of African American Religious Experience* (2008), and numerous articles and book chapters. He is also a coeditor (with Lewis V. Baldwin) of *Revives My Soul Again: The Spirituality of Martin Luther King, Jr.* (2018).

LEWIS V. BALDWIN is emeritus professor, Department of Religious Studies, Vanderbilt University. A cultural and religious historian by training, he is the author of *There Is a Balm in Gilead: The Cultural Roots of Martin Luther King, Jr.* (1991), *To Make the Wounded Whole: The Cultural Legacy of Martin Luther King, Jr.* (1992), *Toward the Beloved Community: Martin Luther King, Jr. and South Africa* (1995), *Never to Leave Us Alone: The Prayer Life of Martin Luther King, Jr.* (2010), *The Voice of Conscience: The Church in the Mind of Martin Luther King, Jr.* (2010), *Behind the Public Veil: The Humanness of Martin Luther King, Jr.* (2016), and numerous other books and articles on various aspects of African American religion, culture, and history. He is also a coauthor (with Rufus Burrow Jr., Barbara A. Holmes, and Susan Holmes Winfield) of *The Legacy of Martin Luther King, Jr.: The Boundaries of Law, Politics, and Religion* (2002) and (with Amiri YaSin Al-Hadid) of *Between Cross and Crescent: Christian and Muslim Perspectives on Malcolm and Martin* (2002). He is the editor of *"Thou, Dear God": Prayers that Open Hearts and Spirits—The Reverend Martin Luther King, Jr.* (2012) and *"In a Single Garment of Destiny": A Global Vision of Justice—Martin Luther King, Jr.* (2012). He is a coeditor (with Rufus Burrow Jr.) of *The Domestication of Martin Luther King, Jr.: Clarence B. Jones, Right-Wing Conservatism, and the Manipulation of the King Legacy* (2013), coeditor (with Paul R. Dekar) of *"In an Inescapable Network of Mutuality": Martin Luther King, Jr. and the Globalization of an Ethical Ideal* (2013), and coeditor (with Victor Anderson) of *Revives My Soul Again: The Spirituality of Martin Luther King, Jr.* (2018).

RUFUS BURROW JR. is emeritus professor of Christian thought and theological social ethics at Christian Theological Seminary in Indianapolis, Indiana. He is the author of *James H. Cone and Black Liberation Theology* (1994), *Personalism: A Critical Introduction* (1999), *God and Human Responsibility: David Walker and Ethical Prophecy* (2003), *God and Human Dignity: The Personalism, Theology, and Ethics of Martin Luther King, Jr.* (2006), *Martin Luther King Jr. for Armchair Theologians* (2009), *Extremist for Love: Martin Luther King, Jr., Man of Ideas and Nonviolent Social Action* (2014), *A Child Shall Lead Them: Martin Luther King, Jr., Young People, and the Movement* (2014), *Martin Luther King, Jr., and the Theology of Resistance* (2014), *Making Good the Claim: Holiness and Visible Unity in the Church of God Reformation Movement* (2016), and numerous articles. He is also the coauthor (with Lewis V. Baldwin, Barbara A. Holmes, and Susan Holmes Winfield) of *The Legacy of Martin Luther King, Jr.: The Boundaries of Law, Politics, and Religion* (2002), coauthor (with Mary A. Mulligan) of *Daring to Speak in God's Name: Ethical Prophecy in Ministry* (2002), coauthor (with Mary A. Mulligan) of *Standing in the Margin: How Your Congregation Can Minister with the Poor* (2004), and coauthor (with Mary A. Mulligan) of *Holy Word and Holy Work: A Call to Prophetic Ministry* (2006).

VICKI L. CRAWFORD is director of the Office of the Morehouse College Martin Luther King Jr. Collection and an associate professor of African American studies. Also, she is a cocurator of the Voice to the Voiceless Gallery at the National Center for Civil and Human Rights, which exhibits the papers of the Martin Luther King Jr. Collection. Among her publications is an edited groundbreaking volume, *Women in the Civil Rights Movement: Trailblazers and Torchbearers* (1990), one of the first scholarly works to address the underrepresented roles of women in the civil rights movement. Her other publications include "Remembering Coretta Scott King and the Struggle for Civil and Human Rights: An Enduring Legacy," in the *Journal of African American History* (Winter 2007), and the foreword to *"In an Inescapable Network of Mutuality": Martin Luther King, Jr. and the Globalization of an Ethical Ideal* (2013), a volume coedited by Lewis V. Baldwin and Paul R. Dekar.

CRYSTAL A. DEGREGORY is the inaugural director of the Atwood Institute for Race, Education, and the Democratic Ideal at Kentucky State University, where she is also an associate professor of history. She is the founder and executive editor of HBCUstory, an advocacy initiative supporting the future of the nation's historically black colleges and universities by preserving, presenting, and promoting inspiring stories of their past and present. Her research explores the interrelationship between black struggles for freedom, justice, and equality worldwide, with a special focus on the activist qualities of historically black academic institutions. She is a contributor to *Freedom Facts and Firsts: 400 Years of the African American Civil Rights Experience* (2009), edited by Linda T. Wynn and Jessie Carney Smith, and to *"In an Inescapable Network of Mutuality": Martin Luther King, Jr. and the Globalization of an Ethical Ideal* (2013), edited by Lewis V. Baldwin and Paul R. Dekar. Her scholarly work has also appeared in the *Tennessee State University Journal*, *Encyclopedia of African American Popular Culture*, *Tennessee Historical Quarterly*, and *African American National Biography*.

TERESA DELGADO is director of the Peace and Justice Studies Program and professor and chair of the Religious Studies Department at Iona College in New Rochelle, New York.

She publishes on diversity in higher education, constructive theology and ethics, and justice for racial, ethnic, and sexual minorities. She is the author of *A Puerto Rican Decolonial Theology: Prophesy Freedom* (2017) and a number of book chapters and articles in journals. She is coeditor (with John Doody and Kim Paffenroth) of *Augustine and Social Justice: Tradition and Innovation* (2015). She also serves as president of the board of directors for WESPAC Foundation (Westchester People's Action Coalition), the leading force in Westchester County, New York, for peace and justice work for four decades; on the board of the Hispanic Theological Initiative (HTI), as a mentor in the consortium of the Forum for Theological Exploration, and as a member of the advisory board of the Wabash Center for Teaching and Learning in Theology and Religion.

WALTER E. FLUKER is the Martin Luther King Jr. Professor of Ethical Leadership, the director of the Martin Luther King Jr. Initiative for the Development of Ethical Leadership (MLK-IDEAL), and the editor of the Howard Thurman Papers at Boston University's School of Theology. He is the author of *They Looked for a City: A Comparative Analysis of the Ideal of Community in the Thought of Howard Thurman and Martin Luther King, Jr.* (1989), *Ethical Leadership: The Quest for Character, Civility, and Community* (2009), and *The Ground Has Shifted: The Future of the Black Church in Post-Racial America* (2016). He is also the editor of *The Stones that the Builders Rejected: The Development of Ethical Leadership from the Black Church Tradition* (1998) and a series based on the papers of Howard Thurman, among which are *The Papers of Howard Washington Thurman*, vol. 1, *My People Need Me, June 1918-March 1936* (2009), *The Papers of Howard Washington Thurman*, vol. 2, *Christian, Who Calls Me Christian?, April 1936-August 1943* (2012), *The Papers of Howard Washington Thurman*, vol. 3, *The Bold Adventure, September 1943-May 1949* (2015), *The Papers of Howard Washington Thurman*, vol. 4, *The Soundless Passion of a Single Mind, June 1949-December 1962* (2017), and *The Papers of Howard Washington Thurman*, vol. 5, *The Wider Ministry, January 1963-April 1981* (2019). He is also a coeditor (with Catherine Tumber) of *Strange Freedom: The Best of Howard Thurman on Religious Experience and Public Life* (1998) and a contributor to *Revives My Soul Again: The Spirituality of Martin Luther King, Jr.* (2018), coedited by Lewis V. Baldwin and Victor Anderson.

ROBERT M. FRANKLIN is the James T. and Berta R. Laney Professor of Moral Leadership at Emory University. He served as president of the Interdenominational Theological Center (1997-2002) and of Morehouse College (2007-2012), both in Atlanta, Georgia. He has also worked closely with the American Academy of Religion (AAR), the Society of Christian Ethics, the Council of Past HBCU Presidents, and the Human Rights Campaign Project Council on expanding LGBTQ rights. He is the author of *Liberating Visions: Human Fulfillment and Social Justice in African American Thought* (1990), *Another Day's Journey: Black Churches Confronting the American Crisis* (1997), and *Crisis in the Village: Restoring Hope in African American Communities* (2007).

MARY E. KING is professor in the Department of Peace and Conflict Studies at the UN-affiliated University for Peace, main campus Costa Rica. She is also a Distinguished Rothermere American Institute Fellow at Oxford University in Britain and the director of the new James M. Lawson Institute. Her *Freedom Song: A Personal Story of the 1960s Civil Rights Movement* (1987), which highlights her experiences working for four years with the Student Nonviolent Coordinating Committee (SNCC) and at times with Martin Luther King Jr., won the Robert F. Kennedy Memorial Book Award. She has received numerous other awards and honors, including a James M. Lawson Award for Nonviolent Achievement, the 2003 Jamnalal Bajaj International Award in Mumbai, India, and the 2009 El-Hibri Peace Education Prize. Her other books include *Mahatma Gandhi and Martin Luther King, Jr.: The Power of Nonviolent Action* (1999); *A Quiet Revolution: The First Palestinian Intifada and Nonviolent Resistance* (2007); and *The New York Times on Emerging Democracies in Eastern Europe* (2009). She is also a contributor to *"In an Inescapable Network of Mutuality": Martin Luther King, Jr. and the Globalization of an Ethical Ideal* (2013), edited by Lewis V. Baldwin and Paul R. Dekar.

HAK JOON LEE is the Lewis B. Smedes Professor of Christian Ethics at Fuller Theological Seminary. His research focuses on covenant, public theology, the ethics and spirituality of Martin Luther King Jr., global ethics, and Asian American theology and ethics. He is the author of *Covenant and Communication: A Christian Moral Conversation with Jurgen Habermas* (2006), *We Will Get to the Promised Land: Martin Luther King, Jr.'s Communal-Political Spirituality* (2006), *The Great World House: Martin Luther King, Jr., and Global Ethics* (2011), two books in Korean, and numerous articles. He is also a coeditor (with Scott R. Paeth and Harold Breitenberg Jr.) of *Shaping Public Theology: Selections from the Writings of Max L. Stackhouse* (2014).

ALTHEA LEGAL-MILLER is an assistant professor of American history and culture at Canterbury Christ Church University in the United Kingdom. She has written extensively about ritualized jail-based sexual violence against female civil rights activists and has received numerous prestigious awards, including an AHRC British Research Fellowship at the John W. Kluge Center, Library of Congress, Washington, D.C., and the Mae C. King Distinguished Paper Award on Women, Gender, and Black Politics from the Association for the Study of Black Women in Politics (ASBWP). She is a contributor to the forthcoming edited volume, *Black Lives Matter: The Past, Present, and Future of an International Movement for Rights and Justice.*

MICHAEL B. MCCORMACK is a professor in pan-African studies at the University of Louisville, with a secondary appointment in the Division of Humanities (Religious Studies). His research interests focus on the intersections of African American religion and cultural studies. His dissertation examined and analyzed the contested relationships between the prophetic tradition in black religion, black moral panic, and the cultural productions of the hip-hop generation. He teaches a range of courses in African American religion and the religions of the African diaspora. He is a contributor to *Revives My Soul Again: The Spirituality of Martin Luther King, Jr.* (2018), coedited by Lewis V. Baldwin and Victor Anderson.

LARRY O. RIVERS is an associate professor of history at the University of West Georgia. His scholarship focuses on religion, the African American experience, and the civil rights movement in the United States, and his articles have appeared in *Florida Historical Quarterly*, *Journal of African American History*, and *Sunland Tribune: Journal of the Tampa Historical Society*. He is currently writing a book on James Hudson, a personalist philosopher, university chaplain, and civil rights activist.

ROSETTA E. ROSS is a professor of religious studies at Atlanta's Spelman College, and founding chair of the Daughters of the African Atlantic. A strong supporter of women's rights, civil rights, and larger efforts for human rights, she is the author of *Witnessing and*

Testifying: Black Women, Religion, and Civil Rights (2003). She is also a coeditor (with Jung Ha Kim) of *The Status of Racial-Ethnic Minority Clergywomen in the United Methodist Church* (2004), and (with Rose Mary Amenga-Etego) of *Unraveling and Reweaving: Reimaging Sacred Canon in Africana Womanhood* (2015).

GARY S. SELBY is professor of ministerial formation at Emmanuel Christian Seminary, Milligan College, and previously served as the Carl P. Miller Chair of Communications at Pepperdine University. He has published articles on Martin Luther King Jr., Ralph D. Abernathy, and Frederick Douglass, as well as on early Christian rhetoric and religion and politics, in *Quarterly Journal of Speech, Rhetorica, Southern Communication Journal, Journal of Communication and Religion, Rhetoric Review,* and *Rhetoric and Political Affairs*. He is the author of *Martin Luther King, Jr. and the Rhetoric of Freedom: The Exodus in America's Struggle for Civil Rights* (2008).

AMY E. STEELE is the assistant dean of student life at Vanderbilt University. Her scholarly interests extend into the areas of social ethics, spirituality, philosophical hermeneutics, homiletics, aesthetics, and pragmatic theology. She is a contributor to Ronald J. Allen and Dale P. Andrews, eds., *Preaching God's Transforming Justice, a Lectionary Commentary, Year A* (2013).

NIMI WARIBOKO is the Walter G. Muelder Professor of Social Ethics at the School of Theology at Boston University. A lively transdisciplinary thinker with a strong background in economic ethics, Christian social ethics, African social traditions, Pentecostal studies, and philosophical theology, he is the author of several books that are characterized by a creative and rigorous interweaving of original insights from each of these disciplines or fields of study. Among his many publications are *Financial Statement Analysis: A Workbook* (1994), *The Mind of African Strategists: A Study of Kalabari Management Practice* (1997), *100 Great Bible Mysteries: Digging Deep for Revelation Knowledge* (2003), *Pattern of Institutions in the Niger Delta: Economic and Ethological Interpretations of History and Culture* (2007), *God and Money: A Theology of Money in a Globalizing World* (2008), *The Depth and Destiny of Work: An African Theological Interpretation* (2008), *The Principle of Excellence: A Framework for Social Ethics* (2009), *Ethics and Time: Ethos of Temporal Orientation in Politics and Religion of the Niger Delta* (2010), *The Pentecostal Principle: Ethical Methodology in New Spirit* (2011), *Accounting and Money for Ministerial Leadership: Key Practical and Theological Insights* (2013), *Methods of Ethical Analysis: Between Theology, History, and Literature* (2013), *Economics in Spirit and Truth: A Moral Philosophy of Finance* (2014), *The Charismatic City and the Public Resurgence of Religion: A Pentecostal Social Ethics of Cosmopolitan Urban Life* (2014), and *Nigerian Pentecostalism* (2014). He is also a coeditor (with Amos Yong) of *Paul Tillich and Pentecostal Theology: Spiritual Presence and Spiritual Power* (2015).

INDEX